# ARABIA
## AND THE ISLES

By HAROLD INGRAMS, C.M.G., O.B.E.

*With Foreword by*
Lt.-Col. Sir BERNARD REILLY, K.C.M.G., C.I.E., O.B.E.
Governor of Aden, 1937–40

*The mountains shall bring peace to the people, and the little hills, by righteousness.*
Psalm 72. v. 3.

LONDON
JOHN MURRAY, ALBEMARLE STREET, W

*To My Wife*

| | | | |
|---|---|---|---|
| *First Published* | .. .. | *June* | *1942* |
| *Reprinted* | .. .. | *January* | *1943* |
| *Reprinted* | .. .. | *October* | *1943* |

*Printed in Great Britain by*
*Wyman & Sons, Ltd., London, Fakenham and Reading.*

## CONTENTS

### PART I

| | PAGE |
|---|---|
| Foreword by Sir Bernard Reilly, K.C.M.G., C.I.E., O.B.E. | ix |
| Author's Foreword | xi |
| Prelude | xv |

*Chapter*

| | | |
|---|---|---|
| I. | The Erythraean Sea | 3 |
| II. | A Pooh Bah in Pemba | 12 |
| III. | The Green Island: Men of Oman | 26 |
| IV. | Men of Shihr | 40 |
| V. | Antres Vast—In Zanzibar Town—A Dhow from Kuweit—Latham Island | 47 |
| VI. | Mauritian Interlude and Oriental Encounters | 63 |
| VII. | Aden Town | 84 |
| VIII. | The Aden Protectorate | 91 |
| IX. | Lahej, Museimir and the Qāt Trade | 103 |
| X. | Troubled Waters | 113 |

### PART II

| | | |
|---|---|---|
| XI. | The Far Off Hills of Hadhramaut and the Lands of Genesis | 137 |
| XII. | The Gateway of the Hadhramaut | 147 |
| XIII. | Travel in the Hadhramaut | 154 |
| XIV. | Wadis and Jōls to Du'an | 164 |
| XV. | In the Valley of Du'an | 169 |
| XVI. | A Peace-making Patriarch | 177 |
| XVII. | Into the Wadi Hadhramaut | 184 |
| XVIII. | The Tomb of Salih and the Sei'ar Country | 193 |

## CONTENTS

| Chapter | | PAGE |
|---|---|---|
| XIX. | Seiyun and Tarim . . . . . . . | 203 |
| XX. | The Tomb of Hud in the Valley of the Floods . . | 210 |
| XXI. | A River of the Rivers of Paradise—The Mahra Country | 217 |
| XXII. | Last Days in Shihr and Mukalla . . . . | 235 |

### PART III

| | | |
|---|---|---|
| XXIII. | Return to the Hadhramaut and the First Move . . | 243 |
| XXIV. | Over the Hills to Tarim . . . . . | 251 |
| XXV. | Tribal Warfare and Seiyid Bubakr . . . . | 258 |
| XXVI. | Visits to the Tribes and the First Peace Conference in Seiyun . | 265 |
| XXVII. | An Incident and the Trial of the Bin Yemani Tribe . . | 275 |
| XXVIII. | Royal Air Force Action and the Submission of the Bin Yemani | 285 |
| XXIX. | The Signing of the Truce . . . . . | 298 |
| XXX. | The New Road . . . . . . . | 312 |
| XXXI. | Trouble With the Sei'ar and Other Tribes . . . | 318 |
| XXXII. | The Social Round . . . . . . | 331 |
| XXXIII. | Present and Future . . . . . . | 338 |
| XXXIV. | The Future of the Hadhramaut . . . . | 341 |
| | Index . . . . . . . . | 355 |

## ILLUSTRATIONS

### From Photographs by the Author, except*

Sa'id and his pipe .. .. .. .. .. .. — Frontispiece

Mukalla from the air* .. .. .. .. ..  
The Bazaar, Mukalla .. .. .. .. ..  
Camel park, Mukalla .. .. .. .. .. } between pages 152 and 153  
The Guest House, Mukalla .. .. .. ..  
Notables at Mukalla, including Sultan Salih and 'Awadh  
Mukalla from the Customs .. .. .. .. ..

Gateway in the Hadhramaut .. .. .. ..  
Date palms in Wadi Du'an .. .. .. .. ..  
Wadi Du'an. Women carrying firewood .. ..  
Ba Surra family at Masna'a .. .. .. .. .. } between pages 176 and 177  
Farewell group at Masna'a .. .. .. .. ..  
The Mansab of Meshhed. Sa'id Ahmed and drummer boy  
Meshhed .. .. .. .. .. .. ..

Shibam .. .. .. .. .. .. ..  
Shibam .. .. .. .. .. .. ..  
Shibam from the air* .. .. .. .. ..  
At Umar's house, Tarim .. .. .. .. .. } between pages 192 and 193  
Group at Reidat .. .. .. .. .. ..  
Seiyid Umar's house .. .. .. .. ..  
Tarim from the air* .. .. .. .. .. ..  
Wadi Hadhramaut from the air* .. .. .. ..

vii

## ILLUSTRATIONS

| | |
|---|---|
| Qabr Salih, Mosque .. .. .. .. .. | |
| Seiyun from the air. Kathiri Sultan's Palace* .. .. | |
| Seiyun .. .. .. .. .. .. .. | |
| Einat. Mosque .. .. .. .. .. .. | |
| Seiyun. Mosque .. .. .. .. .. .. | between pages 216 and 217 |
| Qabr Hud .. .. .. .. .. .. .. | |
| Group at Qabr Hud.. .. .. .. .. .. | |
| Drawing water .. .. .. .. .. .. | |
| Cave dwellings at Sena .. .. .. .. .. | |
| Shihr .. .. .. .. .. .. .. | |

| | |
|---|---|
| Through an Arab doorway .. .. .. .. | |
| A meeting of Peace Makers .. .. .. .. | between pages 304 and 305 |
| The Bin Yemani surrender their arms .. .. .. | |
| Youth of the Hadhramaut .. .. .. .. | |

| | |
|---|---|
| D. (on camel) in Sei'ar country .. .. .. .. | |
| Zaidi, Salim and Ganess .. .. .. .. | |
| Sei'ar chiefs .. .. .. .. .. .. | between pages 320 and 321 |
| Sei'ar types .. .. .. .. .. .. | |
| Hamumi surrender ceremony .. .. .. | |

\* *Crown Copyright Reserved: by kind permission of the Royal Air Force.*

## MAPS

| | FACING PAGE |
|---|---|
| Eastern Aden Protectorate: The Hadhramaut .. .. .. | 354 |
| By kind permission of the Royal Geographical Society. | |
| Indian Ocean .. .. .. .. .. .. .. | 354 |

## FOREWORD

THE name of Harold Ingrams is already so well known to all who are interested in Arabia and the Arabs that it is superfluous to introduce him to those to whom primarily this book will appeal. Its attraction will not, however, be limited to Arabian experts and enthusiasts: it is a book that will interest and entertain a far wider public, and for this reason and also because for several years I watched at close quarters the author's work in the Aden Protectorate I venture on some introductory remarks on his achievements in that country.

Mr. Ingrams is an officer of the Colonial Administrative Service who has had a varied career. In the war of 1914-18 he served for five years with the King's Shropshire Light Infantry and was wounded in Belgium in 1916. He entered the Colonial Service in 1919 and held appointments in Mauritius and Zanzibar, descriptions of which appear in this book. With a great capacity for work, he combines a wide vision and a power of planning for the future with a capacity for assiduous application to the details of everyday administration. It is in his nature to be an enthusiast, and it was not long before his gaze fell upon Arabia, and he felt the attraction of its ancient culture, of its fascinating history, and of the possibilities of a revival of Arab fortunes in the modern world.

In Zanzibar Ingrams came into contact with Arabs from southern Arabia, and he learnt from Hadhrami visitors of their strange native land, so close to the activities of the outer world, and yet so remote from them, so prosperous and so poor, so civilized and so savage. The Hadhramaut is indeed a country of contrasts, with its wealthy Seyyids and its impoverished peasants, its handsome towns, country houses and estates, and its turbulent tribes, banditry and blood feuds. Although part of the British Protectorate of Aden, the wide valley of the Hadhramaut had remained isolated by its natural barriers of mountains on the south and desert on the north. Its seclusion remained undisturbed by Europeans, except for the visits of a few adventurous travellers, until exploratory airmen of the Royal Air Force at Aden, taking swift bird's-eye views of obstacles that had proved so formidable to those on the ground, flew over this little known country, and were surprised both by its unique aspect and by the warmth of the welcome with which their appearance was received.

Many of the Arabs of the Hadhramaut had for some time emigrated in large numbers to Malaya and Java, and there they had seen the results of internal security and settled government. Never losing their love for their home in Arabia, they came to realize how much better and happier a place it might be if the curse of tribal and private warfare could be lifted

# FOREWORD

from it. At the same time it became all too apparent to them that there was in their country no local force or institution strong enough to deal with the mischief, and their eyes turned hopefully to the envoys of the Power which had brought peace and prosperity to India, to Malaya and—near at hand—to Aden.

This was the picture that was portrayed in tempting outline to a man who was already deeply stirred by the pioneering spirit from which the British Empire has grown, and by a belief in the capacity of its representatives to ameliorate the lot of their Eastern fellow subjects. A country calling for help, and above all one that was peopled by Arabs, who, as a race, appealed vividly to his sympathies and his imagination. Here indeed was a task to fire the enthusiasm and determination of a character like Ingrams. It became his ambition to serve in the Hadhramaut and to try his hand at solving its problems.

It was not long before the way was opened. The Colonial Office wishing to establish closer contact with this outlying part of the Aden Protectorate, found in Ingrams an eager explorer of the country, of its needs and of its possibilities. A journey through the length of the Hadhramaut valley, in which Mrs. Ingrams shared with her husband the discomforts and local dangers, resulted in an invaluable report which provided a foundation for the evolution of British policy in the Eastern Aden Protectorate. In due course Ingrams was entrusted with the work of implementing the schemes of pacification and development for which the country called.

In this land of turbulence and blood feuds there were but puny forces to support any form of law and order. Stronger means of keeping the peace had still to be organized. In the meantime there was the power of the Royal Air Force, but this weapon could be used only sparingly and with the greatest restraint in a country where we wished to penetrate as friends, not as enemies. The work of pacification had thus to depend to a supreme degree on persuasion and personal influence, on a judicious blending of firmness and conciliation and above all on sincerity of purpose and a capacity to gain the confidence of a people easily roused to suspicion and hostility.

Ingrams seized on the very real desire for peace, and under his guidance internal warfare was suspended, and a network of inter-tribal truces spread over the land. As Resident Adviser to the Sultans of Mukalla and Seiyun he was able to inaugurate a series of reforms, which, in spite of difficulties and inevitable delays, have set a country long distraught by anarchy on the path of order and progress.

In all his work Ingrams has been encouraged and supported by the indefatigable collaboration and help of his wife. The name of Doreen Ingrams is as widely known as that of her husband, and in this story of life and work in Mauritius, Zanzibar and southern Arabia will be found a vivid description of efforts in which they have shared in the toil and in the success.

*January, 1942.* BERNARD REILLY.

## AUTHOR'S FOREWORD

A DOCTOR once told me that almost every one of his women patients who had a baby said "Never again." "But later," he added, "they come along and ask me to see them through with the next." That is the stand I take, never again, but I hope that I shall be sufficiently firm to stick to this resolve.

The period of gestation of this book has been so abnormally long, and the travail so acute and so prolonged that I do not feel I could face the ordeal again. By the nature of things a Civil Servant is probably more handicapped as a writer than most others. Apart from the fact that he has to spend so much time writing anyway thereby acquiring a distaste for holding a pen more than about ten hours a day, he has little time for it. Most of this book has been written in ships. Part I was written in the *Orion* in 1936, some of it in Union Castle, British India, French and Dutch ships, and some in the islands of Pemba, Zanzibar and Mauritius. Part II was also partly written in the *Orion* and ended in Aden before we left for Mukalla in October 1936. Part III was started in the *Narkunda* and *Canton*, continued in Aden and Mukalla and in the *Chitral*, ploughing its way through the Gulf of Bengal to Penang and Singapore on a grey monsoon day. With the speed of present events it has been difficult to bring the story up to date. In Aden this was scarcely possible, but here in brief and comparative leisure and in the cool mountain air of a Sana spring before a window which looks on a garden of English flowers and shady apricot trees with a load of yellow fruits one is diverted only by the desire to take out a deck-chair and read someone else's book.

That this book should have been written mostly in ships is therefore understandable as I have had little time for writing it elsewhere, and it has had the added advantage of enabling me to look at the subject from a distance. The periods at which the book has been written will account for the changing atmosphere from the Aden chapters to the end of the book. This is the result of writing at intervals, of a country in which I am still living, but of which my knowledge naturally increases with the passage of time and which is itself undergoing rapid changes. Had I written

## AUTHOR'S FOREWORD

Part II now and not referred to all the voluminous notes and reports we made on our first journey through the Hadhramaut, it would certainly have been different—whether for the better or the worse I cannot say. But now that the country has become so familiar it would not be possible to describe it with the detail I used before. Perhaps this would have made it less tedious to some readers, but I feel that much of the value that is obtained from first impressions would be lost, for much of it describes country up to that time unseen by European eyes and which in fact still remains unseen by others.

I have had another compelling motive in writing this book. Since the earliest days of my Colonial Service, and before, amongst my favourite reading has been the works of the pioneers and explorers of the last century, in these days some of those who live in the colonies may lay more emphasis on the amenities and comforts of daily life than they do on its adventures. But there are adventurous spirits in the service and there will continue to be: and so in the first place I have written my book for them that they may know that even in these days when many of the difficulties and disappointments our pioneering predecessors had to face have gone, there still are adventures and hardships to be found.

It is not for me to write about Colonial policy and I do not propose to attempt to do so. But at the same time I have an idea that at a moment when our enemies blackguard us daily about the races who "writhe under our yoke" it is not a bad thing to tell the story of an attempt to carry out the policy of trusteeship and of teaching people to govern themselves in a corner of the world which is mostly desert and in which we can have no material ends to serve. A lot of nonsense has been talked about "Imperialism" and the word has been given a meaning of exploitation of backward races. I do not think anyone will be able to find much about exploitation in the story of the Hadhramaut and I have not found it anywhere else in the Empire. I should not be in the Colonial Service if I had. But I am quite certain I am an Imperialist and equally certain that the vast majority of the Arabs in the Aden Protectorate are too, because we all believe in belonging to an Empire which runs itself on a basis of the mutual interests of all who belong to it. As it has turned out we have gained a great thing out of doing our best for the Arabs in the Hadhramaut and that is their friendship and their firm confidence in and desire for our ultimate victory. No one can doubt that if the Italians or Germans had been in our place in Aden they would have had endless anxiety and trouble

## AUTHOR'S FOREWORD

from the tribes, whereas we have only had a handful of political officers trying to pursue amid the difficulties of war the peaceful policy of progress in the Protectorate. And in that lies perhaps one of the most important aspects of their work. There are 100,000 Hadhrami in the Far East, in East Africa and in the centres of Islam. There has been plenty of evidence that our care for their homeland has done much to make them ally themselves with our cause.

I have dedicated this book to my wife, not because (though it is quite true) "without her help it would never have been written," but because without that help there would have been little to write about. I hope I may be forgiven for saying that she, like many others, is an exception to Freya Stark's dictum that "The British appear to be popular wherever they go until they come to settle with their wives." Nevertheless, as we all know, there is a lot in that statement and if I may add one word more to those contemplating a Colonial service career, it is, choose a wife who will not only share your life but that of the people amongst whom she and you will live.

I started by saying (and I hope the public repetition shows I am in earnest) that I am never going to write another book, but if I were I would dedicate it to those who have made possible the progress of the Aden Protectorate during the last few years. Firstly to our predecessors from Captain Haines onward to Colonel Lake who made and kept the friendship of the Arabs through a hundred difficult years of little encouragement and little money, and secondly to Sir Bernard Reilly, the Colonial Office and the Royal Air Force who have encouraged and made possible every forward move.

My next book I think would be dedicated to the Royal Geographical Society and the Royal Central Asian Society, not because they have so generously given medals to my wife and myself but because they have done so much to encourage interest in these lands and thereby stimulated much of the progress made.

Thirdly, I would dedicate one to all the unofficial travellers and particularly to Freya Stark, not because she paid us the charming compliment of dedicating her last book to us, certainly not because, like many another traveller, she has caused officials many an anxious moment, not alone because of precious friendship, but because her sympathy with and understanding of these people expressed with her eloquent pen has also contributed greatly to widen interest in them.

## AUTHOR'S FOREWORD

Last, but by no means least, I would very much like to dedicate a book to John Murray. Not because he has bravely ventured to publish this book, not only because publishers are too often forgotten (how many people remembering a book and an author also remember who the publisher was?), but because he has for a hundred years published almost every English book about the Hadhramaut—those of Welsted, Theodore Bent and his Mabel, Anna Virginia (why, oh why, did she not describe or depict her costume in the Hadhramaut) and Freya Stark. Mr. Murray is therefore also to be numbered amongst the benefactors of the Hadhramaut. And here I wish to record my unfailing gratitude to Mr. John G. Murray for endless help, advice and patience. Indeed if the book is at all readable it is due to him and Mr. Alan Watts, to whom also I acknowledge my indebtedness for his skilful help in revision.

*Bir al Azab, Sana,*
  *June* 1941.

## PRELUDE

*Naught befalleth us save that which God hath decreed for us.*   QURAN.

I USED to think it was pure chance that sent me into the Colonial Service, but Chance, we are told, is a nickname of Providence and looking back on events it seems to me that I followed unquestioningly the beckoning of the Moving Finger. There was nothing in my ancestry (unless a grandfather who wandered and died in Africa years before I was born), in my education or in my environment to encourage me to travel; rather the reverse. Yet despite every discouragement and without any realization that it was leading anywhere, my interest lay in books of discovery and exploration and the nearer East made most appeal. I owe to my father a fondness for natural history, for his hobby was British butterflies and moths, and this interest hand in hand with the other absorbed my attention to the detriment of a classical education and the cult of games.

My first interest in Arabs was aroused by an old missionary book called *Far Off*, and this led me, at eleven, to learn to read and write the Hebrew alphabet out of the 119th Psalm and a number of Hebrew and Arabic words from the glossary of a book on the Holy Land. Three exploits of which the records survive gave the same thrill as exploration on a larger scale. They were the crossing of a large and uncrossed bog to find what plants and animals were there, the finding of a rare fish in an unrecorded locality and during the war the discovery on a night patrol of an unmapped ditch in No Man's Land.

After I had been wounded and was a temporary home Civil Servant, I took an interest in Reconstruction and the Empire. One day early in 1919 I went into the smoking-room of my club after lunch and looked on the table to find something to read before going back to work. I picked up a discarded pamphlet called "Colonial Appointments." The title caught my eye because the problem of my future was interesting me. I read it through and this passage particularly stuck in my mind:

The duties of an Administrative officer are of a very varied character. In his district he is the immediate agent of the Government, and his

## PRELUDE

responsibility extends to all departments of the Administration which have not a special representative of their own at his station. Thus, in addition to his primary functions of magistrate and of political officer (i.e. the officer responsible for the maintenance of satisfactory relations between the natives and the Central Administration), he may be called upon to take charge of a detachment of police, to perform the duties of accountant for his district, to superintend the district prisons, or to supervise road construction, the clearing of waterways, or other public works. . . . Every officer is expected to do a certain amount of travelling, in the course of which he inspects the outlying portions of his district, transacts any necessary business with native chiefs, settles disputes between individuals or communities, and generally deals with all matters requiring the personal attention of a Government representative on the spot.

As things have turned out, I don't think it was chance that made me pick up that pamphlet, or strange that that passage made its appeal. I applied for appointment and it came about in due course that Lord Milner approved my selection as an Assistant District Commissioner in Zanzibar. On July 4th, 1919, I embarked at Tilbury in the *Durham Castle* bound for Zanzibar via the Cape.

## PART ONE

*Leave your home behind you,*
*Your friends by field and town*
*Oh, town and field will mind you*
*Till Ludlow tower is down.*
                              HOUSMAN.

## Chapter I

## THE ERYTHRAEAN SEA

*On this sea extending from China along India, Faris, Oman, Al Basra, Al Bahrein, Yemen, Abyssinia, Al Hejaz, Al Kulzum, Az Zanj, As Sind and the islands which it surrounds, are so many and various nations that their description and number is known only to the Almighty. . . . From the countries which form the coast of this sea, come different sorts of perfumes, scents, ambergris, various drugs used in medicine, plantains, cinnamon, cinnabar and incense.* MASUDI.

*India mittit ebur, molles sua tura Sabaei* VIRGIL.

TWENTY-TWO years of the Indian Ocean have made it seem like home to me. For this reason I may be prejudiced against other oceans, but when I consider their histories I feel that of all the waters of the world there is none to compare for romance and glamour with the one by whose shores I have worked. For one thing no other has been so long known to mankind. The first ships that sailed the seas came out of the Persian Gulf on to its broad waters. The Sumerians and their successors spread their culture far and wide in the lands surrounding it, and, in the sixth century B.C., the Phœnicians under the auspices of Pharaoh Neco made the first great voyage of which we know by sailing down the east coast of Africa and circumnavigating the whole continent. The earliest known civilizations are still being uncovered in the lands between the Euphrates and the Nile, and somewhere in this area lay the traditional cradle of our race. It cannot be doubted then, that of all mankind, those who live in these regions have the deepest interest for us, and not even yet have we learnt all we should like to know about them.

I have enjoyed nothing more than the many hours I have spent digging into books which might help me to picture the early history of these parts, and particularly that of the east coast of Africa. Of course this history is extremely shadowy, for East Africa boasts no early written records, and to gain some idea of what may have happened one can only point to analogies in the speech, manners and customs of its people with those of the people of the Persian Gulf and the Red Sea.

Zanzibar's story was largely written by the winds, for the regularity of the monsoons made it possible for sailors from many lands to visit it. No more vivid book on the Indian Ocean has been written in the last nineteen centuries than the *Periplus of the Erythraean Sea*—the first Sailing Directions to the Indian Ocean—and yet we do not know who the author was, beyond the fact that he was a Greek of Alexandria. It is clear from his book that he was no stay-at-home compiler of facts, like Pliny, for he gives his information as one who has seen the things he describes. His sentences are short, but each calls up a picture, not only of places as he saw them, but of their distant history. He was, perhaps, a merchant or a trading sea captain, for he gives much information on the trade of each port he visited. He shows himself so familiar with the scenes he describes that it is clear that he made many voyages, down the Red Sea, about as far as Dar es Salaam on the East African coast, and eastwards along the Arabian and Indian coasts to Malacca. I have this at least in common with him, that we both saw East Africa before Arabia.

He tells of a trade in East Africa which had already grown old and of a Zanzibar which had for long been a possession of "the state that is become first in Arabia." The Zanzibar coast was called the Ausanitic coast, and though, seven centuries before he wrote, the state of Ausan had been first in Arabia, its power had long passed away: that the name had endured so long shows how strong it once had been. Ausan had been swallowed up by Qataban, Qataban by Saba, or Sheba, and Himyar had succeeded to the glories of Saba before our author wrote. These four South Arabian kingdoms grew up in the Yemen, the south-west corner of Arabia, the Arabia Felix of the classical geographers.

At the time he wrote the Ausanitic or Zanzibar coast was governed by the Mapharitic chief, the Sheikh of the Ma'afir, a tribe which still exists in the Yemen lowlands. He had farmed it to the people of Mocha (which has given its name to the best Arabian coffee), "who send thither many large ships using Arab captains and agents who are familiar with the natives and intermarry with them, and who know the whole coast and understand the language."

Menuthias was the name by which the writer of the *Periplus* knew Zanzibar, though it was probably Zanzibar's sister and northern island of Pemba, called by the Arabs the "Green Island," to which he referred in particular. It was, he says, "low and wooded." There were "sewed boats, and canoes hollowed from single logs." The people also caught fish "in a peculiar way in wicker baskets." All this is true of Pemba to-day.

Two days' sail beyond Menuthias was the town called Rhapta, "the very last market town of the continent of Azania": it owed its name to the sewed boats that were made there, for the Arabic *rabta* means "he bound or tied." Azania is, no doubt, a form of Zanzibar, which means "the Land of the Blacks." Rhapta was the last place on the coast our author visited; beyond he believed the unexplored ocean to curve round to the west. When he has described Rhapta he goes back and describes the South Arabian ports east of Aden, "Eudaemon Arabia" (Araby the Blest), "a village by the shore, also of the Kingdom of Charibael." Kariba-Il Watar Yuhannim was his name in Arabic. He was the King of Himyar and the title Kariba-Il means "God blessed him." Aden had "convenient anchorages and watering-places, sweeter and better than those at Ocelis, opposite Perim."

This sounds as if the Aden of those days had something better than the famous tanks visited by almost every passing traveller, for if the water had come from rain-water tanks he would probably have said so.

Beyond Aden along the coast were "Nomads and Fish-Eaters living in villages," just as they do now. Then came "Cana, of the Kingdom of Eleazus, the Frankincense country," near the modern Balhaf and Bir 'Ali, trading with East Africa, as the men of Shihr, a near-by port, do to-day. After Cana were two islands, "one called Island of Birds, the other Dome Island," tiny islets to-day called Sikkah and Jezirat Borraka which I have seen from the air white with guano, much sought after in Mukalla, and with the surf breaking over them. Beyond comes the frankincense country and when I saw it from above his words came back to me— "mountainous and forbidding, wrapped in thick clouds and fog." What a tale is here in this book now nineteen hundred years old! I can testify to its accuracy for I have journeyed not once but often in his wake through Azanian and Arabian waters.

It is a tale of a most romantic trade, the trade of East and West, of the men who sought the "ivory, apes and peacocks," gold and silver, frankincense and myrrh, the spices of the East and the black human cargo for the service of the rich. Fearing no hardships they journeyed far, by sea and land, bringing luxuries to deck the temples and adorn the women of the West. The tale of this trade has continued through the ages and London shared in it at an early date: old John Stow quotes Fitzstephen's twelfth century boastful plagiarism of Virgil:

Aurum mittit Arabs: species et thura Sabaeus:
Arma Scythes: oleum palmarum divite sylva.
Pingue solum Babylon: Nilus lapides pretiosos
Seres purpureas vestes:

After the *Periplus* we do not for long centuries get such a clear light on the life and history of these countries, nor of Arab dealings with East Africa, but we hear enough to know that through all that time the intercourse has continued. We read of men from the Yemen flying from religious persecution to the East African coast, probably in the eighth century, and they would not have gone there had it not been for their traditional connection with it. But by this time Yemeni influence in East Africa was declining. A century earlier Suleiman and Sa'id, sons of 'Abbad, chieftains of Oman in the opposite corner of Arabia, the south-eastern, had sought refuge in the "land of Zinj" from Muja'ah, general of the Caliph 'Abdul Malik's tyrant governor Al Hajjaj. De Barros, the Portuguese historian, tells us of immigrants from Al Hasa in South-East Arabia, and in 924 came the Al Harth Arabs from Oman. So the Yemen fugitives disappeared, and driven inland by the men of Al Hasa, their religious opponents, became wandering traders and were absorbed by intermarriage with the negroes.

Islam is divided into two great camps, Sunni and Shia. The men of Yemen who fled to East Africa were, and the rulers of the country still are, Shias of the Zeidi sect. The men of Hasa were orthodox Sunnis and belonged to the school of Shafi, one of their four great Imams or teachers. As in Christianity, so in Islam there are many sects; many more than the two and seventy of which Omar Khayyam speaks, but in the main a Muslim can be classed as either a Sunni, a Shia, or a Khariji, a seceder. The split belongs to the very early days. 'Ali, son-in-law of the prophet Muhammad, was a modest self-effacing man and when there was a dispute as to whether he or Muawiya should succeed to the Caliphate, he wished to submit their respective claims to arbitration, although he himself had been elected. This was the rock on which Islam split, for many of 'Ali's followers broke away from him because he did not insist on his being the prophet's heir, which they thought gave him the divine right to succeed: these were the Shias. A smaller number broke away because he did not insist on his right as elected Caliph: these were the Kharijis.

The inhabitants of East Africa and South Arabia are mostly followers of the Sunni Imam ash Shafi, buried in Cairo, who started his mission in A.D. 813. It must have been after this date and before A.D. 975 that East

## EARLY EXPEDITIONS OF DISCOVERY

Africa adopted the faith of Islam, for in that year came a Shia invasion from Persia when Hassan bin 'Ali of Shiraz founded the Zenj or Zinj Empire. Hassan was Sultan of Shiraz and had six sons. One day he had a dream of a rat with an iron snout gnawing at the walls of his city and foreboded the ruin of the country. His first thought being naturally of his own safety, he determined to escape while the going was good and he and his six sons sailed in seven ships. The fourth stopped at Mombasa, the fifth at Pemba, the sixth at Kilwa on the East African coast, and the seventh at Henzuan in the Comorro Islands. Thus was founded, so legend says, the Zenj Empire. Lacking cohesion, and, with the usual dissensions of oriental states, it soon split up into a loose federation, and later into quite independent city states which warred against each other. Their coins are still found at Kilwa and on Chole, the third island of the Zanzibar Archipelago, better known by its Portuguese name of Mafia or Mönfiyeh in which they perpetuated the ancient Menuthias.

The rulers of these petty states were:

> "... the less maritime kings,
> Mombasa, and Quiloa, and Melind,
> And Sofala (thought Ophir) ..."

of whom Milton speaks.

In 1498 the great Portuguese navigator Vasco da Gama discovered the Zanzibar coast. By rounding the Cape of Good Hope and finding the sea road to India, he had sounded the death-knell of Venice which had for centuries controlled the trade from the east. In 1503 the Portuguese discovered the Grand Comorro, and 1506, Madagascar, and at about the same time the islands now called Réunion, Mauritius and Rodrigues, one of which had been long known to the Arabs as "Margabin"—Maghrabin the Western.

The Portuguese took little interest in Madgascar and Mauritius, but used the East African route to India. In 1591 Sir James Lancaster sailed in the *Edward Bonaventure* to "the Isles of Comoro and Zanzibar, on the backeside of Africa." On his report the merchants and adventurers of London founded the East India Company in 1599, and in 1600 their first expedition started out. The competitive trade with India had begun.

The French were next on the scene and in 1616 de Nets and Beaulieu reached India by sea. Unlike the Portuguese, the French and the Dutch never made any attempt to establish their ports of refreshment on the

7

east coast of Africa, and although the first voyages of the English were up the coast they, too, soon abandoned that route. The probability is that as the Portuguese were firmly established on the coast by that time, other nations felt that they would be more secure if they sought other routes, for, apart from the Portuguese themselves, there were hostile Arabs and tribes to be taken into consideration. The people of the East Coast had learnt from the Portuguese what might be expected of Europeans, and Sir James Lancaster heard at Zanzibar the tales that had been spread of his countrymen. The other nations were wise in avoiding the East African coast, for it was pestilential enough in the eighteenth and nineteenth centuries and there is evidence it was bad in the sixteenth and seventeenth. Certainly its fevers made serious inroads in the strength of the Portuguese who lost many men and much money there.

The Dutch took quiet possession of Mauritius in 1598, and after two hundred years of exploiting its ebony they left it, defeated by the rats imported by the Portuguese, and by wild bands of maroon or runaway slaves, mainly of African extraction and uncontrolled by any tribal or political system, whom they had imported themselves. When the Dutch had left the island the French annexed and developed it, chiefly under the great colonist Mahé de La Bourdonnais, who was Governor from 1735 to 1747. Faced with the need of a labour supply, La Bourdonnais established a flourishing slave trade with Madagascar and the coast of Africa. Mauritius now became, and continued until the eighteen forties, the principal centre of European influence in the South Indian ocean and earned its motto of "The Star and Key of the Indian Ocean." In 1767 the celebrated agriculturist and botanist, Pierre Poivre, was appointed Intendant of Mauritius, and, wanting to develop its resources, sent a secret mission to the Moluccas to steal clove seed, which was jealously guarded by the Dutch.

Mauritius did not long stick to her cloves and early abandoned them for sugar, but if a chance made her Zanzibar's debtor over the slaves she had taken, another allowed her to repay by passing the cloves to Zanzibar—but this is anticipating.

The Portuguese were never popular in Zanzibar and at other east coast towns, owing to their misrule. In 1652 they were attacked in Zanzibar by an Omani expedition, and in 1698 the Imam of Oman, Seif bin Sultan, broke their power in East Africa for ever by driving them from Kilwa, Mombasa and Pemba. The rulers of Oman were followers of 'Abdulla bin Ibadh, founder of one of the principal Khariji sects, and so, by Seif's conquest, the Ibadhis established themselves in Zanzibar where they have flourished. Their founder lived in the days of the Caliph Merwan who reigned from 744 to 749, and the root of his teaching was that the leader of the Muslims must be above reproach, pious and just; he was to be elected for those qualities, but it was not the election alone that placed him above his fellows, as in the case of the Pope, for if he proved unworthy he was to be removed. Nor did divine right have any part in his election, nor a hereditary principle, as the Shias vainly say. These principles of the importance of piety and justice and the unimportance of form find their expression in all that distinguishes Ibadhi from Sunni. In 1741 Ahmed bin Sa'id was elected Imam and became the founder of the Albusaid dynasty which to-day rules in Zanzibar and Oman.

Relations between the French in Mauritius and the Arabs in Oman and Zanzibar were very friendly until a French privateer seized an Omani frigate in 1781. Negotiations resulted in a climb down by the French who presented another ship in exchange for the one seized. The Imam Ahmed's letter acknowledging the restitution is amusing:

> "Your words have had their effect; your generous gift has reached us; and although the ship which has been sent to us is very small and is not worth a quarter of the one we lost, it is to our eyes much larger, it is infinitely more pleasant; and our possession of it gives us greater pleasure; for everything is common between us, and this would have been no less even if we had not received this present."

In 1832 Ahmed's grandson, Seiyid Sa'id, greatest of Zanzibar Sultans and founder of its fortunes, transferred his capital from Muscat to Zanzibar. By this time Mauritius had become British, for it was captured in 1810. British relations with Oman were conducted then, as the French had been, through the Governor of Mauritius. Sa'id's name was well known in Europe, and Oman had become the first state in Arabia.

With the transfer Zanzibar became the capital of a short-lived empire which included the whole of Oman with certain islands in the Persian Gulf, and the coast of Africa for 960 miles from Guardafui to Cape Delgado. In addition Seiyid Sa'id's sway was acknowledged in the interior from the coast to beyond the great lakes. He had set his eyes even further for he had sent Arabs to settle in Nossi Bé in Madagascar, and had even sought the hand of Ranavolana Manjaka, its queen, in marriage. A reply came in English from the lady and a rejection of the proposal from her ministers; they offered a princess instead. No one could read English at the Zanzibar court, so the Master of a brig in harbour was called in to read it to the interpreter who translated it into Arabic. Captain Hart, of the *Imogene*, mentions this affair in his report on Zanzibar and says that the solemnity observed upon the occasion can better be imagined than described. The queen, after various good wishes, said she would be very much obliged if he would have the kindness to send her a coral necklace of a thousand dollars; she hoped their friendship would increase and that they would become better acquainted. "His Highness," says Captain Hart, "was disappointed that there was not more said about love in the queen's letter; but the Master of the brig consoled him by saying she had said as much as she could say in a first letter."

All that we know of Seiyid Sa'id show him to have been a man of imagination, a student of history. Soldier, sailor, diplomat, and first merchant of his realm, he made Zanzibar more than a trading centre: he saw the possibility of clove cultivation. Probably he knew of the eternal quest of Europe for the spices, as well as for the ivory and precious stones, of Asia and Africa. Poivre in Mauritius had distributed the contents of his stolen chest of cloves to the West Indies as well as to Mauritius, Bourbon and Madagascar. Poivre had failed to create an industry capable of rivalling the Dutch—but he, Sa'id, might succeed. Even the Dutch had succeeded for a time in establishing the clove in alien soil in Amboyna and had ordered the destruction of the trees in their native isles of Ternate and Tidore. An Arab brought the cloves from Bourbon: Sa'id issued an edict that every plantation owner should plant three cloves for one coco-nut. It was a wise move for the Arabs were not keen to plant cloves. Their uses were unknown to them and they must wait long before the problematic crop flourished. Sa'id succeeded, and it is principally as a landowner and clove grower that one sees the Omani settler to-day, for in course of time Zanzibar, with Pemba, produced 97 per cent of the world's clove supply. Though the prosperity of the Arabs declined after the abolition of slave labour, the industry continued to flourish until the depression of the last few years and the competition of Madagascar and synthetic vanillin.

Under Sa'id's direction Zanzibar soon became both politically and commercially the principal city in East Africa. To him and to his son Barghash, who reigned from 1870 to 1888, is largely due the prestige of Zanzibar to-day. "If you play the flute at Zanzibar," said the well-known Arab proverb of the time, "all Africa as far as the Lakes dances."

Sa'id died at sea in 1856 and was brought back to be buried in his

Zanzibar. His contemporaries recognized his greatness and desired to erect a domed tomb over his remains. But the tomb rests roofless to-day; before the walls were finished the 'Ulema, the bench of jurists, ruled the project impious: the tomb best loved and known of God is the one unknown to man. Perhaps they ruled wisely. As Cæsar says of Pompey in *The False One*:

> Nothing can cover his high fame but Heaven
> No pyramid set off his memories
> But the eternal substance of his greatness
> To which I leave him.

## Chapter II

## A POOH BAH IN PEMBA

*the Isles
of Ternate and Tidore, whence merchants bring
Their spicy drugs.* MILTON.

THERE are places where one instinctively feels at home. I did in Zanzibar and in the Hadhramaut, and I am sure I would in Oman. On the other hand I have not the same feeling for the Yemen. Before I went to Zanzibar there was talk of my going to Nigeria, but I knew that it was Zanzibar I wanted and I had even bought an Arabic grammar in anticipation. As I go to each new place I make a habit of watching it draw nearer, and I always hope it will be the dawn that gives me the first glimpse of a new home. So far I have been lucky and the impression left on me with the sun rising on the shores of Zanzibar on the morning of August 25, 1919, is ineffaceable.

I came up from the rat-infested hold of the ship in which I had made an unpleasant week's voyage from Durban (it was in the days of a shortage of shipping), and saw first a low, purple streak on the horizon. As we drew near, and as the sun rose, feathery palms appeared standing amid a vivid green of grass and undergrowth. A coral shore of dazzling whiteness and a sea shaded from pale green to dark blue made an unforgettable foreground. The tall white houses of Zanzibar town, standing high and square, reached almost to the water front, dominated by the verandaed palace with high clock tower called the Beit al Ajaib—the House of Wonders. Its clock seems always six hours wrong to the newcomer, for it keeps—and may it always keep—Arab or Biblical time and is set at sunset each day. There is but one minaret on Zanzibar's water front, at its northern end, Malindi, where the dhows congregate. It is a minaret of Hadhramaut pattern and was built by a man from Shihr. The Ibadhis think that decoration of mosques is wrong and their architecture is therefore plain and severe.

I saw little of Zanzibar on that first arrival, for in a week I was sent to Pemba and travelled there in His Highness' ship *Cupid*, one of the two

## A FIRST SPEECH

little steamers that formed Zanzibar's fleet. Though in the war they were armed, their calling is a peaceful one, for they maintain a weekly service with the sister isle and bring its cloves to Zanzibar. On state occasions they carry their royal master, His Highness the Sultan, on his visits to Pemba.

I arrived at Weti in Pemba in the last day or so of Ramadhan, and was faced with the necessity of making a speech to the notables of the little township, when they paid a state call on 'Id al Fitr, the day of fast breaking. I could make it, I was told, in English which would be interpreted, or in Swahili which I did not know. As my visitors were to be Arabs, I asked if I could not make my speech in Arabic, of which my knowledge was no less than Swahili. This idea went down well and the office set to to translate my modest oration. I made it short for I meant to learn it by heart. It was written in Arabic and transliterated, but I asked for it to be written as it should be pronounced, and then I learned it off.

The great day came. The Liwali, the Arab Governor, Sa'id bin 'Isa al Isma'ili, leader of the Isma'ili clan which was the principal family of Weti district, arrived with the Qadhi, the Arab Judge, Sheikh Muhammad of the Albusaidi tribe from which come the Aulad al Imam, the royal family of Zanzibar, and several other notables. The interpreter, 'Abdulla 'Ali, brought up the rear. Up the steps they came clad in full dress—a joho, a long dark blue overcoat with corded seams and braided facings of gold, over their white kanzus. At their waists the silver heads of their jambiyas —curved daggers—peeped out from gay sashes of silk. Their little white everyday skull caps were practically concealed by their imposing turbans of blue, gold and red. I found afterwards that these turbans when unfolded are large enough to serve as bedspreads. Their sandals they had left at the foot of the stairs, but their gold- and ivory-hilted swords clattered on the steps. I awaited them at the top and led the way into the sitting-room where coffee was served. At last the fatal moment arrived. I got up, cleared my throat, and began.

"Ya ayuha al Izzer," started my phonetically written speech. It was received in solemn silence—not a smile on any of those grave, bearded faces. At the end they all said "Amin" which made me feel all the more that we were taking part in a solemn ceremony. They got up—they made their good-byes. Next morning I asked 'Abdulla 'Ali how he thought the speech had gone off.

"Very well, Bwana," he said. "They asked me what it was about when we left and I read it to them from my copy. They liked it very much."

13

## A POOH BAH IN PEMBA

In the months that followed 'Abdulla 'Ali taught me to write Arabic. I learned the letters from him and never forgot them, but the Arabic did not progress. However, the letters came in useful for writing Swahili which I *had* to learn. Indeed my days were pretty full with picking up information of all kinds, and I soon found that that Colonial Office pamphlet had described the duties of District Officers with extreme economy of words.

Some say that the best way of teaching a child to swim is to throw it into deep water. How effective the method is with swimming I do not know, but I know that it did me a world of good to be left entirely alone to worry out the problems of a district for myself. Perhaps is was not always so good for those on whom I experimented, but in the only two cases I remember where this happened the sufferers became thereafter my firm friends. The cases were court cases, for I was vested with the powers of a third-class magistrate and could give up to six months' imprisonment. The very first case I tried was one of criminal trespass and assault. I was not entirely clear as to what this meant, but the meaning grew on me as the case proceeded.

The first witness told the story of how the accused claimed that his next door neighbour's shamba or plantation was his. This did not sound very serious but then it transpired that when the neighbour declined to admit the claim, the accused went into his plantation and tore up three young coco-nut plants. By this time I was beginning to wonder what sort of sentence I ought to pass. Perhaps a fine of ten rupees or a week or so. It seemed that the owner of the shamba had been very forbearing about this, and other witnesses said the accused had, after an interval, torn up a lot more coco-nuts. The option dropped out of my calculations; it must be at least a month, I thought. Then I heard that the owner had lain in wait for our trespasser and got really angry with him when he came to pull up more coco-nuts. The accused had knocked him down. The penalty now rose in a steep curve, as the mathematicians say. I thought of three months and waited to hear what the accused had to say in his defence. He said nothing in his defence; in my mind he was making things much worse by glorying in his pulling up of promising coco-nuts. "It is my shamba," he said. "Why shouldn't I pull them up?"

When the case was over I quickly wrote my judgement. I did not want to show hesitancy as I had an idea that I had to show unfaltering decision. I gave him six months. I thought the court looked rather taken aback at this, but the police, though surprised, were obviously pleased.

The prisoner just smiled. I was also Deputy Governor of the local prison (the Governor of Prisons lived in Zanzibar), so I saw a good deal of the man in the next six months, and in fact took rather an interest in him as he belonged entirely to me, so to speak. He always smiled and greeted me cheerfully when I inspected the prison and no prisoner was ever more assiduous in collecting firewood for me. I began to think I had conferred a boon on him and when he left the jail he brought me a present of eggs. A year later, when I was in Zanzibar district, I found him living there and he did his best to supply me with milk free of charge. I am not sure what broke our friendship, but one day I insisted on paying him, and I never saw him again.

The other case was of an Arab fresh from Arabia, who, in a brawl with a friend, knifed him on the main road. He got six weeks, but it seemed that it was not usually done to give an Arab imprisonment in the local jail with the natives, so he appealed. The appeal was dismissed on technical grounds. In Zanzibar there are two sets of courts, His Britannic Majesty's and his Highness the Sultan's. District Officers were magistrates in both. As the man was a native of Oman he was a subject of the Sultan, but I, inadvertently, had charged him on a charge sheet printed "In His Britannic Majesty's court for Zanzibar." The man's pleader took the case to the Sultan's court, where it was dismissed as the court had no jurisdiction. This man, too, became a bosom friend and was always coming to call on me. All this court work made it very easy to learn Swahili, and I soon discovered I knew what a witness said before the interpreter translated it.

Apart from court work and the jail, I was also in charge of the local detachment of police and used to drill them every Saturday morning. It shocked my then fairly recent sense of military propriety when the Jemadar —the sergeant-major—came on parade not only with a sword but also with an umbrella. He was quite hurt when I made him give it up.

But I had many other jobs: I was the local Pooh Bah. I was Port Officer, Collector of Customs, Postmaster, Registrar of Births, Deaths and Marriages, Probate Agent, Registrar of Documents, Sub-Treasurer and I dare say other things as well. At my office, in my main capacity of Assistant District Commissioner, I found myself giving advice to husbands whose wives no longer loved them, settling disputes between neighbours over each other's fowls, and many other things. In the intervals of learning my work I made friends among the Arabs, for society in Weti was principally Arab.

Arabs in Zanzibar and Pemba were of three kinds and the Swahili in his language is extremely apt and particular with his distinctions. Before Mr. Ford produced a vehicle that looked like a motor-car, there was a marked difference between *fodi* and *motokari*. Then a bus or a lorry is plainly neither a motor-car nor a Ford car. The Swahili called it *mtwana* (the slave), because the lorry carried loads and the bus was at anyone's beck and call. He made no distinction because in Zanzibar both carried freight and passengers in happy and almost complete indiscrimination. So with Arabs. There are *Wa Arabu*, *Wa Manga* and *Wa Shihiri*. The *Wa Arabu*, the Arabs, are the settlers—creoles—of Zanzibar. The *Wa Manga* are immigrant Arabs from Oman and even the crews of dhows from other parts. The *Wa Shihiri* are immigrant men of Shihr, and, by extension, of anywhere in the Hadhramaut. Even the newcomer soon learnt to distinguish the Arab and the Manga. The Shihiri, almost of another race, was even more obvious. Though the Arab and the Manga come from the same tribes, and some may even be closely related, there is no confusing them. The Zanzibar Arab is a slow and stately mover, and the older generation is somewhat apt to run to flesh. His cousin, fresh from Oman, is quicker and wirier. The beard of the Zanzibari seems bushier and more cultivated than the long but often thin and straggly one of the Manga, whose eye, too, deep set under shaggy brows peers wild and penetrating, and has not the gentle glance of one who for two or three generations has lived a peaceful, protected life in town or clove plantation. The Arabic of Zanzibar, influenced by the soft Swahili, has grown less guttural than that of the tribesman newly come, and even when the latter has learnt Swahili "his speech betrayeth him."

All the Arabs of Zanzibar speak Swahili as their *lingua franca*, though they write in Arabic, so that once I had mastered the former language conversation never flagged, and it became more of an effort to learn the latter. Most of the Arabs were well-to-do landlords who spent their time in pleasant ease on their plantations in the district. Many lived a few miles out of Weti and used to come in to market or to transact official business. On these occasions some of them made a habit of visiting my office to pass the time of day.

One of the more frequent—and the more impressive—of these visitors was an old Sheikh of the Filahi tribe. He was fat and jovial, but always dignified; a humorous smile forever lurked on his face and he had one of the finest, bushiest, iron-grey beards I have ever seen. He also had a splendidly hooked nose of true Semitic type. He belonged to the minority who wore a *bushti* and not a *joho*. The *bushti* is a brown or cream cloak—my old friend favoured the brown—heavily embroidered with cloth of gold over the yoke, it is made of camel's hair and, cooler than the joho, it is a much fuller garment. The Sheikh used to come in and apologize for not taking off his sandals, and he was quite right for the office floor was generally filthy. There was a little quiet conversation, crop prospects, the laziness of his hands, politics, the weather, and then he left, and I watched him through the office window walking majestically, for all his moderate height, down the centre of the road, his sandals flapping and his left hand behind his back under his ample *bushti*. A corner of his turban hung saucily from the crown of his head like the feather in a Tyrolean hat. In his right hand he carried a stick with which, and a slight bow, he acknowledged the salutations of the passers-by. He was almost aldermanic in his style and had an alderman's bow window. Sometimes he asked me out to lunch on Sundays on his plantation, five or six miles away, and I have the pleasantest recollections of lazy days spent there on the veranda of an inner courtyard; of afternoon walks, slow and stately, through his clove plantation; of the afternoon sun shining through the mangrove trees and the warm yellow light on the mud-brick walls of his house.

These Sunday lunches in the country were a pleasant feature of life. Other Arabs who invited me to spend the day with them were three young brothers of the Riami family, living at Selem. Starting at about eleven I rode on my donkey through six miles of shady avenues of cloves to their large, rambling, mud-built brick house with untidy courtyard like a French farm. There were always excellent fried and spiced eggs for lunch as well as stuffed chicken. In the evening, before I rode home, we sat in the shade of the trees amid the smell of frangipani and ylang ylang. They always gave me a few red roses to take home; familiar flowers seem more pleasant in a foreign land. I became fast friends with the family, and when his father-in-law died Ahmed bin Sultan, the eldest, broke the sad news to me in the following note:

"We are very glad to notify you that the father of my wife is dead, on date 26/2/20 thusday last."

Most of the rich landowners of Zanzibar and Pemba were Arabs, though they are a small minority of the population. In 1924, for instance, when the total population of the Sultanate was about 202,000 only 16,000 were Arabs. There were the same number of Indians and other foreigners and the rest were African natives of the country. The Arabs did not give a District Officer much trouble or work, and contact with them was, for the most part, a pleasant way of filling leisure hours. But their indebtedness was a constant source of worry; for their plantations were in many cases heavily mortgaged to moneylenders.

I had only been in Weti nine months when I was transferred to Mkokotoni in Zanzibar, and there I was soon involved in the annual business of obtaining pickers for cloves. If clove trees are to bear freely the plantations have to be kept regularly weeded. In old days this was done by slave labour, but after the freedom of the slaves the labour deteriorated and plantations became less productive. Many of the freed slaves remained on their former owners' plantations, referred to themselves as slaves and were often proud of their title. Their masters, too, liked to have them there. They regarded them as their children and it added to their prestige. The slaves also helped with the picking, but as a general rule most of it, both in Zanzibar and Pemba, was done by the Wahadimu, one of the aboriginal tribes who lived mostly in the south and east of Zanzibar, growing coco-nuts and native crops rather than cloves. The search for labour involved much travelling and I had soon covered the whole of my district on donkey or by boat, visiting the Wahadimu villages and arranging with the Shehas, the native headmen, to persuade the young men to go picking. I had, too, to visit the plantations seeing whether the owners had enough labour and whether the pickers had any complaints.

IT was clove picking time that I first met Sheikh Sa'id bin 'Abdulla al Kharusi, who for long has called me his "brother." He came into my office at Mkokotoni to make my acquaintance and I liked him at first sight. Short and stocky, he had then only a few grey hairs in his black beard. I think he has as honest eyes as any man I know, eyes that never waver as he looks you in the face. He asked me to spend the following week-end with him at his plantation at Kinyasini, some seven or eight miles south-east of Mkokotoni. Thus began a friendship which has lasted through twenty-one years.

The week-ends I spent with Sa'id were among the happiest I remember. During the rest of my time at Mkokotoni they were frequent, and not the least enjoyable part was the donkey ride there, for my way lay through shady clove plantations, groves of coco-nuts, open country and bush. There was a difficult river to ford but above its banks beautiful *gloriosa superba* lilies grew in profusion. At the village of Chaani, with its huts built of red earth, I used to stop and drink with the Sheha a fresh-cut, cool madafu, the milk of the unripe coco-nut. The last mile or two lay between shady avenues of cloves till I came to the well-kept ride that led to Sa'id's pleasant bungalow. The clatter of my donkey's hoofs on the sikafu brought him from the shade of the veranda. On this first visit in clove harvest time he was in working garb, a kanzu made of Muscat homespun unbleached cloth called khudhurungi.

"Karibu—you're welcome," as I dismounted from my donkey which was at once led away to the stable. I took Sa'id's outstretched hand and answered and countered all the enquiries as to health, and my ride. I was taken to the cool veranda and put in a deck-chair. Sa'id took another.

"Bring a madafu," and again the welcome cooling drink appeared. Members of the family who were there came up to be introduced, for Sa'id sent his sons to the Government school and some were in town. 'Abdulla and Muhammad, the two eldest at the awkward ages of seventeen and eighteen, came and talked in schoolboy English. Their education was over. Hamud, sick, but not sick enough to be miserable, was, like any schoolboy, glad of the excuse to be free. His favourite weapon at the time was a catapult. Here in the shambas he would use it as he liked and was good at knocking crows off the coco-nut trees. In town it was not so popular and his father had administered, as he told me at our introduction, a beating when he broke a neighbour's window. Hamud hung his head, but next morning he was showing me what he could do. Suleiman, the youngest, a baby of five or six, was too young to be at school. "Suleiman has just been circumcised," said his father. "Show the Bwana your cut, Suleiman."

Suleiman and I were equally embarrassed, but he was caught by his father and the ngariba's handiwork displayed. When he had recovered his dignity he sat on my knee and thereafter spent much of his time with me, telling me all about the events of the day. How a picker had fallen off a tree. How Hamud had killed a wood pigeon with his catapult. Of a snake in the rice field below the garden.

At lunch-time the family were banished to the back of the house where Mrs. Sa'id reigned supreme. Sa'id and his one wife were a devoted couple; she had borne him ten children of whom nine were living, eight boys and one girl, Assia, then about fourteen. Assia was always her father's favourite, but on this first visit I did not meet Mrs. Sa'id or Assia.

Sa'id led the way into the dining-room. It astonished me, for I expected the usual bare room and the usual tray of rice and curry. But it was far more homelike and inviting than my own sparsely furnished bungalow. The walls were painted white with a dado of green. The ceiling was supported by brown beams and from the centre hung suspended a punkah pulled by a servant outside. Though door and all four windows stood open, the punkah tempered agreeably the hot February weather. Polished silver shone invitingly on a snowy white tablecloth, and the floor was deep in Shirazi rugs into which my feet sank. What a contrast it was to the usual shamba house of bare, white-washed mud walls and mat-strewn floor!

"Tafadhl—Draw up and make yourself at home."

I sat at one end and Sa'id at the other.

"Leti chakula—bring the food. You must excuse this poor shamba food. Chakula cha kiarabu—Arab food, you know."

But I was already loud in my admiration of everything.

"Ah, it's nothing; all very rough. Our people don't know how to cook food properly. Not a proper feast, you know, just ordinary."

The soup came. The boys were not skilful waiters but they did their best.

Soup was disposed of. Sa'id knew that Europeans drink soup, but Arabs do not usually have it, and though it was somewhat watery it was most hospitable to produce it at all.

Fish followed—fried and hot with spices and onions but served cold. It was good. There was a wait. Sa'id kept shouting all the time:

"Ya nini hii—why all this delay?"

Plates were changed; along came a kabab of chicken, and though he served me liberally (we used our own knives and forks for there were no servers), it was so excellent that I cleaned my plate. More wait. Another change of plates. Kuku wa kukaanga—braised chicken. I opened my eyes —what a lunch! It was hard work to dispose of a moderate helping.

"Have some more. You're eating very little."

"I couldn't really, I've had an awful lot."

"It's poor food, I know. You ought to have brought your cook."

So I had to have another go. We shall be about finished now, I thought; perhaps a sweet.

Kababs of meat. Help!

"This is good," said Sa'id, "a little."

I was nearly exhausted, but he was a marvellous trencherman.

Sambusa—small meat pasties. Each time the plate was changed. I had ceased to wonder when it would end.

Braised meat.

Skewers with pieces of roasted meat on them.

"Ah, you must have more of this. We always have this," said Sa'id, pulling off half a dozen pieces and putting them on my plate. Even the boys were laughing at me. I manfully kept up.

Mkati wa kusukuma. Thank heaven! The meat courses were finished.

"This is very light. Nyepesi sana. This doesn't make any difference at all."

Mkati wa khokho. Another kind of pastry.

Al kemati. "Something sweet," said Sa'id. "You must have something sweet."

Villosa. Another sweet. I had just one. Then I gave out. I was more than full, I could hardly sit upright. I wanted air.

"Very hot," said Sa'id. "Boy, pull the punkah harder. Have some sherbet?" A pale purple concoction was poured into my glass. Thank heaven it must be over. Soon I could rest. I was already beyond speech. The plates were taken away. Others appeared. What could it be?

A mountain of curry and rice made its appearance. I just gasped.

"A meal isn't a meal without some rice," said Sa'id cheerfully, piling my plate with the well-cooked white grains and picking out a few wings of chicken to put on top.

He was soon busy at a similar helping. I could do no more than toy and stir it up. It was taken away.

"We'd have done better with our fingers," sighed Sa'id.

Cooked fruit.

"Pudin." A caramel pudding, another concession to Western tastes. I poured down a spoonful or two, for it would have been dreadful to pass this compliment by.

A plate of farne, a dish I always liked—a kind of ground rice with special flavouring and sweet—appeared. A teaspoonful was all I could do.

Then came bananas, pineapples, and oranges, fresh from the shamba. But I was beyond all help. No drunken man was ever more incapable of speech and motion.

I stretched myself with difficulty on the floor and slept... and slept.

\* \* \*

"Tea," said the voice of Sa'id. It seemed distant, but he was there, calling me up. I had slept for three hours or so and rose from the floor where I had lain. Tea was on the table. There was a Chinese tea service with red dragons crawling over it. Arabs are so wholesale in their kindness that they cannot really understand making a pot of tea with two spoonfuls of leaves. It was black, but sugar and plentiful milk helped and I think I felt better after it. I could do no more than sample the delicious sponge cakes which Assia makes and which I now met for the first time.

Sa'id suggested a walk, which I thought a good idea. He showed me the fruit trees near the house, coloured crotons and cannas. The ylang ylang, with its curious, sweetly scented but otherwise uninteresting flowers hidden at the joints of the twigs. We wandered among the clove trees. Work was ending now and men and boys were making their way back to the sikafu.

We returned at sunset. Fires were alight and meals cooking. A chattering crowd of women stemmed and the men carried the baskets along to be measured. A grave young Arab, the overseer, poured in the cloves and heaped up a pishi (about six pounds) in the wooden measure, watched anxiously by the picker. The copper pice were paid over. The wage was then about six pice a pishi, though it varied from shamba to shamba and year to year. It might be as little as four or as much as sixteen, equal to four annas, the quarter of a rupee.

Sa'id had disappeared into the house. He came out with a kettle and made for the wash house across the sikafu. He was clad now only in vest and kikoi—the futa of Arabia. It was of Muscat pattern, white with coloured borders. He had wooden sandals on his feet held by a stud between the first two toes.

His feet, arms, and beard were wet, and spreading a little coloured mat made in Mafia he proceeded to say his sunset prayers. Sa'id is an example to all men in the matter of religion. He lives his religion but he never parades it, and I have never known him miss his prayers wherever he may be. He may disagree but it is impossible to provoke him to a religious debate. Of all men I know the Ibadhi is least bigoted in religion, and this is especially true of Sa'id. When I stayed with him there were often other guests, not only Arabs, but Parsees and Indians. If Sa'id found them tired and needing a rest, they would be brought out for a few days in the country. He would remind his Muslim guests of the hours of prayer, and if they prayed, fetch them water and their mats. The Ibadhi does not believe in too much formality about the observances of his faith: thus while prayer he does not adhere to the attitudes laid down for the Sunnis, and moves his head and arms as he pleases. It is a nonconformist type of faith and insists on its elected leader being a good man.

Night had fallen now for in these latitudes there is little twilight. Fires twinkled and lanterns passed through the darkened groves.

I will draw a veil over dinner: there were twenty-six courses.

When the ordeal was over our deck-chairs were put out on the sikafu. Boys brought the little handleless coffee-cups, pouring half-cups of bitter coffee from a graceful, slender-waisted, long-spouted pot. The Arab of Zanzibar hates to miss this black coffee after a meal, and it certainly does help to settle things. Amongst Omanis it is not good manners to pour more than half a cup at a time, and up to three might be taken. I had learnt by now to give the little shake to the cup when handing it back to the server, which means that one has had enough. As we sat there in the soft night air heavily laden with jasmine and ylang ylang, white figures approached.

"Salaam aleikum."

"Wa Aleikum as salaam," replied Sa'id as we hoisted ourselves with difficulty from the low chairs.

"Qarib, qarib. Boy, leti viti—bring some more chairs."

These were neighbours, Mangas who had rented near-by shambas for the harvest. Few of them could talk Swahili or at any rate not more than the few words necessary to summon servants or give orders to their labourers. When they were settled and the coffee circulated again there was the usual discussion on the progress of the pick and the state of the crop, which often varied on different shambas. Sa'id explained to me where they came from and who they were, and gradually the conversation turned to Oman and to the contrasts of its mountains and barren lands with the low-lying fertile green island in which we lived. One thing they found missing in Zanzibar and that was their beloved dates. Sooner or later conversations such as these were sure to turn to the joys of the season of fresh dates.

Coffee continued to circulate and we sipped it noisily, listening the while and talking of men and events. Tales of raids and tales of the sea. Tales even of witchcraft, for there were powerful wizards among the Wahadimu near-by. Gradually distant fires died down and the talking of the labourers lying round them ceased: just one or two voices continued and an occasional chuckle came from the distance. The guests got up and went. I was led sleepily to a comfortable bed and was soon between the

cool scented sheets. The night was given up now to the song of the crickets
—best of lullabies. All night they chirp in varying keys. Some are harsh,
but there is one that has a note for all the world like that of a tiny silver
bell. There was no other sound now but this chorus and the occasional
bark of a lemur about its nightly promenade among the tops of the coco-nuts.

\* \* \*

I stirred at the clatter of clogs when Sa'id was saying his dawn prayers,
but the world was light when I woke to a cup of the strong black tea. A
servant told me my bath was ready, and I made my way across the sikafu
in my dressing-gown to the wash house. There was not only the usual
tub of cold water, but a cauldron of boiling water as well, Pears' soap and an
ample soft Turkey towel. Soaped from head to foot I ladled hot water,
over me and finished with a cold shower.

The fresh early mornings were the best part of the day. When I was
dressed I went out on to the sikafu. Like most boys, Sa'id's sons were usually
late up. As each appeared they went to their father and took and kissed
his hand.

"Sabalkheri, Bwana."

"Sabalkheri, Hamud," or whoever it might be. The boys always
called their father "sir" and did his bidding at once. He knew how to keep
them in order and there were few fathers like him. Many of the older
Arabs complained of the lack of discipline in the younger generation and
that they had no respect for their elders. But Sa'id's family life was of the
patriarchal kind.

I was asked how I had slept. We all commented on the paucity of
mosquitoes. It was always a point of honour in these places to say how
free they were of these pests and how many there were on our neighbours'
places.

Sa'id called for breakfast.

Europeans could not do without porridge, he had thought, so it had
been specially fetched from Zanzibar.

Four boiled eggs.

Two chickens.

Meat patties.

Afterwards I walked round with the family. They told me stories
against each other, trying to make me laugh. Hamud picked up stones
and catapulted at birds and coco-nuts with cheerful indifference. Sa'id
called us. The deck-chairs had been placed under a shady avenue of mangoes,

## END OF A VISIT

like a park drive, below the house, but planted as a fire break. A pleasant breeze was blowing and we sat looking over the waving rice fields where small boys sat on platforms slinging clods of earth to frighten away the birds. As the clods fell, flocks of red-breasted bishop birds and yellow canary-like weavers started up and made for another place.

"Yoi—yoi."

A companion fifty yards away took up the cry and again a sling twanged. The birds got little rest but they were persistent.

Sa'id talked of the iniquities of a 25 per cent clove tax, the cost of labour, the cost of living, the little profit.

So the day passed, pleasantly enough except for the business of doing justice to those enormous meals of excellent food. On Monday my donkey was brought round after breakfast. I mounted it with difficulty. I asked the donkey boy why he was carrying our bag of grain, expecting it to have been finished.

"Bwana Sa'id gave the donkey food, and Zip." (Zip was my pariah dog, found as a puppy in the mangrove swamps of Weti. Finding her there reminded me of Moses but as she was a lady she was called Zipporah, which I believe was the name of Moses' sister. All Pemba and Zanzibar grew to know her as Zip and she followed me everywhere on my journeys.)

I learned that the donkey boy and the other retainers had also been fed. They were all loaded with the remains of the food to carry home. Indeed neither the donkey boy, the donkey, nor I could proceed at more than a very stately and careful walk.

A few days later I met Sa'id again.

"Bibi (his wife) was sorry the food was so bad; you ate nothing."

When I was better known at Kinyasini she would shout out from the back regions: "What's the matter with my food, do you never eat anything?"

## Chapter III

## THE GREEN ISLAND: MEN OF OMAN

> *Sweet is the music of Arabia*
> *In my heart, when out of dreams*
> *I still in the thin clear mirk of dawn*
> *Descry her gliding streams.* DE LA MARE.
>
> *That Prophet ill sustains his holy call,*
> *Who finds not heav'ns to suit the taste of all.* MOORE.

SA'ID BIN 'ABDULLA is not the only friend of Mkokotoni days whose friendship has continued. There is also Zaidi, who has been not only a friend, but a faithful retainer during all my subsequent wanderings. Although I had known him for several months before he came into my service, he was introduced to me as a possible servant in the guise of a perfect stranger.

It was Cokkai who brought him to me. Cokkai's real name was 'Isa and he was Sheha of the village of Potoa, a mile or two north-west of Mkokotoni. He was a little man, round but not gross, with a stupid face pitted deeply with smallpox. He was quiet and unassertive and spoke in rather a husky way, but he was not really stupid at all. In fact he had more influence than most of the Shehas in the district. He was always good at finding clove pickers, and helped me much, not only in getting me animals and birds for the Zoo I kept in my yard, but also in collecting me examples of native handiwork. He had even taken me on nocturnal excursions to watch the activities of the local wizards. 'Isa himself attributed his influence to a wall-eye which looked to me like an advanced cataract. A predecessor of mine had named him "Cock-eye," and he himself, not knowing the meaning, had adopted the word as a cognomen of honorific significance. He was known as Cokkai throughout the district. I once suggested that an operation might restore the sight to his eye, but he decided against it because as he said, if he gained the eye he would lose his influence and he preferred things as they were.

Knowing I wanted a servant he appeared one morning, gliding in his usual almost imperceptible way into my office. "Bwana, you want

## STORY OF A FAITHFUL RETAINER

i?" (*Boi* plural *maboi*, English "boy.") "There's a chap here wants to kazi ya uboi," (boy work).

I did not expect to be able to obtain a servant in Mkokotoni where mine as the only European household, however I said "Bring him in, Cokkai." One of the boys who manned the station rowing-boat appeared. Now might very well have come on his own, but in the East it is almost impossible for anyone to make a personal request personally. Cokkai too ould use an intermediary if he wanted something for himself. As I und that the boat boy in question had had previous houseboy experience Zanzibar, in Pemba and in Dar es Salaam, I took him on, and thus it as that Zaidi came into my service. He was native of Mkokotoni, and, suppose, a year or two older than myself. Like most Africans he did t know his birthday but he told me that he was small enough to be put a soap-box and hidden by his mother under a bed when, in 1896, Seiyid halid, a son of the famous Sultan Barghash, in an effort to usurp the throne d barricaded himself in the palace and been bombarded by the guns of e British fleet.

The event has never been forgotten. The palace square at Zanzibar istled with the old Arab muzzle-loading cannon manned by slaves, while rabs thronged the palace. They had no fears as to what would happen, r the soothsayers had told them that the British guns would only discharge ater. The palace clock struck the hour of nine. The *Thrush*, *Racoon* d *Sparrow* discharged their batteries. The Sultan's ship *Glasgow* was sunk mediately by a six-inch from the *St. George*. In half an hour the palace d its surroundings were a shambles. All was flames and ruins. Five mdred dead and wounded lay in the square. There must have been any mothers as terrified as Zaidi's that day.

Thereafter he had had a varied career. Like most children he had been nt to the little village Quran school, but he had no liking either for theology t for the often-applied stick of the mualim (teacher), so he had left before had even learnt his alphabet, let alone completed the learning of the entire Juran, which forms the only education many Muslims have. He was ught and returned, but ran away again, and then his uncle in whose uardianship he had been placed gave it up and apprenticed him to a tailor. here he learned embroidery, and he can still embroider a kanzu front ith neatness; but he wanted money so he became the driver of a donkey art on an agreement which gave a third of the takings to his master, a ird to the donkey and the cart, and a third to Zaidi. Most nights, he has told me, he used to spend on the twenty-three mile journey from Mkokotoni to Zanzibar, arriving in the morning with coco-nuts and other produce for sale in the market. When he was tired of that he became a sailor, working on a dhow between Pemba and Zanzibar. About twenty years ago he first entered domestic service, and he told me that he had parted from his previous master in Dar es Salaam on account of the way that the master had treated his cook. Then he returned to his native Mkokotoni as a boat boy.

He is a Mtumbatu (plural form is Watumbatu) by tribe, and his home is the little island of Tumbatu, lying about a mile across the harbour from Mkokotoni. The people are exclusive and will not tolerate strangers living in their midst, though many of them live around Mkokotoni and go far afield to seek a livelihood. They are of those who go down to the sea in ships for their living, and the *African Pilot* speaks of them as the best pilots in Zanzibar waters.

One day, when office work was over, I embarked in the station whaler at the little jetty below my house to make the first of many visits to the island. It was a popular expedition for all the crew were of Zaidi's tribe, dressed like sailors in blue shorts and blouses with white pipings on the collar, but they wore red tarbushes. As the evening breeze had not yet risen the boys took out their oars and rowed, their songs echoing across the harbour:

> Mwana Juma twende zetu,
> Daughter of Juma let's be off

sang bow, and the crew took up the refrain as their oars plunged in unison into the water:

> Nangojea kitambaa changu kwanza
> I'm waiting for my clothes first.

Across the bay there is a delightful approach up the narrow channel to Kichangani village, and as the boat passed close under the rocks I saw coneys playing on the coral ledges. They are pleasant little beasts, not much bigger than rabbits, but their nearest zoological relation is the hippopotamus. As we came into view of the beach I could see the natives at work mending their fish traps or otherwise occupied. But as soon as they saw the boat the shore was deserted and I landed, as it were, at a village of the dead, for the doors were inhospitably closed. Walking through the maze of huts and stooping to avoid the projecting poles of the eaves, I saw the end of a coloured kanga disappear round the corner as a frightened woman rushed to seek safety from the invader. Once or twice I came unawares upon a child playing in front of a hut. No sooner was I seen than there was a terrified shriek and the child bolted as though for its life. At the Sheha's house, before which flies the red flag of the Sultan, I was more hospitably received, and sat gratefully drinking the madafu he brought, while the male element of the population, gradually picking up its courage, collected in a crowd behind, in doubt, and wondering what had brought me there.

I asked the Sheha why his people were so shy, for in the villages of the Wahadimu and Wapemba, the aboriginal tribe of Zanzibar and Pemba respectively, there was never this fleeing away as though from danger. He told me that in the old days slave raiders used suddenly to descend on the island and kidnap any women and children they found. It must have been twenty or thirty years that had elapsed since this could have happened, but the people had not lost their instinctive fear of strangers. The Sheha said that the Arabs would entice the children with sweetmeats, capture them and carry them off. This was an ancient method, for Chau Ju Kua, an inspector of customs at the Imperial Court of China in the thirteenth century, speaks of the Arabs doing this in Madagascar, and the historian Idrisi says that the Arabs of Oman kidnapped children on the Zanzibar coast in the same way in the twelfth century. The reason was that the slave traders were endeavouring to turn an extra dishonest penny. In Zanzibar they had to pay for their cargo, but if they succeeded in capturing a child or two on their own, it was all clear profit.

The Watumbatu claim that as a race they were never enslaved and boast that their ruling dynasty was descended from the Shirazis who came with Hassan bin 'Ali. The geographer Yakut tells us that in the thirteenth century Timbat was a town to which the inhabitants of Zanzibar fled when they were in danger, but two hundred years later it had faded into insignificance. Once it counted queens amongst its rulers, and Mwana wa Mwana, after whom a little island with a lighthouse to the north of Tumbatu is named, married into the royal house of the Hadimu dynasty of Zanzibar.

* * *

From Mkokotoni I went, after a leave, to Chake Chake ("Each for Himself") in Pemba where I spent nearly two years. The town, the biggest in Pemba, was stretched out on the edge of a ridge looking down a long creek. In the distance was a small island, Mesale, associated with stories of buried treasure and apocryphally with the name of Captain Kidd

## THE GREEN ISLAND: MEN OF OMAN

Behind Mesale lay the Pemba channel with the African mainland beyond. I grew very fond of my little Arab town with its one main street. Its houses were really Arab homes built of coral and lime-washed, and not the usual mud huts, though to be sure there was the large Swahili quarter of Kichangani which was African enough. The town had also a mosque and with it even a modest minaret. It had been built by Bedwi, the grandfather of the Liwali Suleiman bin Mbarek al Mauli, and was called after him. The Arabs of Weti used to say that Weti was derived from "Waiti," "call them all," because they were so open-handed and generous. They said that the Arabs of Chake Chake were mean, hence the name "Each for himself." This was a libel for I found as much hospitality in Chake Chake as anywhere else, and nowhere more than among the Maulis.

I have said that the Isma'ili were the principal family in the north of the island in Weti district, but here in Chake Chake and down into Mkoani district the Maulis held almost undisputed sway, and, I think, had done since Seiyid Sa'id defeated the Mazruis. Before that happened, in 1822, Pemba—Jezirat al Khudhra as the Arabs called it—the Green Island, had been more connected with Mombasa which was the chief Mazrui stronghold. There were a few Mazruis left in Pemba, but they were unimportant and the great names were those I read on tombstones or heard in the history I took down from Arab friends. Of old, Pemba had been ruled by a Persian dynasty, which lasted throughout the Portuguese period, getting more mixed with the native element and becoming feebler as the years went by. When the Imam, Seif bin Sultan, expelled the Portuguese he settled Mazruis as rulers on his behalf at Mómbasa and the Green Island. In time, as often happens in Arabia, they made themselves practically independent and Seiyid Sa'id had difficulty in reducing them to his authority. Scenes of the battles were often pointed out to me in the district. At Chwaka, near the ruined town buried in the bush where once the Persians had ruled, was the tomb of the greatest of their sheikhs, Mbaruk bin Rashid who died "on the night of a Monday" in 1806. Then at Birikau, on the northern side of the Mkumbuu Peninsula, where lie the ruins of the famous town Kambalu, spoken of by Chau Ju Kua, the historian Masudi who visited it, and others, a great battle was fought when the Mazrui brought warlike Wanyika tribesmen from Mombasa as mercenaries. They were beaten, but came again the following year and encamping at Wesha, on the northern bank of the Chake Chake creek, made a final stand. Various tales are told of who shot Rizike son of Sheikh Mbaruk and the credit has been claimed by several families, but his death broke the power of the Mazruis in Pemba for ever.

After their defeat Seiyid Sa'id appointed Liwalis, Governors, to represent him, and in due course my old friend Suleiman was appointed. He served long and loyally and had had a difficult time at the abolition of slavery. His name had even been mentioned in debates in the House of Commons, and I remember his kissing a newspaper picture of Lord Curzon who had defended his actions, because, Suleiman said, he had been as an advocate for him and pleaded his case.

Although Suleiman was so much the lord of Chake Chake he was not the family sheikh. This dear old man—Sheikh Salim bin Khalif—lived at Kaole, half-way down the creek. In England we often look to a particular house with affection as the place of our birth or the scene of our childhood. In Africa and Arabia this affection is more often turned to a locality, for houses rarely outlive their owners and indeed there is often a curious reluctance to dwell in a house after the owner is dead. Hence you find in Zanzibar scattered ruins of the palaces of bygone sultans. The Maulis regarded Kaole as a sacred shrine, a place of pilgrimage, and paid regular visits to their sheikh.

In Zanzibar and Pemba the only duties left to the sheikh of the clan concerned matters affecting its social life and standing, and the settling of disputes between members of the family. The Sheikh al Mauli can have had little to do in this way, for the Maulis were the most united family I ever knew. Though it must have been years since any of them had visited Muscat—whence the family had migrated about a hundred years before—they corresponded regularly with their relations there and any wandering Manga Mauli who came to Pemba were sure of a warm welcome.

When the Maulis emigrated from Muscat they started by growing sugar, but under Seiyid Sa'id they had taken to cloves and most of them stayed in Pemba year in year out, though Suleiman had a little shamba a short way out of Zanzibar town which he visited from time to time. The rest of the family always rather apologized for his departure to the sister island and I think the Arabs of Zanzibar were inclined to look down on them as country cousins, almost men of the backwoods. They were a curiously psychic family and had a banshee who announced the death of a member of the family in Muscat to those in Pemba and vice versa. They said it never went wrong and that a confirmatory letter always followed. All of them were good Muslims and touched no alcohol, and yet they told me of many ghosts and devils they had seen. Indeed, it was in Mauli company that I saw the only "ghost" I have ever seen.

It happened at Pujini, on the east coast of the island, where there are the ruins of a walled Persian town. Pemba legend associates the place with a chieftain called Muhammad bin 'Abdul Rahman, nicknamed Mkame Mdume—the Milker of Males—on account of the impossible tasks he set the unfortunate people of Pemba. He is chiefly famous for his inhuman cruelties, and for his powers over devils and familiar spirits. A manuscript book of his sermons is still preserved at Pujini and I found in it a magical formula for summoning up Efreets:

> *If there be one who wishes to summon up and have at his bidding an Efreet of the Efreets of Solomon, the son of David, on whom be peace, let him dwell apart in a clean place, clad in clean apparel and his person clean. Let him fast for seven days, and let him read every day forty-one times the Chapter of the Quran beginning " Say He is one God."  There will come to him that night, the third, the fifth, and the sixth, the Efreet he has summoned, he and his people. He will do your bidding, he and his people.*

To-day Pujini is still a place of mystery. Though its extensive ruins have now been explored, they have not been thoroughly excavated, and nothing is known beyond legend of the history of the place, or, for that matter, of most of the substantial ruins scattered in Zanzibar and Pemba and up and down the East African coast. Apart from the more material aspect of its history, the ruined town is a place of terror by night to the superstitious natives. They will not willingly be there after the sun has set, for, they say, manifestations still linger there of the devils that obeyed Mkame Mdume's bidding. Even by day things are said to happen. A policeman, among others, told me that when walking along the path, between the high grass and the bush behind the southern rampart, he had heard the shrieks of a woman, though there was nothing to be seen.

A mile or so north of Chake Chake, on a little plateau overlooking the Mkumbu Peninsula, lay the family seat of Bwana Liwali ("Mr. Governor") as we all called Suleiman. Here at Mkanjuni the old man held his court, for he loved to play the part of a country squire.

"He thinks he's like Harun al Rashid," whispered his brother to me with a smile one day. We all played up to his little weaknesses for they were amiable and there was not a kinder soul in the district. He had built himself a two-storied house—rare in Pemba—which towered above the more modest dwellings of his relations living near. He always had four wives on the establishment and several concubines. Though, of course, they were harem ladies, I was admitted to the family in the same way as I had been with a few Zanzibar friends. The two I knew were the eldest and the youngest. Bibi Mkubwa—the great lady—had been his first wife and I was told they had never quarrelled. She was a remarkable old lady and lived a few miles away, managing her plantation in a way that would have shamed many men. There were no frills on her except for the marinda, the high-necked old-fashioned shirt she always wore. She had a real sense of humour and was full of anecdotes when I dropped in for tea. On my first visit I went with the Liwali. I think she was the only person who treated him as a joke to his face.

"Well, Suleiman, how are the young women?" was her greeting, and he said to me that there was no fool like an old fool. Suleiman sat sipping his tea noisily and listening to her sallies the while. He loved the treatment and she, I know, had a deep affection for him.

The Liwali had had a goodly number of wives, but the only other one I met who was on the roster in my day was Panya who was young and frivolous. Like many Arab girls she had a Swahili name and hers meant "mouse." "Puss" would have been more appropriate. Her sister was married to Habib, the Liwali's brother, Mudir of Kisiwani. Panya was usually referred to as Binti Juma ya Bwana Liwali and her sister as Binti Juma ya Bwana Habib. The sisters often stayed together in a small house belonging to the Liwali, not far from my bungalow in Chake, and they often came over to have tea. They were always well dressed and I rarely saw them wearing the same clothes twice. Their marindas were cut from the very newest pattern in kangas. Kangas were originally so-called because they were grey and spotted white like a guinea-fowl, for kanga also means guinea-fowl. But days when they were as plain as that had long since passed, and among the Swahilis all sorts of extraordinary patterns had their brief mode. You would see a lady with a flat-iron or a standard arc lamp pictured across her shoulders. You might even see a wondrous multirayed sun rising on her back: but Arab ladies of high degree did not go in for devices such as these. Their kangas were more expensive and of flowered cloths that did not come amiss as curtains. Kangas for the most part used to be made in Manchester but I believe there has been considerable Japanese competition in late years. There is quite an element of gambling about their manufacture, for patterns may fall absolutely flat. As a general rule the commercial travellers would consult the big wholesale Indian merchants in Zanzibar. If they were lucky in their choice of design the kangas would sell well. But where one succeeded ten would fail to tickle woman's fancy.

What a rustling of stiff silk there was as the Binti Jumas climbed the steps into the bungalow! They were enveloped from head to foot in black cloaks with thin silk veils over their faces. Beneath the cloaks peeped out coyly white trouser legs with saucy frills above the ankle. With a clatter of bangles and necklaces they threw their cloaks aside as they settled themselves on the sofa in the safety of the drawing-room, displaying rows of closely-braided plaits from brow to nape of neck, and half a dozen tightly twisted pigtails beneath. They had copied from the Swahili the ugly fashion of piercing their ears and enlarging them with close-wound rolls of coloured paper glittering with gold and silver tinsel. Their noses were adorned with small gold studs. They crumbled their cake and sipped their tea, chatting and laughing for an hour or so like inconsequent painted sparrows. Panya had a way of giving invitations to "come up and see me some time" in Mae West style, but the return parties were rather prim.

Sometimes I was asked to spend the week-end at Mkanjuni where I was given the best bedroom which occupied the Liwali's top storey. The veranda in front was an excellent vantage point for watching the activities of the little community. The children of the family and those of the "slaves" played happily together on the open wanja, as the bare space in front of the house was called. Biubwa and Zamzam were quite without shyness and climbed up to talk to me, to bring me jasmine flowers, or look for a sweet. Sometimes at night there were wonderful ngomas (dances). The liwali was a great believer in massage and once or twice he made me suffer the ministrations of one of his female slaves, a skilled masseuse. While I lay on the bed having my joints kneaded, he and Bwana 'Abdulla would sit on chairs and tell the masseuse where to pummel next. The three of us had lunch together on the back veranda with a view over the tops of the clove trees falling away to the valleys beneath. The speciality of the house was saffron pilau, and the great mountain of yellow-dyed rice concealed plentiful pieces of chicken, raisins, onions and other garnishings. I ate better pilaus at Mkanjuni than anywhere.

On Sunday afternoons we went for walks and once Bwana 'Abdulla took me to the top of Pagale hill, just a short distance from Mkanjuri. It is only 281 feet high, but that is a lot for Pemba, and after Zanzibar, Pemba gave the impression of being a hilly country, for Zanzibar is as flat as the

overbial pancake. This was 'Abdulla's favourite view for below he
ould see the country round Kaole where he had lived as a boy. The crest
of the hill fell almost sheer away at our feet, and we looked immediately
n to the top of high coco-nut trees growing in the valley below, while
the Mkumbuu Peninsula stretched away before us like a peninsula on a
relief map. On the left was Chake Chake pier, tiny in the distance, and right
own the creek the *Cupid* lay at anchor looking like a toy steamer. To
the right the view was still more varied with the Bay of Birikau and the
much indented coast. The peninsula itself was green with cloves, coco-nuts,
mangoes and other trees, a pleasant medley of varying shapes and colours.
Here and there were huts and blue smoke rising from some tiny homestead.

Though I knew all the Maulis well, my closest friend and associate was
Bwana 'Abdulla. Like everybody over fifty he deplored the decadence
of the modern generation, but he was wise about it and did not try to
suppress the young. One day, to show me how times had changed he told
me of the way his father used to spend his day and compared it with the
day of the modern generation. Here is the day of bygone times:

| | |
|---|---|
| 3.30–4.00 a.m. | Wake up, brush teeth, bathe and put on clean clothes. |
| 4.00–4.30 a.m. | Wake up any of the boys over ten and make them wash. Stern parents even woke those younger and made them bathe and dress. |
| | Then read the Quran and at dawn pray the Al Fajr. The men of those days prayed not only the compulsory prayers, but regarded it as compulsory to pray the recommended ones as well. |
| 5.30 a.m. | Read the Quran. |
| 7.00 a.m. | Breakfast: bread, bokoboko curry and milk. Then the day's work started. The plantation overseers came for their orders and the slaves were sent to their work. The sons of the house were sent out to supervise and then the master would go too. |
| 11.00 a.m. | Lunch: cooked rice, meat and curry. After it work again for a short while. |
| 12 noon | Siesta indoors. |
| 1.00 p.m. | Get up and prepare for prayers. |
| 1.30 p.m. | Prayers, but the Sunnis prayed earlier at one o'clock. |
| 2.00 p.m. | Work again. |
| 3.30 p.m. | Prepare for prayers. |
| 4.00 p.m. | Prayers. |
| 4.30 p.m. | See the horses and donkeys and then recreation— backgammon or talk, coffee and halwa. |
| 5.00 p.m. | Evening meal: dry bread, meat, milk and dates. |

| | |
|---|---|
| Sunset | Prayers. |
| 6.30–7.30 p.m. | Read Quran. |
| 7.30 p.m. | Prayers. |
| 8.00 p.m. | Retire to harem and talk to the ladies and the children. Eat a little. |
| 10.00 p.m. | Go to bed. At bed-time they wore a kikoi and covered themselves with a sheet under a mosquito net of silk. Double beds were not known. |

It seemed a pretty full day to me, but even the modern day, which 'Abdulla deplored, would not suit many of us:

| | |
|---|---|
| 5.00 a.m. | Wake up, brush teeth, dress and pray. No one bothers about the children. |
| 5.30 a.m. | Go to bed again. |
| 7.00 a.m. | Get up and do any of your toilet you did not do at five o'clock. |
| 7.30 a.m. | Breakfast: tea, bread and eggs. |
| 8.30 a.m. | Work. |
| 12 noon | A light lunch. |
| 1.30 p.m. | Prayers. |
| 2.00 p.m. | Work. |
| 4.00 p.m. | Prayers in a hurry. Tea. |
| 4.30 p.m. | Go out for a walk. |
| Sunset | Prayers and possibly some reading. |
| 7.30 p.m. | Prayers. |
| 8.00 p.m. | Dinner: rice, meat and bread. Go out and see friends or walk about. |
| 11.00 p.m. | Bed. |

Bwana 'Abdulla used to accompany me on my journeys round the district, and became very interested in my researches into the customs of the people and the history of Pemba. We even went off together to nocturnal meetings of a guild of witch-doctors. I do not think he really approved of these undertakings, for, of course, the Arabs strongly disapproved of black magic, but he recognized that it was all done in a scientific spirit, and I believe he hoped with me that if we found out something about it, it might some day come to an end. This is not to say, however, that he did not believe in it, for like most other Arabs, he was convinced that wizards had supernatural powers.

One visitor whom 'Abdulla brought to see me was Hamed, a Manga member of the Mauli clan, down on a visit from Muscat. Hamed liked Pemba but he loved his native mountains more, and whenever we said something good about Pemba he would say "Yes, but in Oman . . ."

## ROUTES TO OMAN

ou pictured Oman as having far more than the flowing milk and oney of Canaan. Nowhere were there such fine grapes, such large walnuts. Nothing could touch the camel's milk, and the karamas (feasts) f Pemba were nothing to those of Muscat. If a man offered his guest a goat in Pemba, in Oman it would be a couple of camels at least. We suggested lack of water and green grass. He countered with mountain torrents and made us laugh at a description of a piece of green grass a short way behind Muscat, where, he said, all the people went of an evening. To me it sounded like Hampstead Heath on a Bank Holiday. Hamed used to come and see me often, firing my imagination and making me long to visit his country to which he gave me frequent invitations. He taught me all the routes he knew. From Muscat to Barbeg is eight hours in an easterly direction, then you go north by Taramid and Hobra to Muslimat of the Maulis, where Hamed lived, in eight or nine hours. Soon I knew this and other routes by heart and often carried my knowledge to other Arabs, who flattered me and said I must have been there. Hamed bought a penny note-book and wrote down the routes and other information for me.

When you leave At Taramid you come in three hours' march to the Wadi al Mā'awil (the Valley of the Maulis) along which lies first the town of Al Wāsit. Then, an hour's march on is Hobra and after another hour is the headquarters of the Sheikhs. Every dwelling place has its name, such as Hujrat ash Sheikh, Hujrat al Kharij and Hujrat as Sufala in which there is a mosque, Hujrat al Mulālla, Mahillat al Qala's and Mahillat Antala where Sheikh Nasir bin Muhammad and his sons live. They are like lions and are generous and hospitable to all friends and relentless to foes. There are deep rivers in this town.

When you leave this town you come to Muslimat, where the people are known for control, authority and bravery. In this town there live some of the Al Mā'awil, such as the sons of Bin Zamil, the sons of Muhallal and others. Every section of them has its own head and all are rich and famous people.

I still have Hamed's book. Perhaps some day I may use it.

One day 'Abdulla announced that a dhow had come from Oman. Such an event is rare in modern times as all foreign trade is dealt with as far as possible at Zanzibar. Of course in the old days this had not been the case, and Chake and Jambangome owed the fact that they are the only two stone-built towns of Pemba to their position at the head of long, shallow shelving creeks, the worst of harbours for modern shipping but ideal shelter for the old craft and good hiding-places for slave-runners. Bad weather with consequent damage to the dhow and lack of water had forced the crew to seek shelter at Chake. I asked them all to tea. They were Sūris and it was my first contact with them. What struck me most was the fact that they were all black. They had, however, finer features than our negroid Bantus and were bearded. They wore kanzus which looked—and smelt—as if they had been dipped in cow dung. They rather alarmed me by coming to tea armed to the teeth with sticks, swords and round shields of rhinoceros hide, as well as the usual *jambiya* round their waists. Some also carried small war drums. After the gentle manners of my Zanzibar and Pemba friends the uncouth habits of the seafarers at first surprised me, but they were friendly and appreciated the party even if they were not entirely at home with cups and saucers and cakes. However they were quite happy with the sherbet and black coffee in Arab cups, and afterwards proposed to dance a Razha for me.

The reason of the armament now became clear. Their intentions were peaceful but the display they gave was extremely warlike. The orchestra of drums struck up and the rest, pairing themselves off, indulged in mimic contests on the lawn, which I thought might end fatally at any moment, for they made great sweeping lashes at each other with their swords, which were apparently only avoided by dexterous countering with shields or by leaps in the air over the passing sword which would have made any skipping enthusiast envious. Some performed with *jambiyas*, making circular downward strokes parried by shield. When one overcame his opponent he would sit astride him and make as though to gouge out his eyes with horrifying realism.

These seasonal visitors did no more than give a savour of what Zanzibar and Pemba must have been like in the middle of last century. Lawless and untamed, they were quite foreign to the peaceful ordered existence of two sleepy idyllic coral islands in the twentieth. They came on the wings of the one monsoon, like blustering ghosts of a violent past and were exorcized on the other, spreading their great lateen sails and flitting silently away, and the place pursued its even way, knowing them no more till the following year.

It was otherwise with the Mangas, like Hamed, who came to stay with their relations. They were like Australian cousins coming back to the old country, only in this instance of course it was the other way round, for we were the colonials, only it was the home land which seemed to me more like the new country of wide-open spaces. They took an interest in local affairs and society, were accepted accordingly, and the place was home to them.

Although the other Arabs, the Shihiris, were always with us, they never seemed anything but strangers in a strange land. I made friends, however, with the local butcher, who was one of them, and, through him, made connections which drew me finally to the Hadhramaut, as I shall relate.

## Chapter IV

## MEN OF SHIHR

*He is calling people to say their prayers; he calls so loud that all the people below can hear and the sounds he utters are like sweet music.* FAR OFF.

*Till a voice, as bad as conscience, rang interminable changes*
*On one everlasting whisper day and night repeated—so:*
*'Something hidden, go and find it. Go and look behind the Ranges*
*Something lost behind the Ranges. Lost and waiting for you. Go!'*
KIPLING.

"Foq al mez—juu ya meza. Taht al mez—chini ya meza—on the table, under the table."

"Hurma—mwanamke," as a woman passed below us. She was covered in the all-enveloping black cloak called—descriptively—buibui or spider, which tradition says Zanzibar borrowed from the Hadhramaut.

Karama was instilling a little Arabic into me, mostly in a kind of Berlitz-Montessori technique which he had developed. But there was not much vim about the lesson: Karama was twelve and the instruction was rather spasmodic. I did not keep him at it for I wanted to know about the home which he had left a few short months before. Besides it was hot, and, still more tiresome, it was Ramadhan. So there was more conversation than Arabic. In the short time he had been in Pemba, Karama had acquired an astonishing amount of Swahili: I hoped that Arabic would come as easily to me, but alas! So we talked mostly in Swahili. He had only been with me a couple of days, but there was something about a small boy who had travelled from the interior of Arabia and sailed on a dhow with the north-east monsoon all the way to Zanzibar which commanded interest. A compatriot of his, Ahmed Sa'id Baziad, the butcher, had brought him to me in the office.

"Bwana, there's a small boy here—just a mtoto—if you took him on Zaidi could teach him to be a house boy and you would learn Arabic from him."

In came Karama. He was clad simply in his native futa. He can have had no further wardrobe to his name, for its condition was almost indescribable. He did not look too clean and his straight hair was too long. My immediate reaction was that this was something that could not be taken into a house, but there was something about the bright, fearless eyes that looked me over so frankly which made me decide to try.

Five rupees did the trick. A small kanzu, a new white kikoi, an embroidered cap, a wash and a hair-cut, and here sat Karama on the grass beside me all in white with his knees drawn up to his chin, contemplating the long stretch of creek below us. He was telling me of his family. Of his father dead in a raid, of his mother whom he had left behind in order to join his uncle who ran a coffee shop in the bazaar behind us. He came from Tarim.

"Where is Tarim?"

"Inside, behind Shihr."

I had of course heard of Shihr but Tarim was new to me.

"Wait, Karama, I want to fetch a map."

I went into the bungalow. There were books on Zanzibar and one or two that dealt with Oman. Only one seemed possible. *The Penetration of Arabia*. I took it out on to the lawn and unfolded the map. Karama looked dubious. I found "Sheher" and nearly an inch above it Tarim. Triumph. I told Karama. He plainly did not think much of the discovery for he himself had told me. I read "Shibam, Saiyun." That woke him up.

"What, are they written there? But how did the Wazungu—the Europeans—know that?"

I told him they must have been there, but his tongue was unloosened. Three days from Tarim, through Seiyun, to Shibam, he told me, and six from Shibam to Mukalla. Nine days journey into the interior. At once it seemed a possible project for a leave. We talked of camels and caravans as the sun sank lower to the horizon.

Chake Chake town, just behind me, was silent. All day long it had lain sweltering under a broiling sun, and man had gone about his various occasions with a lassitude born of the stifling heat and aggravated by an empty stomach. Karama spoke of the heat and the rocks and I wondered if it was like this. But the day was nearly over. Down the long creek on the far horizon the sun sank lower to the sea in a blaze of gold, while fantastic cloudbanks, heavily fringed with dull red, hung suspended above it. In them I saw tall houses—ceaselessly plodding camel caravans. All the scene was tinged with glory: mud and mangroves became like fairy gardens filled with trees of gold and jewels. The sea beyond seemed turned to blood. The nearer sand formed to ripples by the falling tide, gleamed opalescent. Lower and lower sank the sun beneath the sea. Duller and duller became the tints. Just one last gleam and it had gone. I looked back at the town where the minaret of the Bedwi mosque was silhouetted against the darkening sky. At the top a white-robed figure stood, his hands cupped to his mouth:

"A————llahu Akbar, A————llahu Akbar."

His voice proclaimed to a weary world the eternal truth: "There is no God but God. Come to prayers—come to salvation." The appeal sounded irresistible as it came over the hot, quivering air. It was over. The Muadhin turned and slowly descended, pausing at each step like a priest returning from a solemn rite at the altar.

"Time to break fast," said Karama. He flitted away in the dusk, his new kanzu frou-frouing like a debutante's party dress.

I sat there, thinking. . . .

In the western sky the young Ramadhan moon sent a path of silver over the waters of the bay, its surface just broken by a breath of wind. Now the night awoke. Crickets shrilled, a chorus of frogs struck up. In the bazaar the musical clink of cups proclaimed the progress of the itinerant coffee vendor, while the persistent, strident and still remembered tones of hare-lipped Laddad bin Sheddad, the Baluchi date seller, exhorted passers-by to "eat dates and grow fat."

\* \* \*

That was in 1923. I read what Hogarth had to say in the *Penetration of Arabia* about the Hadhramaut, and in particular this passage became fixed in my memory:

> Interest in Hadhramaut should not be suffered to decline yet. About half the trunk wady still remains unexplored and the least-known part is that upon which border the ancient Mahra tribes.

Then I read Bent. But I learned a lot more about the Hadhramaut and the life of its people from Karama and Ahmed Sa'id than from books. There was a small community of people from the country in Chake Chake, mostly coffee sellers, but it was not until I was transferred to Zanzibar, that I met them in large numbers.

As a general rule natives of any part of the Hadhramaut were called

Shihiris in Zanzibar and the word Hadhrami was not often heard, but when it was uséd it meant a man from the interior. Shihiris did not belong to society in Zanzibar. More even than the Indians they seemed men apart. It appears, in the East, that when you do not have Jews you have Hadhramis or Chinese and all are alike in their exclusiveness. In Zanzibar the Hadhramis traded and made their money from the rest of us, but they did not look on Zanzibar as their home and kept themselves largely to themselves. None the less they claimed that their ancestors were the pioneers of colonization in East Africa and certainly their connection was an ancient one, for they are among the descendants of Saba and Himyar. They also claim to have spread the Sunni tenets. Trade is their principal strong point and they took a large share in the slave trade: in 1876 they were described as the largest slave holders in Zanzibar. But it was not only with trading that they occupied themselves, for certainly since the early part of the nineteenth century many have entered the service of the Sultan as soldiers and also as Liwalis, Qadhis, treasurers and clerks. In modern times they have maintained a reputation as soldiers, for many from Zanzibar fought and died in Wavell's Arab Rifles.

Best of all the Hadhramis in my time was one of the older generation, the chief of the Sunni Qadhis in Zanzibar town. Seiyid Ahmed bin Abibekr bin Sumeit al 'Alawi was a jurist of renown. His legal opinion was sought from afar and he had been decorated by the Sultan of Turkey and by the Khedive. More than that, he was a broad-minded kindly cleric, with a ready humour and racy perception of a characteristic kind. There was a good-natured twinkle in his eyes when he spoke, and a kindly smile was rarely absent from his fine ascetic features as he stroked his long white beard. I do not suppose he ever had an unkind thought or did an unkind deed. I think his funeral was the most moving I ever attended. I was private secretary to His Highness the Sultan at the time and as his representative followed close behind the bier. The crowds were estimated at some twenty thousand, from all classes of the population, though most were poor. Many, rich and poor, were in genuine tears. I think that many of us were feeling the gap there would be, that we should not see again that familiar figure in pale blue robe and Hadhrami Seiyid's embroidered cap and close-bound turban of white passing on his daily journey to and from the law courts. I had met Seiyid Ahmed frequently for we served on a commission together. The little Swahili children learned their Quran in Arabic and understood not a word of it. Our task was to make recommendations for its better teaching. It was a matter in which the old man took a great interest. "Parrot talk, parrot talk," he used to say to me, "they can't understand it, it does them no good."

I confided in him my hopes of travel in his country, for he was a native of Shibam. He gave me letters of introduction and I stored them up till such a day as I might be able to use them. Nevertheless, though everyone revered him and held him in affection he did not seem to be of Zanzibar. Perhaps his dress and his religion, both different from those of the other Arabs, had something to do with it, for all his tradition was different. Seiyid Ahmed, though, was not typical of the Hadhramaut Arabs. Even in his own country he would have stood apart by virtue of his ancestry—a son of Ishmael and descendant of the Prophet himself. The great bulk of his compatriots were men in lowly callings, hewers of wood and drawers of water. Fair of skin they stood out sharply from the Africans with whom they competed. You picked them out at once, with their short but spare figures, as their guttural speech mingled with the soft Italian vowels of shouting Swahili men and women who gathered round the town fountains. Many of them were bow-legged: indeed it seemed that they must become so, for they spent their lives carrying two four-gallon petrol tins full of water suspended from a pole about their shoulders. Never had they time to walk; they moved eternally in a curiously uneven run, litting their feet "like cats on hot bricks" and splashing water as they went.

But Seiyid Ahmed and the water-carriers represent only the top and bottom of the scale. The 1931 census gives the number of Hadhramis in Zanzibar and Pemba as 2,800. As their women rarely emigrate, the Hadhramis who settle in the islands mostly marry local women with or without Hadhrami blood, so that many of those included were by no means of pure stock. This number includes, of course, many visitors from dhows, who bring with them clothes, loin cloths, honey, henna, dried fish, salt, ghee, livestock, dates and shark oil (sifa), some of which are obtained *en route* on the Somaliland coast. Most of the visitors sail back to the Hadhramaut a few months later with the south-west monsoon, taking with them locally grown millet. Others, finding employment, stay on for several years until they have gained enough money, two or three hundred rupees or so, to return to their homes.

The occupations of those who remain in Zanzibar are varied. The commonest are those of general traders, labourers, water carriers, private servants, Government employees, fishermen, tailors, and gold and silver-

## OCCUPATIONS OF THE HADHRAMI

smiths. There are also coolies, stevedores, coffee shop and small store keepers.

There is no more pleasant sound in the bazaars of Zanzibar and Pemba than the clink of the coffee cups. The coffee vendor needs neither cry nor bell to tell his passing. Far down the street you hear him coming. In one hand he carries his big brass pot with charcoal brazier fixed beneath, and in the other two or three tiny handleless cups which he clinks together between his palm and forefinger as he goes. This is a trade particularly Hadhrami and though in the Hadhramaut he fills his cup full, he knows in Zanzibar, as he skilfully splashes a thimblefull into a cup, that it must not be filled. There is a story in Zanzibar of an Omani who took it as the deepest insult when he was offered a full cup and upped and stabbed the server right away.

Other Hadhramis deal in the shark and dried fish products of their native Shihr, and the meat trade between Zanzibar and the East African coast has been in their hands for the last sixty years or more. In Pemba this was the work of Ahmed who had brought Karama to me and he employed other Shihiris to slaughter and cut up his meat. Some trades were practised by men of the coast and of the interior indifferently, but a few were special preserves. Fishing and hawking were the occupations of coast men alone, while none but those of the interior made the baskets and mats used for packing Zanzibar's cloves for export. At one time Hadhramis owned shambas of cloves and coco-nuts and much house property in Zanzibar town; but all that is changed and now they own little of either kind, for much of it has passed to the Indians.

Absorbed in trade and the accumulation of money, the Hadhramis in Zanzibar are comparatively indifferent to politics. Although hot-tempered by nature they are as a rule law-abiding and loyal, but from 1923 to 1928 a series of affrays took place in most of which they were the aggressors. The victims of their attacks were the Baluchis, Khojas and Hindu Indians, and the Muscat and Sūri Arabs. The most serious disturbance was in 1928 when fighting between Hadhramis and Omani Arabs continued intermittently for four days and four persons were killed and some thirty wounded. Nasir bin 'Abdulla al Kathiri, the chief ringleader, and others were deported. Nasir went to Java and in 1934 returned to his tribe in the Hadhramaut. The up-country and coast Hadhramis are now organized into two associations which endeavour to compose disputes between individuals.

# MEN OF SHIHR

Hard-working and thrifty, absorbed in their own work, the Hadhramis have few forms of entertainment even amongst themselves; dancing and sitting in coffee shops are the only ways in which they relax. They do not easily adopt the manners and ways of those around them, and though European dress is becoming popular among the younger Arabs and Africans, the Hadhramis are little affected by the change in fashion. They also, as far as possible, continue with the diet, to which they are accustomed, of fresh and salted fish, shark, wheat porridge, millet, rice, meat, dates, bread, milk, coffee and tea.

Both up-country and coast Hadhramis normally share places of worship, but in practice those from up-country congregate and largely control the Juma' and Mzaham mosques and those from the coast the Malindi Mnara mosque. Here in their worship they may feel at home, for the Hadhrami minarets tell of their love for the things of their country. If you asked them what was the best country in the world they would tell you the Hadhramaut, and you would find that their one hope in life was to return to end their days on its shores or in their beloved valleys. The exiles who die in Zanzibar are in death not divided for they share one burial ground. After all it matters no longer whether the white houses of Shihr and Mukalla or the mud-built dars of the wadi called them home. They are in the eternal gardens, which are the bourn of all true Muslims.

*Chapter V*

## ANTRES VAST—IN ZANZIBAR TOWN—A DHOW FROM KUWEIT—LATHAM ISLAND

> *The monsoon brings the white-winged dhows*
> *That come to Zanzibar*
> *Laden with shimmering Eastern goods*
> *From India, and afar.*    ELLIOTT-LYNN.
>
> *Once there was a sailor man singing just this way—*
> *(Too much yawl-o, sickum best fiend!*
> *Singee all-same pullee lope—haul and belay.*
> *Hully up and coilum down an'—bite off end!)*
> *But before, and before, and ever so long before*
> *Any sort of chanty crossed our lips,*
> *The Junk and the Dhow, though they looked like anyhow,*
> *Were the Mother and the Father of all Ships ahoy!—aships!*
> *And of half the new inventions in our Ships!*
> *From Tarifa to Formosa of our Ships!*
> *From Socotra to Selankhor of the windlass and the anchor,*
> *And the Navigators' Compass on our Ships—ahoy! our Ships!*
> *(O, hully up and coilum down and bite off end!)*    KIPLING.

WHEN I left Chake Chake on transfer to Zanzibar, though I did not know it, I had said good-bye to Pemba for good. I was glad of the move for I had not seen the southern part of Zanzibar island where the customs of the people, the Wahadimu, are different from those of the north and of Pemba. Cloves did not grow there, and though there was a fair amount of copra, for the most part the Wahadimu lived on their own crops planted on the rough coral outcrops of the Wanda land. As I was doubling with my district work the appointment of Registrar to the High Court, I did not at first have much chance of travelling by land through the district. On Tuesdays I used to motor across the island to the District Headquarters at Chwaka with a great friend, Sheikh Tahir bin Abubekr al Amawy, the Qadhi, who claims Moorish descent. He has the merriest twinkle in his eye, never looks grave and his gold teeth flash continually. He and I used to hear our cases, I did my office work and we returned in the evening.

On Friday afternoon I again left Zanzibar town and drove to Chwaka

## IN ZANZIBAR TOWN—A DHOW FROM KUWEIT—LATHAM ISLAND

on district work where I met Sheikh Muhammad bin Hashil, the Arab District Officer. He was one of the tallest Arabs I have ever seen. He must have been at least six-foot-three or four, and he wore a tarbush that added several more inches and crowned a large black bushy beard. He was a stepson of the famous Tippoo Tib, a slave trader and a merchant, as well as a great explorer and traveller, who had many associations with men such as Livingstone, Stanley and Cameron. He was known far into the interior and had even been made Sultan of Utetera. In the late 'eighties King Leopold made him Governor of Stanley Falls. He died in Zanzibar in June, 1905.

Muhammad bin Hashil was not a well-read man and he was somewhat of a free thinker in his religion, but he knew a lot about the Wahadimu and had great influence with them. Most unusual in an Arab, sport was the ruling passion of his life and he was keen on big-game shooting and fishing. He had a motor-boat and we often went trailing off the south of the island. On one of our best days we caught seven twenty- to thirty-pound fish in less than an hour, though occasionally fifty-pounders also came our way.

Every Friday evening we embarked at Chwaka and chugged off southward on district work, inside the reef which protects all the east coast of Zanzibar. One week-end was to Makunduchi, four hours distant. It was a delightful village with a lovely rambling native-built Government house with a thatched roof. One of the things I liked best about Makunduchi was the camel riding, for it was the only place in the Sultanate where camels were still the mode of transport. I had a string of them myself at Chwaka and the one I rode was called Adolphus.

The people of Makunduchi had many unusual customs including a peculiar dialect of their own. They had a dance in honour of a devil of the sea—an old man with a long beard carrying a trident in his hand who had been seen approaching the place in a canoe. The dance was played with tridents and model canoes, and I feel sure that it was a relic of the worship of Poseidon which had survived from the days of the *Periplus* and the old Greek traders. I had not the remotest idea that a dance like this was played at Makunduchi when we arrived there. It just happened to be on; but I had not watched it for five minutes before I felt certain that I was watching something the Greeks had left behind. When I asked its origin and was told of the old man with the beard I felt more sure and further investigations confirmed me.

The people derived the name of their village from Konduchi, a village on the mainland, a little north of Dar es Salaam, whence they told me they came. Near Konduchi is another village called Msasani with a bay and harbour of a kind most pleasing to the ancients. Here at Msasani was found in 1907 a coin of Ptolemy X Soter. Piecing all the facts together I had no reasonable doubt that this must have been the Rhapta of the *Periplus*, the "very last market town of Azania." Here, no doubt, the Greek sailors built a temple to the presiding god of the sea who had brought them so far in safety and to whom they prayed for a safe journey home.

Next week-end we went to Jembiyani, a spacious village just north of Makunduchi. It is built on sand and pleasantly shaded by coco-nut palms. All round it was short close-cropped turf growing to the edge of the shore of white coral sand. We arrived there by moonlight and when we were about half a mile from the shore I shed all my clothes and dived into the warm water, making a brilliant path of phosphorescence. The great stretch of white sand gleamed like snow in the moonlight and all the palm trees were turned to silver. The coco-nut is the most conversational of trees, especially on a moonlight night with a slight breeze. Its fronds become silver and darken again, bob up and down, and in their rustling seem to be talking among themselves. We pitched our tents on the soft grass, leaving them open to the pleasant warm wind which blew continually across the Indian Ocean. We said, though I never verified it on an atlas, that we had only sea between our tents and Java. At high tide the waves came thundering up to the very threshold, and we bathed for hours at a time in the warm water.

When we had dined off curried chicken and rice made by Zaidi and washed down with madafu, we went to watch a dance. Zaidi loved these performances and presently came up to tell me of another show. He took me to the veranda of a house curtained off by mats, and there I first saw a native Punch and Judy show. I have since seen Kargoss, as it is called, in Zanzibar and Aden, and it has grown familiar, but I do not think I have ever seen it as well performed as at Jembiyani that night. The Wahadimu who played it had been taught by a Shihiri, and like true travelling showmen they went from village to village by day and set up their show in the evening, charging a modest halfpenny for admission.

Muhammad Hashil and I spent much of our time exploring caves, for the south of the island was full of them.

On one occasion we both entered a leopard cave on a small island called

Vundwe in most picturesque surroundings. Our guide was the custodian, for the Wahadimu have what they call a Mwana Vyale to look after the places where the spirits dwell. Before he entered the grotto where the cave was he called "Hodi, hodi," just as one always does when entering a house in Zanzibar. I rather liked this politeness to the spirit of the cave and found out afterwards it was universal. On the spirit's altar outside was a queer collection of offerings including fragments of old Chinese and Persian ware and the lock of an antique flint-lock gun almost lost in rust. It must have been old, for there are no people left who remember anything more ancient than a matchlock.

* * *

*Many days he wandered in the bazaars beholding and marvelling at the people and the palaces.* TREASURE OF MANSUR.

During this time I got to know Zanzibar town well. I lived in a house in the main street with a veranda overhanging the road, a vantage point from which to watch everybody's coming and going. One regular passer-by who became a friend was a cheerful Shihiri woman who sold cakes. She would pass every day about half-past one with her basket on her head and crying out:

'Ala babak, ya Karim—mufa'a
At thy door, Oh generous one—cakes.

I loved my rambling house, though it collected a great deal of dust. It had thirteen rooms and none of the floors were level. There was a modern sleeping-box built on the roof and various small alterations had been made inside, but it was a real old Arab house with cool, thick walls and pleasant Saracenic arches inside.

One Sunday when I was out at a lunch party I sat next to Dr. Spurrier, who, after service as Medical Officer of Health, retired and settled down to spend the rest of his long life in the Zanzibar he loved better than anywhere else. The talk round the table was of ghosts, and Spurrier had been made to tell the story of the ghost he had seen in the old palace of the Mwenyi Mkuu, the King of the Wahadimu, at Dunga in the centre of the island. The rest of us contributed our quota and I said that I thought there was something queer about my house.

Every day when I came back from the office at twelve I had my lunch and at once went up to my sleeping-box to rest until two, when it was time to go back to work. After lunch the boys always cleared off and did not come back till tea-time. So I was sure of being undisturbed unless anything urgent happened. But almost every day I heard heavy footsteps coming up the steep and creaky stairs. At first thinking it was a boy I used to call "Zaidi, Zaidi." But there was no answer and as I was sure there had been someone there I ran out to see. There was no one. So I got used to it, and sometimes I heard from my bed a deep sigh when the footsteps had reached the top of the stairs.

I had no sooner told this than Spurrier said: "Why, that's the old general. He always used to sigh like that when he got to the top of those stairs." My house had a certain historic interest for it had belonged to General Sir Lloyd William Mathews, who lived for long, and died, in Zanzibar. He was Prime Minister first of Seiyid Barghash and then of subsequent Sultans, and no European has given more to the country or been more loved by its peoples. His was a gentle ghost and never alarmed me.

It took me a long time to know my way thoroughly about the maze of the old Arab town without getting lost. The city is divided into a number of quarters. Shangani was that particularly favoured by Europeans, while Malindi, the most tumbledown, was favoured by Shihiris and Mangas. Most of the more important Arabs lived in Baghani and Kajificheni, and there were others where the Bohoras, Memons and Banians congregated.

Most of the charm of Zanzibar was due to the haphazard way in which it had grown up. Comparing Zanzibar and Dar es Salaam I used to think at one time how much wiser the Arab town planners had been than the Germans, for the shady narrow lanes between the high white-washed coral houses, with their thick walls, meant that the inhabitants walked abroad and lived in far greater comfort than those who used the wide sunlit streets and mosquito-wired thin-walled bungalows of one storey. But I realized later that the town planner had had nothing to do with Zanzibar. Indeed, if it had not been for an ancient law which made every man set up his scaffolding poles on his own land there would not have been any streets at all! Zanzibar was never planned: like Topsy, it just "growed."

No people except Arabs could ever have built it. It is equally true that only Londoners could have built London. Towns reflect much of the mentality of the people who build them. London, in its individuality and its compromise, is rather like an Arab town and that perhaps is why English and Arabs usually get on so well together. A town planner had far better keep his town planning to his own country. He only makes a mess of

## IN ZANZIBAR TOWN—A DHOW FROM KUWEIT—LATHAM ISLAND

things when he tries abroad, for I do not think any town planning expert has yet absorbed enough of the mentality of foreign races to be let loose in rearranging their towns. When European architects and town planners get together in "embellishing" purely Eastern towns the results are often even more deplorable than when the Arab, thinking that everything Western must be good, builds in European style. It is only on matters of plumbing that West can speak to East with authority, but plumbing is, or should be, decently concealed.

There was a great fascination about the bazaars of Zanzibar with their varied life and colour, and the richly carved doors of Zanzibar were as remarkable for their beauty as for their symbolism. By day or night the town was interesting. When the little shops were open Indians sat cross-legged on their thresholds, shouting at their neighbours and spitting the red juice of betel on to the roadway. One shop was gaily decorated with multi-coloured kangas, while next door was a Banian hammering away at making brass pots and clad only in a white dhoti, the rolls into which his paunch was creased telling of the fattening effect of a milk diet. The top knot on his head by which he hopes to be lifted to heaven hung loose round his neck. In the grain shop next door sat impassive a large Indian woman in a loose gown, her untidy hair dyed red with henna, while ever and anon she drove marauding chickens with a long wand from the miscellaneous baskets of rice, lentils and millet. Chickens were not the only bazaar thieves. Tied up on barazas, or even loose in the streets, were goats nibbling from bundles of grass or stray waste-paper. As I passed by one open door there came out a warm breath of fetid air and I saw dimly in the interior the uncouth figures of gaunt camels ceaselessly turning the mills that grind sesame to oil. In the street of the money-changers Indians sat on platforms in shop doorways in which were piled dollars and notes. Amongst their coins I used to find not only Maria Theresa and the dollars of Abyssinian Menelik, but the beautiful Madonna dollars and Spanish pillar pieces of eight known as Riale ya Mizinga or Cannon dollars.

Beside the creek runs the most fashionable Arab afternoon promenade. Here the élite of the town walk after four in spotless white linen; their turbans and johos are laid aside and over their kanzus they wear white coats, and carry tamarind sticks in their hands. Here I often met Sa'id bin 'Abdulla and other friends. I saw much of Sa'id in those days, and he used to take me to call on a number of Arabs. With him I met the Naqib 'Abdur Rab, the representative of the exiled Kasadi family once rulers of

## SHEIKH SULEIMAN BIN NASIR

the Hadhramaut. The Naqib belonged to a Yafa'i tribe and was a Sunni, but he had adopted the dress and manners of the Omanis and was a respected member of the community. Another friend, Seiyid Qeis bin Azzan, a relative of the Sultan, came from Oman to spend his last days in Zanzibar. There was no mistaking the "grand seigneur," for he was of imposing size and presence. There was Sa'id's own brother Muhammad, and there were many others. But perhaps one of the most striking personalities of them all was Sheikh Suleiman bin Nasir al Lemki. He was a man for whose sagacity I had always the greatest respect and whose friendship, which lasted till his life's end, I valued highly. He had already had a distinguished career when I met him. When the Sultans of Zanzibar ruled supreme on the African mainland he had been appointed Liwali of Bugamoyo and later of Dar es Salaam. When the Sultan was made to sell his mainland territory to the Germans, Sheikh Suleiman remained behind at his request to lead the Arabs. He had travelled extensively, met the German Emperor, by whom he had been decorated, the Tsar of Russia and many of the pre-war personages of Europe. He had been to China and America and conspicuous among his belongings in the little den to which I used to climb to have tea was a much belabelled and much treasured top-hat box.

These were private apartments and there there might even be a "drop of something" available. Sheikh Suleiman was a religious man in a real sense, but he was no dry as dust formalist. He believed with St. Paul in "a little wine for the stomach's sake," but it went no further than that. At nights he was usually "at home" to Arab friends in his sebuleni, the downstairs hall of all Zanzibar houses, which has a stone seat running all round it. I used often to drop in here while the coffee circulated of an evening, and most Zanzibar news came up for discussion. Indeed, apart from His Highness, Sheikh Suleiman was the best informed man in Zanzibar of daily happenings. Curiously enough he spoke no English or other European language, though he understood more than most people believed. He had a great liking for the society of Europeans and he was always popular with them.

One of the best things in Zanzibar at this time was the real friendliness between all communities, and no two were more intimate than the European and the Arab. Much of this was due to Sheikh Suleiman, for he frequently gave parties where they mixed freely. When the Navy came he was amongst the first to call and they all liked him. In 1924 H.M.S. *Hood* and *Repulse* reached Zanzibar on their Empire cruise, and Sheikh

Suleiman gave a picnic to some fifty of the officers which he commissioned me to organize.

It takes some organizing to cater for seventy guests in a place like Zanzibar, especially when they and the entertainment have to be transported to the other side of the island, for the picnic was to be at Chwaka. I sent hunters with 12-bore shotguns down to the south of the island and in a few days they came back with about a dozen guinea-fowl which I put in the local ice factory. I bought ducks and chickens, and on the previous day all the birds were cooked. In the morning they were delivered at my house packed in petrol boxes. There were salads: we had the famous Zanzibar dish of kelele (the heart of a coco-nut tree). It costs a whole tree to produce a salad, but there is no other like it. The kelele is the heart of the head of the tree, the embryo fronds. It is solid and white like ivory when ready for eating, about two feet long and about six inches in diameter. Without being cooked it is cut transversely in slices and is crisp and nutlike and quite delicious. Another exotic salad was of avocado pears. You can eat them with Worcester sauce or sherry, but they are equally good as a salad and also made excellent sandwiches mixed with egg. There was fruit both tinned and fresh, including the great luscious pineapples for which Zanzibar is famous. Andrade, an old Zanzibar District Commissioner, won the Order of Christ by sending pineapples weighing eleven kilos each to the Queen of Portugal.

There was bread to be thought of and endless cakes for tea, not to mention all the other obvious necessities. China and silver were quite a problem. "And the beer," said Sheikh Suleiman. "Don't forget the beer. Lots of it. And we want ice and whiskies and sodas and vermouth. They must have whisky and soda after sundown."

However it was all ready in time and we left for Chwaka in a long procession of cars, and after a large lunch the guests bathed, explored the shambas on foot or by donkey as they liked. But the best turn of all was my camels. There were no saddles and many a rider took a toss from the unbroken barebacked beasts.

The old man went to all the parties in the *Hood* where he was sometimes the only Arab, and yet he soon contrived to be the centre of attraction and I was hard put to it with interpreting for he had a quick and ready wit. One evening we were drinking beer in a circle of our hosts in the immense wardroom of the *Hood*. With no disapproving Arab eye upon him Sheikh Suleiman was thoroughly enjoying himself. Alcoholic beverage was forbidden to Muslims by local law as well as by the Sharia, and the Attorney General, seeing Sheikh Suleiman with a large glass in his hand, came up and jokingly said: "We shall have to see about this in the morning, Sheikh Suleiman."

"You can't catch me here," replied the old man. "This is British territory."

\* \* \*

One hot January afternoon I got out of my rickshaw at that corner of Malindi in Zanzibar town where 'Abdulla the Persian sat in his shop waiting for customers to buy the brass and copper pots, the trays and chests, carpets and curios, for which he used to ask inordinate prices in a charming manner. I used to spend many an hour in 'Abdulla's shop drinking coffee and bargaining with him, but this day I wanted to go on one of the large dhows, which had come from the Persian Gulf, to buy carpets.

I made my way among the crowds of fierce-eyed, black-bearded men, wearing dirty drab green kanzus, and with pink and brown turbans loosely twisted over their heads to the house of Bā 'Āmr. It was one of a row, old with wooden stairs, somehow reminiscent of an English labourer's cottage. It was spotlessly clean. I shouted "Hodi" up the stairs, and Bā 'Āmr's familiar "Karibu" answered me back, so I climbed the narrow steps to his little bed-sitting-room. It was tidy and home-like. Bā 'Āmr was there in the doorway to receive me. Old and wizen-faced with a stubby beard and but one eye, he was not an elegant sight, but he was well set up and straight, and had a heart of gold. After mutual enquiries as to health and business I suggested carpets. He looked thoughtful a minute and then proposed that we should sally forth while he made enquiries.

Bā 'Āmr, though a regular resident of Zanzibar, was a native of Shihr, and as we crossed the square we stopped time and again while he exchanged greetings with friends just arrived. It was only from December to February, while the north-east monsoon was blowing, that Malindi Square showed such a scene of activity. At this time you might meet in the streets representatives of all those races who had helped to make Zanzibar's history, and Malindi was transformed into an Arabian seaport. We made our way through the crowds to the shop of Muḥammad, another native of the Hadhramaut. Bā 'Āmr and Muḥammad consulted together for a few minutes then Bā 'Āmr went off, while I sat on Muḥammad's baraza and discussed, over the coffee and halwa which he hospitably produced, the quality of the carpets that had come from Persia with the monsoon.

## IN ZANZIBAR TOWN—A DHOW FROM KUWEIT—LATHAM ISLAND

"Yes, they are better than the trash that came last year. Wallahi, they are. I have bought two for seventy rupees that last year would have been sixty each. And dates and figs," he said, "are plentiful, and it is said that plenty of ghee is on its way down from Barawa."

Bā 'Āmr returned bringing with him a young, tall and sharp-featured Arab to whom I was introduced.

"Good luck," said Bā 'Āmr in an aside. "They have come to-day and say they have carpets."

We cut down an alley to the shore, and passing a group of peculiar little men from India, with large gold rings in their ears, sitting gambling in the sand, embarked in a boat. The boat was small, and there seemed to be so many of us in it that the gunwale was perilously near the turbulent water. I did not do this every day of my life and felt a little nervous at the lurches and at the quantity of water we shipped. The fleet of dhows for which we were bound was a long way off. My new friends also were evidently either not quite comfortable or not satisfied with our rate of progress, for when we were some way from the shore one of them stood up and shouted something in Arabic in a piercing yell. He repeated his shouts and waved his hands and signalled, miraculously retaining his balance. At last he was heard and four or five figures scrambled over the side of a large buggalow and entered a boat tied up to it. The boat pushed off and was propelled towards us at some speed. We soon met it and transhipped, not without further misgivings on my part as neither craft was very stable.

> One foot in this boat, one foot in that
> Both push off and you fall flat,

said the Chinaman, and that was what I expected would happen. However the transhipment was safely accomplished and I was introduced to the captain, an old bearded man with a weather-beaten face.

We had more room and some leisure to take in our surroundings. There were forty or fifty dhows in the harbour ranging from the big buggalows, bedeinis and batilis of the Persian Gulf to the small twenty-ton jehazis of Indian origin, but built in Zanzibar and on the coast. A dhow always seems to me a vehicle of history at its most romantic and picturesque, and of all dhows the buggalow calls up the clearest pictures of long voyages and strange ports, of Sindbad the Sailor, of piracy and the slave trade. There is a touch of the galleon about its high square stern with its carving and the windows of its cabin. Its main and mizzen masts, raking well forward, carry huge lateen sails, the descendants of the square sails of the Egyptians. With its tall poop and its long prow it is a graceful sight when, with its white sails stretched, it plunges forward into the waves, as a circular saw eats into a log, and now, as it lay at anchor with sails furled. The crew pulled with great energy at their curious oars—long poles with round boards nailed to their ends. As they pulled they chanted, and we moved over the deep blue water with high speed and tremendous splashings. Two of the oarsmen were but children, sharp, intelligent-looking lads, who gave me the impression of having had a rough time and hard life for all their tender years. One of them was minus an eye, and that led to an exchange of jokes between him and Bā 'Āmr. But the little boys pulled with as much vigour as their elders, even if more erratically, and when one of them splashed us with water the incident was only an occasion for humour.

We were soon alongside the dhow from the stern of which flew the red flag of Arabia emblazoned with the word "Kuweit" in large white Arabic letters. We had to ascend a rope-ladder hanging over the side—a difficult performance on the calmest sea. However we were soon at the top where we were invited to sit on the folded carpets laid down for us on the poop. The inevitable coffee made its appearance, and a large wooden tray with a pile of dried figs, and walnuts which one of the crew cracked for us with a piece of iron. We had come for carpets but it would never have done to broach the subject straight away, so we sat at ease eating and talking on a variety of subjects. I asked what sort of voyage they had had.

"It was rough at Soqotra and Ras Hafun."

"Have many dhows been wrecked this year?"

"A few, but not so many as last when several were lost in that place of storms."

What is the news of Kuweit? How was Sheikh Salim? Is he on any better terms with the ruler of Nejd? So we talked. Then we asked about trade. What quality and quantity of commodities were being brought down this year? What is the price of dates in Basra? Has there been a good crop? Are carpets plentiful? And so gradually the subject was reached. Then we asked a question about the carpets we were sitting on and the captain offered to show us others.

We went down to the main deck and while he and his minions delved somewhere in the cabins under the poop I made a brief survey of the ship.

It was large and had a crew of thirty, carrying also a number of passengers. I asked what the fare was from Zanzibar to Kuweit and was told: "Twelve dollars without food."

By our feet yawned a black hole down which I looked fully fourteen feet to the bottom of the hold. After seeing it I understood better where the camels, sheep and oxen which the dhows carry are stowed, and I understood also how, in those unregenerate days, such large numbers of black human cattle could be carried.

By now the deck was covered with a variety of brightly-coloured rugs. Bā 'Āmr looked at me and winked with his one good eye.

"They're good," he whispered to me, and then said aloud in a bored way: "They're an indifferent lot."

"Have you none better than these?" he asked the captain.

No, the captain had no more and did not seem much disturbed by the disparaging remarks of my friend.

"How much do you want for this pair?" said Bā 'Āmr.

"Say what you will give," replied the captain.

"That is not the custom of commerce," said Bā 'Āmr. "Tell us your lowest price."

After some discussion as to who should name the price the captain suggested one hundred and fifty rupees. Bā 'Āmr laughed in a scornful way.

"Why, that's more than the price I gave for four far finer ones from Muscat but a day or two ago, and carpets are cheaper at Kuweit." I stifled a laugh at his impudence for I knew well the old rascal had not bought any carpets that year.

"I will give you fifty for the two," he said. "And that is more than they're worth. Never did I see such poor carpets."

Then it was the captain's turn to laugh scornfully and he made as though to fold up his carpets and put them away. "I thought you had come to do business, but apparently you have only come to joke."

"Fifty-five I will give you and not a pice more," said Bā 'Āmr.

"One hundred and twenty-five is my lowest figure," said the captain. "And that barely leaves me a profit."

"Well, sixty," said Bā 'Āmr. "And you will never get such a price again."

The captain burst into a voluble stream of language but Bā 'Āmr brushed it all aside.

"Khalas, it is finished," he said, and despite the captain's protests, reinforced by those of his crew, Bā Āmr picked up the carpets, folded them neatly, and put them aside on a spar.

"Now about these two," and so the argument went on until he had selected six for which he had named his own figures. We were beginning to congratulate ourselves on the acquisition of six very respectable rugs for one hundred and eighty rupees or thereabouts as Bā 'Āmr made calculations of the total sum.

"Sixty for the first pair," he said.

"Wallahi, I will never sell them for that," broke in the captain. "I paid sixty-five for them myself in Basra," and so the argument began all over again.

However, that pair were finally acquired for seventy rupees, and the six for the sum of about two hundred and ten. The harsh words that had been flung about, and the sour looks, were now forgotten and we sealed the bargain over a further cup of coffee. When we got up to climb over the side into the boat we were fast friends and the captain gave us as we left a large bag of dates, figs and walnuts. I was very grateful and thanked him accordingly, but Bā 'Āmr did not understand the precept of not looking a gift horse in the mouth, for he opened the bag and critically examined the contents.

"Can't you give us any better dates than these?" he asked plaintively, holding up a few squashed specimens. The captain looked sheepish but despatched one of the small boys down the hold, from the depths of which he presently returned with a few pounds of much finer dates, and we set off for the shore.

As we rowed back I realized that in one afternoon I had witnessed the tale of much of Zanzibar's history. Since dim antiquity these great dhows or their prototypes had come on their trading voyages southwards from the Red Sea, from the Hadhramaut, from Muscat and the Persian Gulf, and from India, and the men who manned them were sons of those old sea captains who knew the coast of which the *Periplus* speaks, men of Ausan and the other states of ancient Araby. The East is indeed a living museum, for what was, is now, and probably will be to the end of the chapter.

* * *

*What matter in what wreck we reached the shore*<br>
*So we both reached it?*      W. S. BLUNT.

In 1924, just before I went on leave, Sir Claud Hollis, then Resident at

Zanzibar, was kind enough to take me with him in the *Cupid* to visit Zanzibar's most distant possession. Miles away from land, low and flat and sandy, surrounded by inhospitable rocks on which gigantic waves beat tirelessly, Latham Island is an extraordinary contrast to the green fertility of Zanzibar and Pemba. It lies about thirty-five miles south of Zanzibar and is only a thousand feet long by two hundred wide. As it is very low it is a danger to shipping, and the main object of the journey was to plant casuarina trees to make it more conspicuous.

We left Zanzibar at night and in the morning woke to find ourselves tossing about some distance off the island, which was barely visible, for there is not a feature that stands out on it. We were anchored; the *Cupid*, of about three hundred tons, simply bobbed up and down, rolling and pitching and tossing like a cork anchored by a string in a whirlpool, and for the first and only time in my life I was seasick. But so was Charlewood, the Port Officer.

Presently a lifeboat was launched: the casuarina seedlings were put into it and the rest of us, including Fritz, the Resident's dachsund, embarked and made for the beach. This was a variable affair; the *African Pilot* says that it is to be found at one end or the other of the island according to the monsoon. As the south-west monsoon was blowing it was due to be at the north end, but as we approached I could see nothing but a bank of sand, perhaps a hundred feet high at an angle of about sixty degrees. Against it mountainous seas were breaking, and at each wave the shore was completely submerged.

The manœuvre at which we aimed was to be carried by a wave and deposited on the top of the wall of sand. It will be appreciated that a second on the wrong side might make all the difference. We were about a second late. We just failed to reach the top of the bank and the next thing I knew was that we were thrown on to jagged rocks at the bottom and the boat came apart under us. We all seized something and my share was Fritz. Then the next wave was upon us and when I saw the sun again we were struggling in a white foam of surf with buoyancy tanks, which had broken loose from the wreck of the lifeboat, bobbing up and down round us. We and the bits were washed ashore, soaked but undamaged.

It did not take long to explore the island but what there was of it was interesting. It was at least a couple of feet deep in guano, with a crisp surface which shone like snow in the sun. My feet sank in through the crust at every step and the stink is in my nostrils as I write.

The first half of the island had been appropriated by great white gannets, literally thousands of them. They sat on their eggs or with their chicks, cheek by jowl. How they did not get their families mixed up I cannot imagine, in fact I expect they did. There was barely room to put a foot down without stepping on them, and though they made no attempt to move, the din was frightful. As I picked my way through them they made ferocious jabs at my feet and sometimes really hurt even through the leather of my boots.

The southern part of the island was covered by a succulent creeping plant, the only vegetation, on which gulls and terns had eggs and young. As I walked across it the birds flew round me in hundreds and I had to beat them off with my arms. They were like clouds of gigantic flies, so closely and in such packed throngs did they surround me.

The captain of the *Cupid*, who had seen our "landing," sent a motor-boat to rescue us. Charlewood signalled to it not to come too close and gallantly swam off to it. Getting the boat as near the rocks as he dared he threw a line to us and with an endless cord and a lifebuoy we were all rescued, being pulled one by one through the raging surf. I was the last to leave, hugging Fritz to me.

As to the casuarina trees; we had embarked them in the lifeboat ("hold them carefully, whatever you do don't break them") neatly planted in boxes in a way which would have done any nurseryman credit. Alas! Between ourselves and Fritz the seedlings came off quite the worst and only a few poor battered fragments were cast up after us by the sea. But these were borne tenderly, almost reverently (it was all rather like the burial of Sir John Moore) by Charlewood and the crew to the one patch of soil that seemed free of birds and there planted—interred I feel would be the better word. But there was no sure and certain hope about that ceremony and I feel that mariners may still sweep the horizon in vain for a glimpse of lofty trees to warn them of the perilous presence of Latham Island.

\* \* \*

Soon after this visit I went on leave. It was the year of the Wembley Exhibition. Sheikh Suleiman came home to see it and I was to look after him. He had a following of five, two sons, a secretary who in Zanzibar was his chauffeur, a Swahili houseboy and an Indian friend of us both. Wherever we went by train we all travelled together, first class, and whenever we went to the theatre, which was most nights, we had the greater part of a row in the stalls. The party was dressed in European

IN ZANZIBAR TOWN—A DHOW FROM KUWEIT—LATHAM ISLAND

clothes; Sheikh Suleiman wore an astrakhan cap and a frock coat. He had the most amazing collection of flowered silk waistcoats. As neither he nor any of his party could understand English sufficiently, our plays were never very serious, and musical comedies and revues were most appreciated. If there was a laugh I had to interpret the joke. This I did in a whisper to Sheikh Suleiman who would laugh uproariously and pass it on. So it went down the line to the seventh man with a series of loud guffaws which must have been disconcerting to players and audience alike. By the time we had visited the Tower, the Zoo, and all the other sights of London, I began to feel like a small circus proprietor, and was glad when we retired awhile to the peace of Shrewsbury.

Back in Zanzibar I left the country districts for good and in 1925 held several posts in addition to my new work in the secretariat. Amongst other jobs I was Private Secretary to the Sultan and to the Resident at the same time. But apart from occasionally writing letters for the Resident to the Sultan and answering them for the Sultan to the Resident, the double rôle did not worry me much except during the naval visit, when day after day I would see the Admiral off from a Residency party and, very often with a hasty change of uniform, make my way as fast as possible to one of the palaces to receive him on behalf of the Sultan. They were the most considerate masters. I owe much to Sir Claud Hollis and so does Zanzibar. For His Highness I developed the most sincere admiration and affection. In domestic affairs it was very much the Sultanah who had the last word; if any problem with a domestic issue arose in the course of my work for His Highness, he would always say: "I must consult Her Highness first." They were an affectionate couple and after the Sultan took to a motor-car they were often to be seen driving out together. I never knew a man in a position such as his with more natural dignity and charm. On State occasions no country could have had a fitter representative, and in matters of State concern he had a surer instinct for what was right than many of those who advised him.

## Chapter VI

## MAURITIAN INTERLUDE AND ORIENTAL ENCOUNTERS

"*Ce sont de bons gens.*" *Ainsi des violettes, sous des buissons épineux, exhalent au loin leurs doux parfums, quoiqu'on ne les voie pas.*
ST. PIERRE.
*God sends meat, and the devil sends cooks.*

ONE morning in May, 1927, as I was sitting at my work in the Beit al Ajaib a decoded telegram was put before me. It began "Offer Ingrams appointment as Assistant Colonial Secretary, Mauritius..." It is strange how in one moment the course of one's life can be altered in this way. You may, so to speak, be flung half round the world, from Fiji to the Falklands, or Jamaica to Jerusalem. More often than not the offer of transfer will be one which you have barely contemplated as a possibility. Although Mauritius was only about fifteen hundred miles in a direct line from Zanzibar I had scarcely heard more than a mention of the place, and the manner of life was to be very different.

After a leave I came back through Zanzibar where I picked up Zaidi, and if Mauritius was to be strange to me it was much stranger to him. Previously, it is true, he had been to Dar es Salaam, to Mombasa, Nairobi and Nakuru with me, but though they were different it was still his own language that was spoken.

In the few hours that we stopped in Zanzibar I had much to do and many people to see. I was late for the ship and Zaidi was later, for I had to wait for him on the shore while the siren of the French mail blew urgently. A day or two later we arrived at one of the Comorro Islands where we were to stay for twenty-four hours. Our very delightful captain was standing at the head of the gangway, watch in hand and twinkle in eye, as I was leaving to go on shore.

"Mr. Ingrams," he said, "we leave to-morrow afternoon at five o'clock."

I was glad to see the Comorro Islands, for they were extremely beautiful, but quite different from the coral isles of Zanzibar and Pemba; they are not only much smaller but mountainous and volcanic. These physical differences apart, however, their civilization is an extension of the Swahili and Arab cultures. They owe their name, so it is said, to the Qamr or Moon Mountains of the Mahra country, and were settled by Jews in the time of Solomon, but later they were governed by the Persians who founded the states of the Zenj Empire. Mayotte, one of the four islands of the Archipelago, has also Malagasy connections. The Sultanates of the Comorro lasted until the French occupation, and the archives of Zanzibar, Mauritius and Aden contain much about their affairs, for at one time British influence was paramount.

On this journey we called at Mayotte and anchored between it and Dzaudzi, the ramshackle and unkempt headquarters of the Archipelago, where I explored the Boulevard of Crabs, a causeway over a stretch of shallow water which joins Dzaudzi to the Island of Pamanzi. It owes its name to the familiar little blue and pink crabs of the Indian Ocean—lopsided creatures with one tiny and one very large claw which they wave threateningly at intruders as they retire into the water.

Over the Boulevard a long walk past villages and through a valley led me to the extinct volcano of Dziani. From its summit I looked down on a cup-like crater fringed with mangoes and coco-nuts, but there were no inhabitants, for the place is believed to be haunted. The principal products of Mayotte are vanilla, ylang ylang, lemon grass, balm mint and basalisk and thinking that people who grow such pleasant things could not fail to be pleasant themselves, I called in, on my way back, at the large village o Pamanzi Keli and was at home as soon as the people knew that I spoke Swahili. They have a language of their own, allied to Swahili but owing also a good deal to Malagasy, and they sat round me while I took down a vocabulary. Like all Swahili villages Pamanzi Keli was clean and charming and it was in the women that I noticed marked differences with Zanzibar. I confess that the Maore women looked superior, for they were tall and graceful and had an air of arrogance lacking in the friendly women of Zanzibar and Pemba.

The port of Madagascar which interested me most was Nossi Bé, and quite by accident I found there my Happy Village. The place was of great interest to me, for early in the nineteenth century Seiyid Sa'id had sent colonists to Nossi Bé and protested without effect in 1841 against French intrusion.

I landed and walked up the street called Hell, memorable for the incongruous presence in it of a church—incongruous unless one has heard of the

## MARADUKA

Admiral Hell to whom the Sakalava surrendered the island. I came at length to a large Sakalava village where a Sakalava lady, speaking a little Swahili, invited me into her small, cool and clean palm leaf home, floored with boards lifted above the ground. She advised me to go to Maraduka, a village on the shore, for she told me that all the people there spoke Swahili, so after sharing a dish of bananas and fish, called katakata, with her I went back to the beach and chartering a rowing-boat set out on a voyage of discovery to find Maraduka.

It lies at the top of a wide creek whose high banks were covered with leafy woods. Outrigger canoes called laka, differing from those of Zanzibar in that they had one outrigger instead of two, moved with their little square sails up and down the creek. We came at last to the tiny jetty of Maraduka where several dhows and a number of canoes lay up on the mud. The place reminded me of Chake Chake for the architecture was much the same and there was just the one main street about half a mile long. It consisted of the usual Indian dukas, and it is probably from this word for "shop" that the village takes its name.

Zaidi and I soon had a crowd around us, for they told us that they never met people who spoke Swahili. Indeed their emotion at hearing about their old homeland was quite extraordinary, for these were the descendants of Seiyid Sa'id's colonists. Old men came up and beating their chests said: "We are all subjects of the Sultan."

There were, of course, some who had migrated to join their relations since Seiyid Sa'id's time. One of them had left in the 'eighties, when the great Barghash sat on the throne of Zanzibar and sent Tippoo Tib on his journeys. He came hobbling along when he heard of my presence, and repeating protestations of loyalty to the Sultan, asked how Seiyid Barghash was. He was full of grief when I told him that he had died nearly forty years before.

As we were shown round the little village of Swahili huts we came to one solitary Sakalava hut over which a beautiful purple bougainvillea trailed. There were ferns on the veranda and the house was gay with green and red paint. It looked as much out of place here as an eskimo's igloo would look in an English village. I sat for an hour or so outside the hut in a circle with my friends, while the friendly owner brought out his valiha, the typical Malagasy instrument, made out of a piece of giant bamboo with threads of the fibre lifted out and tautened by bridges. He played soft tuneful music, and sang in a pleasant low voice love songs in the Sakalava language.

And at last, after a voyage of forty-five days, I came to Mauritius. Never had I been to a place that felt so much like the end of the world. For in those days there was hardly a ship that came in sight; all turned back home, and on this journey I was almost the only passenger left by the time we arrived. It presents the most peculiar contrast to anyone who approaches it by the east coast route. Port Sudan—Jibuti—Aden—Mombasa—Zanzibar—the Comorros—even Madagascar—all seem to have something in common. The policemen, for instance, are all much alike with their khaki tunics, shorts and tarbushes. But when I stepped ashore at Mauritius I saw blue-serge-clad policemen, with blue and white good conduct badges and friendly black faces looking at me from under London bobbies' helmets; and then a real white London bobby, who had not been home for seventeen years and longed to see the Vauxhall Bridge again.

But there or thereabouts my "home" feelings ended for a while, and it was not long before I was wondering why everybody, including myself, was not wearing knee breeches and flowered coats and ruffs and wigs and things, for I discovered I was living in a fragment of eighteenth-century France, cast in some strange way into the Indian Ocean four hundred miles east of Madagascar. After the policeman the next man I saw was properly dressed. He stood on a pedestal looking seawards and, I hoped, welcoming the strangers. I confess now that, rather surreptitiously, I always used to take my hat off to Mahé de La Bourdonnais as I passed him, in token of his great achievements. You have only to read Macaulay's *Essay on Clive* to learn what kind of a man he was, and, in time, when I had learnt more about him I classed him with the greatest of pioneers.

At first Zaidi and I were lost in Mauritius. For a start we went to stay in Phoenix, where there was a good service of trains running over the top of the island through Phoenix and Curepipe, 1,800 feet up, down to Mahébourg, in all a distance of thirty miles. A few days after we had arrived Zaidi had to travel alone from Port Louis to Phoenix. He could not read and could not speak Creole, so a Swahili-speaking friend bought his ticket for him and put him on the train. In due course the train stopped for good. A kindly station-master fetched him out, took his ticket and, helping himself to his cash, charged him the excess fare from Phoenix to Mahébourg, bought him a new ticket and put him on the train again. He arrived safely at Port Louis and was again helped to pay his excess fare. This time he got his friend to bring him home.

Altogether the trains were a source of much amusement. At night

Port Louis was a city of the dead and few people of substance lived in it. Until about 10 a.m. trains from the highlands deposited people at the capital, and from about 3 p.m. to 6 p.m. proceeded to move them back again. It was a completely suburban life and people travelled in bowler hats and black coats, just to make it more realistic. To make it even more homelike evening papers were produced in French, English, Hindi, and Chinese. I never saw such a place for newspapers; there must have been more than a dozen periodicals of one kind and another.

The total population of the "cher petit pays" is about 400,000. Some 130,000 of these formed the "General" population—comprising about 7,000 of pure French descent, perhaps 250 to 300 English, some 40,000 Creoles of more or less pure African or Malagasy descent, and the rest a mixture of French, English, African, Malagasy, Indian and Chinese blood. Then there were about 245,000 Hindus, either Tamil, Telugu or Hindi speaking, 8,000 Chinese and the rest "Arabes." Why they were called Arabs I never discovered; there was not a single Arab among them, for they were all Muhammadan Indians, mainly Hanafis but a few Shafis. Many of them are descendants of Indian settlers from French times. They also included a number of Shias, principally Bohoras and Memons, and I believe I had friends among all these communities.

I have said that I felt (in spite of the black coats and bowler hats) as if I was living in eighteenth-century France and amongst the descendants of the old French colonists the feeling was inescapable. I have met no kinder, more hospitable community anywhere, and I was continually attracted by the delightful oldworld courtesies that were current. No conversation was more amusing or company more "sympathique." There were relics of a past, bygone in other countries, which were startling. It was not *comme il faut* for unmarried girls even if they had reached—shall I whisper it?—a safe thirty to be seen about with men friends. They could not even go to a dance or a picnic with a party unless properly chaperoned. One of the most astonishing survivals—nearly extinct I confess—was the chaperones' pen at a dance. In this enclosure sat the chaperones; some of them knitted, others gossiped. When a dance was over a man returned his fair partner to her chaperone, or perhaps he might walk up and down with her. But "pas de sitting-out." Yet I should admit that I only saw this happen once or twice.

Once I heard of a lady arrested because she kept company her husband did not approve; I was told that the procedure in such a case was for the

## MAURITIAN INTERLUDE AND ORIENTAL ENCOUNTERS

husband to seek an order from a judge in chambers. If the lady did not obey the order when the bailiff served it, the bailiff obtained the assistance of the police and the lady was arrested and handed over to her husband's custody. He could keep her locked up until she came to a better frame of mind. I remember, too, the case of a lady teacher with a wastrel of a husband who did not work. The husband obtained an order for the wife's salary to be paid to him. I think this moved opinion so much that ultimately an arrangement was made allowing the wife a proportion of her own salary. Such cases as these were rare, but I mention them as interesting survivals of darker ages; on the whole I do not think that you could find happier or more devoted couples than in Mauritius.

But while the Mauritians retain much of the eighteenth century, there is nothing behind the times about the way the ladies dress. At a race meeting or a dance you will find the "dernier cri." Many have their own dress agents, often compatriots in Paris, who forward to them the advance "modes." Mauritian functions are truly brilliant affairs and if you ransacked Europe you would not find a higher percentage of charming girls. Government House balls and garden parties, race meetings, weddings, dances, "chasses," these are the occasions in which to see Mauritians at their best. There is no more picturesque race-course in the world than the Champ de Mars at Port Louis, even if there are rarely more than three horses in a race. It is not in fact an occasion for racing; it is *par excellence* a social gathering. On the big days the vast field, and even the encircling amphitheatre of hills, thronged by the Indian women in all their coloured silks, look like brilliant beds of exotic summer blooms swayed by the winds. A brilliance only to be matched with the vivid pinks and yellows of the cakes and sweets that are offered for sale.

I seem to have wandered far from Arabs, but there were many things in the structure of Mauritian society that reminded me of Zanzibar. Since leaving Mauritius I have found them again in Aden. The Mauritian indeed seems to have absorbed something of the Orient in which he lives; a liking for curry and rice, a lavish hospitality, even the almost harem-like seclusion of women.

Historically too Mauritius, as I have shown, is by no means out of the Arabian picture, for in the eighteenth and early nineteenth centuries there were constant relations with Muscat. The archives of Port Louis contain a host of interesting documents including treaties with Oman. So too at Caen among the papers of General Decaen, the last French Governor,

## MUSLIM FESTIVAL

I found much correspondence with Muscat and even the Yemen. The period is perpetuated for ever in Mauritius where you find the names of Moka, Medine, La Mecque, Yemen and other Arabian places. There was a fair trade, too, in donkeys, dates and dried fish. The creole word for date, indeed, is Arabic and not French.

The first British treaty with Seiyid Sa'id was contracted on behalf of Sir Robert Farquhar, the first English Governor, and the first British representative at Zanzibar was an Arab on the Mauritius pay-roll. In old gazettes you can find records of frequent arrivals of dhows from Zanzibar: Seiyid Sa'id's famous ship the *Shah Allum*—Lord of the World—came there. With the African side of Zanzibar the contact was, of course, more extensive. Thousands of slaves came from the market in Zanzibar and the language of the people in Mauritius is, as a consequence, Bantu African in construction though it is French in its vocabulary. (The language of society, of course, is purest French.) You may hear in the creole of Mauritius the same folk tales you have heard in the Swahili of Zanzibar.

But all that has passed and to-day contacts are few. There is a small Swahili-speaking community of Comorrian origin, but there is only *one* true Arab in Mauritius, the Imam of the Juma' mosque. He, poor man, is really an exile, for he comes from Medina, and as he cannot speak a word of anything but Arabic, can only talk to the two or three Indians who know it.

There is a Muslim festival which is one of the sights of the island. It is the Shia commemoration of the great day of mourning, the martyrdom of Hussein on 10th Muharram, and although in other countries the ceremonies are so particularly Shia, here they have lost much of their original and their factional significance and men of all creeds join in. The processions in Mauritius are known as yamsée, and the tazias, the funeral cars of the Imams Hassan and Hussein, as ghoons. The field of Kerbela is transferred to the Rivière des Lataniers and there for the occasion those who venerate Hussein seek his dust in the river mud. Most imposing of the processions is the Levée des Ghoons on the night of 10th Muharram. For once I saw Port Louis no longer at night a place of the dead. My first impression on leaving the car in the market place was of noise; from every direction crowds were coming towards this quarter of the town, and in the public gardens they congregated round the sweet and cake sellers, the merry-go-round, and the groups of men dancing, playing, singing and chanting the Quran. The moon and the street lamps and the lanterns shone upon the

## MAURITIAN INTERLUDE AND ORIENTAL ENCOUNTERS

gathered groups with a soft and varied light. Soon I began to distinguish sounds in the babel around me, cries of the street sellers of "Bananes, bananes, gâteaux piments!" Creole was not the only language, some of the better educated talked French, occasionally I heard English and varied Indian dialects, while the chanting of the Quran gave a touch of Arabic.

While there was an Eastern splendour in the vari-coloured saris of the Indian women and the white silk coats and trousers, and the pigtails of the Chinese girls, the men, unfortunately, preferred to ape the West, and the result was distressing. Trousers of dirty white, of khaki and of black; coats of the same but rarely agreeing with the trousers; the awful slouch hats from which the only relief was the smart tarbushes of the Muslims. There was no age limit and babes in arms and old men and women were all there. It was an amazing display of races and of their intermingling.

In 1929 the time came for Zaidi and myself to go on leave. He had taken unto himself a temporary wife as he had left his other two in Zanzibar. She was Creole and I had some misgivings when he told me that he proposed to bring her to live in the "dependance" at the back of my house in Curepipe. I was a little doubtful what the neighbours might think, but as my friend, the Sub-Inspector of Police, was sure that I should not be compromised, I consented. In due course Zaidi informed me, with pride, one morning that he had become a father. I congratulated him the more as hitherto his Zanzibar wives had not been able to produce heirs for him. As the time drew near for our departure he told me that he intended to take the child back to Zanzibar with him, and that its mother was quite prepared to part with it. She no doubt had enough maternal cares, for my police friend told me that she had already five children by different fathers.

I asked Zaidi what his chief wife in Zanzibar would have to say about this. He said he was going to give the child to her as a present as she had none of her own and that all would be well, and so, in due course, we left, Zaidi via Madagascar for Zanzibar, and I via Ceylon for England. There, shortly after, I met a doctor and his wife home on leave from Zanzibar, bringing with them a Swahili ayah. I asked her about Zaidi and was told that though he had arrived safely with the baby, his principal wife had refused to have anything to do with it, saying she did not mind how many babies he had as long as she did not have to take care of them. He married another wife to look after it. The boy had been registered in Mauritius under the name of Kassim, but was henceforth known as Maurice—a delicate compliment to the island from which he came.

*       *       *

A year later I returned to Mauritius with my wife, calling at Zanzibar for Zaidi, and visiting once again the Comorros and Madagascar. This time the ship called at Ngazija—the Grand Comorro—the home of the Mkokotoni Qadhi and many Zanzibaris. Nothing much is known of its ancient history for the natives fled when the Portuguese came and settled there at the beginning of the sixteenth century, but in the middle of the nineteenth there were five Sultans ruling in different parts of the island. Of these Seiyid Ahmed at Mroni, which is to-day the capital, was paramount in name, though Musa Fumu, the Sultan of Itsandra and Bambao, was more powerful, and one was a woman, Ayesha by name. By 1881 Seiyid 'Ali, grandson of Seiyid Ahmed, had become leader and five years later he persuaded the French to proclaim a Protectorate. He was exiled to Réunion, where now languishes the Riff chieftain 'Abdul Krim, but was restored in 1910 and died in 1916. Since then there has been no Sultan.

The day we came in sight of Mauritius I took D. on deck before dawn to watch sunrise over the island. Mauritian sunrise has none of the loving warm glow of the nearer tropics; it is an angry blaze, glowering from behind the dark mass of the Morne, most glorious of all mountains of the Isle de France. And against this background of fire are silhouetted the island's fantastic peaks, so strange in their resemblance to natural objects that a quasi-serious study has been written of how they were carved by a bygone race of giants. The Mauritian landscape has changed little since Bernardin de St. Pierre, and the gentle spirits of Paul and Virginia still roam in hidden corners; you still find names of the period, and not only on tombstones, for there are many descendants of the old *noblesse* who emigrated in the days of Louis XIV, XV and XVI. There are even those whose ancestors escaped from the very shadow of the guillotine, and there are others, descendants of those hardy Bretons, the corsairs.

I had a minor tragedy to face on my return to Mauritius; the white ants had eaten much of my furniture, many of my books and all my pictures. I was inclined to credit them with a supernatural system of intelligence, for while I was at home, working in the Colonial Office, I had put forward a suggestion that the possibility of investigating the easy annihilation of the termite race should be considered. Something of this kind was done, though I remember a prophetic note being put on the papers:

"*Vixere anti-termitites ante Ingramemnona*—the white ant always wins." The wholesale holocaust of my property looked like vengeance and amongst my papers destroyed were the carefully hoarded-up letters of introduction which Seiyid Ahmed had written for me. The Hadhramaut, indeed, seemed very distant in those days, though I got Van der Meulen's book as soon as it appeared and found that he had not visited the wadi which Hogarth had catalogued as awaiting exploration. D., bitten with the Arabian idea, obtained a teacher, a young Indian who knew only a little Arabic. Through the medium of French, for he spoke no English, he taught her the elements. I took lessons twice a week in Hindustani and Persian from the Court Interpreter whose name was almost unrecognizable in the queer transliteration of Mauritius. "Amode" seemed to be a poor attempt at "Ahmed."

Andrew Lang says in his book *Magic and Religion* that the Europeans of Mauritius "take no interest in the doings of the heathen" and I determined that this reproof should not apply to me, so after enquiries for guides I made visits among the Eastern communities.

The Chinese in Mauritius are a self-contained and exclusive community and have little to do with the rest of the population except by way of making a living out of them. They carry retail trading to extraordinary lengths. At their little "boutiques" you can buy one cent of a rupee's worth of sugar, salt, tea, cheese, dried fish or grain, a few matches, a single slice of bread or a single sardine out of a tin. In their own shops you find all sorts of exciting things, like eggs black with age, shark fins, dried *bêche de mer* and other queer fish. Grave, impassive, and usually immobile of countenance, a Chinese shopkeeper has yet a dry sense of humour.

I was told the tale of a young black woman who went into a "boutique" and asked for a "pair of flesh-coloured stockings." John Chinaman turned silently to his shelves (I suspect he disapproved of these fripperies), brought down a pair of black stockings and without a word handed them over the counter to her. The young lady of fashion was furious.

"I asked for flesh-coloured stockings," she said.

"*Qui to causé?*" asked the old Chinaman in the Creole language. "*Ça napa coulère to cere?*" ("What are you talking about? That's the colour of your flesh isn't it?")

The men always wore European dress but the Chinese ladies wore mostly black wide trousers and a black collarless tunic, doing up their hair in a plain bun at the back of their heads and wearing no hats. Port Louis has a Chinese quarter where there are gambling dens and a Chinese theatre.

## CHINESE THEATRE

Once I was taken by some friends to a performance. We were given front seats—deck-chairs—in the orchestra stalls, but the theatre was not at ill crowded. I was not surprised when I heard the performance had already lasted continuously for two days. Most of the audience were fast alseep and every now and then a newcomer, doped with opium, was carried in by the attendants and dumped in one of the deck-chairs. The play was acted by a travelling company from China. As I could not read the playbill I had not the remotest idea what the play was about, but the players, who were all men, were dressed in the beautiful costumes of old China and the stage was brilliantly lit.

The orchestra was equipped with an exotic-collection of instruments, chiefly percussion. One old gentleman whose job it was to beat a number of drums of different sizes, including one of enormous proportions, as well as a huge cymbal, must have been at it since the show started for he was functioning in a state of coma. At intervals he suddenly galvanized himself to life, beat everything within reach with extraordinary vigour, and then relapsed into insensibility again: while in this state he occasionally administered a mechanical tap to something close at hand. Now and then a lady came to the edge of the platform behind him, and waking him up by pulling his sleeve, handed him a small cup of tea which he drank and slept again.

A delightful Chinese, the President of the Chinese Chamber of Commerce took me to their principal temples. It is rightly laid down that a Chinese temple shall have a pleasant aspect and be open to the most fortunate wind. It must also have an enclosed courtyard open to the sky. How much more comfortable and happy we should all be if we adopted a law like this for our own homes. Both the Chinese temples in Port Louis fulfilled these requirements: one looked over the lovely Champ de Mars and the other across the harbour, whose waters lapped at its front veranda. They were pleasant places within with their black wood carving and the peaceful faces of the gilt figures. There is a figure of Buddha in one of the temples only, for the Chinese of Mauritius pay most attention to the worship of their ancestors. In the Champ de Mars temple, called Namshun Foykoon, there were wonderful carvings in relief illustrating the rewards and punishments of the next world. The principal personage among the calm artistic figures in the temple was the general and sage Kwan Ti. On the altar in front of him stood a bronze lion with the pleasant smoke of sandalwood coiling from its mouth. There was also a lamp burning and three cups of tea poured out for Kwan Ti. These are changed at a short ceremony every morning when the temple gongs are beaten and fresh incense sticks are lit.

D. went with me to the other temple. Here there was a famous oracle Shin Kao, whom a queue of Chinese were consulting. D. wanted to ask the oracle when we should move from Mauritius, so our friend produced a priest. He took two kidney-shaped pieces of wood from the altar: one side of each was rounded and the other flat. He threw them on the floor and one fell round side up and the other flat side up.

"You may ask Shin Kao your question," he said. "If both are round side up or both flat side up, questions may not be asked."

Then he handed her a jar of divining rods—slips of bamboo about eight inches long with Chinese numbers on them, and showed her how to manipulate it. You shake the jar with an upwards and forwards movement until one rod falls out. When this happened he picked up the rod, looked at the number, and took her over to the wall where there was a board on which were nailed bundles of vari-coloured printed slips. He tore off a slip from the bundle bearing the same number as the rod. It read "It is good to journey." Not very helpful, I thought.

One specially useful thing in the temple was an automatic doctor. It worked in the same way as the oracle. When you had shaken out a rod you went to a board and got the prescription which the oracular doctor prescribed for you. All you had to do then was to take it into a Chinese pharmacy and get it made up. In this temple were many images including one of the Virgin Mary, whom the Chinese identify with Kwan Yin, the virgin saint. They gave us a present of incense sticks when we left, and sometimes we burn one even now in our Aden home.

There are two groups of Hindus in Mauritius, those of the north or Calcutta and those of the south or Tamil. They are together far the greatest section of the population and came to take the place of the slaves as workers on the land. I visited the principal temples of both groups, but the one I liked best was that of the southern Hindus just outside Port Louis. The most spectacular ceremony of the southern Hindus is firewalking, called Ti-mithi. The northern Hindus have only one festival which provides a show. It is the Cavadee which takes place on Great Siva's night. For some days before the ceremony the devotees make their way from different parts of the island to Grand Bassin, a large and beautiful lake in wild country in a crater in the middle of the island.

## INTRODUCING GANESS

The Hindus hold that it is connected by a submarine channel with Mother Ganges. It is believed that if a man does the Cavadee pilgrimage to Grand Bassin for five consecutive years he will go to Paradise without any question when he dies.

It must not be thought that all my time was given up to enquiries of this kind or to attending weddings and chasses and the other pleasant functions of Mauritian life. I had, in fact, heavier office work than I had met before. During my last year or so I acted as Colonial Secretary, and at one time, from January 1932 to about July of the same year, I generally did about fourteen hours work a day. The financial depression had hit Mauritius hard and a financial commission came out. The work of reorganization consequent on its report, and the preparation of the budget, fell mostly on me under the direction of the Governor, Sir Wilfrid Jackson. He was a kind chief and very considerate to me, or it would have been much harder than it was. Actually I enjoyed it. I motored down to my office from Vacoas where we were living and was generally there before nine. I stayed there till at least five, and often till eight in the evening, working with candles round my desk, for there was no precedent for such times and no electricity. I drove home and after dinner used to work till two, three or four in the morning with D. heroically adding up figures, taking down dictation or typewriting. At one o'clock mid-day I went up to a top room of the pleasant old French Government House and had lunch. The room in which I had it had been La Bourdonnais' bedroom and his great four-poster was still there. Sometimes after lunch I would gaze for a few minutes over the burnt grass slopes of the mountains which hemmed in Port Louis, and wondered if we should ever see the brown sands of Arabia.

* * *

The trio of D., Zaidi and I was increased to a quartet on my second tour in Mauritius, for Ganess joined us. Since the death of 'Uthman, the hero of the omelette, I had not had a cook as faithful as Zaidi had been a servant until Ganess came. Cooks came and went in a mixed procession of age, race, temperament and skill. Some stayed only a week or two, others even a year, but none had personalities that impressed themselves on my memory. To me a cook is not ordinarily such a reality as a personal servant. I gave up visiting my kitchen when I found the cook filleting a fish on the floor. As the food always tasted perfectly good I saw his successors only when they wanted money for market and I checked up their books, and at the end of the month when they wanted their pay. Otherwise they were intangible presences in the background and when I think of my cooks it is chiefly by their stock dishes. There was the boned chicken cook, the coco-nut soup and coco-nut curry cook, the dressed crab cook and the ice and chocolate sauce cook. There was also the "Bombay toast" (bread fried in butter) cook and there were several banana fritter and caramel pudding cooks. These last were poor, and their confections, together with the eternal kuku (chicken), were sent up *ad nauseam*.

When I first came to Mauritius there was a rascally cook called Joe with an oily lock over his forehead. He was merely a rosbif cook for he had had only English experience, but his bills were as big as any French chef's. He was followed by two nondescripts, one of whom was a Muslim with a tarbush and beard but otherwise unsatisfactory, and then came Gustave. What a change it was. When I gave a party I would say: "*Qu'est ce que nous avons pour dîner ce soir* Gustave?" I did not talk Creole to him for I did not know it well enough at the time.

Gustave checked it off on his fingers: "*Nous avons, Msié, premièrement des croûtes et secondement crême d'asperges. Puis il y a des jolis poissons frits avec une sauce un peu spéciale. Alors nous avons un bon plat des petits pois, un canard garni avec des legumes et puis comme désert, un soufflé chocolat.*"

Gustave had only been in French houses and I never knew how cheap food was till he dealt with it. When I came back from leave he came to see me. "I would like to come back, Msié, but I am in another job, with a priest. I can't leave him yet, *mais j'ai un frère*...."

And so Ganess came. He was not really a "frère" only a "cousin." I liked Gustave and was sorry he did not return, but we grew so fond of Ganess that I was quite relieved when the months went by and Gustave did not reclaim the job.

Ganess is still young, twenty-seven he says. He is Hindu by origin and nebulously Roman Catholic by profession of faith, having been brought up in an orphanage when his parents died in the 1918 epidemic of flu. He had had both French and English experience, but the latter had not spoilt him, because it was under the competent eye of Lady Read at Government House where he was second cook. He had gone with the Governor on a local leave to Bourbon, so he felt a very travelled man.

Quiet and unostentatious in his way, we very soon saw that he was a personality. He was not just a presence in the kitchen. He was Ganess. And he had peculiarities.

He had, too, a wide range of curries and he was fond of "conceits," the most artistic being a broody hen sitting on her eggs. The hen, made of whipped cream looked so like a white leghorn sitting there with her currant eyes, her roseleaf comb and her almond beak, that I could scarcely bear to carve a bit out of her. Her eggs were made with infinite patience. Ganess bored a hole in a real egg, abstracted the contents, and poured drop by drop a mixture of cream, gelatine and some flavouring. He broke the shell carefully when it was set and out came what looked like a hard-boiled egg.

Ganess and Zaidi are "buddies," though there are curious contrasts between them. Ganess smiles only occasionally, a gentle restrained sort of smile. Zaidi laughs all day long, except in his rare sulks, with a wide display of shining teeth. Ganess spends his money carefully and wisely. He buys something useful like a bicycle or a trunk. Zaidi bursts his pay on endless new clothes. He is a man of fashion and always follows the fashion of the country in which he lives. In Zanzibar he wore spotless kanzus, carried a small cane and had a white coat like the better Arabs in undress. In Mauritius he had pin-striped suits, a gay tie and co-respondent shoes. In Aden he wore a silk shirt outside a brightly coloured futa, like all the best people in the bazaar.

*   *   *

WE left, on what was to be our last leave from Mauritius in a Dutch boat, the *Barentz*, and spent six days in Bourbon, or Réunion, the "Ile soeur" of Mauritius. It is a fascinating island in its natural aspects, but as far as I could see many of the inhabitants had no other occupation than drinking, for rum and red wine are cheap. But if Bourbon has been damned by man, Nature has dowered it lavishly with variety of climate, luxuriance of verdure and magnificent scenery. It rises to a height of over 10,000 feet and has not only snow-clad peaks, but a live volcano. A railway runs round much of its coast and we followed this to St. Pierre in one direction and to St. Denis, the capital, in the other. There was nothing whatever to attract in Pointe des Galets, the port, which was drabber, dirtier and more desolate than the blackest of the Black Country, and was not even dignified by honest labour. The only thing of interest I have ever seen there was Alain Gerbault's boat, the *Firecrest*, which was lying in the harbour when I passed through in 1927. It was astonishing to think of that tiny vessel carrying him solo over all the world's oceans.

The railway of Mauritius is like a real railway, but I have never seen people felt it a pity that they wanted to leave aside their lovely Eastern garments, but I am sure Mrs. Johnson was right in letting them have their own way. The girls learned not only needlework and embroidery but also to read and write, quite a new thing for girls in Zanzibar. They were also taught cooking and child welfare, and a delightful Sheikha of the old school, with marinda and all complete, taught the Quran. The school is behind the palace in a large Arab house with a courtyard enclosed by high walls. All approaches are surrounded by a high fence with barbed-wire on top so that the parents need have no anxiety as to the breaking of harem rules. The children were not all pure-bred Arabs for there were woolly heads next to long silky locks. This school is perhaps the most important social development in Zanzibar history, for it means that nowadays the educated young men have educated young wives and the lives of both are made fuller and more interesting.

At Mombasa we had three or four days to spend and went to call on Sir 'Ali bin Salim Albusaidi in his office in the old town. If anyone has earned the right to be called the Grand Old Man of Kenya it is Sir 'Ali, the wise friend of all communities. He has now retired from active work as Liwali of Mombasa, but he has been a great and good influence in the country. Mombasa is still a part of the Zanzibar dominions, though Kenya administers it and pays rental to Zanzibar for it. The Liwalis of the coast are the Sultan's representatives and head the important Arab communities.

The most attractive view to be had of Mombasa is from the sea when you see Mombasa—not Kilindini—harbour opening up. Mombasa harbour is much smaller than Kilindini and for this reason has been practically abandoned by all craft except dhows. The rocky cliffs on which the white surf breaks continually are crowned with the green of grass, casuarinas, coco-nuts and the weird baobab. The old Arab town creeps down to the water-front as though trying to escape from the modern invasion of red-tiled houses and bungalows, and the scene is dominated by the old Portuguese fort where flies the Sultan's flag. The fort is a large quadrangular building, yellow and weatherbeaten with age, still not very different from what it was when built by the Portuguese in 1593. It is now a prison, and a Colonial judge who served in Kenya in the early days told me that when he was appointed a visitor to the jail he started by making a thorough inspection. After seeing all round the jail he requested that the prisoners should be paraded and checked against their warrants of committal. This resulted in one prisoner being left over and search failed to find the missing warrant.

anything in the world like that of Réunion. The rolling stock was so old that we wondered how it stood being pulled about. The "Hommes 40, Chevaux 8" wagons of the war seemed more luxurious than the first-class compartments, though it is true that the latter had seats. It was a terrific business leaving Pointe des Galets. There was the usual French performance of not being able to buy a ticket until a short time before departure—in fact all the paraphernalia of French railways, such as Salle d'Attente, Hommes, Dames, Bagages, even the clock, were there to make you remember the *chère patrie*. But there the resemblance ended, for efficiency was utterly lacking; not even the clock worked.

When at last we were in the train there was a long wait. Then a bell rang and later a whistle blew. In undue course we started unannounced. The performance was repeated at every station: a bell rang and a whistle blew. Sometimes the train started on the whistle, sometimes it did not. It moved at a stately crawl along the country-side until it reached a bridge which it always took at a rush, fearful that unless it got over quickly the bridge might collapse.

Our Dutch boat brought us on May 17th, 1933, to Zanzibar, where we stayed for a wonderful fortnight with Crofton, an old friend and then Chief Secretary. There had been many changes since I had left it six years before, and we visited by car many parts of the island which formerly I could only reach by donkey or boat. Crofton drove us down to Makunduchi and Kizimkazi where I saw again the ancient mosque with its Kufic inscription dated A.D. 1107, 500 of the Hejira. It is a unique inscription, and speaks much for the artistry of some of the ancient immigrants.

Perhaps the most surprising and the most interesting development of all was the success of the Arab Girls' School, which had just been mooted before my departure for Mauritius. It is really the creation of Mrs. Johnson, the Headmistress, and reflects the greatest credit on her. It had now been going for about six years. At first, of course, the Arabs would have nothing to do with it and many people were pessimistic as to its chances of success. His Highness, however, brought his influence to bear and the school opened with six or seven small girls. But now it was crowded out and there was a waiting list. Mrs. Johnson had very properly started with adhering strictly to Arab custom. In learning needlework and embroidery the children made Arab clothes, and the fact that now many clothes of European pattern are made was due not in the least to European pressure but to the desire of the pupils themselves. I think, indeed, most

The superintendent, who had been there for many years, told the judge that the prisoner had been there when he took the jail over, and nobody could throw any light on the matter at all. The prisoner when asked why he was in jail simply said: "Sijue Bwana, shauri ya serkali (I don't know, Master, it's the Government's idea)" which any one of them would have answered.

"But don't you know when you came here?" he was asked, to which he replied: "tangu zamani sana (a very long time ago)" which again might mean anything.

"But don't you remember if you had any paper or anything when you came?"

Here the man was more helpful. He had come, it appeared, with a cheti (piece of paper). Search was now made again, this time amongst the prisoners' clothing. By a process of elimination one bundle was claimed by the man in question. It contained a note to a bygone superintendent asking him to lunch. It is probable that the prisoner had been selected as a messenger by the man who had written the note and sent to deliver it to the superintendent. Not being blessed with any bountiful intelligence he had stood about in the jail for some hours waiting to deliver the note, until an Indian warder, or jemadar, had no doubt thought he was a prisoner awaiting the issue of jail clothes. The rest is easy to understand, and for one who knows the East African native not difficult to believe.

The native name of Mombasa—Mvita, War—tells its history in a word, for long before the Mazruis resisted Seiyid Sa'id there, Africans, Arabs and Europeans fought to possess it. Even after the Mazruis had been beaten by Seiyid Sa'id in 1822 they continued to give trouble, and in 1824 they induced Captain Owen, of H.M.S. *Leven*, to declare a British Protectorate. It is not generally known that this Protectorate made Mombasa for a short period a dependency of Mauritius, for Sir Lowry Cole, the Governor at that time, corresponded with the Mazruis and received their deputation in Port Louis. In the Mauritian archives I found many interesting papers of the period, and here is one written by Salim bin Rashid Mazrui, an interesting contemporary document which gives some of the history of the period from Mazrui point of view:

> Towards the middle of the last century, Seif bin Sultan, rightful Chief of Oman, captured Mombasa from the Portuguese (who had been in possession of the place a long while before) and established there the Arab tribe of Mazrui This tribe continued in obedience to Seif bin

## SIR 'ALI BIN SALIM ALBUSAIDI

Sultan so long as he lived. Seif bin Sultan was succeeded by Imam Ahmed Bu Saidi, grandfather of the present Imam, but the tribe of Mazrui did not acknowledge him as Sovereign of Mombasa, nor have the people of Mombasa ever submitted to any Chief of Oman save only Seif bin Sultan before whose time Mombasa had no connection at all with Oman.

About twelve years ago the people of Lamu rose against Pate (a separate Principality of which Lamu was at that time a Dependency), and the Pate Chief solicited aid from the then Hakim of Mombasa, 'Abdulla bin Ahmed Mazrui. 'Abdulla sent troops to Pate, more with the aim of restoring union than of making conquest. Matters, however, were not brought to an agreement and during these disputes the people of Lamu sent proposals to Seiyid Sa'id, the present Imam of Muscat, offering to deliver up the Island of Pate to him if he would assist them against Mombasa. Seiyid Sa'id accordingly occupied Lamu with his own troops and then demanded the surrender of Pate. Pate was at that time held by 'Abdulla Mazrui, Chief of Mombasa, who refused to deliver up the island to Seiyid Sa'id and in the battles which followed many of the Mombasa ships were destroyed by the Imam's fleet. At length the Imam sent a letter to 'Abdulla stating that Lamu was already in his hands and that if he would give up Pate to him also, he, the Imam, would cease all operations against Mombasa. This letter to 'Abdulla containing the Imam's proposal to relinquish his designs upon Mombasa on condition that Pate was given up to him, is now to be seen at Mombasa, with the Imam's own seal and signature affixed.

'Abdulla, trusting in the good faith of Sa'id, withdrew the Mombasa troops from Pate which then fell easily to the Imam. The Mombasa force had no sooner retired from Pate than the Imam sent vessels and suddenly took possession of "Jezirat al Khudhra," then a part of the Mombasa territory. On this act of treachery the people of Mombasa determined to break off all relations with the Imam and apply for protection to the King of England.

Next day we were to spend with Sir 'Ali and he sent a motor-boat from his mainland home of Peleleza to fetch us from the Kilindini wharf where our ship was berthed. He met us on the steps of his jetty and took us to the cool veranda of his drawing-room. Sir 'Ali's is not, strictly speaking, a house: it is a whole series of houses scattered over a wide area and he gets plenty of exercise walking from one to another. It is an original and attractive idea, for he has quite a walk from his bedroom over gravelled paths to his dining-room and another from his dining-room to his drawing-room. All of them are like bungalows, one-storeyed buildings with red roofs, and there is a superb setting of coco-nuts and shady mangoes.

Sir 'Ali, as an old friend, was interested in my future. He said he thought

I should get a move soon. He knew I wanted to go to an Arab country, but was sure it had been good for me to have gone to Mauritius. He had a slow delightful way of speaking and his words were always wise.

"You have had fish once," he said, "and the Colonial Office don't give you fish twice, next time you will have cake, I am sure of it."

D. thinks it is good magic if we want to be transferred to a place to spend money ourselves in going there: then we shall probably get there at Government expense afterwards. We tried this on when we got to Aden and did it more thoroughly than I had ever done before. We went ashore and started off through the tunnels cut out of the mountain. At Sheikh Othman we discovered our taxi-driver had deceived us. We could not get to Lahej without a permit. An inexorable policeman stood by a barrier like a continental level-crossing gate and could not let us pass. It was tantalizing, for there beyond lay a wide desert of Tribal Arabia. There was nothing to be done so we drove to the Sheikh Othman gardens, where D. caught grasshoppers to feed the Round Island lizards.

\* \* \*

Towards the end of a holiday in Normandy I heard that a friend in the Colonial Office was enquiring when I should be back, as he had something to tell me. It was not until we got back to England that I learned what it was—the chance of a job as Political Officer in the Aden Protectorate.

D., of course, said that her magic had come off, but as it was not absolutely certain we continued to apply magic and spent vast sums of money on intensive courses of Arabic at the School of Oriental Studies. The course was extremely thorough. I did eleven hours of classes a week, but the work of preparation made it up to rather more than four times as much. We found it not only interesting but entertaining. We had, for instance, a curiously varied class at which we learned phonetics. Here we were taught by a young man who had the most extraordinary throat I have ever known. I do not mean that it was odd to look at, even inside, though he did show us how his throat organs worked. But he could make any sound from Chinese to a Zulu click come out perfectly and, of course, Arabic was child's play to him. Not so with the rest of us, who included some cadets bound for the Sudan, a colonel, an old lady and a young one who had Persian ambitions. It seemed as if we should never be able to cope properly with a sound like the letter *qaf* for instance, when the old lady, asked to try again, said she had been trying to get it for sixty years. In my Quran class there was another old lady. One day I asked her where she was going, thinking

## MORE PREPARATIONS

she was a missionary, but she told me that she was going nowhere. She was just learning the Quran because she thought it was one of the things one ought to know.

Arabic was not all I studied. I hoped that the Hadhramaut might now be in the offing and learned how to make an exploratory survey with the instructor of the Royal Geographical Society. It was not exactly fun to a tropic flower like myself trekking and mapping the untrodden wastes of Richmond Park in the winter. Like Jacob, I had waited seven years, for I went to Mauritius in 1927 and it was 1934 when we sailed for Aden.

*Chapter VII*

## ADEN TOWN

*The fourth haven is called AHADEN, and stands in a certain little island joining, as it were, to the main, in the land of the Saracens.*    MARINO SANUDO.

> At the Gate of the Orient, sentinel stands
> Aden, majestic, o'er Araby's sands.
> What legend and lore of the mystical East!
> What glamour romantic what riot and feast!
> It beckons and calls like a Siren; but then
> My heart is athirst for old Sydney again.
> Trooper Bluegum in "The Old Country".    ED. ERNEST RHYS.

BOOKS by casual travellers through the Red Sea usually describe Aden in one of three ways: (*a*) by sheer fiction, (*b*) the description of a bawdy adventure in Harlots' Row at Sheikh Othman, or (*c*) the old-fashioned "Coal Hole of the East" business, dismissing the place as too frightful for contemplation and too uninteresting for description. There is much to be said for the last. A stranger with an hour or two to spare, who comes off a comfortable ship in the heat of a summer's day into the dust of Aden, and climbs in a fit of conscientious sight-seeing to the top of the Tanks, is not likely to go away with much sense of having experienced a taste of the Romantic Colourful East. Even a visitor who stays a day or two at one of Aden's hotels is not in much better case, unless he has someone to look after him. For a soulless, military officialdom did its best to see that nothing picturesque or beautiful was ever allowed to raise its head amongst the depressing, severely practical, and utterly uncomfortable barrack-like structures it erected itself. It says much for the British soldier that he has been able to maintain even in Aden his reputation for rising above his surroundings, for those once stationed there will say they enjoyed themselves.

I have been told that I am utterly exceptional in having liked Aden before I came there to live. It was familiar enough to me in its externals from the short visits I made to it on my way to and from Zanzibar and Mauritius, but if I try to justify my early affection for it I shall probably find it difficult after living there. As far as I remember it was the camels, the brightly-clad Arabs with their long curls, strange gutturals and wild eyes like those of freshly-caged beasts in the Zoo, which principally appealed to me.

Then, too, I never failed to sense the awe of the flaming sword of sunrise on the naked height of Shamsham, the beauty of the purple shadows and the rose-tinted sand piled below it. Soldiers, of course, rise early and should see these glories, but I suppose their poor earth-bound eyes must willy-nilly be confined to the parade ground, or surely they could never have allowed the horrors that pass for houses, offices, churches, even war memorials, to rise against that magnificent drop scene which Nature has provided.

A Portuguese artist produced a picture of Aden in the sixteenth century which you can see in Yule's *Marco Polo* and doubtless in other books. When you compare its turret-crested heights, its minarets and battlemented walls, with the low squat-looking cubes neatly arranged in square blocks with rectangular streets—it is all very mathematical—you may well wonder where is the Aden of which Ezekiel spoke to Tyre:

> *Haran, and Canneh, and Eden, the merchants of Sheb, Asshur, and Chilmad, were thy merchants.*
> *These were thy merchants in all sorts of things, in blue clothes, and broidered work, and in chests of rich apparel, bound with cords, and made of cedar, among thy merchandize.*

You had far better live at 53A Laburnum Row, Peckham or Clapham, London, than at House 523 M Street, Section D, Crater Camp, Aden.

Some people thought that April 1st was a very suitable date for D. and myself to arrive at Aden, but it started being interesting at once. As usual we had risen early, and soon after the ship had anchored there was the din that greets every ship arriving at an Eastern port. Confusion was added to by the fact that His Highness the Sultan of Lahej was departing on a visit to India, and the alleyways of the *Corfu* were crowded with numberless bare-legged, wild-looking, but exceedingly friendly Arabs mixed up with late bath-goers. On the whole I think that the East takes much more interest in the way that the West lives and has its being, than the West takes in the customs of the East. "Manners none; customs beastly" is too often the occidental attitude, and the Englishman plunges Eastward, golf bag on shoulder, till he sees the small red flag and someone to carry his bag and bring him his whisky and soda when he has finished his round. The East had not yet taken to golf, but it watches what is comprehensible with a keen and eager eye and imitates what it thinks worth imitating. I saw many curious peeps taken that day through open cabin doors.

* * *

Zaidi arrived from Zanzibar on the same day that we landed from the *Corfu*. His great ambition was to learn Arabic thoroughly so that he might return and "put it across" his friends, for a Swahili who knows Arabic in Zanzibar has gone up several steps in the social scale.

We went, first of all, into a well-built house in "Front Bay, Crater." Its surroundings were rather deplorable and as we preferred sleeping outside there was little privacy. We took on as second boy a rather quarrelsome Yemeni called 'Ali, who had seen most parts of the world as a sailor and had consequently acquired a somewhat astonishing vocabulary of English, French and Swahili. It was a bit difficult to practise the colloquial Arabic of Aden with him but I certainly increased my knowledge of my own language.

'Ali's tales of South America, Australia and other far corners of the globe made me realize how Sindbad the Sailor's yarns grew from genuine travellers' tales. I asked him of all the world which country he liked best, and he told me the Yemen hills and after them Scotland, for the people and the mountains were so like those of his own home.

After a month or so we migrated to a house with the best situation in Aden, perched on the ridge, some 150 feet high, which separates Holkat Bay from the Crater. It is a rambling tumbledown house flanked by a precipice on either side, and from a distance looks like a medieval castle. In this eyrie we were overlooked by no one and caught every breath of wind that strayed across the heavens. It was sometimes difficult to get our Persian landlord to do much in the way of repairs, and the stairs were apt to break under my weight, but every now and then a man came along and nailed a piece of packing-case somewhere or splashed some paint about. It leaked, of course, but as it rarely rains in Aden that did not matter much. It had no windows, only trellis, and packing-case affairs for doors, so that when sand storms blew we got more than our share.

And then Ganess arrived. We went to the French mail to meet him, with a ready rolled turban in a parcel. Fearing the worst I had imagined he might arrive in one of the unspeakable slouch hats dear to Mauritian cooks off duty. My precautions were justified and Ganess had a clean start, though for some weeks he lived in almost dumb bewilderment. His wish to come to Aden showed a spirit of adventure unusual to the ordinary inhabitant of Mauritius, and it must have required courage to step alone on to a strange ship for a country where his own language would be useless.

I soon discovered in Aden that Ganess had a quality usually totally lacking in native races, namely the desire to climb to the top of a mountain with no other object than to find out what is on the other side. When we were settled down we started exploring our rocky home in earnest, and Ganess often used to ask to come with us: Zaidi came when he was asked but it was more out of politeness than personal interest.

A boy in the Government School was recently asked in an examination paper to say into what parts the world was divided. His reply was: "The world consists of four parts, Aden, Maala, Hedjuff and Tawahi." I prefer, like Caesar, to divide our little world into three. The first consists of Tawahi and Tarshein, with an extension to Gold Mohur Bay and Khormaksar. The second part, which is ours, consists of Aden town. It has an extension to Maala-by-the-Beach (Maala-on-the-road is merely used to pass through on the way to Tawahi) and another to the deserted beach of Khormaksar and beyond. The third part consists of the fairly well-known town of Sheikh Othman and the almost unknown territories of Imad, Hiswa and Little Aden.

I am afraid I know little of the first part except Tawahi, the business quarter, where I worked, though I have paid an occasional nocturnal visit to the bathing-pool at Gold Mohur. The quarter is inhabited mostly by Europeans who, roughly speaking, work at Tawahi (called Steamer Point), sleep on the rocks of Tarshein and either swim at Gold Mohur or play golf and polo at Khormaksar in the afternoon. In many ways the third part is the most interesting and I shall have something to say about it later. But the second part, in which we ourselves live, has many charms.

It is divisible into two realms—that of men and that of the mountains. The division between the two is to some extent clearly apparent to the naked eye, for the kingdom of the mountains consists of the bare rocky ground and the steep crags of the old volcanic walls, practically unbuilt on, and entirely uninhabited. Psychologically, though, the boundary between the two is much more subtle, for while quite ordinary mortals walk the fortifications, climb to the Parsee tower of silence, or even follow the steep but well built path to the summit of Jebel Shamsham, 1,725 feet above the sea, there is really only one man who walks amid the greater solitudes. This is the "chieftain" Besse whose position as king of the mountains is unchallenged —indeed a former Resident recognized his spiritual supremacy in this realm. He is not selfish about his world and often invites his friends to "come for a walk." D. goes regularly with him and even I have been for one of the milder rambles. At the occasional moments when I was able to take my eyes off the "path," and, loosing hold of the rock, to straighten up and take stock of my surroundings, I did wonder why more people did not come sometimes and look at the deep cobalt of the sea far below, or the wild rock masses—"sheer igneous brutality" someone called them recently—towering above. There were queer aromatic plants and lovely flowers growing in hidden corners, an occasional fox and groups of shabby bald-headed vultures.

Sometimes you find in the mountains fishermen from as far afield as Mukalla, carrying their catch from some secluded bay to the Aden market, and in the nearer part there are stone-cutters living in caves. They seem to have no part with the life of the town, but even they cannot follow Besse in all his ways. For all his sixty years odd, mountain goats have nothing on him nor could they melt up a vertical chimney like he can.

In the world of men it is the life of the place that is interesting. Amongst the deplorable buildings there is just one relic left of the older Aden of the days of Suleiman the Magnificent—an old minaret near the Treasury. The mosque it served has long since disappeared and it stands there like a lovely lady of other days drawing her skirts close round her ankles as she finds herself left alone in the midst of a midden, with her sedan chair gone.

Although it is not all ancient, the mosque of 'Aidarus, patron saint of Aden, huddling up in a corner away from the parade ground order of the modern town, is a real work of art inside as well as out. Here are the tombs of the founder and his family in richly-carved wooden covers. The legend has it that the pious builders were at a loss for wood to make the doors, and that ready-carved doors floated miraculously up to the shores of Aden from India.

As we came, one Sunday night, over the edge of the plateau above Aden on our way back from Shamsham, the echoes of a brazen gong came startlingly clear from a near-by gorge. Thus we found, and later visited, Aden's only Hindu temple, built right up against the rocks at the head of a deep gorge, resplendent with its white-wash and yellow and green decorations. It was locked, but a temple servant took us up to the veranda and told us a grisly tale of a murder that had taken place there.

Aden's best known sight, the Tanks, are to my mind dull. The only interesting feature is the quantity of water they can contain, more than twenty million imperial gallons. They have been so restored and built up and fenced in by a tidy-minded military administration that it is difficult to know what they looked like originally. There is little definite knowledge of them. They may be Himyaritic or they may belong to a later age, possibly Roman or Persian. But if you climb up the steep steps above the Tanks you get a good idea of the catchment area and can come down again by the Tower of Silence—of melancholy interest. Happily the Parsees of Aden seem a healthy community, for in two years I never knew it used. Deaths, however, did take place among the Hindus and we sometimes saw a yellow-shrouded corpse born to the burning ghat below our house, and for hours at night the flames of the consuming funeral pyre leapt high and threw flickering lights on the surrounding mountains.

In Crater cemeteries there lie buried Western, a young engineer who planned the now obsolete fortifications which cost £7,000,000 to build, and Ion Keith Falconer, founder of the Sheikh Othman mission, one of the few Christian missions in Arabia. Another little cemetery contains the remains of those who fell at the capture of Aden and on its wall is painted the badge of the King's Shropshire Light Infantry, which of course has an interest for me.

> It dawns in Asia, tombstones show
> And Shropshire names are read;
> And the Nile spills his overflow
> Beside the Severn's dead.

If the few sights of interest in Aden are mostly concerned with the dead, the bygone past, or man's many guesses at a problematical future, the affairs of the living, as they can be observed daily in the bazaar, always interested us. There the show is a daily and continuous performance— a kaleidoscopic eddying stream of Arabs, Jews, Indians, Somalis and other Africans shouting in a dozen tongues. Men, camels, honking cars and grubbing goats jostle each other in utter confusion. The coffee shops are always full of an afternoon and small traders carry on curious businesses. Quite a number of people earn an easy living by charging a pice for a few shots at a target. There is a large paper-covered board stuck up on a wall with rows of brown dots on it. Here many an up-country tribesman, anxious to raise his percentage of direct hits on neighbours at home, seeks to improve his marksmanship. He is given an airgun loaded with a dart, and standing about four paces distance tries to hit the brown dots. If he succeeds there is a small explosion, for they are painted with gunpowder. The proprietor pulls out the dart with a pair of pliers and he starts again. A few minutes watching this very serious business gives you ample explanation as to why the sudden-death roll in the Protectorate is so low, even though every tribesman has a rifle.

In the late afternoon the camels are fed. They sit in semi-circles of up to seven or eight while the herdsman sits facing them on a bed, like a nurse telling bed-time stories to children. He has beside him a pile of qasab, stalks of millet or maize, which he folds into small bundles and pushes into the mouth of each couched camel in turn. Goats, cats and dogs forage happily all day long in the refuse heaps and dustbins. The goats usually get most to eat as they are least particular, browsing through the streets quite content with bits of leather, newspaper and other rubbish. Next time you buy an *Evening Standard* from a street seller, think that the ones you do not buy may in a short time be feeding an Aden goat. Great bales of unsold papers, principally *Evening Standards*, *Daily Sketches* and *Daily Mirrors*, find their way to Aden and are distributed far into the interior to be used by shopkeepers for packing rice and grain.

But the sight of Aden which intrigues us most is mysterious No. 13 the Crater. In one of our wanderings we saw a door half-way up the steep cliff leading to the plateau. We climbed up and found great double doors, locked, flanked by pillars and with "13" painted over it. It was built right into the mountain. No one has been able to tell us what is behind the door, and we sometimes wonder if anybody else can see it, for they never seem to know of its existence. We hope it leads to the authentic Arabian Nights' cave, but we fear it is probably something military.

*Chapter VIII*

## THE ADEN PROTECTORATE

ἔν τ' Ὠκεανοῦ πελάγεσσι μίγεν Πόντῳ τ' ἐρυθρῷ.

PINDAR.

WHEN I arrived in 1934 Aden itself had been administratively a part of India since its capture in 1839 and it did not become a colony until 1937, but the Protectorate had for several years been under the Colonial Office and there was and is no part of the dependent Empire in the least like it. The key to the matter is, of course, that it is not administered. Soon after the capture of Aden—the first annexation to the Empire in Queen Victoria's reign—the Resident, Captain Haines of the Indian Marine, started to cultivate friendly relations with his Arab neighbours and in these relations the Protectorate of to-day had its origin. Haines' dealings with the tribes of the hinterland were directed towards making the safety of Aden itself more assured, and gradually treaties began to be concluded. The keynote of all of them was friendly relations and later the safety of the caravan routes to Aden. In due course they developed into Protectorate treaties which extended the protection of Her Majesty to the tribes concerned, and included an engagement on the part of the tribes not to cede their territories to, or negotiate with, foreign powers.

Until 1937 Protectorate meant in practice what is now called the Western Aden Protectorate. Up till 1933 or 1934 official documents had generally spoken of the Aden Protectorate and the Hadhramaut, but the distinction, if ever there was one, was dropped at that period as the treaties with the chiefs east of the "nine cantons," a term which included the territories of the 'Abdali, Aqrabi, Amiri, Haushabi, Fadhli, Yafai, Aulaqi, Alawi and Subeihi chiefs, were of old standing and precisely similar in character to the others. But until 1937 there was, owing to scarcity of political staff, little contact with what is now called the Eastern Aden Protectorate and in this chapter I propose to deal principally with the western part of the Protectorate.

To-day throughout the whole Protectorate there are upwards of fifty chiefs of varying status in more or less direct correspondence with the Government at Aden. Some thirty of these are in treaty relations, and seven are gun chiefs.

There is a great deal of difference in social standing and importance between the treaty chiefs. They range from rulers as important as Their Highnesses of Lahej and Mukalla, through lesser Sultans such as the Fadhli and the Haushabi, and Sheikhs with as little control as the Mausati and Muflahi of Upper Yafa', to rulers of single towns such as the Sheikh of 'Irqa, and petty chieftains such as the Rija'i Sheikh of the Subeihis. Amongst the non-treaty chiefs are the Dathina Sheikhs and the Mas'abi Sheikh who is partially dependent on a treaty chief, the Sharif of Beihan. The Mas'abi are probably the Marsuaba of Strabo, the furthest people to whom Aelius Gallus penetrated.

A glance at the map will show that the two most important chiefs in the Protectorate are so geographically situated as to make them the natural leaders of its western and eastern portions. The Sultan of Lahej has already gone a long way towards establishing a hegemony over his neighbours. He is *de jure* suzerain of the Subeihis, and to a lesser extent of the Haushabis. Without interfering with the internal affairs of his northern and eastern neighbours, he has shown such wisdom in his dealings with them, that they naturally seek for and accept his arbitration in their troubles. There are occasional tiffs it is true, but even the independently minded mountaineers of Upper Yafa' show more and more of a tendency to seek his advice, and this tendency is naturally carefully fostered. The Sultan of Mukalla has not yet succeeded in establishing his leadership to the same degree as the Sultan of Lahej.

Many of the chiefs have stipends, some granted by treaty and some by grace. They also receive certain presents, and until recently some had the privilege of issuing a fixed number of recommendatory letters each month in favour of their tribesmen and these were usually automatically honoured by the present of money, generally a small amount. Regular yearly visitors received the sum they had been accustomed to get. Often persons of influence or who had rendered service were given a personal arm and a hundred rounds of ammunition. Chiefs also received presents of, or were allowed to purchase, supplies of arms and ammunition for defence purposes. The principal object of the presents was to encourage the good behaviour of the recipients and in particular to try to secure safety on the main caravan routes.

## CHANGES IN ADMINISTRATION

The matters that used to take up most time at the Residency were tribal quarrels, raids, murders, loots or breaches of the peace upon the main trade routes. As a general rule these would be disposed of by writing letters of advice to the chiefs of the tribes concerned. The injured party was adjured not to let retaliation follow, the offenders were urged to pay up the compensation or blood money which might be due by Arab custom, and the chiefs were pressed to punish the perpetrators.

During the administration of Sir Bernard Reilly changes were made. Presents, recommendatory letters and the distribution of arms have ceased and instead he encouraged schemes of agriculture, dispensaries and education. Tribal feuds and quarrels still take up a lot of our time but there is a great contrast between the files of to-day and those of five years ago. At that period the principal decisions of a morning's work were whether So and So should be given a rifle and 100 rounds or whether a letter of advice should be written to some so-called Sultan counselling him to make peace with his relatives or saying that the instigation of some raid or murder "was not what we should have expected of you, oh friend." Nowadays we give more attention to the construction of dams in Abyan, the extension of potato and onion cultivation at Mukeiras, the constitution of Tribal Guards at Beihan, the establishment of a school at Museimir; and slowly, too slowly for some of us, the patient labours of the Political Officers in the field and the Agricultural Officer begin to bear fruit.

\* \* \*

Most of the chiefs are entitled to pay an annual visit to Aden and to be entertained for a number of days, according to their rank, at Government expense, together with varying numbers of tribesmen, followers, camels, horses and so on. Some of them are given cars to go sightseeing in the afternoons. The more important are received by the Governor. Gun chiefs have a guard of honour of the very smart Aden Armed Police in their red turbans. While the chief concerned inspects the guard, the gunners at Fort Morbut thunder forth eleven or nine guns as the case may be.

The states of the Protectorate are perhaps remarkable more for the differences of their internal arrangements than for their similarities, and manners and customs vary widely from one state to another. State is in fact a misleading term, for while it can be applied with some accuracy to comparatively well-knit organizations in the few fairly civilized areas of the Protectorate such as Lahej and Mukalla, it has no meaning at all in the case of a Subeihi tribe. In some of these states the chief is all powerful and the sole fountain of law and justice. In others he is little more than a figurehead, while yet again there are cases in which although he rules, he rules in effect only so long as his tribes are content with him.

There are well marked social differences in the classes of the people, and roughly speaking the hierarchy conforms to a fairly general pattern. There are first of all the chiefs—sometimes rulers and sometimes merely *primus inter pares*. Most states or tribes have royal families from which the chiefs are elected by the 'Aqils or heads of the tribal sections. Their titles vary—many are Sheikhs, but there are a number of Sultans, an Amir and a Sharif. There are also the Naqibs—co-Shiekhs of Mausata. Like continental barons each male member of the royal family has the title of Sultan, Sheikh, Amir or Sharif. The title of Sheikh is the most capricious in its application. Almost any Arab who reaches a certain standard of living and gains sufficient "heshima," as we called it in Zanzibar, may be styled Sheikh and in this instance it has no more meaning than the English Esquire. Then there is the proper tribal use of the word referred to above, and in the Hadhramaut are whole tribes of Sheikhs whose position is almost ecclesiastical.

After—or in a sense even before—the chiefs come the Seiyids, descendants of the Prophet through his grandson Hussein. They are often keepers of shrines and are socially useful as they are professional peacemakers. Then there are the Qabilis, the tribesmen, the independently minded men-at-arms. After them come the merchants and townsmen, freeborn Arabs but not arm bearers, and then the slaves.

In the western part of the Protectorate they were never numerous and in some tribes they have never existed. The word slave has now come to indicate a social class instead of an oppressed people and in practice where the name is still employed they appear to do much as they please though technically not permitted to leave their district without sanction. Lastly come the Khadims or Hijris who perform the most menial of functions. Neither slaves nor Khadims can be the subjects of blood feuds, the most obtrusive feature of the social system.

The Arab modes of trial are compurgation and the ordeal. Compurgation means that anyone sued in a civil action, or accused of crime, can bring ten men to swear on his behalf that they believe his account of the case. Ordeal is the essentially Arab method of proving facts and it consists in an appeal to the supernatural. The person accused first solemnly swears to his innocence. He then has to undergo one of two tests, the ordeal by fire (bish'a) or the "accursed morsel" (lukhmat al khānuq). The accursed morsel is a piece of hard dry bread specially consecrated by the "priest." The accused first calls on the Deity to make the bread stick in his throat if he is guilty: and then proceeds to eat the morsel slowly. If he swallows it freely he is innocent; but should he choke in any way he is guilty. The assessment of all criminal wrongs at a price in money is a notable feature of the tribal law. A complicated tariff is formed—every wound has its price: for a broken arm so much, for a damaged leg so much; even life has its price for the slayer must pay to the relative the diya of the slain man. In the blood feud the offender is only left unprotected by the law as against those who have suffered by his misdeeds—not against the world at large.

Such are methods practised to-day in the Protectorate and yet—the account I have given is taken almost word for word from the account of Saxon methods in Storey Dean's *Legal History*, pages 7 to 9! Among these Arabs human life is cheap; the people have not yet developed the consciousness of being shocked at murder. Many of the tribes live in a state of savagery. It is of course not so shocking as the savagery of American gangsterdom or of revolution in Russia or Spain, because it is more innocent—it is nearer the animal and that is where the surprise comes, that in the twentieth century there remains a place where man in his code has progressed so little and is at least a thousand years, in time, behind ourselves.

At the time of my arrival the Saudi-Yemeni war had just begun and not unnaturally I imagined references to "the war" referred to that. But not a bit of it; Aden had a small "war" of its own on. The Resident had recently successfully concluded a treaty of friendship with the Zeidi Imam of the Yemen. This was a considerable diplomatic triumph for the matter had hung fire for years, while several of the better parts of the Protectorate, which Britain had engaged to protect, were in the hands of the Zeidi forces. Not only that, but much to the damage of Aden trade, the Imam had closed the routes leading from the Yemen to the port. As a result of the treaty the Zeidi forces were withdrawn and the trade routes reopened.

As I have said there are agreements with some tribes for the protection of these routes and amongst others the Quteibi (probably the representatives of Qataban of old) is under an obligation to maintain a force of road guards. For this purpose its chief, Hasan 'Ali, received a regular monthly payment.

When the treaty had been signed, the Imam opened the routes again, being duly assured that they would be safe. Now the Quteibi lie across one of the main routes from the Yemen and it did not look good when the Quteibi road guards proceeded to plunder almost the first caravan to come down. It was further learnt that most of the plunder had found its way into Hasan 'Ali's house. A demand was therefore made for the payment of five hundred Maria Theresa dollars—equivalent to about £40— to cover the value of the loot and certain donkeys which had been slain by the road guards. In accordance with Arab custom hostages were also demanded for future good behaviour. Of course hostages are not really much good to us, because all we do is to arrange for some friendly ruler to keep them in ease and comfort as honoured guests. Arab rulers do more than this with their hostages if there is any further trouble among the friends and relations of their prisoners, and I suppose people never know if we might not turn Arab.

Anyway the fine was not paid, nor the hostages surrendered. So an ultimatum was sent, threatening air action if they were not forthcoming by a given date. They were not forthcoming and the "war" began. Now there is a great deal of ignorance about these "brutal" tactics, and, to start with, it is remarkable leniency that levies only a fine upon a chief and his guards who shoot up peaceful merchants on a public high road, which as the Arabs will tell you belongs to God for the use of all men. I dare say even the most pacific of pacifists would not object to the police barging in and breaking a few heads. But the Royal Air Force does not adopt these violent methods.

First of all messages are dropped saying that bombing will start at a given hour on a given day and warning the inhabitants to clear out. When the notice has expired, machines reconnoitre to make sure no one is left and then smoke bombing begins. The principal product of this performance is smoke and noise and it is intended to make sure that everyone understands that business is meant. Personally I never heard of any of the inhabitants being left to watch the performance close at hand.

Light bombing then begins and a certain amount of damage is done. If this had no effect in expediting the payment of the fine, then heavier bombs are used, and finally the inhabitants are kept uncomfortable by not being allowed to return to their homes at night and by being warned off their crops. Usually they get fed up before long as the women plague them for their obstinacy. Even if material damage is done it does no amount to very much. Houses are easily rebuilt and in fact it would no

## THE TRUTH ABOUT "BRUTAL" TACTICS

take much more than a box of matches to destroy many Arabian villages, made mostly of brushwood.

We had not been in Aden long when Colonel Lake, the Political Secretary, took me up to Dhala to see how the political side of the war was getting on. We went by air. It was my first flight in a British service machine and it made me thirst for more. We started about half-past seven and soon climbed to 8,000 feet. The air was intoxicating. Fresh and cold it stung my face as I leaned over the side while the mechanic in the cockpit with me pointed out the sights. We were soon over Quteibi country and I saw the landing ground of As Soda with its white markings and circle in the middle, rather like a giant football ground.

In about forty minutes from Aden we were over Dhala and circling round for a landing. A Verey light was fired—the last I had seen fired was in Flanders in 1916—to show the direction of the wind and we had soon bumped gently on to the Dhala landing ground, 4,000 feet above the sea.

There was no sign of the Amir, who had been warned by wireless—for there is a small station for political purposes at Dhala—so we sat under some 'elb trees, overlooking a wadi or valley, to have the breakfast of sandwiches and coffee in thermos flasks that we had brought with us.

As we contentedly munched, word came that the Amir drew near. With the Sultan of Zanzibar as my only example of an important Arab chief and pictures of fierce Amirs with jewels in their turbans and curling moustachios in my mind, I looked for something rather resplendent in the highland chief I was to meet.

Lake and I went to meet him: an aged Chevrolet bumped over the edge of the landing ground and tore across it in a cloud of smoke and dust. It came to a standstill and disgorged a crowd of indigo-painted warriors and their rifles. You could tell the Amir because he wore a coat, the rest simply wore a futa—a coloured cloth wound round their waists, and blue turbans. The Amir had on a turban done in the Indian style, but it was not jewelled. He was short and his legs were bare from the knees, and he had also a good dagger at his waist.

The sun was now getting hot so Lake and I together with the Amir and 'Ali 'Abdulla the interpreter adjourned to the shade of the aeroplane wings and sat uncomfortably on the gravel. The Amir's coffee maker was hailed and came along with an aged and black coffee pot and a couple of small slop bowls of pottery about half an inch thick. Lake, perhaps wisely, declined, but I, on my usual principle of trying anything once, accepted. I was poured a brew made of coffee husks and ginger. I confess it was not bad, but where, oh where, were the clean little cups and lovely decorated pots of Zanzibar, with the good bitter brew of black coffee? It seems that the economically-minded folk who grow the real Mocha coffee export the bean and have schooled themselves to like the valueless husk. The Amir produced a cigarette-case; I was interested to see that he has good taste for they were 555's.

I admit my first shocks on these encounters were considerable, but they were not fatal. Indeed on reconsideration I began to see that in fact the Amir did look exactly what he was, a highland chief, and I should not be surprised if the Scotsman's garb has not grown out of something very much like the dress of the Yemen highlanders.

We listened to the Amir giving the latest news of the situation, as he sat crosslegged on the gravel playing with a couple of pebbles. It appeared that the Quteibi were still holding out and the principal trouble was Uncle Muqbil, uncle of Hasan 'Ali, who had a great deal more character than his nephew, an attractive figure but who from a fondness for intrigue was the principal *trouble-fête* of that part of the Protectorate. After a long discussion about the necessity for security along the trade routes we took our leave.

The "war" carried on for some weeks and neither side would give in, though the Royal Air Force were almost as fed up with their daily and nightly patrols as the Quteibi must have been with living in caves. Six members of the Aden Protectorate Levies, who were Quteibi, were sent on leave while the war was on and lived in a cave on a sheep a day. They said when they came back that they had been keeping their eyes in by shooting at aeroplanes. No one seemed to see anything peculiar in such a proceeding and I do not think it ever occurred to the Quteibi, loyal soldiers of His Majesty, that there was anything humorous about their firing at their British comrades. They could be both tribesmen and soldiers and there was no ill will on either side.

At last the Amir, trying to increase his authority with the Quteibi of whom he is in a small way suzerain, and at the same time to stand well with the Dōla (Government), made an "arrangement." He would pay the fine and house the hostages. To us he proposed that he should be reimbursed out of the Quteibi road subsidy, but the Quteibi, sharp as

## EDUCATING THE SONS OF CHIEFS

rsecopers and knowing their Amir, got it in writing from him that he ould stand the racket. So the "war" ended and for a time traffic was in peace on its way to and from the Yemen.

It is actual fact that at the conclusion of one of these "wars" the enemy ne in and asked to see the aeroplanes which had bombed them. When y had been shown them they asked to see the kind of bombs and the icer who had dropped them. One of those present pleaded guilty and y warmly shook him by the hand and thanked him. Tribesmen who ve offended and been made to give in, are glad to have their faces saved. ne of their friends can make fun of them if they have had to give in the overwhelming force of air control.

Experience of these inter-tribal conflicts seems to show that much of the trouble is due to the chiefs and there is evidence to show that if they uld be brought up to consider the interests of their subjects, many of se problems would never arise. It was about thirty years ago that aptain Warneford had proposed the idea of a college for the sons of chiefs, d the idea was eminently sound. From time to time it was taken up ly to be dropped again for some reason or other, and it was not until r Bernard Reilly became Resident that the idea really looked like taking ape and it was proposed to cut down the expenditure on presents to chiefs d start a school with the savings. Sir Bernard turned the job over to me d I felt that at last I had something constructive to do.

There were in Aden, here and there, a number of ruined or half-ruined arracks and I was told I could take my choice. The principal ones were the Crater but these I rejected as being too near the bazaar, and I was ite certain that the last thing that would be good for up-country children ould be to be anywhere near the Aden bazaar. On a ridge in the area nown as Little Isthmus in the outer perimeter of Aden's rocks there stood other barrack. It was quite an impressive, solid sort of a place and had nce been the officers' mess of an Indian regiment.[1] Later it had served as e place of detention for a time of the exiled Egyptian leader, Zaghloul asha. When I first saw it, it had been left unwatched and every particle f floor and stairs and anything wooden that could be removed had been olen for firewood. Below the ridge lay further collections of ruins and me flat ground. Up the ridge in the afternoons D. and I climbed daily nd brooding over the place pictured how it was to look when it was a chool. Of course the planning of a school required other considerations han site alone, important though that was. I spent time and thought

## THE ADEN PROTECTORATE

on the social background of the boys who we hoped would come to it and on the type of product we wished to turn out.

What was wanted was a type of chief who had other thoughts than his pocket and pleasures, one with a sense of duty who would rule his tribe with an eye to its progress and with justice and equity. He had not got to be highly educated, at any rate the next generation of chiefs had not, but he had to appreciate, for example, the value of agriculture and of medical science. No advanced literary education was required and only enough English was necessary to enable him to have contacts with Royal Air Force officers and others visiting him who had no Arabic. As a matter of fact I would have been quite ready to dispense with English but that the chiefs themselves had shown a desire for it to be included in the curriculum. After thought, then, I decided that the objectives of the school were to be character training, physical training and literary education, in that order of importance. The school was not to be a cheap imitation of European things, but an attempt to teach the best of Arab things and so importance was to be laid on good Arab manners and as far as possible we were to bring Arab institutions and games into the place. It seemed to me that religious teaching must be taken more seriously than it is usually taken in Government schools, and that apart from insistence on religious observances, such as prayer, the reality of religion and the carrying of it into every action of daily life must be insisted upon. Too often in South Arabia you find that religion and the everyday things of life are entirely divorced from each other, and though the mosques in the town are full, the lives of many of those who fill them would hardly bear the lightest investigation from a moral standpoint—cheating, lying, defamation, oppression and dishonesty of all kinds are only too common, and in fact it is generally amongst the beduin, many of whom barely pray or fast, that the highest standard of honour and of patient resignation to the will of God is to be found. I felt indeed that much of what a public school in England tries to impart in the way of character training was required, and the discipline such as it gives was sorely needed for these children who are brought up without any at all. Believing, too, in the necessity of a sound body, I laid emphasis not only on games, such as codified nature games and football, but on a sound diet and a day which was properly proportioned into hours of work, recreation and rest.

As for the lessons themselves, these were to start with the three Rs. The sort of standard aimed at was that a boy should be able to write an

## A DREAM REALIZED

telligent letter, and to think clearly, and little emphasis was laid on ammar and literary niceties. Tribesmen anyway bother little about such rt of things and most of them can neither read nor write. They were be taught history and geography with most of the emphasis on that of eir own country; as they got further away from it the subjects became etchier. Nature study, agriculture and hygiene came into the syllabus id it can be seen how with, for example, the life of the mosquito, various bjects overlapped. I preferred for instance that reading and the writing essays should deal with practical matters wherever possible, and in arithetic problems of how to fill a bath with the plug open were barred. the last years such subjects as citizenship and the art of government were be taught in elementary fashion.

Sitting on the hill-top, I laid out in my mind's eye the mosque, the irdens (the soil would have to be brought from afar and watered by aste water, as water was far too precious in Aden to be poured :w over a garden), the football ground, the swimming-pool and so on. he ruins below and around me transformed themselves into a tailor's 1op, washing places, kitchens, store rooms and the like. By dint of perilous ymnastics I had climbed to the top storey of the main building and, alanced on girders from which the floor had been ripped, estimated the ccommodation available as enough for thirty-six boys. I had seen the eds in place each with a slumbering form on it, and below desks made to 1easure with heads bent over them. In the dining-hall messes of six boys ach with a master to teach them "table" or floor manners sat round white loths spread on the ground, while the portrait of His Majesty, whose ikeness was unknown to them, gazed down on them from the end wall. pictured their uniform clothes for every occasion, khaki shirts, "futas" 1ot shorts, and turbans for everyday use, vests and shorts for games, and ;reen and purple kilts, turbans and Scotch jackets with embroidered nonograms for walking out on Fridays.

When the whole picture was complete down to what they would have o eat on every day of the week, I wrote out my report and sent it in.

In due course it came back approved and work then started. That was in October of 1934 and the school was to open on the 1st April, 1936 somehow many of my ventures start on that day!). I had to get staff, ind for the teachers went back to Zanzibar where I could at any rate be sure of getting decent rural-minded lads. Later a headmaster came from the Sudan, one who had the vision to grasp the idea behind the school, and then

## THE ADEN PROTECTORATE

there was the usher. This post was the most unusual of the lot for he was really the matron and added to that the business of discipline outside the classrooms. He was the only local member of the staff, a bearded 'Aulaqi with many years service as an officer in the Aden Protectorate Levies.

We wrote round to the chiefs, hoping but not expecting that there would be a response. As I thought it would, the idea soon got round that we wanted their sons as hostages for their good behaviour and we started with only the promise of three of his children from the Fadhli Sultan. For the rest I looked over the boys who, under an old arrangement, were having free education in the Government day schools in Aden and from them I chose four of the smallest who did not seem demoralized with bazaar life. The scheme as yet went no further than boys of eight to fifteen. I hoped that in time, if it was a success, a school for those from fifteen to twenty could be undertaken.

On April 1st I drove to the Government school and collected seven frightened boys in my car, took them down to Jebel Hadid and put them into a classroom there. The Aden Protectorate College for the Sons of Chiefs had started.

The first day or so was difficult, breaking them in to regular hours. Muhsin the usher and I saw them through their meals and games and at night had to bath them ourselves and put them to bed, for these were things they knew not how to do themselves.

Time went on and slowly the numbers rose and there came a day when we could sit on the ridge and see everything in its place and everything happening as it had been planned. There too, stood the mosque. I had done one rather revolutionary thing. Hitherto it had been the chiefs who had demanded money from Government. I had demanded contributions from the chiefs and collected nearly three hundred pounds, as marble tablets in the mosque bore witness. Above the mihrab in the mosque carved in marble was the school motto, which I had found by opening the Quran and putting my finger blind on a text:

"Verily God ordaineth justice and kindness."

## Chapter IX

## LAHEJ, MUSEIMIR AND THE QĀT TRADE

*Indeed, what is there that does not appear marvellous when it comes to our knowledge for the first time?*
PLINY THE ELDER.

*It is curious to see the people who have been sleeping on the roof get up in the morning.*
FAR OFF.

JUST beyond Sheikh Othman lies the territory of Aden's nearest neighbour, His Highness the 'Abdali Sultan of Lahej, premier chief of the Protectorate. Beyond the police post and barrier on the Dar al 'Amir road, passing Sheikh Othman, lies the Protectorate. Here the track ahead is in fact the way to the Yemen, for driving through Lahej and the country of the Haushabi Sultan you arrive in the course of a hundred miles or so at Ta'iz. From Ta'iz you can reach Hodeida in a car, and I suppose if you could arrange for fuel and all the permission necessary, and did not irretrievably break down, you could eventually reach London. During the Saudi-Yemeni war the troops of King 'Abdul 'Aziz reached Hodeida in Ford lorries from Jedda, and from Jedda Mr. and Mrs. Philby have driven to London.

We had been ten days in Aden when we set out to make our first reconnaissance of Lahej. The police post we had seen on a visit the year before, but this was an exhilarating moment for we came no longer as strangers, and when the policeman at the barrier had been assured of my identity he pushed up the gate and we drove through into our promised land. It was a sort of neutral ground for a couple of hundred yards, past one of the stone pillars which mark the boundary, to the 'Abdali customs fort of Dar Al 'Amir. Here another level-crossing pole bars the road between the tall mud dar of the commander of the fort and a smaller building—open fronted—where he or one of his minions lies on a raised divan at the receipt of custom. Impassive and completely without emotion he puffs at his hookah, as crowds of yelling beduin couch their camels, or vastly overloaded buses boil furiously, while the baggage of the passengers is searched.

Friendly folk gave us greeting and cleared a way for us through the rabble, for they do not stop the cars of Europeans from Aden, and we were soon scudding across the ten miles of desert sand which separate Sheikh Othman from Lahej town, a journey of about an hour. Generally speaking the best road is not the road and we kept left of it to avoid the well-ploughed tracks.

There was plenty of traffic on the road, ancient and modern, and we crossed many caravans going to and fro between Aden and Lahej. Buses and taxis swept by in both directions at incredible speeds. In one taxi which had stopped we counted fourteen passengers. Buses were loaded to the very roofs. How they ever got from one end to the other I have never been able to understand. Their radiators are always like a volcano in eruption and they cannot possibly have a sound spring between them. Really it is the motor transport which is ancient; the camels with their jaunty spring have quite a modern air. At one point we thought we were looking at some Birnam Wood on the march; on closer inspection it turned out to be a line of haystacks moving towards Aden. Actually there were camels under them but they were quite invisible at a short distance. All the fodder required in Aden and its vegetables and firewood are daily brought from the interior and much comes along this road. The camels know their way well and the drivers are generally asleep on top of the loads. Zaidi, who had come with us, found great entertainment in the sight of a lady peacefully asleep on a bed tied across the top of a loaded beast.

As the mountains of Aden receded into the haze, those of the interior stood out plainer, and larger houses set in green fields with scattered palms showed that we were entering the Lahej oasis. We passed under shady trees and drove by a tent where an 'Abdali police guard checks the travellers in and out to a large square crowded with taxis, camels and men. Actually this is a taxi rank but how many of the museum pieces standing there could move if really put to it I do not know. We drove on to a guard house and left the car there in the shade.

The Sultan of Lahej's army which polices his domains is divided into the Lahej Trained Forces, a smartly equipped body of a few hundred men, his few retainers and the irregulars. The irregular tribesmen are rarely called up and the Sultan keeps their arms locked in his armoury. His brother, Sultan Ahmed, is the Commander-in-Chief of the army, and his nephew, Sultan Salih, who has the rank of Bimbashi or Major, commands the L.T.F. We saw some of them now for the first time sitting on the

## CHARM OF LAHEJ

mud bench which runs round the guard house, where a sentry stood with fixed bayonet.

Like all Arab towns the charm of Lahej lies in its haphazardness. It is mud built and, except for the Sultan's palaces, remains the natural colour of mud. Arabian towns on the sea are usually white-washed, but unless coral or suitable stone for burning lime is available those in the interior melt into the landscape. The Sultan's palaces tower over the town: the old one, stone fronted and solid, lies to the right of the square, through a gateway closed with sliding doors. The new one, white and graceful, stands in a wonderful garden facing the square with its back to the desert.

A few buildings rise to four or five storeys, others do not rise beyond two or three, and most are of one storey only. Dust and sand are everywhere, and as in Aden there are many booths of pottery jars where you can buy a drink of cold water for a pice. The narrow main bazaar street is packed with small shops, in most of which were men gossiping round a water-pipe. Crowds filled the open-air cafés, and on a corner stood a large Café de la Paix with chairs and tables standing well out into the road. Passing through the bazaar we came to the camel park, where beasts from the interior were being unloaded. It was difficult to shake off the hordes of small boys, each with a home made walking-stick in his hand, swaggering along behind us, with cries of "Bakshish, bakshish!"

Once through the town we saw a forest of trees away to the right. Tired of the din, we made for it as a duck makes for water. In the distance it seemed a dense mass of dark-foliaged mangoes with coco-nuts sticking their wavy heads above, but on reaching it we found an abundance of limes, jack fruit, dates and guavas.

Night fell as we crossed the desert and hemmed us in so closely that we seemed to be driving downhill into a dark forest. Occasionally pairs of emeralds and rubies gleaming in the dark told of silent watchers, and once or twice hares and bushy-tailed foxes crossed the beam of our headlights.

Soon after this visit to Lahej we proposed ourselves for a week-end at the Haushabi Sultan's capital of Museimir, some forty miles beyond. From Lahej we had to take an escort of four soldiers and left in a procession of three cars. For some miles the road was fairly easy though sandy and bumpy. It wound through green fields and passed the Sultan's orchards at Husseini where it was lined by a shady avenue of African almond trees (bedam). At the fording of the Wadi Tiban it wound circuitously in ups and downs, and rocks and drifts of heavy sand made driving hard work for D. The once-distant hills drew close and the surface became stony: we passed the fortress of Al 'Anad standing silhouetted on a sandy hill and turning a corner among the low foothills were startled by an outburst of firing. We realized in a second that it was the customary greeting of the country and that we had entered Haushabi territory. To us, of course, it was something more than a formal greeting. Lahej, ruled by its own Sultan, is quite civilized. This was our first welcome to untamed Arabia. There was a post of the Haushabi Sultan's soldiers lining the side of the hill. Tribal warriors persisted in finding a skyline to stand on, which is very picturesque, but they would fare badly in real warfare. They were as black as Africans, though I saw later that some had finer features. They wore only dark-blue turbans and a dark futa round their waists, held in place by a cartridge-belt.

Al 'Abd Al Muntassar, in charge of us and our escort, pointed out Jebel Warwah, quite a striking mountain in which I had a personal interest for it featured in one of the Arabic books I had used at the School of Oriental Studies. A little later we turned round a spur and had our first view of Museimir, dominated by the Sultan's palace, about half a mile ahead. We covered it in a minute or two and got out of the car to a terrific fusillade of rifle fire and several rounds from an old ten-pounder. We walked with the Sultan and his son into the rough stone-built palace under an old and attractive archway between lines of troops blazing off a lot of ball ammunition a few inches from our ears. After the bright sunshine we could see nothing in the darkness into which we were plunged. The ground floor was the State prison and on one side straw and brushwood were spread as night quarters for the prisoners. In the day-time they appeared to be free to do pretty much as they liked and they walked about holding their chains up with a piece of string.

We were led up the dark and difficult stairs by hand, stumbling on the rough stones and dried mud of which they were built, and taken by the Sultan into a guest chamber with a low ceiling supported with twisted trunks of trees. The room was long and narrow, and the small windows opened flush with the floor of dried mud, covered with straw mats, Shirazi rugs and quilt-like ferrashes. There was a marble-topped table reminiscent of Lyons, and four folding chairs, while hard oblong cushions covered with bright silks lined the wainscot. The Sultan motioned us to the chairs but we insisted on sitting on the floor like our hosts. Four or five men came in with the Sultan, and outside the army was still busy banging off guns in salute. Sultan Sarur was dressed in shoes with stockings, a kilt-like futa with a handsome jambiya in a belt at his waist, a white drill coat and a turban of several sombre hues.

After lunch we started off on a "private" walk accompanied by the Sultan's principal factotums. The Lahej soldiers came too and so did twenty or thirty Haushabis all armed with rifles. We walked down into the Wadi Tiban and crossed among healthy looking maize to the Sultan's shady garden of fruit trees. On returning to the palace the Sultan asked me to come upstairs where he showed me a room in which he thought we should be more comfortable. In shape it was much like the other but it contained a very narrow single bed on which he suggested we might sleep, a number of locked boxes filled with household stores and the Sultanas' wardrobes, an elaborate gramophone with a large selection of records, and one corner partitioned off by a low wall behind which the Sultan thought we could wash more comfortably than in the room below.

We liked our new room better than the old but the prospect of sleeping indoors was too grim to be thought of, for the heat would have been appalling, so we were also given a roof surrounded by a parapet about four feet high. There were magnificent views of Jebel Warwah to the north and the mountains of the Subeihi country to the west. Through all this wild and majestic country of barren rock the Wadi Tiban, winding through maize fields, cut a brilliant and beautiful slash of green. There was a lovely sunset getting ready and a half-grown moon already visible. The roof also commanded an excellent view over all the other parapeted flat roofs in the village.

We ate our dinner on the roof and afterwards walked out, escorted with armed men as usual, to watch some dancing outside the palace walls. A semi-circle of men and women, their arms round each other, moved up and down, bending their knees (in what seemed a strangely modern style) absolutely rhythmically, to the accompaniment of a drum, sounded by one of the prisoners with a chain on his leg. He was quite happy as he stood or squatted beating his little barrel-like drum and smoking cigarettes. He sang the solos and refrains were caught up by the dancers. Much of the impromptu song was a tuneful good night lullaby to us—"Al Wali wal Madama, mesalkheir." At the end of the dance we said good night and went up to the roof where our bedding had been spread. The moon shone down on bodies laid out to sleep on all the house tops, and we too were lulled to slumber by the dull thudding of the drum, the singing, the barking of dogs and the braying of donkeys.

The next morning I was awake a good deal earlier than the rest of the little town, for looking over the roofs of the village I saw recumbent forms lying wrapped in coloured cloths on ferrashes or mats and not a soul was stirring. I was surprised as it was already light, but gradually sleepers wriggled and heaved, sat up, uncovered their heads from the cloths swathed round them, yawned and stretched their arms. After a moment's somewhat distasteful contemplation of the new day they got up, tightened their waist cloths and staggered indoors.

It was a delicious morning but by the time we had breakfast the roof was very hot. I went down to have a talk with the Sultan about the arrest of certain murderers. We do not, of course, interfere with domestic affairs in the Sultanates; if a Haushabi kills a Haushabi it is nothing to do with us, nor, as a matter of fact, are we much concerned when a member of one tribe kills a member of another. It is the place that matters. If travellers from other countries or tribes are molested on the trade routes then there is trouble, and the responsible Sultan has to arrest the culprit and make full restitution for any robbery committed. In this instance there were two outstanding cases, and the Sultan seemed to have very little hope of being able to arrest the real criminals and said that they had fled the country. Our talk was inconclusive and when we had touched on the ever-present question of the supply of arms and ammunition, the Sultan told me that he wanted to send his son to pay his first visit to Aden, which the Arabs of the interior look on as a sort of Paris.

Then the Sultan took us sightseeing. It is curious how great a sight water is in Arabia and he told me of it as if it was something unique, emphasizing that it was permanent. It was only a short distance but we set off with an army, the Sultan and his son Muhammad, many warriors and the 'Abdali soldiers and Al 'Abd. We drove with the Sultan in an old Chevrolet which bumped over the loose stones and boulders of the Wadi Tiban and its tributary the Wadi Jirab. When the "road" became too impossible we got out and climbed up the wadi, stopping to look at each pool and stretch of running water, and exclaiming, much to the old man's delight: "Wonderful, wonderful!" The pools were full of tiny fish and numbers of a kind of *xenopus* frogs.

In the afternoon I found a pedlar who had come with a load of wares from Aden. Besides small luxuries like toilet soaps, scents, and so on, we had some toys, amongst them "dying pig balloons" at one pice each. With an outlay of half a rupee I was able to make most of the children in the village happy and add a further noise to the already extensive chorus of donkeys and crying babies.

D. had been visiting the Sultan's mother-in-law who lay very sick on a carpet of filthy cloths, nursed by a gentle-handed male slave. In the hope of effecting her recovery two men brought up a goat and, passing it over her body seven times, cut its throat and gave the meat to the poor. In spite of this, however, she died during the night.

On our last morning the matutinal hymn of donkeys and babies was reinforced by the surviving "dying pigs" and we were driven off the roof early by the smoke from two large mud ovens on a roof below us. A slave was feeding the fire with green shrubs and another woman was making the bread—a paste of flour and water rolled out and rubbed all over with ghee, kneaded, and finally flattened out and stuck on the inside of the hot oven. It is cooked in about ten minutes when the flat round loaves are taken off the side of the oven and piled one on top of the other on a dish. When D. said good-bye to the women they gave her a present of some delicious honey which she thought was a strange but excellent fruit as it is packed in gourds. It is forced in through a tiny hole and it is quite difficult to see how it has been done.

A month or two later we paid another visit to Lahej, but this time as the guests of His Highness the Sultan who had returned from India. He had invited us to breakfast and it may sound as if a bumpy journey through the desert was an extravagant journey for a breakfast, but business was to be combined with pleasure and I was to attend a conference at which His Highness was to deal with some of the Subeihi Sheikhs who own him as their liege lord—as far as they own anything, for the truth is not in them.

The Subeihis had been at their usual game of plundering qāt caravans. They are a disorderly tribe, much subdivided and consequently much divided against themselves, living in the desert and foothills between the 'Abdali State and the Straits of Bab al Mandeb, west of Aden. Qāt, *catha edulis*, is a shrub which grows principally in the Yemen hills, and chewing it is the principal recreation not only of the Yemen and those States of the Protectorate between Yemen and Aden, but also of the Adenese themselves. It is not cheap—a bunch of a dozen or so shoots costs up to twelve annas—but those who like it and can afford it, or think they can, spend more on it than most of us spend on tobacco. It must be a very acquired taste, for I have tried a leaf or two and thought it was filthy, but when you have acquired that taste it makes you feel a devil of a dog so long as the feeling lasts. It is not soporific, but on the contrary wakens you up and sharpens the intellect—at least so addicts tell me. Most of the addicts, I confess, need a sharpening to their wits, and the pity is that the effects last such a short time. It is so expensive that the ordinary man can only afford one day a week in which to feel a superman. This is usually Friday and when prayers are over qāt parties foregather. Each member of the party turns up at the meeting place with a few bunches of qāt, and all the host does is to provide the spittoons. In an hour or so the stories begin to improve. What tales fishermen and golfers would tell if they took to qāt!

Qāt is expensive because it must be fresh, otherwise it is useless. The shoots are gathered in the early morning up in the Yemen hills and carefully packed in grass and green twigs to keep them fresh. The small packets are immediately loaded on to the camels—300 packets to a load—and the caravans arrive in Lahej on the morning of the third day, having travelled continuously. The Aden cargo goes on by bus.

There are three kinds of qāt, named from the localities from which they come, Ta'izi, Sabri and Maqtari. There is nothing to choose in quality between the first two, but Maqtari is inferior.[1]

It is a curious trade and little is known of it. The losses in such a perishable article may well be considerable and may make the retail price prohibitive. But there are many who get a rake-off from this luxury industry and who are unwilling to see it die.

The complaint against the Subeihis was that though they are not entitled to a rake-off they took it. The caravan would be peacefully wandering along when a crowd of toughs belonging to some petty chief would descend

---

[1] The Imam's taxes on each load come to M.T. $3½ for Maqtari and $4 for the other two and these latter are also subject to what are euphemistically called packing charges of $6 taken by the tax collector. Transport to Aden costs Rs. 20 a load for Ta'izi and Sabri and Rs. 15 for Maqtari. The first two pay Rs. 3 a load in taxes to the Haushabi Sultan and Rs. 7 and Rs. 8 respectively to the Sultan of Lahej; Maqtari comes by another route and pays one rupee to the Rija'i Sheikh and Rs. 3 to the Sultan of Lahej. Then the Aden Settlement collects an Octroi duty of Rs. 45 on a load of Ta'izi or Sabri and Rs. 40 on Maqtari, so that by the time the loads have reached Aden town they cost for Ta'izi Rs. 134 in summer and Rs. 265 in winter, for Sabri Rs. 134 and Rs. 280 and for Maqtari Rs. 110 and Rs. 120. Ta'izi is retailed at from eight to ten annas a bundle, Sabri from eight to twelve and Maqtari from four to seven.

om a hill, armed to the teeth, and pulling the loads to pieces extract a
w choice bundles, with the result that the loads arrived at Aden dried
ɔ and "unfit for human consumption."

When we arrived at the palace, His Highness came down the stairs to
ɩeet us himself. Sir 'Abdul Karim Fadhl is a man of about fifty, tall and
ɩim with a neat pointed beard and keen eyes. There is no mistaking the
ɩct that he is a ruler who rules. He was dressed in Indian fashion, tight
ousers, long coat buttoned up to the neck, with a gold turban wound
ɩgh and a flash hanging over the neck. Over his coat he wore a trans-
arent abba—gold braided and rather like a lighter version of the Zanzibar
ushti. He took us up to a large drawing-room lit by french windows
ɩading out on to a small balcony over the porch, and looking over a well-
ept garden with oleanders in bloom, fountains playing and thin pillars
ɩearing electric light globes which at night transform it into a fairyland.
ɽhe drawing-room was very English, rather Edwardian in period: the
ɩarpets had a mellow look and the comfortable chairs and sofas were
ɩovered with soft silk tapestries.

We soon saw that business came before breakfast, for His Highness
ɩent for the assembled chiefs to come up. There was the Haushabi Sultan,
wizened and a little decrepit. His territory lies between the 'Abdali Sultan's
and the Yemen, and he has the lawless Subeihis on his west and the 'Amir
of Dhala, who does not love him, on the east. On the south-east he just
touches two of the most ill-begotten tribes of the Fadhli Sultan—the Ahl
Fuleis and the Ahl Haidera Mansur. Altogether he has little fun. Although
he is independent he acknowledges a vague suzerainty by the Sultan of Lahej
who treats him very well and helps him considerably.

Then there were two of the Subeihi Sheikhs—the Rij'ai, an obstinate
boy of about eighteen, and the Makdumi, rather a pleasant old man. They
all came in, kissed His Highness's hand and squatted on the floor at a respect-
ful distance. Presently Prince Fadhl, His Highness's eldest son, arrived and
after shaking hands with us, kissed his father's hand and took D. to visit the
ladies.

The conference began. It went on for an hour and ended inconclusively.
For one thing the principal culprit, the Mansuri sheikh, was absent, and for
another it seemed impossible to make the Rij'ai boy grasp the fact that an
ancestor of his had signed a treaty in 1871 with Queen Victoria's representative guaranteeing that he would not interfere with caravans in return for a
monthly payment of forty dollars. The lad said in effect, and not unreason-

ably, though it was not for me to admit it, that it simply did not pay him to be good.

We adjourned for four days and on my next visit I found that the Rij'ai had spent the interim as His Highness's guest in the jail. The Lahej jail often brings people to an easier state of mind and as the Mansuri Sheikh had been fetched and kept him company, I went away with the usual promises that the boys would be good in future.

Meanwhile D. had been taken off by Fadhl to meet his mother. When they returned for breakfast, we were taken to wash in a real bathroom, taps and running water complete. The cool dining-room with its black and white marble floor was off the drawing-room, and the table gleamed invitingly with its white linen and polished silver. We had porridge, liver and potatoes, omelette, bread and butter and jam and tea. After this taste of an English country house, with the song of the birds and the fountain in the garden ringing pleasantly in our ears, we went back to Arabian Aden, where there is hardly a house with "mod. cons." and where the daily ration of water comes up our mountain in round tanks carried by three little donkeys.

## Chapter X

## TROUBLED WATERS

*And of their vain contest appeared no end.*     Milton.

*From spiteful words they fell to daggers drawing.*     Harrington.

At the beginning of June, 1934, I was handed several large and unpleasant-looking bundles of paper, euphemistically called files, and asked to study the "Fadhli-Lower Yafa'i dispute." The bundles consisted principally of letters in Arabic, and translations in English, with so-called minutes written on their backs in ink or red, blue and black pencil as struck the fancy of the writer at the moment. The paper was of most inferior quality looped together at one corner and well worn, torn and thumb marked even before they got to me. I give these details not with any sense of grievance, but merely to show that the paper study of the subject was itself formidable. These bundles only covered a period of about ten years: there were 'previous papers" in the records going back for about eighty. Here lies a clue to the really formidable side of the question and also a clue to the high state of civilization that parts of Arabia have reached. We have our ideas of thorny questions in Europe and those of us who have worked in Whitehall are sometimes apt to measure the importance of a question by the amount of paper dealing with it. Take for example the Nile and its importance to Egypt. Think of the various administrations and people through which the Nile has to pass before it gets to Egypt at all. I have no doubt that the archives of the Foreign and Colonial Offices—not to mention Chanceries and Secretariats abroad—must have quite a lot of paper packed away, dealing with the questions of the waters of the Nile. Yet I do not suppose that any other State in the world can boast as much paper on a small matter as there is in the Residency Office at Aden on the Water question of the Fadhli and Lower Yafa'i tribes—the matter of the "canal." Of course with that true political sense which is almost an instinct in Arabs and which they have developed to an astonishing degree, successive Lower Yafa'i and Fadhli Sultans have realized that they had in this canal, passing from the territory of the one to that of the other, matter for first class intertribal complications. The canal was first dug about eighty or ninety years ago. Presumably they started getting fun out of it straight away, but realizing that you cannot have a first class international bone of contention until you have an agreement in writing dealing with the matter they negotiated one in 1872.

At this point it becomes necessary to explain the terrain. The Lower Yafa'i and the Fadhli countries are two of the largest States in the western part of the Protectorate. The Fadhli country, coastal territory, stretches along the coast from Aden for a considerable distance. Behind it, or behind the western part of it, lie the mountains of Lower Yafa'i country, and the rivers that water the fertile oasis of Abyan in Fadhli country rise in the mountains of Lower Yafa'. Perhaps a century ago some engineering genius, no doubt of Fadhli race, saw that by cutting a canal from the river Bana in Lower Yafa'i territory, the waters could be made to irrigate much of the upper part of the oasis. This canal, called the Nazi'a, has been the source, not only of water for irrigation, but of agreements and disagreements, wars and counter wars, ever since. The 1872 agreement made provision for the supply of the water by the Lower Yafa'is to the Fadhlis and for the payment for the water by the Fadhlis to the Lower Yafa'is. Of course there is no real doubt that the Fadhlis would like to have the water and irrigate their crops, and the Lower Yafa'is realize that this is reasonable, but the history of the affair shows that the only really satisfactory solution to the matter will be one which, while it allows the Fadhlis to have the water, will at the same time deprive neither side of a most delightful bone which they can unearth from time to time, and over which they can growl at each other.

Every now and then both sides like to persuade the Residency to take a hand. As the files show, the Residency have sometimes consented to play, though reluctantly, and once or twice there have been quite decent rubbers. As I was a newcomer, it was thought that both sides and I could have some fun out of the business, and that was the principal reason why D. and I started off on a short journey to the Fadhli country. There was at the time a period of truce for eighteen months, but no one was taking it very seriously, and constant raidings of cattle and camels and constant murders took place in the area round Haid Halima, a hill which we visited and which stands on the border of the two countries. A map shows that Haid Halima depends from Lower Yafa'i territory like a tear dropping into the troubled waters of Abyan, and it has indeed, as will be seen, played the part of a tear drop on several occasions.

Then there was another small trouble for me to deal with, a quarrel between two of the Fadhli Sultan's tribes led by the Nakhai Sheikh and the Sultan of Yeramis. This quarrel arose from the mortgage of some Yeramis land to the Nakhai. He had come in to take possession and murder had resulted. He was now determined to have Yeramis land in compensation. So much I gathered from other files, and prepared to set off to try to pour oil on the troubled waters.

On our arrival at the Fadhli Sultan's palace at Shuqra we came up to a fine airy room where we found the Sultan just rising from his siesta. He explained that he had not really expected us until the next morning, but everybody was soon busy getting ready to deal with our arrival The army was hurriedly collected in the bazaar and got busy firing a salute from an old muzzle-loading cannon. They managed to fire off twelve guns during the next hour or so, and a little desultory rifle-fire accompanied it.

We now began to make other acquaintances, first and foremost being the Sultan's small son Hussein, a most engaging boy of about eleven. Full of dignity and good manners, he was amusingly conscious of his importance and very imperious in his speech to his inferiors, whom he treated with a rather attractive haughtiness. He bossed the whole family and had recently distinguished himself by running away from school in Aden. The keynote of his costume was green. His shirt was of pale green silk, his multi-coloured futa looked like a green tartan kilt, and his turban, which he wound in Indian style, was bright green flecked with red. Whenever he left the palace he put on his bandolier stuffed with cartridges and his jambiya and carried a Lee Enfield rifle as tall as himself.

The chief palace official was Sheikh 'Abdulla bin Bubekr who combined the functions of butler, Master of the Household, and principal private secretary. Fifteen years ago he paid a visit to Zanzibar and Mombasa and, amongst others, knew the Sultan, Sir 'Ali bin Salim and Sheikh Suleiman bin Nasir al Lemki. So he spoke a little Swahili and Zaidi was soon thoroughly at home.

While we were having tea the Sultan's eldest son, Salih, came in. He, too, was an extremely good-looking youth, about nineteen or twenty with a strong face full of character. His father was rather afraid—or shy—of him and I heard that they were not on good terms. All he wore was a cloth round his waist with a bandolier and jambiya, and round his curly black hair an indigo-dyed piece of cloth. In fact, unlike his father or young Hussein, he was plentifully indigoed all over. In strong contrast to his sons, the Fadhli Sultan had not, at any rate in his old age, anything like their strength of character, and as a man of affairs he was not a success. His face was almost beardless, his hair was grey and inclined to curl and his turban was bound like a wreath of laurels, reminding me of a Roman Emperor. He was, I should say, somewhere in his sixties, untidy in his dress and personal appearance, again a strong contrast to his sons.

After talking to the family we were left alone to make ourselves at home. Our quarters were delightfully clean, airy and comfortable. The bathroom, too, was all that could be desired, a clean cement floor and a huge jar of icy-cold water which gave me delicious shivers when I poured it over myself.

When we returned to the palace after a stroll in the town we found the Sultan counting the money in the Treasury. He was squatting on the floor near his bed under which he kept a brown tin box—the State Treasury. Later I found that where the Sultan was, there was the box. It was brought with him to Aden and every time I saw him in a taxi the box was there between his knees.

He asked us to sign his visitors' book, which contained two English names, and told D. that she was not the first lady visitor to Shuqra, for not only had Mrs. Fowle, the wife of a former Resident, been there, but forty years before, in the time of his father, an English lady and her husband (Mr. and Mrs. Theodore Bent) had spent some days in the mountains. This was in 1897 and in *Southern Arabia* Mrs. Bent has written an account of their journey. It was much the same as ours was to be, but done in the opposite direction, for they ended at Shuqra.

After breakfast on the next morning the Sultan and I began a business talk which lasted, with interruptions, for the next three hours or more. The subject was, of course, the Lower Yafa'i–Fadhli trouble, and though I shall give a fairly connected account of it, the actual conversation proceeded amid constant interruptions. Every few minutes somebody would come in and the Sultan did not want to speak in anybody else's presence. He could not send them away so we had to pass polite nothings. If nobody came in the Sultan would go out to see about some domestic detail in the pantry. If he did not go to the pantry he would be going to shout to someone out of the window, or to the window to answer a call. If he was doing none of these things he was paying very little attention to what I was saying and turning the conversation off on to every conceivable subject. So everything had to be said about fifteen times, and I never left a point until he had repeated it to me sufficiently for me to understand that he had more or less grasped it.

Early in the conversation he produced an Arabic agreement some twenty years old between the late Fadhli Sultan and the Lower Yafa'i Sultan. Two of the articles provided that the Lower Yafa'is should give the water of the Nazi'a canal to the Fadhlis, and that the Fadhlis should pay for it twenty-five rupees and two qosras of dates annually, in accordance with custom, and that Husn Halima (a fort on the hill called Haid Halima) should be demolished. He said that at first the conditions had been carried out but Husn Halima had been rebuilt recently by the Lower Yafa'is. Then he produced a written award of 1929 by the 'Abdali Sultan and said that although a decision had been given that Husn Halima should again be demolished nothing had yet been done. He also said that he had recently been given another award by the 'Abdali Sultan approving his claims for loots and raids against the Lower Yafa'i Sultan. After he had repeated himself and aired his grievances to an extent I thought sufficient, I took a turn in the conversation and said that while all that might be so, I did not believe that this dispute would be settled until both parties ceased to recite their grievances and approached the matter afresh with a real will to settle it and goodwill on both sides.

"They tell me," I said, "that this row has been going on for about eighty years and no one believes it can be settled. I've more faith in your and the Lower Yafa'i Sultan's good sense than this and I'm sure that if you would only try to approach the affair in a spirit of good will we should get on."

This, of course, was my first acquaintance with an old-standing Arab dispute and I had not yet grasped that in fact nobody really wanted the dispute settled. The Sultan naturally loved having someone new to listen to all the ancient history and to argue with him. I might as well have said nothing, for just as if I had said nothing at all he was back on Husn Halima.

"I'll come to Husn Halima all in good time," I said. "It's like a boil which will go on swelling up until the poison that caused it has been removed. I don't even think of it as the bottom of the trouble, but before we come to talking of it I want to insist on this need for good will."

We went on saying "good will" and "Husn Halima" at each other until a letter was brought in from some Seiyid referring to the necessity of settling the matter, and by a peculiar coincidence using practically the same expressions as I had been using, telling both parties to forget their grievances, and entertain good will. I pounced on this and at last we were off the Husn.

Having got the Sultan to agree to this necessity for mutual good will, I said that I thought that the root of the trouble, as far as the Fadhlis were concerned, was the Nazi'a water.

"Yes," said he, "it irrigates all my fields and my tribesmen's."

"Well then," I said, "if it could be arranged that the Fadhlis get their proper allowance of water at the right time and that the Yafa'is get paid at the right time, and in accordance with custom, the Husn Halima question could be considered dead and no one would mind its being demolished."

I was rubbing in the need for a proper settlement of the Nazi'a question when Salih walked in and butted into the conversation by holding forth about Husn Halima again. So back we went to the beginning. But father had no desire to talk with Salih there, so he retired to the pantry and I changed the conversation and began telling Salih that I hoped he was a good boy and helped his father, until he got tired and left. Father then returned and we set to work again.

"Now we're agreed about the proper settlement of the Nazi'a question," I said, "I can tell you that we think the Husn ought to come down as it is a perpetual source of offence to the side that has not got it. But, when it does you'll have to take steps to keep the Ahl Haidera Mansur and the Ahl Fuleis in order, as it isn't reasonable to expect the Lower Yafa'is to leave themselves open to their incessant raiding."

"We can swap consuls," he replied with an expressive flip of his fingers, "and they will have to tell the Sultan in whose country they live when a raid takes place by his men, so that he can punish them at once."

"Well, there's no harm in that," I said, "but the real remedy lies in your tightening up your control over these two misbegotten tribes and not allowing them to raid.

"You ought to think more of the wrongs the Fadhlis have done to the Lower Yafa'is and what you can do to make up for them, and then a settlement would be closer. It's absurd to find two senior chiefs squabbling like a couple of beduin, and ridiculous to suppose that two men of your influence and status could not settle their differences and walk into Lahej

## ARRANGING A SETTLEMENT

and tell the Sultan, who has agreed to arbitrate between you, that you have done so."

He then began to talk about Sultan 'Aidarus (the Lower Yafa'i Sultan). "You must make allowances," I said, "for the fact that he is a young man while you are an old man with wider experience of the world, and because of this you must do your best for the interest of peace."

"I will try to make friends," replied the Sultan.

I then talked about the claims for loots due to the Fadhlis by the Yafa'is. "You have declared yourself a man of peace," said I, "and it would be a great boon if you could persuade your men to let bygones be bygones, so that the Lower Yafa'is can see you are in favour of peace and are prepared to make sacrifices for it."

"I couldn't do that," answered the Sultan, "because of the great disturbances there would be among my tribesmen who have had to pay eighteen hundred rupees to the Lower Yafa'is."

"I can see there are difficulties," I said, "and I don't want to overpersuade you, but merely ask you to do so if you can as it would be a great mark of goodwill on your part."

After a long discussion he agreed to do so and said he would stand the racket of all the loots out of his own pocket. "But," he went on, "if you mention this to the Lower Yafa'i Sultan don't say that it comes from me, but that it was a suggestion made by you which I accepted conditionally on the settlement of the two questions of Nazi'a and Halima."

I promised him that I would do this and then started talking about the Yeramis trouble. "Until recently," I went on, "the Nakhai has been a good sheikh and the Government gave him privileges because he looked after the landing ground, but as a result of it he seems to have got a swollen head and has been recovering illegal taxes from Yafa'i caravans, creating a disturbance at Yeramis and occupying the houses there of the children of Sultan Ahmed bin Hussein whose wife is a British subject."

"He has discussed these matters with me," said the Sultan, "and he has undertaken to recover no more transit dues from Yafa'i caravans, to leave the houses and to stop disturbances at Yeramis."

"I am very glad to hear it," I replied. "I hope he'll do what he says."

"If he doesn't I'll fight against him," said he thumping the table.

"I don't want you to fight," said I, "but to bring him to reason. I

want to talk to him myself, but I'm sure you could use persuasion withou
force and if you want my support I'll give it to you."
The Sultan said that he would do his best. Then he started telling
me about his system of collecting duty on all that passed through his country
and naïvely told me that he took his whack out of ammunition sent to his
subordinate chiefs.
"That ought to stop," I told him. "Government arms and ammunition
aren't dutiable and they're issued for a special purpose. When Government
assesses how much arms and ammunition are necessary in a particular
case, it doesn't allow for a rake-off by the Chief."
"I don't like Government supplying the Nakhai Sheikh with arms
direct," went on the Sultan, "because it encourages him to create disturbances on the roads. If Government wants to send him arms and ammunition let them be sent through me and I would see that they were distributed
to important Nakhai tribesmen who maintain security."
I said again that this concession had been granted exceptionally and
that these supplies would be given him on condition that he acted in accordance with the wishes of Government. "In any case it's just as easy to
take away a privilege as to give it, and if the Nakhai doesn't behave himself
no doubt it will be withdrawn."
"I've written to the Nakhai Sheikh," said the Sultan, "to come to
Shuqra or Yeramis to see me, but my messenger has not yet returned."
This brought our conference to an end and I was devoutly thankful,
for I was worn out and more than ready for lunch.
The time had now come to arrange a settlement of the dispute between
the Sultan of Yeramis and two of the Fadhli Sultan's tribes concerning the
mortgage of some Yeramis land to the Nakhai Sheikh, leader of the tribes
concerned. Accordingly, on the afternoon of the following day and after
D. had said good-bye to her friends in the Harem, we started on our
journey to Yeramis in the mountains. We were supposed to start at three
o'clock, but naturally there was the usual delay in saddling camels with the
Sultan's luggage, including the indispensable treasury chest, and it was not
until almost five that we actually left the city, accompanied by almost all the
notabilities of the Fadhli realm. It was the most distinguished caravan
that had ever left Shuqra. There was Sultan Fadhl bin Hussein, the Sultan's
brother, young Hussein, his son, 'Othman bin 'Abdulla, nephew of the
Sultana, two Sultans of the Haidera Abu Mansur tribe, six 'Aqils of other
tribes, the son of the Yeramis Sultan and many others including the Sultan's

brother-in-law—Commander-in-Chief Muhammad bin 'Abdulla Abu Haidera, reminiscent of George Arliss and known, on account of his rich bass voice, as "the Bishop" and also as "Uncle Muhammad."

We had not been going long when "Uncle" came galloping past on his camel and shouted out, patting his saddlebags: "If you want water or anything just ask me." When he reached the head of the column he got off his camel and, despite his sixty-two years, ran along like a boy with the escort, leading their songs and encouraging them.

We were heading almost north towards the Guddam range with its many peaks, which appear deceptively close. It was dark soon after we had crossed the Wadi Rakhama deep cut in black volcanic rock and every now and then I heard the piping, imperious tones of young Hussein shouting: "Ya Ahmed Nasir! How much further have we got to go?" And then, whenever we reached a possible halting place: "Oh my Uncle Muhammad! Is this where we stop for the night?"

After a steep climb in the dark and missing our way once or twice, we finally got down into the Wadi Mitwan and thankfully found that this was our camping-ground. The floor of the wadi was perfectly flat and sandy. Its walls were almost vertical, about fifteen feet high, an ideal camping-place. We stretched ourselves out on our saddle-cloths and rested for a short while, which, incidentally, resulted in D's hands and clothes being stained a deep blue. Her saddle-cloth had been dyed with indigo.

We had reached the camping-ground at half-past eight and an hour later the Sultan turned up. He had been delayed with his interminable talks. We greeted him and talked to him for a few moments before he went off to join his 'Aqils at the other end of the camp. Hussein and I went off to gather firewood with the help of a slave. Young Hussein was full of fun and kept ragging our companion by pretending there were snakes in the bushes as we pulled out the dry wood. But it seemed as if the loads with our beds and our food would never come, and in fact we were no longer hungry when they did turn up at half-past eleven. In spite of the commotion on the arrival of the baggage camels, young Hussein lay on his back fast asleep and nothing woke him. We got out our camp-beds quickly, put them up and ate a few biscuits and some water-melon, after which we fell asleep to the accompaniment of the queer noises of the camels just beside us. As Zaidi said, they were singing both ends.

I think that I was the first of our large camp to wake on Saturday morning. It was still quite dark but dawn was breaking. We had arranged to start just after the dawn prayers, but as it seemed to me that nobody as yet had said any prayers, I woke up 'Ali 'Abdulla and told him I thought they ought to be getting on with it. However, he thought that if they said any prayers they would say them to themselves, and if they said any at all on the tour this was certainly the way they did it for, except on our last morning in Zinjibar when I saw the Sultan saying his prayers on his bed, nobody seemed to bother about them. There is, of course, an exemption in favour of travellers, but on a comfortable tour like ours there was really no excuse.

Ahmed the slave was soon astir shaking sleepers and shouting "Arise, the day, arise," and after a perfunctory toilet, we started off about a quarter past five. We went on up the wadi until we came to a blank mountain wall and turned off to the left. There was barely a trace of vegetation on the sides of the hills though plenty in the wadi, and the mountains had the appearance of having been poured out while molten and having set at once in slabs, the strata being all inclined to the ground at an angle of forty-five degrees.

We climbed for an hour or more up the narrow, rocky wadi until we had reached its head, where we dismounted and climbed up over the pass to drop into the Wadi Yeramis, which was almost a downwards repetition of the way up. At about eight o'clock we entered the Wadi Yeramis, with its running water and grass and cultivation on either side. Our party led by "Uncle Muhammad" was well ahead and we stopped to wait for the Sultan so that we might make a State entry into Ar Rôdha. We sat down and drank tea on the bank of the river while the camels munched the bushes. When the Sultan joined us we went along the wadi until we saw Ar Rodha perched on its hill with the Sultan's small dar towering above everything else.

We climbed to the plateau and dismounted some distance from the dar, drawing up in a long line, while our camels and horses formed a second line behind us. Some fifty yards ahead, facing us, stood the hosts' side, the Sultan of Yeramis and his son in the centre facing the Fadhli Sultan, his relations and myself, who were in the centre of our side. The Yeramis were beating drums and howling in welcome, whereafter they slaughtered a bullock, and began a somewhat barbaric edition of "Nuts and May," known as a Murkib. Two men stepped forward and side by side circled about in front of the Yeramis team, and gradually, two by two, others fell in behind them until they had collected about twenty. The procession walked in ever widening circles until they approached our side, and as each couple in the procession passed the Sultan and myself they fired off their rifles, singing an improvised song as they marched. This was repeated several times and then the procession returned to its own side.

It was now our part to return the call, but with all our petty chieftains we considered ourselves so important that we could only do the processing in our own honour. The procession was done in the same way. With the exception of the leaders most of our team were petty chieftains. Three other chiefs mounted their horses and in regular circus fashion circled the walking procession. On the return of this party the court poet was ordered to make up some verses for the occasion, and I was asked for my name to be included in them. Here is what he sang:

"We have come with the Sarkar (the Government) who has especially come with the object of maintaining the security to the frightened.
"He has his arsenal and his soldiers in his hands and is advancing in the world both by sea and by land.
"Ingrams has come out to Wadi Yeramis and made it secure and the army accompanying him is strong and is pushing forward in every part of the world.
"There have been some clouds which have been seen to be about to pour rains both in the autumn and summer seasons."

The words were caught up by the others and we all walked slowly forward in a long line towards the Yeramis Sultan's dar. Here we shook hands with our hosts, and Sultan Haidera, a dear old man with a delightful child-like smile, no teeth and very hard of hearing, seized my hand and led me at a terrific pace through a courtyard strewn with straw, where the animals were kept and which was also the Royal Courts of Justice, into the dar and up a pitch-dark winding staircase at breakneck speed. After a few minutes of perilous scrambling up some four or five flights he pulled me into the guest-room, sat me down on the floor, and plumped down opposite with a toothless smile of triumph and welcome.

The guest-room was rough and poorly furnished with mats, a bed, and a carpet locally made. The windows had neither glass nor shutters but were just ornamental lattice work which could not be opened. The rest of the party were soon up and we were served with cakes, eggs and milk tea flavoured with cardamon. Plain tea without milk but liberally sugared also made its appearance in glasses. We exchanged complimen and then rested for a while.

Presently lunch came. The dinner service, which consisted of wov mats of sizes from a foot to three or four feet across, was collected fro the walls and thrown down for us. Slaves came in with the food; one them carried huge hunks of boiled meat under his arm and threw the down on the mat as if he was dealing cards. It was rather like feedin time in the Lion House. A large enamel platter of sodden rice was flu into the middle and some very hot and greasy native bread was chuck round, one to each leg of mutton. Sultan 'Abdulla, Haidera's son, a with us. When I felt that I had done all that politeness required I sa "Al hamdulillah" and got up. 'Abdulla said: "Al hamdulillah? Ha you finished so soon?" I apologized, but said I had done very well a retired to the corner to wash my hands and mouth and pick my teet Followed ginger coffee and more tea, and a huge supply of really goo milk, after which we lay down to rest.

Ar Rodha or Na'ab stands on the right bank of the Wadi Yeran on a low plateau of earth cliffs. It is an important centre of traffic a until recently there were a number of shops. The wadi round the plate used also to be extensively cultivated. On the words "until recently hangs a tale, for now the shops have all disappeared and the cultivatic is nothing like what it ought to be. Those who are accustomed to mo civilized life will hardly believe that this desolation is due to a fami quarrel.

On one edge of this plateau stands Sultan Haidera's dar in which l and sons and dependants live. He is the Yeramis Sultan and rules ov the Wadi Yeramis as a feudal lord of the Fadhli Sultan. On the other edg of the plateau stands the house of his nephew, Sultan Ja'bil bin Hussei whose two brothers live with him. The houses are not much more tha a hundred yards apart, and the space in between them is as flat and bare a parade ground. Ja'bil and his brothers have quarrelled with their unc and cousins. If uncle shows his nose, or his ox, or his ass, or his goat, c anything that is his, outside the walls of his dar, Ja'bil shoots at it, an vice versa, if Ja'bil ventures into the daylight outside his house his unc and cousins take a shot at him. Not unnaturally, therefore, the shopkeepe and others found that living in between the two was not conducive t comfort or profit and departed. Cultivation on account of this squabbl is, of course, almost at a standstill as it is not safe, and for some years th oxen and sheep and goats have not been brought home at night but hidden below in the wadi, for both sides have their fortresses on the edge of the plateau and can get down under cover.

At our meeting in the morning Sultan Haidera and his son 'Abdulla complained to me about Ja'bil, and I said that I was sorry to hear that Ar Rodha, formerly a big town, had become a desert as a result of their family dispute. I enquired about the real cause of the quarrel. Sultan 'Abdulla said that Ja'bil had killed his father-in-law some seven years ago; that he ('Abdulla) had not taken retaliative action against him, but had tried to persuade him to submit his case for arbitration in accordance with the tribal system, but that Ja'bil had declined to do this. Ja'bil had also taken a man of theirs and sent him up-country for sale. I said that I would like to arrange for a reconciliation to be made between them and Ja'bil, because no permanent settlement of their troubles could be effected while they were at enmity with each other. "Your trouble with the Nakhai Sheikh," I went on, "could be much more easily settled if you were a united family." They agreed to this, so I asked: "Are you prepared to receive Ja'bil if I can persuade him to come?"

"We are," they said, and so I had a talk with the Fadhli Sultan who agreed to appoint "Uncle Muhammad" as an arbitrator between them. I left for our tent, which was pitched almost midway between the rival camps, and sent a note to Ja'bil inviting him to come and see me at my tent as I would very much like to make his acquaintance and talk about several things. 'Ali 'Abdulla took the letter personally to Ja'bil and he and his two brothers, 'Abdul Rahman and Ahmed, came to the camp a little later. I did not particularly take to Ja'bil. I knew he had three murders (later I learned the total score was twenty-one) to his discredit, but although I did not allow this to prejudice me (particularly as one was only a father-in-law) I did not find him an attractive personality. He was perhaps in his early thirties and had protruding teeth and a rather stupid appearance. But 'Abdul Rahman was a great improvement on his brother and quite friendly, though Ahmed was sulky and I could not raise a smile out of him.

After the usual exchange of compliments I said, rather mendaciously, that I was very pleased to make their acquaintance and visit their country. I then said the same as I had done to Haidera and his son.

"Although I have had a dispute with my uncle," Ja'bil replied, "he has brought the Nakhais into the country instead of arranging a settlement between ourselves."

"I have seen your Uncle Haidera and your Cousin 'Abdulla," I sa "and they have agreed to renew friendship with you, and the Fadhli Sult has appointed an arbitrator to look into your differences." Ja'bil agre to this and we then gave them tea and Jacob's biscuits and after sending messenger ahead, Ja'bil with his two brothers and I left the camp for I uncle's dar. When we arrived, Sultan Haidera, supported by 'Abdul and Ahmed, another son, received the three brothers in prodigal son fashio The old man, wearing a more beaming smile than ever seemed genuine moved by the reunion, but though Ja'bil returned his embraces he seeme reserved and lacking enthusiasm. But you would have thought it was meeting of long lost relations from distant corners of the earth rather tha from a hundred yards away. Again we scrambled up dark stairs hand hand, and flushed with triumph I brought Ja'bil and his brothers into tl guest-room, looking rather as if they expected to be knifed any minut

"I have brought you together," I said after we had sat down, "becau: it is shame that a family should act as you have done and you must be united family in other affairs. And you ought to work your fielc again which I hear have been left uncultivated for years owing to th trouble."

Ja'bil jibbed at this and said in not very friendly style that he had sever: claims against his uncle.

"The claims will have to be solved by the arbitrator," I replied.

"Perhaps," said Ja'bil suspiciously, "the judgment of the arbitratc will not be carried out." As he continued to harp on this (he knew Ara ways better than I did), I asked both parties if they agreed to "Uncle being arbitrator and to accept his decision, and they said "Yes."

"You," I said turning to Ja'bil, "must submit yourself to your uncl not only because he is the head of the family but because he is your rulei and you must all be good subjects of the Fadhli Sultan."

The Sultan was present at the interview and chose this moment to pu his foot into it more heavily than usual. I was careful in all my doings t say the Fadhli Sultan had decided this or that, and in announcing tha "Uncle" would arbitrate, he also said he would appoint Salih bin Nasir, one-legged relative of his, as a second arbitrator. There was a shout o dismay at this, so I quickly said that I did not remember his mentionin¡ his name when he decided on Muhammad bin 'Abdulla, but that I wa sure any decision he made would be right and perhaps we might discus it afterwards. He agreed and there was a general sigh of relief.

## CELEBRATING PEACE

"All I am doing," I said, "I do as a support to your master the Fadhli Sultan and out of desire for the maintenance of peace."

Everybody seemed pleased with these arrangements and the party broke up quite happy in order to have another Murkib as a public sign of the new peace.

After leaving Sultan Haidera and his reunited relations, the Fadhli Sultan and I walked across to the tent and here I tackled him about the appointment of Salih bin Nasir as an extra arbitrator and made him drop the idea. While we were sitting in the tent the Murkib was getting ready outside. Our team was drawn up about ten yards in front of the tent and consisted of Haidera and his sons and the visitors, ourselves. The other side drawn up opposite at about fifty yards interval consisted of Ja'bil and his brothers and their supporters. They provided another bullock which was duly slaughtered. Their side also started the visitation which was exactly on the same lines as that of the morning. We followed and our procession included Haidera's two sons and some of the Fadhli petty chieftains, amongst whom young Hussein made his first public appearance in a Murkib. New songs were composed for the occasion.

When it was all over the Fadhli Sultan took me by my left hand and 'Abdulla bin Haidera, shortly relieved by his father, by my right hand, and we walked forward to Ja'bil's house, where we were invited to dinner, climbing up a dark staircase like the one in his uncle's house. Cakes, coffee and tea were served, and the Fadhli Sultan made a nuisance of himself by being rather condescending in paying the visit at all, and by complaining of the stuffiness. He summoned two of his slaves to take the dinner-service off the walls and fan himself and myself with the mats, so I said that there was a very pleasant breeze coming in through the window. I sat here about half an hour talking nothings and then begged to be excused saying I felt very tired and wanted to go to bed early, as we hoped to be off soon after dawn. I found my way down the dark stairs and out through the courtyard which in the interval had become a perfect shambles. I counted no less than seven freshly slaughtered sheep and goats, and made my way between pools of blood outside feeling a little sick.

Ja'bil's two brothers followed me to the tent, firing off in turns a round every two or three paces. I was quite unprepared for this and found it most alarming as they only use ball ammunition and were only a yard or so behind me. However I was told that it was a compliment paid to a peacemaker. We passed the remnants of the slaughtered bullock, which was completely hidden by a squabbling mass of villagers hacking off their hares, and so back to the tent where I bade my escort good night.

Shortly afterwards Ja'bil's brother, 'Abdul Rahman, turned up. He had a sheep for me which he said was for my dinner, a goat for D.'s dinner and a couple of fowls to make weight. We dined off scrambled eggs and I did my best to disembarrass ourselves of the livestock. Then we went to bed. The Fadhli Sultan told me very ostentatiously in front of Sultan Haidera that he proposed to post four soldiers for our safety. I said that he would no doubt do what he thought best, but that I felt perfectly secure in this present atmosphere of peace. Later on Sultan Haidera sent along to say he wanted to put some soldiers to guard us, to which I sent back a civil reply to the effect that I felt very honoured but that I felt very secure. Finally Uncle Muhammad came along to ask if we wanted anything and said that he proposed to put down his mat near-by and look after us. But there was little cause for anxiety, for the principal topic of conversation in the village that night was the fact that the herds were brought back to the houses for the night, and this had not happened for years.

Presently the place quietened down; the squabbling villagers had cut up and carried off the beef, and apart from the occasional barking of dogs, who were clearing up the remains, and the low voices of the sentries, the only other sound was the beating of a drum which went on almost incessantly throughout the night.

\*    \*    \*

After breakfast next morning I went to see the Yeramis Sultan and his relations, including Ja'bil. The Fadhli Sultan was there and we arranged a month's truce between the Nakhais and Ja'bil during which time "Uncle" was to arbitrate on their differences as well as on the family squabble. As none of the Nakhais were at Ar Rodha I suggested calling them and explaining matters to them. When they were asked to come they declined, so at my request the Sultan went off to see them himself. They took such a long time talking that I sent 'Ali 'Abdulla to ask him if he would like me to come. Answer came back that he would, so I went as well.

Ahmed Hassan, the senior Nakhai at Yeramis and brother of the Sheikh, was a genial old man with a white beard who gave me a friendly greeting. When I asked him to come down and be pleasant he took me to a window and pointed out a stone in the wadi, saying: "There is where my two brothers were murdered. I will not sit down with Ja'bil."

Put like that my sympathies were rather with him, but I thought it better to try to make some sort of reconciliation in view of the truce we were arranging, and said that I would like the Nakhais to renew friendship with Ja'bil because no real settlement could be effected between parties who were at enmity with each other. They finally agreed to come with me and, taking Ahmed Hassan by his hand, I led him to the room whe Ja'bil and the others were waiting, and they shook hands all round. Wh coffee had been served I explained the arrangements "which," I said, "ha been made by the Fadhli Sultan, and you must understand that I supp< your Sultan and desire peace to be the order of the day in the town."

"Also," I went on, "if the Nakhais have land here they want to work, they must consider themselves like other subjects of Yeramis and submit to the rulers of the country. They must also understand that they have no right whatever to interfere with affairs of State, but should behave well in subjection to the rulings of the Sultan. One month's truce has been arranged between the Nakhais and Yeramis."

"I am afraid," said Ja'bil, "that the Nakhais will start trouble again with me if the truce period expires without any action having been taken."

"I will do my best in the matter," I replied and added, optimistically, that I hoped that their troubles would be solved before the expiration of the truce.

This done, I said good-bye to Sultan Haidera and his relations, and left his house to go back to the tent, followed again by a peacemaker's escort of two, firing off their rifles.

Then we set out for our next objective—Husn Halima—making our way off the plateau and down into the wadi.

The wadi was green with overgrown vegetation, and the heat was tempered by a good breeze, which, however, did not prevent us from feeling thoroughly exhausted at the end of the day. Added to this I had eaten and drunk so much filth in the cause of peace and friendship that I was not feeling entirely at my best. We rode the whole day along the Wadi Yeramis, reaching the Wadi Bana on the following morning when we saw Husn Halima in the distance. Here a messenger brought me a reply from the Lower Yafa'i Sultan to a letter I had sent the night before:

> We have received your letter date 17th June 1934 regarding your coming to Husn Halima. We in reply inform you, Oh friend, that we hope you will be in our part in the morning. When you approach Halima you will find us ready to receive you there with the usual honourable

salute. We are very much pleased to make your acquaintance and know your good manners.

As regards the Fadhli Sultan and his party we request you kindly allow them to go to 'Ubar ash Shab'a without meeting us.

I thought from this that Sultan 'Aidarus was going to prove somewhat 'intransigeant," but decided it was wiser to go alone to Husn Halima. I asked the Sultan to remain with his party at 'Ubar ash Shab'a where I could send for him if it was possible. As we drew nearer the Husn standing on its hill, D. and I and 'Ali 'Abdulla and two guides gradually diverged from our main party and made for it. As we approached we were challenged from the fort and our guide shouted: "It is the Government." A burst of rifle fire followed and a salute of five guns was fired. When we arrived at the foot of the hill we learned that the Sultan was not there, but he soon arrived to receive me very cordially and with more firing of guns.

Sultan 'Aidarus bin Muhsin al Afifi, Sultan of the Lower Yafa'is, is a good-looking young man in his early thirties. He impressed me at once as being more cultured than most of the people we had been meeting of late. He looked intelligent, his manner was easy and assured, and he was not fulsome in his speech. I was struck with the hold he appeared to have over his men. He had come down from his residence at Al Husn, a town some five or six miles away, to meet me with five hundred men, and, if such words can be applied to a body of undrilled beduin, they seemed disciplined and well-ordered, obeying at once any command he gave verbally or by sign.

'Aidarus was well dressed, if not over dressed, for the heat by now was terrific. He had a brown silk turban wound high in the Lahej fashion, and wore a long Indian pattern heather-coloured coat close-buttoned up to the neck. Beneath this there showed a white lace tunic reaching to below the coat, which was almost down to his knees, and his trousers were black velvet. A pair of brown shoes finished the costume, but he had a dagger well ornamented with gold in his sash at his waist. He was riding a small bay horse.

We had planted ourselves under the only bush in the neighbourhood large enough to give shade and as he approached I went forward to meet him. He dismounted and we shook hands. Somehow we managed to dispense with the usual polite nothings and merely expressed pleasure at meeting each other. One of his followers came forward and spread a Persian rug under our bush. He introduced me to some of his principal followers including the 'Aqil of Husn Halima, a pleasant-faced but very black individual. We sat down to business and tea and coffee were produced.

The Sultan 'Aidarus asked me to go up to the Husn but I thought it would be more tactful to the Fadhlis to decline, so said I was feeling unwell, which was not entirely untrue. I then tackled the big question and repeated to 'Aidarus most of what I had said to the Fadhli Sultan, except that I added: "I am sure a young, able and intelligent man like yourself ought to be able to make a new friendship with the Fadhli Sultan and settle your differences yourselves, and go to Lahej and report that you have done so."

"I am in favour of peace," replied Sultan 'Aidarus, "but the Fadhlis have failed to meet the lawful claims of the Lower Yafa'is for fields, and over murders and loots."

I smiled, replying that the Fadhlis had similar claims against them.

"During the truce period," the Sultan said, "the Fadhlis have continued to carry off the property of my men while they have done no wrong whatever."

I repeated what I had said to the Fadhli Sultan, namely, that there could be no real peace until both parties showed a real desire to settle the affair, "and," I went on, "I advise you to think rather of the wrongs your people have done to the Fadhlis than of what they claim from them."

"The Fadhlis have only one right," said 'Aidarus, "the Nazi'a water, and in all other matters they have wronged the Lower Yafa'is."

"I believe the Fadhli Sultan is sincerely anxious to make peace," I said, "but the Nazi'a water question must be satisfactorily settled and Husn Halima ought to come down as it will always be a source of offence to the side that does not possess it. I have impressed on the Fadhli Sultan the need of keeping the Ahl Haidera Mansur and the Ahl Fuleis in order if the Husn is demolished."

Sultan 'Aidarus smiled. "The Fadhlis never keep their word but will agree to keep it and then act treacherously."

"I don't altogether blame you for smiling," I said, "but if you want peace you must try and have some confidence in the promises of the other side."

I then enquired as to the real reasons of this long-standing dispute, and asked if he did not agree that the Nazi'a water question was at the bottom of it all.

"The original reason," he replied, "was a rifle which was given by my predecessors to the Fadhli Sultan as a pledge, but the Fadhlis declined to return it to him."

I laughed at this, and so did he and said: "That, of course, is a trivial matter, but the essential differences lie in the question of some fields taken by the Fadhlis from my predecessors at Ja'wala and two other places, some forty-six and thirty-two years ago respectively."

I then asked him what stood in the way of the demolition of the Husn and the settlement of the trouble.

"I would require assurances against future raids," he replied, "payments for past loots and the restoration of the cultivable lands."

"I understand from the Fadhli Sultan," I said, "that he is prepared to post one of his men as consul in Lower Yafa'i territory to report raids at once, and he suggested that you should act in the same way."

I also spoke to him about the Fadhlis foregoing their loot claims (in the manner in which the Fadhli Sultan had asked me to put it) and requested him to do the same. While he gave me no definite reply I gathered he would be willing to do this if the other questions were satisfactorily settled.

"I have been very anxious to arrange a meeting between yourself and the Fadhli Sultan," I then added, "but in deference to your wishes expressed in your letter I did not bring him with me although he had been willing to come. I wonder whether you would accompany me to meet him."

He started to make excuses but I told him that that was not necessary and if he did not want to come he had but to say so. He then agreed to come with me, accompanied with five of his men, and I wrote a note to the Fadhli Sultan asking him to come too with five men and meet us half-way. This was sent off on a fast camel to 'Ubar ash Shab'a and 'Aidarus and ourselves mounted and left Husn Halima at half-past ten.

We rode across dried-up cultivation unshaded from the grilling heat until we came to some small clumps of trees at a spot called As Saila. When we were clear of Husn Halima 'Aidarus had signalled with his hand to his men and the whole army had moved off northwards, so that our party all told was reduced to about ten. At As Saila we chose the best-looking bush for shade and lay down on Aidarus's carpet to wait. Getting up after a short time to have a look round I noticed a large body of men about two hundred yards away behind us. These turned out to be some of 'Aidarus's followers so I asked him to tell them to move, which he did, and presently a rumour came that the Fadhli Sultan was arriving with a large army. Investigations showed that there were only seven of them all told.

As they drew near 'Aidarus and his followers and myself went forward to meet them. The two Sultans embraced like long-lost brothers and their men fired salutes. We returned to the carpet and I gave the Sultan and Uncle Muhammad some tea and water as they were very thirsty. We then got down to business and I repeated to them both together most of what I had already told them separately.

"Sultan 'Aidarus," I said to the Fadhli, "has mentioned certain fields to me, that you yourself have said nothing about, and so tell me your side of the story."

As the Fadhli Sultan consistently evaded the question I began to feel that there was something in it.

"I can explain," said Uncle Muhammad, "the question of the lands has been discussed before the 'Abdali Sultan and was ruled to be dead."

"The case is pending at Lahej," broke in the Fadhli, "and I've not come here to discuss business but merely to pay a friendly visit to you and the Lower Yafa'i Sultan."

"I'm surprised at your speaking like that," I said, "you know quite well that I have spent most of my time since being your guest trying to persuade you to come to some sort of arrangement and I've been saying the same things to Sultan 'Aidarus as I have said to you. I haven't the least wish to interfere but only to help and if that's your attitude I'm sorry I've wasted my time and tired myself out for nothing."

"I'm prepared to give a pledge," said Fadhli, "that I will submit to any decision which Sultan Abdul Karim[1] may pass."

After some discussion Sultan 'Aidarus agreed to do the same. Each Sultan then drew a *jambiya* from the belt of one of his followers and handed them to me, repeating that they would accept any decision given. When the pledges had been given to me we drank a loving-cup of somewhat tepid water from the lid of my thermos flask and the party broke up amiably.

We parted from the Yafa'is with mutual hopes for an early meeting and rode on to 'Ubar ash Shab'a. Here the tent had been pitched and Zaidi had some very welcome tea ready. We drank gallons of it but ate only three biscuits between us. After this we lay on the floor and slept for an hour and a half and then started for Zinjibar after I had thanked the 'Aqil for his hospitality and told him not to indulge in any more raids.

[1] Sultan of Lahej.

## TROUBLED WATERS

"On the head and on the eye," he replied tapping his turban, but I had not the least doubt that they would soon be back at their usual pastime.

We were extremely camel sore and tired but it was a nice ride down the Wadi Bana towards the sea, in the cool of the day. There were a good number of trees and much scrub, but on the whole the wadi was dry and barren of recent cultivation owing to this internecine strife between the Yafa'is and the Fadhlis, and the Sultan pointed out to me places like Al Khor where he had previously had a great deal of cultivation. Later we came across the Nazi'a canal again, quite dry, and he complained as usual of the Yafa'is. I pointed out that he had only to settle his differences for this barren desert to be blossoming again. Presently we passed out of the mountains and were once again on the flat plain of the coast.

A long trek brought us to Shems ad Din near Zinjibar. Here the country was green and trees and date palms were plentiful. During the last half hour of our ride we let the camels graze freely from the *shahr* growing on the outskirts of the Abyan settlements, and we reached Zinjibar after seven, where the Sultan, who had ridden on ahead, was waiting for us. A salute was fired from the top of the house which we were lent and where we were soon comfortably installed.

And after a restful night we left early next morning by the beach for Aden, bidding our farewells to the Sultan and all his relations, standing in a row beside him and waving as our car bumped on its way to the shore.

*
**

## PART TWO

*That which is on our foreheads
We must indeed fulfil.*
                              ARABIAN NIGHTS.

*How pleasant it must be to stand on the side of Ararat and to think
"Here my great father Noah stood and my great mother Noah's wife."*
                                             FAR OFF.

*Chapter XI*

## THE FAR OFF HILLS OF HADHRAMAUT AND THE LANDS OF GENESIS

*Tout vient a point qui peut attendre.*     RABELAIS.
*Near acquaintance doth diminish reverent fear.*
                                                SIR PHILIP SIDNEY.

IN the Aden Protectorate we do not, as I have said before, administer the tribes; we hope that contact will lead to harmonious relations and that gradually the tribes will learn to administer themselves. Unlike most other parts of the dependent Empire, the formation, if I can call it so, of the Aden Protectorate was not preceded by a period of exploration or missionary penetration. Most of the country had not even been seen by Europeans before the treaties of protection were signed. In this instance the mountain came to Mahomet and it was in Aden itself that the chiefs and tribesmen learned what a European looked like and what his funny ways were. Perhaps the most important function of Aden from the point of view of the Protectorate is educational, for Arabs, like other people who live in a primitive style, are good imitators.

It is only in very recent times that Mahomet has started going to visit the mountain. Before that there was not enough political staff for it to be customary to travel afar merely to shake hands with a chief. Much contact has been made lately by the Royal Air Force and I expect one day, if justice is done, a statue to Squadron Leader Rickards will be put up in recognition of the fact that most of the thirty-five landing grounds in the Protectorate were planned and built by him. Nowadays a tayāra (bird machine) is a familiar object in the country and no visitors are more welcome than when they drop down out of the skies. Of course contact visits may mean a great increase of work. Even if you only say "how d'ye do" the chief may say lots of other things to you which he would not have thought of or bothered to write if he had not seen you, and you may find yourself embroiled in all sorts of affairs. "Let sleeping dogs lie" is a motto which still has point, even in Aden.

## THE FAR OFF HILLS OF HADHRAMAUT AND THE LANDS OF GENESIS

It was on contact visits that in 1934 I saw some of the remainder of the western part of the protectorate, such as Mukeiras, the 'Audhali capital, the Subeihi country and Habil Jabr in the Redfān mountains. In the sticky heat of an Aden summer it was a pleasant break to soar up in the clear cold air and alight not far from some running stream as at Habil Jabr: or high up in the mountains to look down upon Al Qara, the capital of Lower Yafa'i with its six-storeyed house and its graceful minaret perched as if upon an inverted tumbler in the middle of a deep wide basin.

It was about the time of these visits that the Resident spoke to me about the Hadhramaut. During the previous year he had been there himself, by air, on a four-day visit, but he had always felt that we knew far too little about the eastern part of the protectorate and wanted a more thorough examination to be made of the country than had yet been possible. He hoped, too, that it would be feasible to work for some sort of understanding between the two chief rulers of the country, the Qu'aiti Sultan of Mukalla and the Kathiri Sultan of Seiyun, who were hereditary foes.

We soon began preparations in earnest. At the back of my mind were those words of Hogarth which I had first read in Pemba more than ten years before.

> Interest in Hadhramaut should not be suffered to decline yet. About half the trunk wady still remains unexplored and the least-known part is that upon which border the ancient Mahra tribes.

Since then Rickards and Cochrane, together with Lake as a passenger, had flown down the wadi, and Rickards' sketch map was the most reliable information. It was important that I should also go to the country to the north of the wadi. Boscawen, an East African settler from Tanganyika with a wanderer's instincts, had been there and collected some birds, but he had written nothing about it and all I knew was that he had passed through the country of the Sei'ars and spent a week hunting the oryx with them in the Rub'al Khali. I met Boscawen at the time of his return, just after I arrived at Aden, but when we were making our preparations he was not available. He came again to Aden when we had returned and I asked him why he never wrote anything. His reply was: "I can't spell"; that evening we played Lexicon at Besse's house and as Boscawen tried to get away with CABY for CABBY perhaps there was something in it.

138

The latest travellers to write about the country, Van der Meulen and Von Wissmann, had not been north of the wadi, and the only person who had and had written about it was Mrs. Bent. The Bents had travelled up the Wadi Ser, past the tomb of the prophet Salih, and said that just beyond their furthest point the great desert began. I asked Arabs who had lived in Shibam about this, and the general opinion was that the desert was about fifty miles north of Shibam and that the edge of the mountains and the sand running eastward came within twenty miles of Tarim. They thought that a round trip up to the desert from Shibam and along its edge to some wadi that would bring you back to Tarim ought to take about eight days. So I planned that we should go from Mukalla via Du'an to Shibam and from there make a round trip to Tarim. From Tarim we would follow the wadi, which had been waiting for me so long, to Seihut. From Seihut I proposed to sail back to Mukalla by dhow.

There was, of course, much more to it than that: to make a survey of the social, economic and political condition of the country many contacts were necessary. Our friend Hassan Muhammad kindly volunteered to come with us. Hassan has many friends and contacts. He is a Persian by race, and his family history is one of service to the British Government. Indeed Hassan's peculiarity is his absolute belief in the infallibility of the Government.

Packing things ready for the Hadhramaut reminded me of going to France in the war for the first time—we had so many gadgets. Most of the things I had to take to France were lethal, and most of these we took to the Hadhramaut were scientific, that was the only difference. But bearing France in mind I determined we would not look like Christmas trees, so reduced our baggage to a minimum. Indeed when the time came we were laughed at in Mukalla for having so little. But then Sultan 'Umar, who went round the Hadhramaut just before us, took two hundred soldiers and a brass band, not to mention suites of furniture. So perhaps Mukalla ideas of what constituted a little were based on higher standards than ours.

\* \* \*

## LAND OF GENESIS

The country for which we were bound has long seemed to me the most ancient in the world. In strict accuracy this may not be so, but since I have come back from it the impression has grown stronger on pseudo-scientific grounds as well as on those of sentiment and tradition. The immensity of its barren plateaux and the awe-inspiring, deep, precipitous abysses made me feel alone on top of the most primeval world. It takes me far enough back in time to think that perhaps this land has hardly altered since the last ice or pluvial age carved it out, for nature has done little to clothe it in the soft colours on which we in richer lands are accustomed to rest our eyes.

But all this apart there remains the inner consciousness of the first literature with which most of us became familiar and, study we geology never so hard and believe in evolution firmly as we may, when we think of the beginnings of our world a thought of the Book of Genesis passes automatically through our minds. And in the Hadhramaut Genesis is ever present. As I stood under the firmament of heaven on the barren eocene heights of the Hadhramaut steppes for the first time, I remembered the words: ' In the beginning God created the heaven and the earth."

Here it seemed that Creation had stopped at the very beginning.

And my first breathless look over the mighty wadi of Du'an recalled the Heavenly muse:

> Thou from the first was't present
> And Dove-like sat'st brooding o'er the great Abyss
> And mad'st it pregnant.

In all, I saw the graves of seven giants and heard of three others, not to mention the stories of the whole giant race of 'Ad. I felt that it needed a race of giants to pace the far-spreading steppes and to bridge the vast chasms, and all this could only remind me that: ' There were giants in the land in those days.'

And when I thought of the generations of Adam, why, the whole country breathes of them and I felt it was but a short yesterday since they passed away. The wadis tell of the waters returning from off the face of the earth and the neighbouring island of Soqotra is brought into the story, for there are those who say that it was the Isle of the Blest to which the hero Gilgamesh repaired through the waters of Darkness, the Straits of Bab al Mandeb, to learn the secret of immortality from his ancestor Uta-Napishtim, who told him of the abating of the floods on the mountain of Nisir:

## SONS OF JOKTAN

When the seventh day had come
I brought out a dove and let her go free
The dove flew away and came back
Because she had no place to alight on she came back
I brought out a swallow and let her go free,
The swallow flew away and came back
Because she had no place to alight on she came back
I brought out a raven and let her go free
The raven flew away, she saw the sinking waters
She ate, she pecked in the ground, she croaked, she came not back.

and so I like to think of Uta-Napishtim-Noah talking to his descendant on the shores of the Blest Island of Soqotra where he slept in a reed hut like those we met on our journey.

And when we come to

The children of Shem; Elam, and Asshur, and Arphaxad, and Lud, and Aram.
And the children of Aram; Uz, and Hul, and Gether, and Mash.
And Arphaxad begat Salah; and Salah begat Eber.
And unto Eber were born two sons; the name of one was Peleg; for in his days was the earth divided; and his brother's name was Joktan.
And Joktan begat Almodad, and Sheleph, and Hazarmaveth, and Jerah,
And Hadoram, and Uzal, and Diklah,
And Obal, and Abimael, and Sheba,
And Ophir, and Havilah, and Jobab: all these were the sons of Joktan.

Have I not walked the land of 'Ad the son of Uz and visited the grave of four hundred and thirty-three-year-old Salah and his four hundred and sixty-four-year-old son Eber, which is Hud? And do not all the tribesmen of that land say, we are of Joktan? And does not the land itself bear the name of Hazarmaveth or Hadhramaut? I have seen much of the dwelling of the sons of Joktan which "was from Mesha, as thou goest unto Sephar a mount of the east."

You cannot help it, in the Hadhramaut you are living in Genesis. It is just as if the beduin had realized the latent possibilities of their land as a setting and had staged in it the story of the creation and of the peopling of the world. After telling who were the sons of Joktan the Bible is silent as to what became of them, so that you come to a country as if it were lost to you, and there feel you have discovered them and seen their life and adventures—the living story of the sons of Joktan in a world that lives

## THE FAR OFF HILLS OF HADHRAMAUT AND THE LANDS OF GENESIS

still in the fashion of the Old Testament. You have seen the descendants of Joktan and their life as you have read of those of his brother Peleg.

Now any seriously-minded historian will tell you that all this is veriest legend and the mythologist will tell you that I have not told it critically or even correctly. The historian will say that in face of the South Arabian inscriptions the legend and tradition have been shown to be without foundation, and the mythologist may point out that even if you identify Soqotra with the Isle of the Blest, that the story of the Deluge is an interpolation in the Epic of Gilgamesh. But what they think and say is of no importance when you realize that the giants are the tribal ancestors of the people and that they believe it all, and that it is of vital importance to them that they are descendants of Joktan. It is of far more importance than the forgotten truths of the old kingdoms of Ausan and Qataban and Saba and Himyar and Reidan and their forgotten trinity of Sin and Shems and Athtar and their forgotten language. What they built is still there and stands, the work of the sons of 'Ad, who lived 1,200 years and begat 4,000 sons and daughters.

"And when the sons of 'Ad had passed away," said the Hadhramaut historian to me, "there arose in the valley the sons of Hadhramaut, the son of Qahtan (Hazarmaveth the son of Joktan). His name was 'Amr but he was nicknamed Hadhramaut—'Death is present'—on account of the troublous times in which he lived." Then came the tribes of Kinda, a descendant of Hazarmaveth's brother Ya'arub, through Kahlan, and the tribes of Hadhramaut and of Kinda were always fighting but finally Kinda prevailed and the Hadhramaut tribes became beduin. Kinda had four kings in the country of Hadhramaut and they had an idol called Haslad whom all the people of Hadhramaut revered as their god. And the Kinda kings ruled for many centuries until Islam came and the Prophet of God sent Ziyad bin Dhubeid, who converted the tribes of the Hadhramaut without bloodshed, and four kings and a queen were appointed. But when Abubekr became Commander of the Faithful, the tribes in the Hadhramaut fell away from Islam, so Ziyad brought an army and slew the five rulers. After this the Hadhramaut again followed Islam until in the 128th year of the Flight (A.D. 746) the tribes revolted and became seceders, followers of the Ibadhi creed. But twelve years later Ma'n bin Zaida came with an army and defeated the men of Hadhramaut at a battle at Furt al Hussein, which was between Henin and Qatn, slaying 15,000 of them

142

# HADRAMAUT HISTORY

Then Ma'n bin Zaida ruled over the Hadhramaut for the Abbasides and compelled the people to wear their black dress.

Hadhramaut remained loyal to the Abbasides till 263 (A.D. 877) but when their dynasty came to an end it was independent until Yemen tribes occupied it as well as Aden in 410 (A.D. 1019). There were three Yemeni dynasties until in 745 (A.D. 1344) the Al Yamāni of the Āl Tamim occupied Tarim. At this time there were three ruling tribes, the Tamimi, the Nahd and the Saberat, and the first two are still important. In 894 (A.D. 1489) the Kathīris began to rise to power and gained fame under their great leader Bedr Bu Tuweirak, but his people were not loyal to him and in his time the Portuguese came to Shihr. He brought mercenaries from the Zeidis of Yemen, the Yafa'is, and Turks from Suleiman the Magnificent, and from this rose another period of Yemeni domination and two Yafa'i dynasties, that of the Kasadis and the present one of the Qu'aitis.

In 1246 (A.D. 1830) 'Umar bin 'Awadh al Qu'aiti was a soldier in the army of the Nizam of Hyderabad. He had lived in Shibam and sent his family from India to Qatn. At this time all the small villages round Qatn were Yafa'i but Shibam was under the Āl 'Isa Kathīris, ruled over by Sultan Mansur.

Sultan Mansur, however, had no money so he sold half the town of Shibam to the Qu'aitis of Qatn and both he and they ruled in the town. On the occasion of the 'Id al Fitr the Yafa'is went to visit their relations in Qatn and Sultan Mansur killed all the Yafa'is who remained in Shibam, declaring that the country was his. This was the beginning of the Qu'aiti-Kathīri trouble. Fighting was continual but the Kathīris were more powerful. Some of the Yafa'is then sent a mission to 'Umar bin 'Awadh in India and it was for this reason that he sent his three sons to live at Qatn. He also sent soldiers who besieged Shibam for sixteen years, during which the inhabitants were reduced to eating leather. At last the Seiyids of Āl 'Aidarus were called in to arbitrate and they decided that the Qu'aitis should have one half of Shibam and the Kathīris the other half. This was agreed to and in 1274 (A.D. 1858) Shibam was divided.

Sultan Mansur, however, was not satisfied. He prepared a certain house for a feast and placed gunpowder in the building and then invited the Yafa'is to dinner, including the three sons of 'Umar bin 'Awadh with their slaves. But they were warned of what was to happen, so one of the sons sent an excuse saying that they had received good news from their father and were celebrating the occasion. However he sent small groups of

143

THE FAR OFF HILLS OF HADHRAMAUT AND THE LANDS OF GENESIS

territory; here and there are towns and districts under direct rule and there are towns which are little city states allowed autonomy by the Sultans. The tribes, nomad and settled, are not subjects, but to a greater or lesser degree under the influence of one of the two Sultans, allied to them perhaps, and to a certain extent controlled by the fact that the Sultans hold the ports and the markets.

The seat of the Government of His Highness the Sultan of Shihr and Mukalla—the Qu'aiti Sultan—is at Mukalla. His dominions are divided into five provinces, Shihr, Mukalla, Du'an, Hajr and Shibam, each under a governor. There are also other areas under his influence or control but not included in any province. The capital of the Kathiri Sultan is Seiyun.

*Chapter XII*

## THE GATEWAY OF THE HADHRAMAUT

*And in due course landed at Makalla of Hazramaut.*
ARABIAN NIGHTS. BURTON.

PREPARATIONS for our journey moved on to completion and we began counting the days before we should start, like schoolboys ticking off the days left till holidays. When you have wanted anything as badly as I had wanted this journey, you are always in a fever lest something should happen to prevent it. But at last on October 29th we embarked on one of Besse's ships, the *Al Amin*. Meryem, his daughter, and he took us on board and we had a good dinner, "honest talk and wholesome wine," on the bridge over which the captain presided. Afterwards, as we talked, we watched the loading of sugar and bales of old newspapers and at about ten o'clock we said good-bye and were off.

The next day we spent at sea. The blue of the sea was just sufficiently disturbed to sparkle with the sunlight. The sky was quite cloudless and the coast, which was visible all the way, stood on the horizon as a long yellow line of sand and rock. To Ahwar the way recalled previous journeys but after that it was new.

At five o'clock the next morning we were drawing very close to the land. It was still dark but the houses of Mukalla were dimly visible through the mist. As the sun rose over the horizon on the seaward side it lit up the white town and gave a pink glow to the steep face of the mountains behind. Entering the harbour we were reminded of Zanzibar, though the minarets of some of Mukalla's thirteen mosques are an added beauty. Tall, white-washed houses come right down to the sea, most of them having four or five storeys, or more. Looking from the sea the Sultan's new palace, built about five years ago, lies on the extreme left at the very edge of the town, for near-by is an archway leading out to the caravan halt where the camels are tethered. The full extent of the town to the east was not yet visible. Mukalla, long familiar to me in picture, had become a reality.

There were a number of dhows in the harbour when we steamed in. Several rowing-boats were soon out and the doctor and two others came aboard to welcome us. The doctor, a young Hindu called Ranade, was a new introduction to Mukalla engaged by Sultan 'Umar. With him were 'Ali Hakim, a well-known character in Aden and Mukalla, and for all his littleness of stature one of the most kind-hearted men imaginable, and Msellem Bal'ula, who is the Treasurer and speaks English. Soon after six we said good-bye to the captain, our luggage was stowed into one boat, ourselves into another, and to the chant of the oarsmen we were rowed to the stone steps of the Customs. At Mukalla the term Customs house is more than a courtesy title. There is a well-built quay, where dhows can come alongside, and good godowns. Over the gateway is the inscription AL GAITY CUSTOMS. This recalled to me a certain theatre in the Strand, and in fact, until we got fussy at Aden about Arabic spelling, the Sultan was generally known as the Gaiety Sultan.

There is a large open space before the godowns which was full of townspeople gathered to witness our arrival. Here bales of sugar, baskets of dates and bundles of old newspapers imported from abroad, jostled with huge packages of Hamumi tobacco ready to be shipped. We got into the Sultan's car and were driven through the archway into the street, and along the water-front where the dhows are built. It is flanked by busy coffee shops and is reminiscent of the Vieux Port at Marseilles with its open-air cafés. Soon we left the sunshine and passing through the narrow crowded bazaar, came out again on the waterfront with a low sea wall on our left. In the town and along the sea-front we had passed police stations and blue-clad police on duty and here were khaki-clad soldier guards who turned out to salute.

We were barely installed in the guest-house when Sultan, or Jemadar as he is more familiarly known, Salim bin Ahmed, the Wazir and Regent during the absence of the Sultan in India, came to welcome us, dressed Indian fashion, with a long coat and tarbush. This was our first meeting with Sultan Salim, and during our stays in Mukalla and Shihr we appreciated greatly his innumerable kindnesses to us. After he had left we had breakfast and then went to return his visit at the palace, Qasr al Mu'in. He met us at the head of the stairs and ushered us into a drawing-room filled with silk-covered chairs, china jars, sideboards, whatnots, mirrors and miscellaneous ornaments. Large photographs of the Sultan, Sultan Ghalit and of the Nizam of Hyderabad, decorated the walls. We were given coffee with sweet biscuits and after a short talk Sultan Salim took us round the palace.

The principal sight was the Sultan's bathroom, which had the largest sunk bath I have ever seen. How I would like to be Sultan of Mukalla and bathe in it every day! But I think I should change the decorations of English country scenes painted on the walls.

With the official visits over we started to make ourselves familiar with Mukalla, where we spent seven happy days. If I was not disappointed with Mukalla from the sea, Mukalla from the inside more than fulfilled my expectations. The immediate reaction was perhaps all the greater as I had just come from Aden. To me modern Aden is almost undiluted ugliness, but Mukalla has a real beauty of its own.

Mukalla has only one city wall: it needs no others for nature has provided the steep cliffs of Qarat al Mukalla just behind the town to protect it from the landward side, and the mountains come so close to the sea at its east end that the approach to the town along the narrow strip of coast could easily be protected. There are four little white forts perched on the edge of the cliff, which would be occupied if there was trouble. The one wall, which protects the west of the town, runs down from the mountains to the sea, a matter of two to three hundred yards. There are only two buildings that overlook it—the guest-house and the palace—and between them the road runs through the city gate to the camel park beyond; the gate is of fine Indian design and the palace is also Indian though not quite so beautiful.

The palace and the guest-house are therefore in the west of the West End of Mukalla, called Bara as Sida. The quarter reaches up to the fine new mosque which Sultan 'Umar was building a few hundred yards to the east of the palace. There is even electric light as far as Sultan 'Umar's mosque and I have seen it turned on, though this does not always happen. This is the residential quarter and contains the finest houses in Mukalla.

Like London, Mukalla has also a city—Al Bilad—which is the oldest part of the town and built on the promontory that forms an arm of the harbour. Towering above the other houses in this quarter is the seven-storeyed palace of the old Kasadi Naqibs, now used for Government offices. It is surrounded by four- and five-storeyed houses, mostly belonging to merchants in narrow dirty streets, and the slum huts of the Somali quarter. In front of the Government offices is the dispensary; and the prison and the cemetery, which occupies a large area, are also in Al Bilad.

There are two other quarters in the town, Haft al 'Abīd, the poorer quarter, which runs from the cemetery to the mountains and along to the east and under the cliffs, and Haft al Hara which runs from the cemetery westwards and includes Sultan 'Umar's mosque and the houses between the sea and the mountains.

From the window of the bedroom in the guest-house I could lie abed and watch the endless activities of the camel park, called Therb, which at the time of our visit was thronged with camels, donkeys and beduin. Towards evening strings of camels would amble slowly along the road from the interior, and in the early morning groups of beduin wrangled as they loaded the camels for the start of the long trek up-country. Frequently there were several hundreds of camels couched outside the wall and the beduin lit their camp-fires almost underneath our windows. Morning and evening they gathered the camels into groups and fed them with stalks of millet bought in the bazaar. All day long two craftsmen sat just outside the gate shaping curved pieces of wood into the frameworks of pack saddles, and every now and again a group of black-cloaked women bearing skins filled with water wandered among the camps selling the water to the beduin.

Beyond Therb across the mouth of the wadi was Sherij Bā Salam, the Subian village. The Subians, whose name, I am told, is derived from the word meaning "youth," come mostly from the Wadi Hajr and so in other parts of the Protectorate are called Hajris. They do all the menial jobs, hewing wood and drawing water, and are not allowed to sleep in the towns but must have their quarters outside. Between Therb and Sherij Bā Salam was the drying-ground, where the fish are spread out on the sand to dry in the sun and then gathered into piles some six feet high and finally taken to the interior for manure, camel fodder or human consumption.

East of Mukalla is another suburb, Khalf. This, too, is dedicated to fish, for recently Sultan 'Umar removed the fish-curing and drying industry from inside the town to Khalf, where he built new godowns. The rocks all round are strewn with large split fish, sun curing. . The manufacture of fish manure and the preparation of dried fish (wazif) is a large industry of the coastal area, and in the list of exports fish products come third in importance. Besides wazif the other fish products are sifa or fish oil, a little of which is made in Mukalla and Shihr, hanit which is cooked and

## A PROGRESSIVE GOVERNMENT

dried tamad fish and sold for local and up-country consumption, safif which is dried tamad and tarnak fish, lakhm, dried shark, of which a great deal is prepared in Mukalla and rish (shark fins), a certain amount of which are sent to China.

The sea teems with fish and one day standing at the Customs we thought the water was black. Closer examination showed it was black with fish which simply had not room to move. What the smell of Mukalla can have been like before Sultan 'Umar removed the industry to Khalf I cannot imagine, for as it is the pervading aroma of the bazaar is fish. The other outstanding memory of it is flies, flies in solid droves. I asked Zaidi what he thought of the bazaar and he said: "The men are made of flies." Indeed everyone walked in aura of them.

According to all the rules of hygiene, dysentery ought to be the prevailing disease, but far from it. When I inspected Dr. Ranade's dispensary in the yellow building in front of the Kasadi palace, he told me he had used nearly two hundredweights of Epsom salts between April and October. There is stagnant water everywhere, but there is surprisingly little malaria. The water supply coming in pipes from springs and reservoirs at Bakezebur, about five miles north of Mukalla, is unprotected at its source and over part of its course, but there is no typhoid. I can only hint at the condition of other sanitary arrangements, but there is no hookworm. Every canon of public health is flouted, but a merciful providence must keep a special eye on Mukalla. The principal ailments are diseases of the eye and rheumatic affections of the joints.

Still, the Mukalla Government has set its feet on the right path. That there is a doctor at all says something, that there is a piped water supply from what would be an unimpeachable source if protected is a lot more. In other ways, too, I saw signs of progress. There are three Government schools, one of which teaches English. The other two are big schools with four hundred and forty boys between them. There is much with which the scientific educationalist might find fault, but the one thing that is important is there, the will to teach and the will to learn.

Mukalla has other industries besides fish, though they are minor ones, such as the preparation of simsim or cooking-oil and a fine grade of lime. There is craftsmanship in Mukalla too: the workers in silver make dagger scabbards which are much sought after, and from here come the baskets wrongly called Aden baskets, bright of many colours, shaped like a broad bin, which the Jews in Aden sell to passengers. The women who

## THE GATEWAY OF THE HADHRAMAUT

make them also make coloured mats and fans, sitting plaiting by the roadside.

We tried to photograph the normal activities of the bazaar and the water-front, but it was practically impossible, for the whole population simply downed tools and stopped to stare wherever and whenever we appeared. If we went on foot we were pursued by a throng of sightseers. In the narrow bazaar street all the traffic we met came to a standstill: the blue-clad police cleared a way with a will, and time and again I begged them to stop, for the crowds were always friendly and I thought they might resent being swept out of the way. After a few days of this things improved, and as we drove or walked through the bazaar there were greetings on all sides. One afternoon the Regent held a military review for us and after the march past there was an amusing programme of sports. There was no particular competition about them and so many men were just told off to run a sack race, a three-legged race or whatever it might be.

We had considerable entertainment in Mukalla one way and another and found the Government very fond of what the Mauritian calls "protocol." Thus if it was official entertainment it was given at the palace, and Sultan Salim dressed up in long coat and trousers, and meals were more or less à l'Anglaise. If he entertained us privately we went to his house and he wore a shirt and futa. Here we had Arab entertainment, and at tea drunk it without milk and with much sugar in little glasses. This is a Javanese habit and tea, to a large extent, is displacing coffee in the Hadhramaut.

One morning Ganess told us we were dining out. It was the first I had heard of it but he said he had been asked to cook dinner at the palace as we were dining there. At about six, when we had come back from our afternoon drive, Msellem came in.

"It will give His Excellency the Minister much pleasure if you will dine with him to-night at the palace."

We accepted solemnly, as if it had been an entirely novel idea. As darkness fell the lights were on early. The palace sprang into a blaze of illumination inside and out, and with this heavy load on the current the guest-house lights were dim. We walked across to the palace and at the head of the stairs were greeted by Sultan Salim and ushered into the drawing-room, where the other guests were already assembled. They were Yusuf Sharif, a leading Indian merchant and the Chief of Customs, Msellem, 'Ali Hakim and the doctor. Later experience taught me that they were the only guests who ever came to these functions, for they included all the

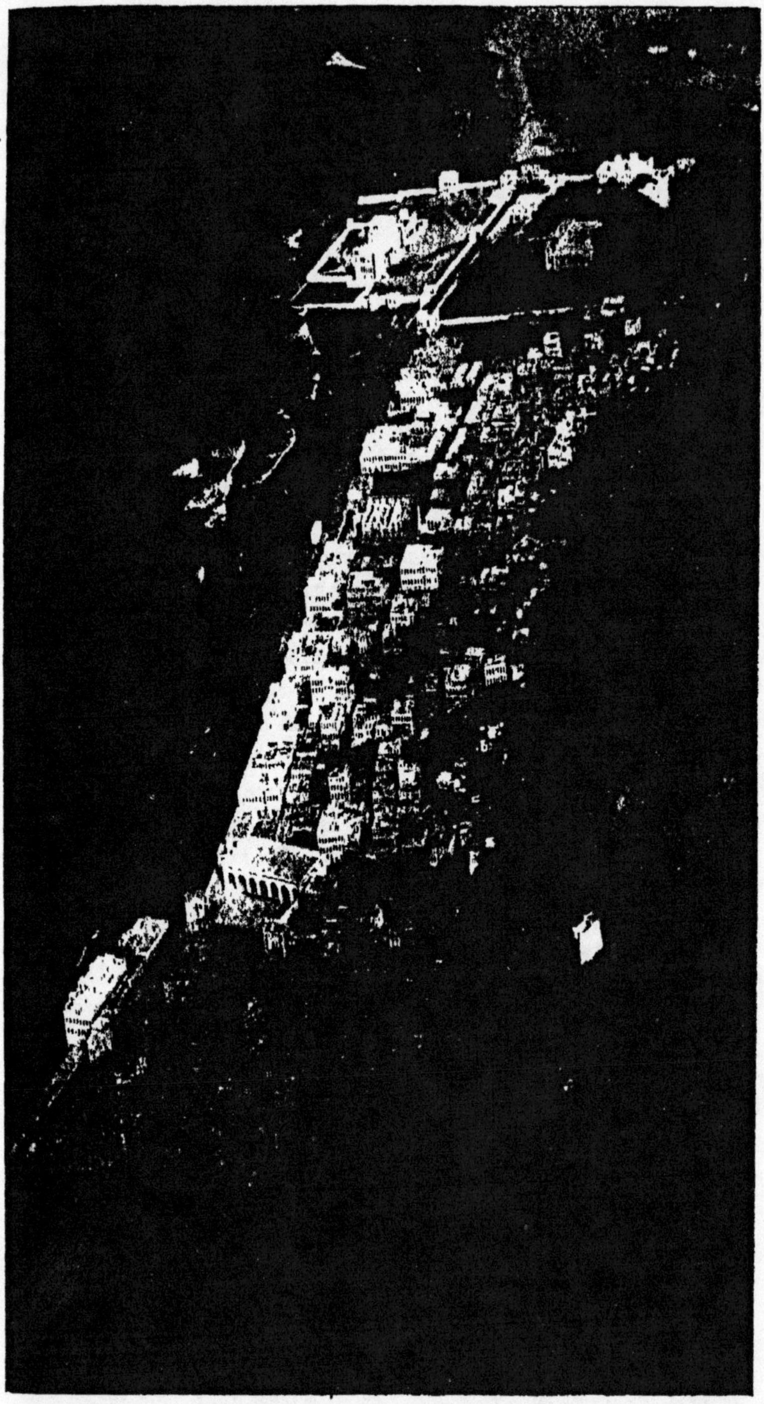

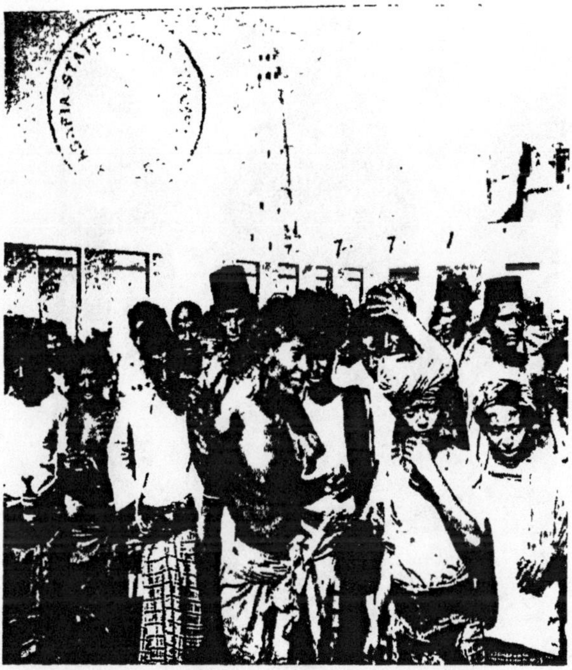

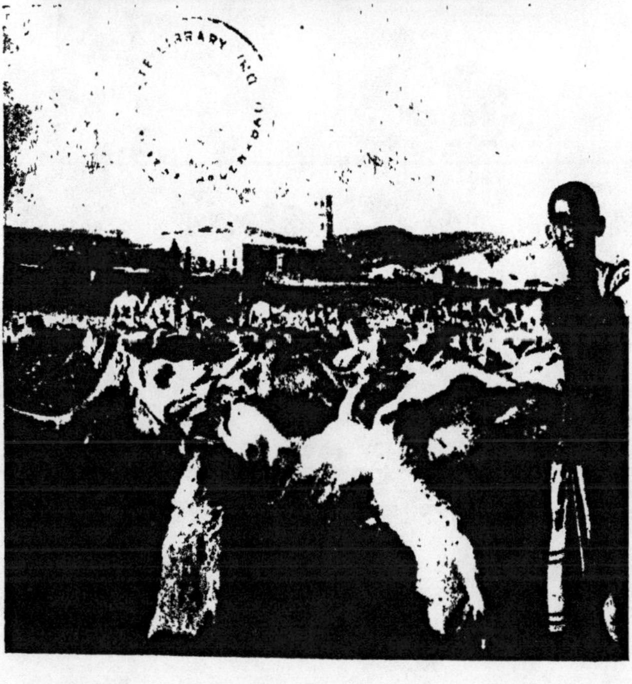

The Guest House, Mukalla,
Standing L.-R.—'Abdul Malik, driver, Dr. Renade, 'Msellem, Salih 'Ali,
Seiyids 'Abdul Qadir, photographer, driver

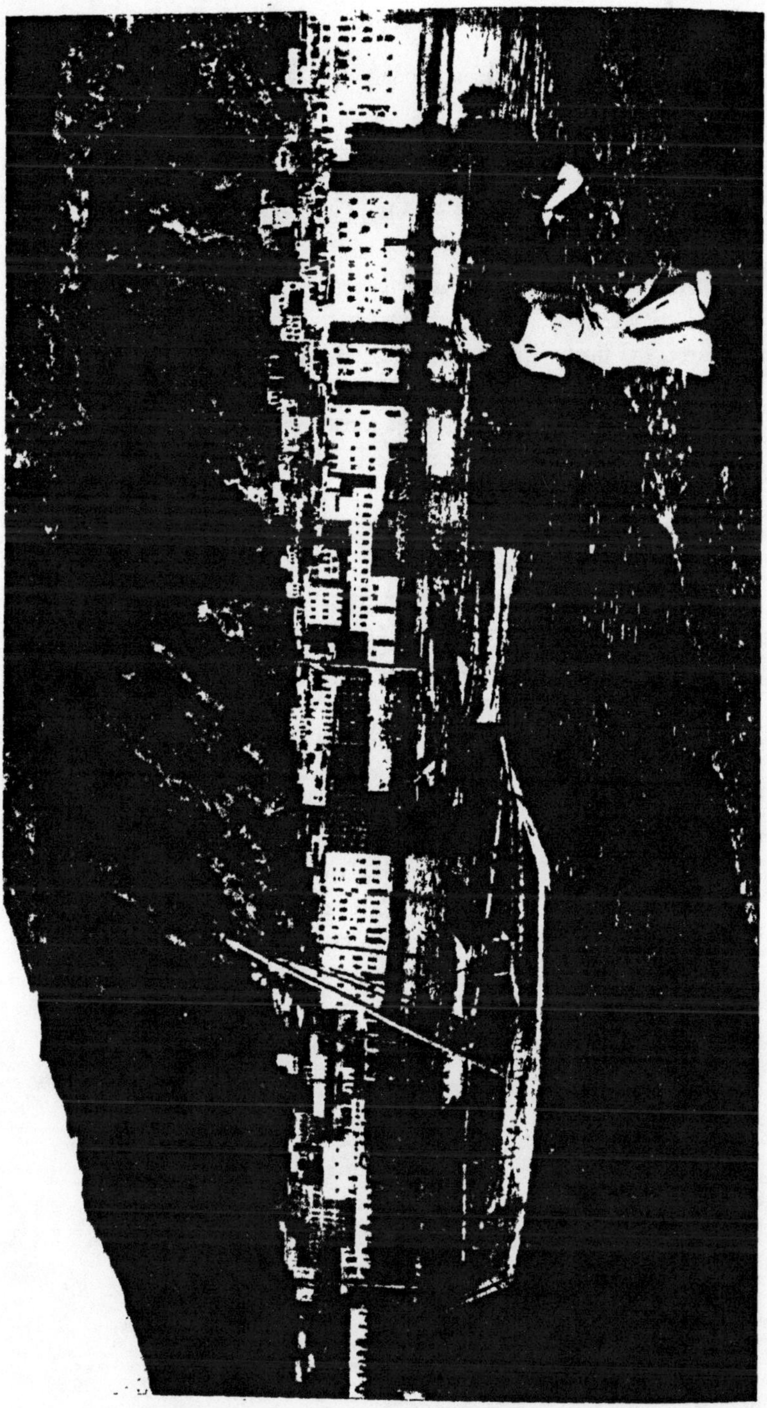

## DINNER AT "GOVERNMENT HOUSE"

people in Mukalla who had a nodding acquaintance with a knife and fork.

The party reminded me more than anything of a party at a Colonial Government House. All the local visitors were Government officials and they brought up little stories of what had been happening in the course of the day's work and the day's bazaar stories. There were titbits intended to make His Excellency laugh, and His Excellency listened and made the usual little jokes. He himself showed us the photographs taken at the tea-party, and they were passed round and admired. The Major Domo announced dinner. It was served in the dining-room in European style, a snowy table-cloth, good silver and a service with an Arabic monogram and the device "Government of Mukalla." The food was the joint production of Ganess and the palace chef, and their efforts made a somewhat overwhelming repast. After coffee in the drawing-room we left early. This was a concession to Arab custom, for when you are invited to an Arab dinner you go for the dinner and not for the talk, the bridge or round games. So, when the dinner is over there is no excuse for delay. As a slight corrective to such a meal we strolled up the main street and through the bazaar, which at this hour was almost deserted. A few shops were still open and groups of men sat round the smoky flares of tin lamps or the now popular incandescent kerosene lamps known as terik. There were two or three cafés open. In one, whose walls were decorated with gay floral paintings, a gramophone was playing an attractive Arabic song. Some of the "locals" and a few beduin sat round beating time. The street still reeked of dried fish, but it was strangely silent, though we glimpsed lights through chinks of doors or shuttered windows which told that the occupants were not yet abed.

The nights were always quiet, though sometimes I lay awake and heard the sentry beating out the hours on a gong, just as it used to happen in Pemba.

153

*Chapter XIII*

## TRAVEL IN THE HADHRAMAUT

*If you will be a traveller, have always the eyes of a falcon, the ears of an ass, the face of an ape, the mouth of a hog, the shoulder of a camel, the legs of a stag, and see that you never want two bags very full, that is one of patience and another of money.*
                                                                                        FLORIO.

WE soon fell into a daily routine at Mukalla. We awoke early and at sunrise sat on our veranda drinking tea and eating fruit. It was refreshingly cool in this morning hour; the sea was calm and even the beduin at Therb were quiet. The only sound was of birds in the dewy garden. Presently Therb woke up; so did the army,[1] and the policeman over the wall beat out seven strokes, whereat we bathed, dressed and had breakfast.

After breakfast the car came at nine, and the morning was generally

---

[1] The Sultan of Mukalla has about eight hundred slaves and they are the best treated section of the population. "Slave" really conveys quite a wrong idea if you think of *Uncle Tom's Cabin* and other heartrending stories, for the Mukalla slaves and generally those in South Arabia are spoiled children. There are two hundred and fifty of them in the army, all of African origin. They receive from one to three dollars a month pocket money, rations and quarters. They are provided with wives and given milk, scarce in Mukalla, for their families. The remainder of the regular army consists of 350 to 400 Yafa'is. They each get nine dollars a month with no extras, so that they are not so well off as the slaves. Most of the regular army is stationed in Mukalla and while we were there we watched—or heard—their morning parades, which took place every two days in the palace yard when they marched and counter-marched to the cheerful beat of tomtoms and kettledrums. But on Thursdays they parade in the estuary behind Therb and we watched them swinging proudly out of the main gate, with the band at full blast. They have only one set of uniform which is kept for special occasions. There are 1,000 to 1,200 irregulars, paid seven dollars a month each and officered by eleven Muqaddams with eleven Muawins. A commando is a hundred men and these troops, who are all Yafa'is, garrison the interior towns. Defence forms the biggest item on the expenditure side of the Mukalla budget—about Rs. 225,000 out of a total of Rs. 300,000 which does not include the civil list. The total revenue is probably about Rs. 700,000 raised mostly from customs, about Rs. 350,000, tobacco industry, Rs. 120,000, and the dues on loaded camels, about Rs. 90,000.

spent in inspections or business talks. We visited the schools, the customs, the police stations, the dispensary, the water supply, the prison and the bazaar. Sometimes we went out to lunch, but more often we had it at home. Till four we worked or saw callers. Then came tea, and at half-past four the car with Afzel Khan Monen Khan, the Afghan chauffeur and the garage boy. East we drove to Ras Mukalla and west to Fuwa, Manawarih and the parts round Dis. Anywhere a car could go we went. At Fuwa, where is the landing-ground, the Governor, complete with hurriedly assumed black coat and sword, came rushing out to greet us; at Manawarih was the lovely house of the ex-Wazir all shut up. The roads in this direction were quite varied and there were charming little lagoons surrounded by green turf and thronged with flamingoes and wild duck, so tame that you could approach within twenty feet of them. We went to Fuwa by the shore and by the overland route. The former was the faster and the driver loved to send his Essex Six along at fifty miles an hour, scattering crabs and gulls in all directions. As we came the line of gulls leant forward as one bird, took off, wheeled round with shrill cries and alighted as we passed. There were casualties among crabs, for unlike their yellow cousins on the beach three hundred miles westward, they had not learnt road sense. Near Mukalla white drifts of sand separated the shore from the land road; just before sunset the shadows on the drifts lengthened and their tips were tinged with rosy pink.

Beyond Dis was Bakezebur and the springs and reservoirs for Mukalla's water. At An Naq'a was the Sultan's summer house, rather in disrepair, but wired for the portable electric plant he takes from palace to palace. Its only piece of furniture was a pathetic derelict Erard piano, whose keys we struck from sheer pity whenever we went there; it was said to have come from a French warship wrecked at Ras Hafun some twenty-five years ago. What stories that poor piano might tell. The garden, with its lovely view over the wadi to the sea, had shady bedams, some coco-nuts, guavas, paw-paws and oranges, and grapes trailed over a framework. There were neat little beds of radishes, and chillies. There is a small swimming-bath in the garden and a swing for children. The Sultan uses the palace for two months during the date season, at which time many of the richer inhabitants adjourn to the neighbourhood to eat the fruit.

One day, as we were returning from this direction on foot, I made the acquaintance of one of the Sultan's gunners, dressed in an old military greatcoat. He was a Mgoni from southern Tanganyika who knew Lake Nyasa and spoke fluent Swahili. He told us he had come to Mukalla as a boy. He was married here and no longer desired to go home.

We also visited Gheil Ba Wazir, the centre of the Hamumis tobacco industry. Our road at first lay along the main Du'an caravan route, dotted with forts and drinking fountains. One of the principal features of the caravan roads of the Hadhramaut are the numberless siqayas or public fountains, which have been set up for the benefit of thirsty travellers. They are roofed in and usually whitewashed and have a number of apertures on all four sides. A vessel, generally an empty tin, is provided, and anyone wanting a drink puts it through one of the holes into the cistern inside. Most siqayas are given by private benefactors and money dedicated for the purpose pays for someone in the nearest village to keep it filled with water. There were many along the road we passed, though where the motor track deviates from the caravan route they were not to be seen.

Soon after passing Shiheir, a small town with a few well-cared-for gardens growing pomegranates, tobacco, dates, coco-nut palms, figs, water melons, tomatoes, guavas, onions, lady fingers, chillies, grapes, sweet potatoes and maize, we saw the walls of Gheil Ba Wazir in the distance and wound round the outskirts of the town walls to the gate leading into the Sultan's garden. Here was a well-built Indian bungalow set amongst shady trees. Immediately in front of the house was a large swimming-bath nearly 100 feet long, furnished with a boat and water chutes.

After a short rest we left again to visit the town, the water supply and the tobacco plantations. The principal tobacco nurseries are at Al Quf, about three miles from the town. In the distance it reminded me of a South Wales coalfield, for its forest of well-tackle looked like pit-head machinery. Round the wells are the beds where the tobacco seedlings are grown. When they are three or four inches high they are taken from Al Quf to Al Harth, which we visited next, and planted out in rows. In due course the crop is gathered and dried; drying barns are unknown. The total annual value of the crop is said to be five lakhs, of which the Sultan gets Rs. 120,000 in duty and ground rent, and the cultivators a profit of Rs. 80,000, the cost of production being estimated at three lakhs.

Gheil Ba Wazir was large but dirty and with more than a fair allotment

## PREPARING FOR AN INLAND JOURNEY

of flies. Outside the western gate of the town are the pottery workers, one of whom kindly made a jar for us. He sat to the side of his wheel and turned it with his foot while he shaped the jar with his hand as it turned round. In this town, as in Mukalla, all the women, however poor, are veiled, and even young children drew their head veils in front of their faces as we went past. The poorer women wear a cloak which falls from the top of the head almost to the ankles at the back and, leaving a hole for the face which is covered by a thin veil, falls to just below the knees in front. This is the buibui, the outdoor dress of women in Zanzibar and here for the first time I saw it in its native home.

Usually we came back from our drives at about six, and from then till dinner either paid or received visits. After dinner came more visits and we worked again till bed-time. Meanwhile we were not idle in making preparations for our journey up-country. We had said that we wanted to leave on Sunday and hoped that with the usual delays we should be able to get away on Monday, November 5th.

The principal caravan routes to the interior are so organized after centuries of common use that there is really no more difficulty in arranging for departure from Mukalla to the interior than in arranging a departure from London to the Continent. In London one probably goes to a travel agency; in Mukalla one goes to one of the brokers of the beduin. As we were going to Du'an we went to the cheerful, smiling Ba 'Ubeid. The Wadi Du'an routes to the interior are worked by the Marashida and Khama clans of the great Seibani tribe, and although the fares are not printed in a local Bradshaw they are settled and well known. Here they are as Ba 'Ubeid gave them to us: By donkey, wata and 'aser, that is to say riding over the level country and over the rough and hilly places, standard rate 15 to 16 dollars. If you are under normal size or over normal size you pay less or more according to weight, very much in the same way as you do when travelling by air. The limits each way are from 13 to 20 dollars. By donkey, wata, i.e., riding only over level country, standard fare 10 to 11 dollars with limits according to weight of from 8 to 15 dollars. Each passenger is allowed free transport of up to three frasilas or sixty pounds of food. The camel fares are, wata and 'aser, 10 dollars, and wata 5 dollars. In the same way there is a free allowance of up to three frasilas of food but no allowance for weight.

From these figures it will be seen that the aristocratic means of transport on the Du'an road is the donkey. Excess luggage is charged at freight rates which are, by camel, 10 dollars for a bahar of twenty frasilas, and by donkey 1½ dollars a frasila.[1]

The really luxurious traveller also engages a couple of *ma'ras* or porters who proceed on foot the whole way carrying, like a Chinaman or a milkman, a pole across their shoulders from which is suspended a basket at each end containing light breakables. These men cost about Rs. 12 each for the journey. They keep by the traveller's side all the way, provide in theory liquid refreshment when required, gather the wood for fires at night and generally perform such domestic duties as may be required of them. Ba 'Ubeid, however, told us that it had been provided in our terms with our caravan-men that they should provide firewood and water at halts. We learned afterwards in the interior that the service must always be stipulated for in advance, otherwise travellers are charged extra.

Negotiations were completed in due course. Ba 'Ubeid got us most delightful Murshidis, little dark men with long curly greasy hair, black cloths wrapped round their waists, a spare one that could be used as plaid or turban, and nothing else except indigo to protect them from sun and cold. They wore jambiyas at their waists and carried fairly modern rifles decorated with silver. In the Hadhramaut more than in the west of the protectorate the rifles seem ancient at first sight because of the silver decoration and because they invariably fix a rounded block of wood covered with hide on to the butts. In the old matchlocks this was intended to take the recoil, but of course it is no more than ornament with a modern rifle.

The little beduin slipped silently into the guest-house, creatures of the wild, as out of place as deer in a drawing-room, their glances darting timidly but curiously at everything as they sized up us and our baggage. It is with humiliation that I confess to being assessed as an extra outsize. A special donkey had to be obtained for me from a day and half's journey away, and I had to pay a supplement of two dollars on the maximum fare. Hassan should certainly have been charged extra too, for at the beginning of the journey he was carrying a lot of superfluous fat and I felt it was most unfair

[1] The traveller's liabilities have not ended with the payment of the fares, for he has to provide rations for his donkey-men and camel-men at the rate of one man to one animal for donkeys, and one man up to three animals for camels. For donkey-men the rations cost from a half to one and a half dollars a head according to whether they eat with the traveller or not. The rations for camel-men cost two dollars a head as they take eight days over the journey instead of six. The rations to be purchased are, flour, oil and ghee, rice, dried fish, dates, spices and onions, coffee and dry ginger. Rations are only paid for if the caravan is accompanied by passengers.

## PROCRASTINATIONS

when he was assessed as normal size. D., also an outsize in height (I ought to say that she protests against the insinuation and says she is *only* five feet eight inches and fairly slim), escaped public humiliation by being provided with His Highness's mule. This extremely kind attention was due to Sultan 'Umar who, before leaving Mukalla for India, left directions that the mule which he himself had ridden on his journey to the Hadhramaut should be offered to D. When we had completed all our arrangements we were overwhelmed by the Qu'aiti authorities stepping in, taking over all the transport and insisting on paying all our expenses from Mukalla to Du'an.

At last dawned Monday, November 5th, the day on which we should have started, and until the afternoon we urged the necessity of going, but of course in the morning, when the baggage ought to have left, neither camels nor donkeys appeared, though Ba 'Ubeid brought along the beduin to make a final inspection of the loads. Two porters also came to see what they would have to carry. It seemed to us that there was very little, though what there was was of rather unusual shapes and included a rangefinder, a tin case of maps, a cinema camera, a plane table and its legs, and some thermos flasks. When they had seen it they said "Is this all?" Were assured that it was, laughed, and went away and that was the last we saw of them. Another pair were then brought and they took the job on.

At three o'clock we sent the baggage downstairs in the hope that something might happen, and an hour later three camels were brought into the garden to be loaded. The camel-men then proceeded to select their packages with customary gesticulation and argument, and tie them together in loads of equal weight. After further delay donkeys were brought as our load was too much for the camels alone. When at last the animals were laden it was much too late to start, so it was arranged that the baggage would go on to Tila as Sufla and we would go there by car the next day.

When at last all the animals were loaded the procession moved out of the garden and through the western gate, and we were not in the least surprised to see it stop there, at Therb, the camel park. The camels were couched and the donkeys were unloaded. Their first day's march, perhaps two hundred yards, was over.

When this excitement was at an end 'Ali Hakim came in to say that the mule was below. 'Ali Hakim, who to paucity of inches combines generosity of girth as well as of heart, got on it to show off its paces. Sultán Salim assisted by applying his stick to the mule's hindquarters, and though the gallant 'Ali was not thrown off he was unable to remain on. Much to my dismay I retired to bed with a sudden attack of fever, and D. was assaulted in bed (short of bedclothes which had gone on with the luggage) by an outsize in beetles. The creature has now gone to its eternal home in the British Museum, but I do not think I am exaggerating if I say that from horn to tail it was four inches long.

Mercifully my attack of fever was practically over in the morning and we were soon ready to start. We found Sultan Salim outside and the court photographer armed with his large camera. This was our third heavy engagement with him; we felt as if we were film stars. We were taken on the steps, under the trees and beside the cars, but at last it was over. We got into the cars and, committed to the peace and safety of Allah, drove off through the western gate.

As far as Harshiat the road was familiar and a few minutes later we saw another village and were surprised to hear that it was Tila. Down in the wadi bed our camels and donkeys were waiting for us, but it took us an hour and a quarter to get away. Loads were sorted again, donkeys were saddled and there was the usual general uproar. Hassan, who for weeks had been talking of the cold he was to experience in the highlands, had discussed the possibilities of oiling his body or of painting it with indigo. As he had brought woollen undies, overcoats and thick English suitings, we thought these enough and vetoed the oil and the indigo. He had, however, been told that honey was excellent for keeping out the cold and thereupon produced a tin of it. We were soon to curse this tin most heartily, all day and every day, for our cherished belongings became sticky with its leaking contents. But the immediate question was that Hassan had not shown his tin of honey to the beduin when they sized up the luggage, and excess-luggage charges were demanded. However all these questions were ultimately settled and we left Tila at noon with a caravan of four camels, one mule and eleven donkeys.

Sultan Salim had sent with us Salih 'Ali al Khulaqi and Salim bin Miftah, a slave sergeant of artillery, to assist us in all our doings and accompany us till we should come back to Mukalla. The former rode and the latter went with us, every inch of our way, on foot. The two porters were Bukheit bin Mansur and Muhammad. Bukheit also stayed with us all through the journey but Muhammad, as will be told later, ran away.

The chief of our beduin was Sa'id bin 'Umar Ba 'Ubeita ar Rashidi as Seibani, one of the most lovable of his kind we had ever met. He was not given to the shouting and screaming of the other beduin, but was quiet and effective and did more than his fair share of the work, for perhaps he was not sufficiently impressive to see that the others always did theirs. He was good-looking with something feminine in his features, in love with a brand-new wife whom we were to meet on the way, and, above all, he played a pipe. Often on the way Sa'id would draw his reed pipe from his black sash and swing along ahead of the caravan playing his plaintive air. How much we would like to have been able to record his melodies, though they are clear in our memories, bringing back pictures of the wadis and jōls. Long may Sa'id continue to pipe his caravans over the road to Du'an. Even when he has passed away his spirit will haunt those barren jōls and travellers will hear borne over the wind the plaintive sound of his pipe.

As we rode away from Tila we followed the seil flood bed of the wadi, which like all seil beds in the Hadhramaut, was troublesome on account of the big round stones. But after a short distance the road leads steeply out of the wadi up a short stony hill and is then flat and good going. It is passable for cars and indeed, until recent floods, it was used by cars as far as Lusb. We rode along this gently sloping surface passing only a siqaya, and although we had only been going for a quarter of an hour the men went to get a drink. We were to learn in the subsequent weeks that it is as difficult for a beduin to pass a siqaya as it is for a hiker to pass an inn. However the siqaya was empty, and Salim and one of the others threw big stones into it as an insult to the man who should have put water there and had neglected to do so.

There was a little scrub but no vegetation until we went down into the Wadi Hawi, where bushes and sumr trees were more plentiful. This is really the sum of one's immediate surroundings when travelling in the Hadhramaut. On the top, usually flat, the vegetation is sparse. In the seil beds of the wadis, amongst the stones, the vegetation is thicker. To-day it consisted of spreading sumr trees with an occasional surah, bushes of senna and hawir from which the beduin get some of their indigo, duma'a scrub and, growing in the loess, harmal (*Rhazya stricta Dene*), khuweira (*Cassia obovata Coll.*), and dhowela plants. The beduin dry and crush the leaves of the poisonous harmal to place on wounds, and this seems to be its only use. The camels and goats avoid it entirely.

Presently I distinguished myself by taking a heavy fall from my donkey. As I picked myself up, rather shaken from contact wtih the stones, I wondered ruefully if my journey was to be a White Knight's progress. However, it may well have been that this misfortune at the outset appeased the jealous gods, for it was my first and only accident. Some of the Arabs of Zanzibar, at the beginning of the unlucky month of Safar, deliberately burn themselves in order to avoid further misfortunes, so perhaps it was my lucky star that saw to it that I took an early toss.

To the Wadi Hawi succeeded the Wadi 'Anana with a view of Jebel 'Anana which formed a landmark for an hour or so, and shortly after leaving it we had a final view of the sea. As we rode across another stony plateau some of our beduin nibbled dates which they carried in little bags slung over their shoulders. Sa'id drew out his pipe and beguiled us with a tune as we rode on towards Lusb. There were about twenty houses in the village mostly of one storey, though there are two of four and five storeys, and round them was the usual cultivation, dukhn (bullrush millet, *Pennisetum typhoideum*), sweet potatoes, imported from East Africa and called from the English, batata and keneb (Italian millet, *Setana italica*). It was not until we had actually passed through the village that we looked down on to the green of the Wadi Lusb below. Here were date-palms, bedam, tamarisk, and ariata trees (*Conocarpus erectus Jacq*). We rode down into the wadi where we found a few pools with fish in them, but apart from two women watching a herd of goats, there was no one within sight.

Soon we passed our first downward caravan. There is little for camels to carry from the interior to the coast, and these were laden with musht (*Grewia erythraea Schweinf*) for camel fodder, and firewood. Near here the longer Du'an road, better for camels, branches off. When we reached Lubeib my donkey had a strange reluctance to move on and I learned that this was where it lived. The men also wanted to stop for the night, but as it was early and we had covered little ground I asked that we might move on to the next halting place with water.

We bivouacked at Al Halāf, a corner of the wadi with nothing else but a water hole among huge boulders overshadowed by the high cliffs. Despite the strangeness of his surroundings, Ganess throughout our tour turned out excellent meals. Sultan Salim had sent a crate of unhappy chickens with us and as long as they lasted we had them for lunch and dinner. We started our morning light, generally nothing but porridge, tea and biscuits. Lunch was cooked the night before, but later when the chickens were finished the three of us usually disposed of two tins of fruit. Four o'clock tea degenerated into a drink of smelly but boiled and tepid water from our water-bottles, taken riding and followed by a cigarette, but dinner was the chief meal of the day. It was rarely that we could get

## BEDUIN CUISINE

anything fresh, but with the aid of potatoes, rice and curry powder, Ganess contrived to make even the tinned herrings, to which we were at last reduced, very palatable.

The beduin's cuisine was much simpler. The saucepan would be dipped in the water-hole or filled from the water skins, the rice, unwashed, poured in and while it was boiling they pounded their dried fish to shreds. This was then well stirred into the rice, some spices added and a handful of ghee, and dinner was ready. They set to, some of them with both hands. Coffee followed; when they had no mortar they ground up the roasted beans with their teeth and with the inevitable ginger made their brew. The donkey-men messed together, and so did the camel-men. Salih and Salim, Zaidi and Ganess formed another mess, and the porters yet another. Zaidi tried beduin food for a day or two, but even his brazen stomach could not assimilate it.

Only on four nights of our whole journey did we use our tent, about which I had been sadly deceived, for it turned out to be a large marquee with two palatial rooms which I was ashamed to ask anybody to erect, and in fact on the four nights that it was set up it was on the proposal of our beduin themselves in the almost freezing cold of the barren Jōls. On nights such as this first one, well sheltered by the wadi walls and great boulders as big as cottages, nothing was more pleasant than to sleep, as we had always slept in Aden, under the stars.[1]

[1] Reading this seven years later I am struck with the contrast of our present methods of travel. The arrangements of this early journey were based on East African practice but nowadays we never have a tent or a baggage camel. Our baggage is limited to one roll or bundle, a bag of rice, some dried fish and other odds and ends. But we still don't appreciate chewed coffee!

## Chapter XIV

## WADIS AND JŌLS TO DU'AN

*The gauger walked with willing foot,
And aye the gauger played the flute;
But what should Master Gauger play
But Over the hills and far away.*
        R. L. STEVENSON.

*Straight mine eye hath caught new pleasures,
Whilst the landscape round it measures!*    JOHN MILTON.

AL HALAF is where Van der Meulen and Von Wissmann also spent their first night. The former writes "our beduin are not quite at ease in their minds as to its safety," but we found its road supremely safe, thanks to the Ba Surras of Du'an for whose roof we were bound. We thought a nursemaid could push a perambulator (if she could get it over the rocks) with perfect safety to herself and her charge from Mukalla to Shibam.

We had blissfully supposed that the hours of travel in the Hadhramaut would be much as in the western part of the protectorate, and that we should travel in the cool of the morning and the afternoon. We had been told in Mukalla that the usual hours were from 6 a.m. to 10.30 a.m. and from 3 p.m. to 6 or 7 p.m., but that they could be varied according to the wishes of the traveller. At any rate we expected seven or eight hours a day of marching. In our innocence we were up early the next morning, November 7th, and ready to move at six, but, despite the easy first day, it was not until a quarter-past seven that we were finally on the way, climbing steadily up the right bank of the wadi. Much of the way we had to walk and in about an hour and a half we had climbed a thousand feet above our last night's camp to Ar Rashih where we had a short rest. The walls of the wadi are awe-inspiring in their height and their slopes are studded with loose enormous boulders down to the wadi bed, where we could glimpse the green of sumr and other bushes. On the hill-side there was little else but duma'a. The massive boulders took curious forms and in places the hills were undercut as if they had been quarried with tools. In many places these cliffs

## A TREE OF MANY PARTS

looked as if they bore giant inscriptions where they were weathered in regular lines, and some of the boulders by the wayside seemed to have measles, being covered with red metallic pimples.

Ar Rashih was nothing but a name, a spot on the side of the wadi of greater width than the ordinary path and therefore allowing for a party to sit down. After a short pause we climbed another seven hundred feet in the next two hours, passing the village of Zemen al Kabir, green with cultivation and dates. We halted at Zemen as Saghir, dismounting at the rest house of Sheikh Muhammad 'Umar Bazara of Du'an.[1] It had windows but the beduin, alas, keep in them not only themselves but their animals, with the accompanying flies and smell. So we chose to sit under a tree and found a place among rocks and under the shade of an 'elb tree, about a hundred yards away near a field of keneb. This tree is generally called in Arabic sidr or nebk and is universally esteemed by the Arabs.[2] In Zanzibar the local Arabs claim that it is under this tree that the resurrection will take place. It is mentioned in the Quran and tradition says it is a tree in the seventh heaven with roots in the sixth. The tree has a Christian interest too, for legend has it that from its spiny branches Christ's crown of thorns was made, hence its Latin name *Zizyphus Spina-Christi* (Linn.). Sometimes called the jujube tree, it was the lotus of the Lotophagi of which Herodotus speaks. It grows a small cherry-like fruit called dōm which, however, to our tastes is distinctly dull. Once in Mkokotoni an old Arab friend, Shinen bin Sa'id, brought me a parting present the night before I went on leave—a fifteen-foot python in a sack and dōm fruit done up in a pyramidal plaited box of coco-nut fronds. I put the python under my bed for the night, but it escaped. The dōm berries got safely home, but no one cared much for them. In the Hadhramaut the leaves of the 'elb are used for washing and are good for cleaning carpets. It is one of the most important trees up-country, for from it comes the best honey and its timber is practically the only one useful for house building.

After lunch, riding past villages with tall date-palms and gardens we came to Himem and presently a stream ran and rippled by our side like any English brook. We stopped for the night at Qa'r al Murakaba, having

---

[1] These rest houses are known generically as murabba'as or cubes. In the lower parts of the Hadhramaut they are called madharab and in the upper sirah.

[2] In Zanzibar the Swahilis call it Mkunazi and one of the quarters of Zanzibar town is called Mkunazini or the place of the sidr tree.

climbed 2,500 feet since morning, and again found good quarters among the rocks. On our arrival one of the beduin declaimed the 'Adhan in a penetrating and untuneful voice. This he did quite frequently, but nobody took much notice of him and none of the other beduin prayed.

The next day we followed the wadi Ankedun to the plateau of Bein al Khorebtain; Salim, who the night before had complained of toothache, was now singing lustily again as usual; but better than Salim's was the song of the birds in the wadi which with the morning light became a brighter and brighter green. And then passing down into the wadi Hisi we came to Sa'id's home, where his new and much-loved wife lived. One of the women had come out to meet us and Sa'id's bride, gay with her new-won jewellery and trousseau, came down to see him. The women, here, mostly veiled, were shy of us but watched us in friendly fashion from afar or hidden behind walls and bushes. I told Sa'id to go away and talk to his wife for an hour or so, but he said no, he was on duty. However we made no move until he told us to come on. The Kor Seiban, the highest mountain in the Hadhramaut, towers majestically over Hisi, huddled precariously on the edge of a cliff, and is the original home of the Seibani tribe.

At Hisi we left the wadi and rode up a gentle slope on to the jōl. There was a vast expanse, to our left, of sloping hills, on our right the Kor Seiban and steep mountains. It was a most impressive sight and time and again I stopped to look back. Geology is the science of the earth's crust, and here was the earth's crust naked and unashamed, stretching far away to the horizons and deeply cleft by great wadis with sheer cliffs. Although it is 6,000 feet up, the jōl was once under the sea, for we found shells on it, and I am told the wadis were carved out by the last ice age. The solid stone of our path had been worn smooth and polished white by generations of travellers during a thousand years and more. The great age of the way we were travelling was brought home to us by seeing Himyaritic names carved on the flat stone. To the Himyarites had succeeded generations of Arab travellers and they, too, had left their names behind. One read: "Muhammad bin Ahmed Ba 'Ashi 1294," and there were others much older.

That night we camped on the top of the plateau near the murabba'a of Ash Shūara, built by Muhammad Ba Tawīl, overshadowed by the great cliffs of Aroba and Mola Matar, making us feel infinitely small and lost in the immensity of space around us.

Our track next morning wound round a narrow ledge on the sheer mountainside. All the places round us echoed the name of Mola Matar, and we were soon above his tomb, which is quite fifteen feet long. The big rocks on either side of our track were piled with small stones to which our men added more for Mola Matar. Mola Matar is distinctly the property of the beduin. No one knows who he really was, but they claim that he was a prophet of the tribe of 'Ad. In an effort at orthodoxy, attempts have been made by the more enlightened folk to identify him with 'Ali bin Abu Talib, the prophet's son-in-law.

Mola Matar was the first of the many giants we met in the Hadhramaut, and on the identification of the giant I would hazard the guess that he enshrines the memory of an old rain god, though in so far as I have been able to trace what is known of the ancient South Arabian trinity, the rain god does not figure though the heavenly bodies were worshipped. The Mola's name is spelt in the same way as the word for rain, and the grave may well be the site of an old shrine or temple, for these lofty mountains are often wrapped in cloud, and where could there be a more appropriate place than this. I suspect, too, that the guardianship of property left for safe custody, as here at Mola Matar, also arises from the ancient South Arabian worship. Men prayed to Athtar Sharqan, the guardian of temples and tombs, that sacrilegeous hands might not be laid on their offerings and gifts. All over the Hadhramaut we found these places where things might be left in safety, and the system is valuable, one might almost say indispensable, in a country where there are no railway cloak-rooms on the route.

We rode along the ledge round the wadi, meeting new vegetation at these heights and listening to the birds. And as we climbed Jebel 'Urka, Sa'id played on his pipe and danced ahead with Hamed and Salim—all flashing their daggers in the sunlight. By evening we reached the edge of Hasar Jōhar, from which lies a panorama over the road to the Wadi Hadhramaut of flat-topped hills, shaven and swept clean and cut by deep ravines. The browns of the landscape turned to a deep blue in the distance so that, looking at it, we felt almost as if we were gazing at the sea on the horizon, while the gorgeous gold of the sunset lit up the banks of cloud over whose crests brilliant blue rays shot heavenwards.

That night we camped near the deserted village of Sarab. For the last twenty minutes of our ride it had been dark and it was bitterly cold when we reached the murabba'a called Dim, where we waited for the baggage to come along, watching small white rats playing along the beams of the ceiling and running up and down the walls. The building was almost square, built of dry stone with no windows and only one door about five feet high. The height inside was just over six feet and one pillar in the centre propped up the roof; on the floor there were remains of a fire from the previous occupants, and though it was littered with dung, it was a warm and cosy retreat from the bitter cold outside.

We camped for our last night before reaching Du'an at the murabba'a of Ba Khāmis, and for the last time we heard through the night the shuffling and snuffling of donkeys and camels at the end of their tethers and every now and then the mule's mournful whinny.

We were on the wide plateau of Jōl 'Ubeid at eleven the next day, the sixteenth anniversary of the Armistice, and during those two minutes my thoughts went back to the war, to the first Armistice Day when London went mad, to the Cenotaph and the other Armistice Days passed on the sea, in Zanzibar and in Mauritius. Memory took me far in that short time during which my immediate surroundings were forgotten. At two minutes past I took a view back on the distant peak of Kor Seiban which we had left two days before, and turned to the business in hand.

## Chapter XV

## IN THE VALLEY OF DU'AN

> *And thy Lord inspired the bee, "Take to houses in the mountains, and in the trees, and in the hives men build.*
> *Then eat from every fruit, and walk in the beaten paths of thy Lord; there cometh forth from her body a draught varying in hue, in which is a cure for men; verily, in that are signs unto a people who reflect."*
> QURAN.

> *Praeterea regem non sic Aegyptos et ingens*
> *Lydia nic populi Parthorum ant Medus Hydaspes*
> *Observant.*
> VIRGIL.

AT the murabba'a of Ba Khabar we were met by a party from Du'an, headed by Sa'id bin 'Awadh bin 'Umar Ba Surra, who had come to welcome us. After a short talk we rode on and soon saw the first signs of Du'an, the white pillars which mark the boundaries within which the beduin may not raid each other. For more than an hour after we had met our hosts we went forward through the same monotonous scenery and never another sign of settled life. Poor Sa'id was not well and his flute was silent. He did not complain or ask for anything, but I saw that sometimes he ran ahead and lay down like a sick animal huddled up in his cloth in the scant shade of some thorn bush. Unwillingly he accepted a lift for a short while, but was soon on his feet again. Then quite suddenly the opposite wall of the Wadi Du'an came into view, a tremendous abyss opening almost at our feet. Dismounting, we began the long climb down the pass, called 'Aqabat al Hibil, which takes an hour and a half. On a ledge we got our first view of the valley. Nine hundred feet below the perpendicular cliffs ran a river of dark green date palms mingled with the lighter green of the 'elb trees and the cultivation. At first we saw no houses; then out of the pale brown, sandy cliffs appeared great castles, so harmonizing with their background as to be invisible at first sight, huddling at the foot of the opposite cliff as though they wanted to climb the wall. Several towns lay below us, 'Ar Rashid, Khoreiba and 'Aura, their high buildings like fantastic fairy-book palaces raised pile on pile.

## IN THE VALLEY OF DU'AN

For a time we gazed fascinated and then continued the descent through a narrow pass and along a ledge with perpendicular walls above and below. As we drew near the bottom, the surface of the track was better and not so steep. Here a long line of the notables was waiting to meet us, headed by Sheikh Ahmed bin 'Umar bin Ahmed Ba Surra, one of the joint Governors. After shaking hands with each in turn, we were led among shady date groves, in and out and round about, until we came to an open slope near Masna'a. The hill led up to the Governor's castle, and outside a massive, intricately carved wooden door stood ready to greet us, Sheikh Muhammad bin 'Umar bin Ahmed Ba Surra, the senior of the two brothers who rule the Du'an province. He led us into his rambling castle, up steps and along passages to our room, one of the most delightful that could be imagined.

Nowhere else in the Hadhramaut did we sense exactly that feeling of peace and calm which broods over the sunlit sheltered depths of the Wadi Du'an between 'Aura and Khoreiba. Down here, below the level of the world, it was difficult even to recall the barren windswept heights over which we had travelled. News seemed somehow to drop into the wadi from the sky; not that there was much news but every letter that came was almost common property and formed a topic of conversation in several scores of homes. Sleep brooded over the place, not just the sleep of out-of-the-way country villages cut off from rails and telegraph wires, but the eternal sleep of a distant past which has never known an awakening. Forgetting the many little wars that have taken place there, it seemed, indeed, as if the last exciting thing that could have happened in the valley was the rushing of the torrents of the subsiding flood. Yet another illusion it gave us, the illusion that the way down its 'aqaba was one of those staircases covered by a trap door which lead to those wonderful gardens of the *Arabian Nights*, full of fruits and delicacies not found in the world above.

The interiors of the houses were of peculiar beauty, particularly in those furnished in the pure Arab style. Fashions have changed to a great extent in recent years in Du'an, so we were told. Old doors were low, often not more than four feet high. Old rooms were also low and dark. All that has changed in the houses of the well-to-do. Their doors are tall, but, still beautifully carved, and the rooms too have grown bigger and higher, while it is becoming a standard practice in Du'an architecture to build the houses on the principle of self-contained apartments. Several house owners told us with pride that every room in their mansions had a bathroom attached.

The door of our little suite in the castle opened on to a narrow white-washed, carpeted passage. The entrance of the living-room, a well-proportioned arch, was on the left and at the end of the passage was a small bathroom. The living-room was perhaps twenty feet square and about ten feet high. There were six windows with exquisitely carved lattice work and one small glass window, in the shape of an old Arab lamp, quite high up. The system gave plenty of light without any glare. The walls were whitewashed and each side of the entrance a door, in a heavy, carved frame, gave on to large cupboards in which rifles, bandoliers and clothes were hung. These doors were studded with iron nails, two inches in diameter and burnished with lead so that they looked like silver. The ceiling was an attractive herring-bone arrangement of slats, roughly hewn in unstained date wood. The beams of carved 'elb wood were supported by four square pillars of the same material with wide capitals. Between three of these pillars there were three plain wooden poles fixed high up over which clothes are hung. The floor was spread with camel-hair rugs striped rust brown, white and black, and a few cushions completed the furniture.

As we wanted to sleep out of doors we were given another flat in the castle with an outside veranda, but it took us several journeys to memorize the ups and downs and twists and turns of the way there. The bedroom had a shapely Moorish arch set in a screen of 'elb wood, carved and studded with these silvered nails. On each side of the door there was a recess in the screen for books, among which I noticed Tabari's history. The floor was strewn with Persian carpets and the brass bed was covered with a blanket bearing the design of a red lion, a popular motif which we saw many times again. In the corner was a large carved chest of sissum wood inlaid with brass of Indian workmanship, nowadays generally known as Zanzibar chests. Later, I saw some well-made local copies of them. Large pieces of furniture like this provided us with a never-ceasing source of wonderment in the Hadhramaut, for they had all been carried through wadi and over jōl on camels.

But some of the rooms in Du'an are positive museums. The owners themselves seemed to know that their decorations were not in the best of taste but explained that they liked them and apologized for them on that ground. The walls were simply covered with 'junk,' cheap brasswork, oleographs, pots and pans, cups and saucers of a ' present from Brighton ' description, trays of tin and brass, glass dishes, coffee-pots, lamps, fly-whisks, primus stoves and kettles.

We could see far down the wadi from the roof on which we slept, and

## IN THE VALLEY OF DU'AN

as the sun rose over Du'an the morning light crept down the wadi wall and illuminated the tops of the houses and then the palms and gardens beneath. And then came the sound of the Call to Prayer echoing round the age-old walls of the wadi, as it had echoed for more than a thousand years, and before that no doubt the priests of Sin and Shems and Athtar had called their devotees to worship.

Du'an is very ancient; relics have been found there of the Himyarites and we were shown some work attributed to them high up on the northern wall. It has been suggested that the Thabane of Ptolemy, longitude 35° 40′, latitude 16° 20′, was perhaps Du'an, and the identification of Pliny's Thoani is even more certain. Du'an is now a retreat to which its rich inhabitants come to rest from the turmoil of the world, but it has an old-world atmosphere and though the principal people are well travelled, the beauty of the houses and the hospitality are purely Arab.

There are men in Du'an who have big business interests in Aden, in Port Sudan, in Abyssinia, in Java and in Egypt. There is no money to be made here and no product for export except the famous luxury honey. The rich men bring large sums of money to beautify their homes and to preserve their gardens. Date trees are sold here for as much as from £50 to £75 a tree, far beyond their possible economic value. It is purely sentiment that keeps Du'an going.

Emigration is the principal characteristic of the Hadhramia and it is interesting to note that to a great extent each colony abroad is connected with a particular place or places in the Hadhramaut. Du'an is mainly connected with the Red Sea, but the largest colony of Hadhramis abroad is in the Netherlands East Indies, where there are about 70,000, mostly from the Āl Kathīr. They are principally traders in batik and sarongs. In Singapore the community, which originates mainly from Tarim and Seiyun, is small but extremely wealthy. It occupies itself mostly with house property. In Kenya, Tanganyika and Zanzibar there are large numbers of Hadhramis from Shihr, the Tamimi tribe and the tribe of Hajr, but the standard of wealth is much lower than in the East Indies. Some are small traders but most are engaged in manual occupations.

The morning after our arrival D. visited Ba Surra's harem and sat on the floor among a number of women wearing long black dresses brightened by an insertion in the front of red, yellow and green silk patches sewn together. They wore orange silk scarves over their heads, tied under the chin, and most of them had their hair cut quite short. D. was bombarded with questions and closely examined, for she was the first European woman they had seen.

"Didn't you find the road very tiring?" they all wanted to know, for none of them had been out of the wadi and it seemed extraordinary that a woman from the West should drop down on them from the jōls. Friends from neighbouring houses came in with a jingling of bracelets as they went round kissing hands. They displayed necklaces and nose rings, too, when they took off their black silk cloaks and untied the piece of black cloth with slits for eyes which covered their faces like a domino. They felt D.'s dress and asked her what she wore underneath and why she had no jewellery. But when she explained that on a journey she left her ornaments behind and only wore the simplest kind of clothes, they thought it was very sensible. The lady of the house took her by the hand and led her round the women's quarters, many small rooms like a convent, sparsely furnished with carpets and cushions, and linked by outdoor passages which made it difficult to realize that all the rooms were in one house. The kitchen was large and airy, with an enormous cauldron in one corner where several women were stirring the dinner.

For the rest of the morning Ahmed, the younger of the two brothers, took us on a tour. As we walked down to 'Aura from the castle I was struck time and again by the almost overwhelming feeling of the mighty cliffs which pressed upon us.

"It seems so extraordinary to find all these people living in a river-bed," I said. "Don't you ever have any big floods?"

"It is a long time since there was a big flood," said Ahmed, "about three or four hundred years ago. The wadi was flooded from Rehab and four thousand date palms were washed away."

"The walls of the wadi are so clear cut that you'd think they had been cut out yesterday."

"Ah, that was in the time of our father Nuh. The whole land was covered with water. Nuh and his family built a big ship and lived in it while the flood lasted. When the flood subsided and the water ran away there were big rivers: that is how these wadis were cut out and why you found the sea shells you told me of."

The way Ahmed spoke I almost felt that he had watched the waters return from off the earth, and the wadis looked so new that it seemed quite possible. He led us through shaded kitchen gardens with dates, 'elb and lime trees, and neat beds of carrots, onions, lady fingers, tomatoes and pumpkins. A common object which aroused my curiosity was a board supported by a string at the four corners and slung between houses. Ahmed told me that it was a hen-roost to keep the birds safe from the fox that wanders by night.

When we returned to the castle he showed us a beehive, a pipe fitted into the wall consisting of circular sections about a foot in diameter. Outside there is a small hole through which the bees enter and leave the hives.

"The bees have an āb (father)," said Ahmed. "Sometimes a new āb arises and it leaves the hive and goes away a short distance followed by some of the others. Then you take a mat and make a roll like a hive, and close one end, and sprinkle inside a perfume of the perfumes used by the ladies. Then you go to the place where the new āb has gone with the other bees round it and you pick up the āb gently in your fingers—it doesn't bite—and put it into a small cage like this." He produced a little wooden cage, like a tea infuser and gave it to me. "Then you put the cage inside the rolled mat and get someone to beat a tin or a copper tray and the bees leave the place where they have swarmed and come to the āb. You carry the bees to a hive, put the āb in its cage into the hive and in go the bees after it."

"Why," I said, "it's just what the bee-keepers do in England. When I was a boy I used to beat a tray for my father when the bees swarmed and he used to sprinkle scent over the bees. Only we call the āb the queen, for she is the mother of all the bees. We put her in a cage, too."

But Ba Surra could not understand this. "But it is the leader," he said, "and whoever heard of a woman leading an army like that?"

"Ah well, you know, the children always go after their mother. It's just that this mother has so many children." I thought of the old woman who lived in a shoe but did not see how she would help the story. "With the bees it is the women who are important; as a matter of fact all the bees who gather the honey are women, but they don't breed."

"But they are the soldiers," said Ba Surra, "they have the swords to sting with. The bee women are bigger and don't sting."

"We believe they are the males," said I, "the strongest of them marries the queen and then is killed by her. The workers kill the rest."

This was sheer revolution. I could see how his mind was working. "There are tribes in other parts of the world where women do the fighting," I added. Ahmed was too polite to contradict me. He just shook his head in doubt. After all, we once thought the same thing:

## PAYING CALLS

>         so work the honey bees;
> Creatures that, by a rule in nature, teach
> The act of order to a peopled kingdom.
> They have a king, and officers of sorts:
> Where some, like magistrates, correct at home;
> Others, like merchants, venture trade abroad;
> Others, like soldiers, armed in their stings,
> Make boot upon the summer's velvet buds;
> Which pillage they with merry march bring home.

If some wise fool had not discovered the truth, women might never have thought of votes.

In the afternoon we paid calls; first to Ar Rashid to the house of the Bazaras. The principal member of the family in Du'an, Muhammad bin Ahmed Ba Zaid Bazara, came to Masna'a to fetch us, and we rode among the dates whose fronds cast lace-like shadows on the shaded path. All the village of Ar Rashid had turned out to watch our arrival and heads looked from every window. From one first-storey window above our path even a goat looked curiously at us. The women and children kept at the sides of the path in the date groves, and as we moved ran forward to seek fresh cover, peeping at us round the trunks of the palms.

It was an attractive room into which we were shown, spread with Persian carpets and big coloured cushions. Coffee, halwa, biscuits and cake formed the first part of the entertainment. Then, as at Ba Surra's place, they brought us honey, lovely round golden combs almost too beautiful to cut. It was the time of the honey crop and all day long these combs were put before us. Sheer nectar as the honey was we could not eat it all day long, particularly neat.

"But you don't know how to eat it," said Bazara. "Take a spoonful of honey and dip it in your glass of water and then see."

From Ar Rashid we rode on to Khoreiba to have another tea with Seiyid Hamid bin 'Alawi al Bār. Khoreiba is the biggest of these three villages, and some of the houses were immense. The streets were steep; sometimes they seemed only a little off the perpendicular, and in places they were stepped. Sometimes they led under the very houses themselves. Seiyid Hamid's house was practically at the very top of the village and he greeted us at the door, covering his hand with a shawl to shake D.'s. By the time we had climbed many flights of stairs to his gorgeous Moorish guest-room at the top we felt we had almost climbed to the top of the wadi wall. Here cream-coloured walls shone like marble, being made with lime polished

## IN THE VALLEY OF DU'AN

with a flat flint, in a manner much more common in Tarim and Seiyun. Our host produced an elephantine tea consisting, besides cake and biscuits, of a large variety of tinned fruits including, the first time we had met the fruit since we left Mauritius, tinned lichis. As we said we had eaten them before and were glad to meet them again in Du'an, he sent us half a dozen tins next day. After we had finished the still heavily-laden trays were passed on to the "second class" then carried away to the "third class," though a small boy seeing them going hastily grabbed as many slices of pineapple in his fingers as he could.

It was dark by the time tea and talk were over, but before letting us go Seiyid Hamid took us over his house. It was a bewildering experience. All the suites were alike and each room full of numberless ornaments from which we were invited to take our choice. He showed us his own bedroom, his son's bedroom, and still more bedrooms in the course of construction, until at the end we felt we had climbed all over some Arabian Queen Anne's Mansions looking for a flat. When we had seen his house he took us over part of the neighbouring palace of Seiyid Muhammad Ba Harūn who had kindly given us letters of introduction to friends in the Hadhramaut. It was night before we had finished our tour. We said good-bye with regret and clambered down the steep streets by the lights of the lamps carried by our friends, then we rode back through the moonlit date grove to dinner. On our return we found this letter from Sultan Salim:

> You have left our part while our thoughts are still with you and sorrowing for the troubles you are being put to, especially Mrs. Ingrams, on account of the difficulties you will face on the road, but we pray God to help you and grant you safety in your journey.
>
> We are sorry that your stay was for so short a period that we could not do everything for you. We admire your gentle sentiments and good manners and wish you a blessed and victorious journey.
>
> We hope that Mrs. Ingrams has comfortably enjoyed riding the mule. On your arrival at Du'an you will find our sons Muhammad and Ahmed Ba Surra, who are the representatives of H.H. the Sultan at Du'an and Leisar. We have already asked them to do all that pleases you. Please inform them of the time at which you will leave Wadi Du'an for Hadhramaut so that they may send letters to the representative of H.H. the Sultan at Shibam to send you the escorts to Meshhed and prepare for your arrival.
>
> In conclusion please inform us of your health as well as that of Mrs. Ingrams so that we may be pleased. We hope to meet you shortly.

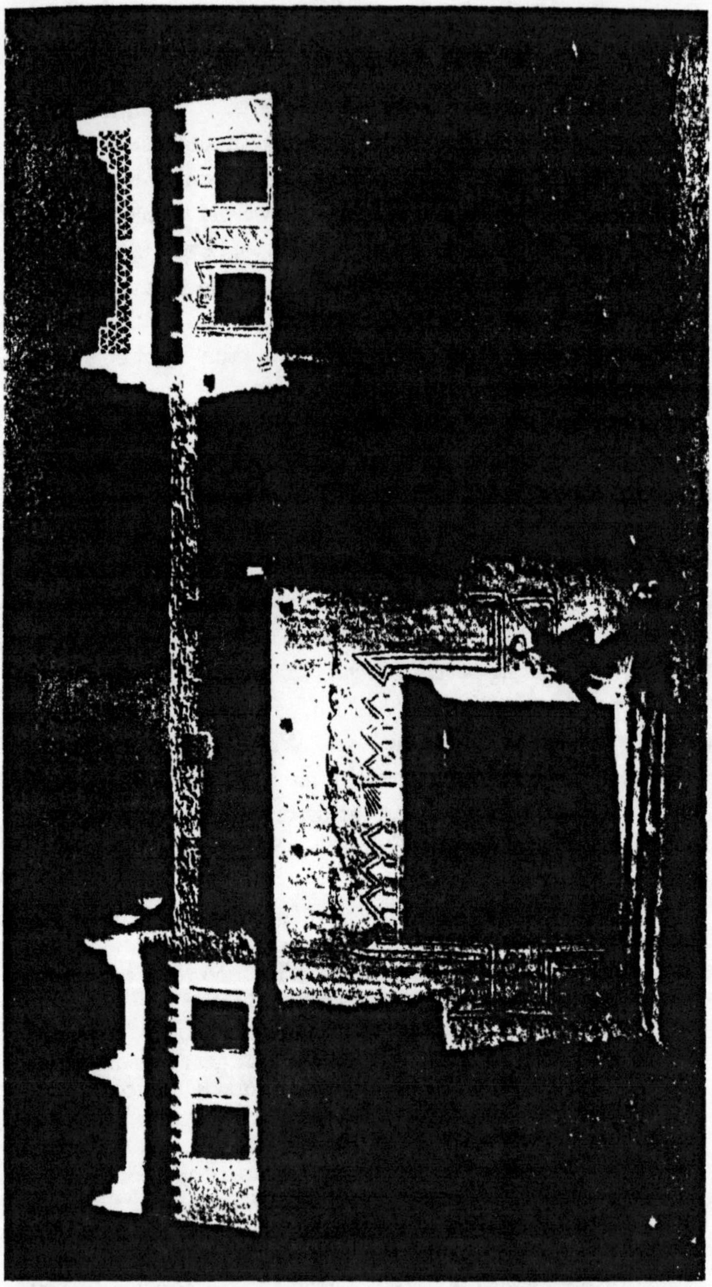

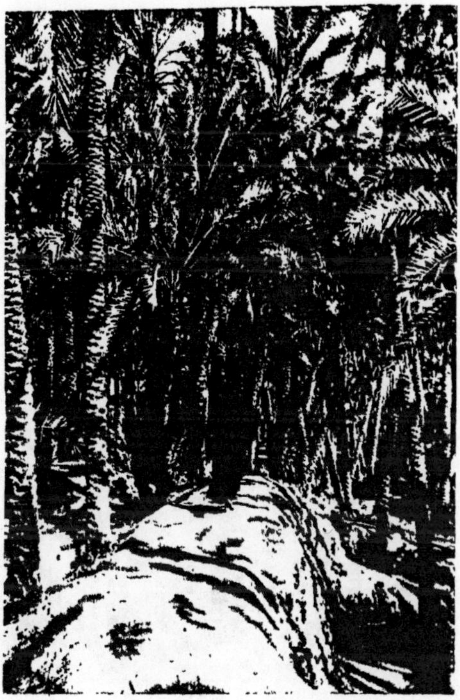

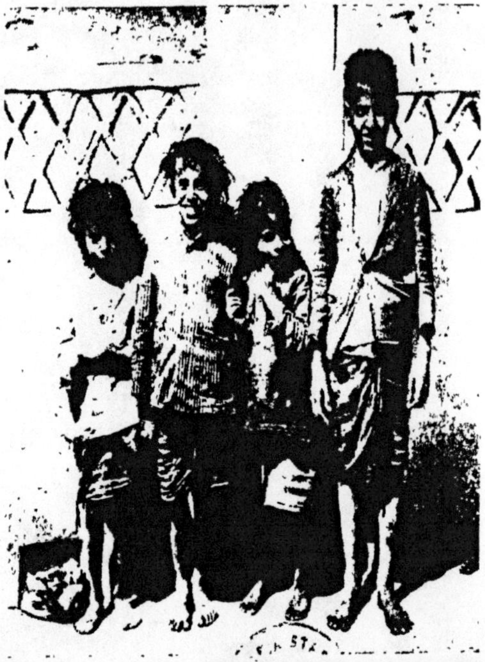

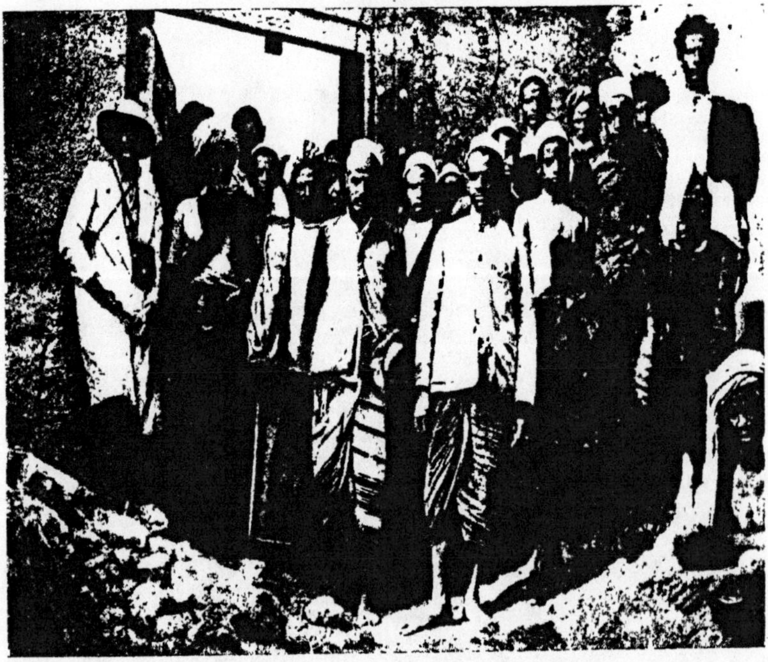

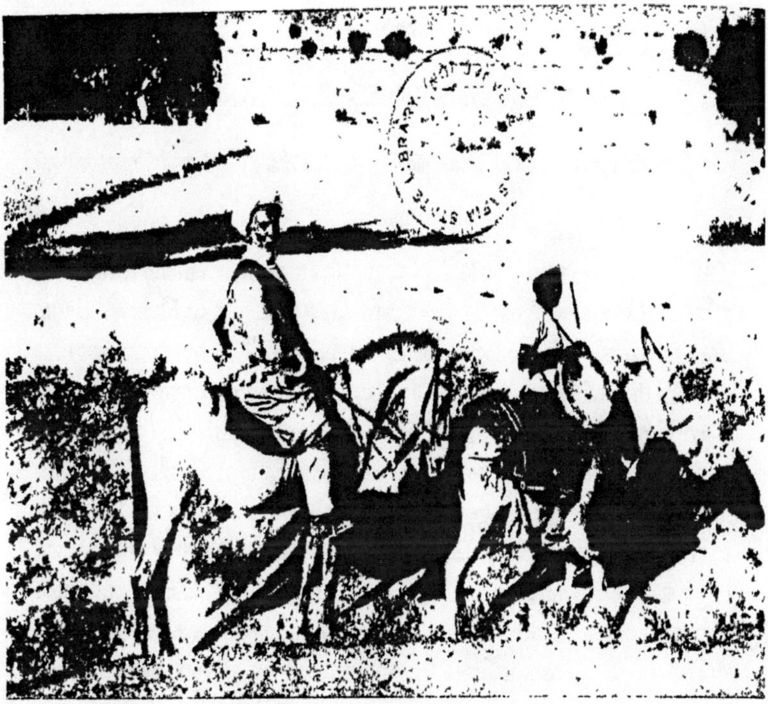

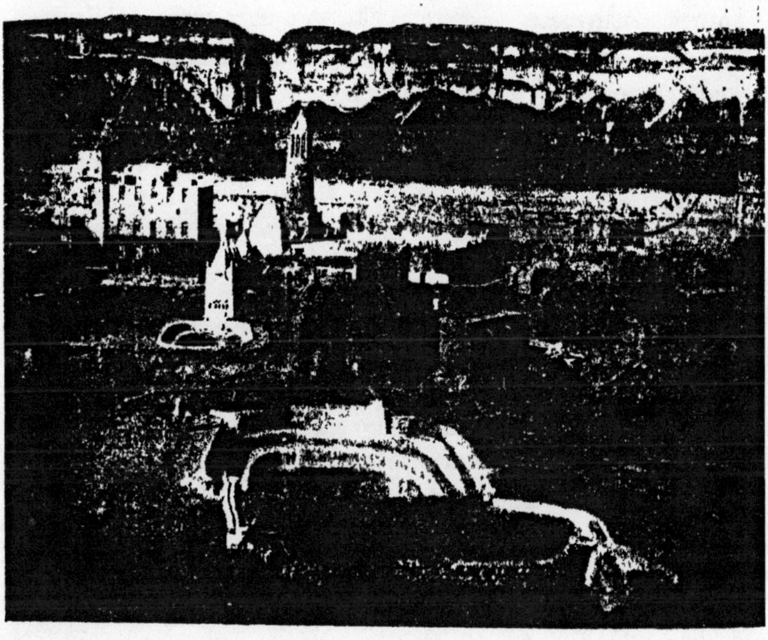

## Chapter XVI

## A PEACE-MAKING PATRIARCH

*How beautiful upon the mountains are the feet of him that bringeth good tidings, that publisheth peace.*     ISAIAH.

THE next day we were due to depart, and again we were embarrassed by the wholesale kindness of our hosts who paid our transport to Shibam. From now onwards, with the exception of one brief spell on our journey to the north of the main Hadhramaut valley, we were to wander for weeks through a world of wadis, never seeing further than their walls. The wadi was as fertile as the jōl had been barren. There were signs of life all our way the first day, village after village on one side or the other of the wadi, and much cultivation round each, dates, durra (great millet, *Sorghum vulgar*) and hashish. Cows and sheep and black and white goats in the charge of women grazed all along our way and there were any number of fine 'elb trees.

The traveller was not forgotten on our road for at very short intervals there were siqayas and murabba'as. Gradually the way became more open though we frequently found ourselves riding between the high stoned banks of terrace cultivation. Amongst the villages we passed were that of Hudūn, named after the son of the prophet Hud, and the autonomous village of Budha.[1]

[1] Budha is the capital of the 'Amudis, the principal tribe of Sheikhs in the country. Before the Seiyids came into the Hadhramaut the Sheikhs were the principal ecclesiastical influence and they probably took the place of an earlier hierarchy formed by the priesthood of the old religion. Nowadays they take precedence after the Seiyids but they have much the same privileges. They are a very respected class, are better educated than the tribes-men, and as a rule do not bear arms. The 'Amudis are descended from one Sa'id bin 'Isa who was known as 'Amud ad Din (prop of religion). All the men of the 'Amudi tribe bear the title of Sheikh and at one time they were paramount in the Wadis Du'an and Leisar, but in 1900 the Qu'aiti broke their power and they fled to the mountains. Later, however, they were allowed to return to Budha and their other towns which were acknowledged to be autonomous, although the tribe is under the actual control of the Ba Surrass of Du'an.

## A PEACE-MAKING PATRIARCH

During the afternoon we first noticed the rakh (*Salvadora persica L.*) which is such a popular camel food. Here it was called rakh haqq ash Sheikh Sa'id (the rakh that belongs to Sheikh Sa'id), and is named after 'Amud ad Din who is buried in Qeidun where he is revered as a weli and a ziyara to his tomb takes place on the 27th Rajab. Tradition has it that in his lifetime he ruled all the Hadhramaut and in some way became connected with the rakh so that the spot where it grew was a sanctuary for those involved in blood feuds. Near it there might be no fighting. Nowadays those who pass pick a piece of the rakh and wear it in their turbans.

That night we halted at Sif, a town with a poor reputation for hospitality. Here Wrede was turned back on his journey and neither the Bents nor Van der Meulen found a welcome. That it is a poor sort of place is true, but we found nothing to complain of in our reception. As we drew near three men came out to meet us and, dismounting, we greeted them. Sa'id bin Ahmed Ba Gheish, the Qu'aiti sub-Governor under Ba Surra, led them and took us through a maze of dirty streets to a tall white-washed house belonging to Salih bin Mbarek Ba Saluh, where we were shown to our sleeping-quarters on the roof.

D. was then called away to visit the harem where ten much-bejewelled women in dark-blue dresses and orange scarves sat on the floor in a cheerful room with a coloured ceiling, painted pillars, and pots and trays hanging on the walls. They pawed her about with exclamations of astonishment. "Poor thing! How white she is. Look, everywhere she's the same colour," said a young woman pulling up D.'s sleeves and drawing back the collar of her dress. "Do you use soap?"

D. admitted she did. "Ah," they nodded their heads knowingly. "That's why you're so fair," said an old woman, "you should use oil like we do and then you'd be all right."

After dinner I went down to the guest-room into which we had first been shown in order to make the acquaintance of Seiyid Ahmed bin Hussein bin Harūn al 'Attas, Mansab of Meshhed, of whose arrival I had just heard and to whom I had a letter of introduction from Seiyid Muhammad Ba Harun. I found the old gentleman having his dinner with Salih 'Ali, while five Yafa'i soldiers, who had come from the fort called Husn ad Dōla just outside the town, sat round another tray. The Mansab was one of the most delightful patriarchs I have ever met, with kindly twinkling eyes and a fine bushy beard.

"I am very glad to see you," he said. "I have never understood why we haven't had a British officer up here before. We have had Dutch, why not a representative of our own Government?"

I explained that for a long time the staff in Aden had been short. "Well, it doesn't matter now you've come at last. The Protectorate has much to thank the British Government for. I have a great admiration for our Government and its efforts at peace-making all over the world. Peace-making is my own job, you know, and as a matter of fact I have come here to-day to patch up a quarrel between some Seiyids in Qeidun. But I can come back and do that when I have looked after you at my own place in Meshhed."

"You musn't do anything of the sort," I said. "I don't want you to change your plans because of us. It is quite sufficient to have met you here."

He had just finished his dinner and was washing his hands. When he had dried them he said: "Now we can shake hands."

"Well, if you don't really want me to come back I will write to my sons and they'll look after you all right."

We talked a bit about world affairs and he showed himself unusually well informed. The Yafa'i soldiers sat in the background listening and I asked them from what tribe they came. "We are all of the Ahl as Sa'd," they said.

"Oh I know, from below Al Qara." Interest was at once aroused.

"Have you been there?"

"Well, I've seen it from the air. It's a wonderful place, perched up on the rock." They loved talking to someone who had seen even a little of their homes. "When do you go on leave?" I asked.

"After some years, Inshallah. What is happening to Sultan 'Aidarus?" They were referring to the Lower Yafa'i-Fadhli quarrel.

"Nothing if he is reasonable," said I. "But the Resident has taken a lot of trouble over that affair and we must have peace."

"Peace is what we all want," said the Mansab; "Inshallah he will see that."

When I had said good night I went upstairs, and passing the door of the harem, was called in. D. and our host were there and when the women heard me coming they all hastily covered their faces. I came in and sat on the floor among the ladies who were rather restrained in the presence of the master of the house, though his wife kept up a whispered conversation with D. from under her blue veil. They were intrigued to see that I was white, too, and I assured them I was the same all over. One lady boldly asked me why we had no children.

## A PEACE-MAKING PATRIARCH

"Too much work," I said, rather unfortunately, for there was immediate giggles. As the conversation showed signs of deteriorating our host changed it and showed us some framed photographs hanging on the walls, in one of which his brother was posed standing beside the seated figure of the Wazir to Sharif Hussein. He said that he knew Philby and had travelled with him. We stayed talking till it was quite late, when we said good night and went up to our roof to sleep.

Next morning we said our good-byes outside the town, being accompanied there by our host, the Qu'aiti representative, the Yafa'i garrison whom I had met the night before, and other notabilities. The atmosphere of Sīf was not unfriendly though perhaps a little disapproving, unlike Seiyid Ahmed.

"Come on now, let's have a good-bye group," he said, catching D. by the hand, and there he stood in the middle looking like the benevolent father of a flock, which of course is just what he was. As our ways were the same for some little distance he came with us, riding a grey horse with a European saddle and preceded by a boy on a donkey rattling a drum. He was in full dress this morning wearing a red sash of office like an order, and we went along like a small circus for some way, people leaving their work in the fields to come and watch us and kiss the Seiyid's hand. When we were in sight of Qeidun we dismounted and said our good-byes, watching the old gentleman ride off with his drummer ahead.

The wadi was a good deal wider than on the previous day's journey and rather more barren, though there was still a succession of villages to right and left. We were soon in sight of Hajarein and stopped not far away in order to have our lunch in peace and then go forward to see the town. Hajarein looked very impressive on its island mountain, but it is a place to which distance lends enchantment, for the town itself is indescribably filthy.

Hajarein was the last town in the Du'an province, the limit of the Ba Surras' jurisdiction. The area under the influence of Du'an is, however, much greater than the two wadis which the Qu'aiti directly rules. It is a well-run province and the Governors' hand carries weight through it. One of the reasons why they are so powerful is that they are also Muqaddams or heads of the great Seibani Zei, a name which is given to three confederations of tribes in the Hadhramaut which have single leaders. The Seibani are in close subordinate alliance to the Qu'aiti.

In the glow of a golden evening we came to Meshhed. The last rays of the sun were fading from the house walls and it was dark when we rode up to the Mansab's house where preparations had been made for us. His sons welcomed us kindly and furnished us with our favourite roof-top on which to sleep. We talked, we dined, and were soon abed.

It was at Meshhed that we expected to be met by cars to take us to Shibam. At Hajarein we were told they had arrived but there was no sign of them at Meshhed, nor did they arrive in the morning, but this did not immediately worry us and we set about exploring the place confident that we should be in Shibam (two hours away by car) that evening.

After breakfast I sat talking to Muhammad while D. went off to visit the ladies. I told him how fine Meshhed looked with its domes from the roof-top and asked how old it was.

"It's quite new," he said. "It was my grandfather who founded it. There were always lootings and raidings in this part of the wadi so he came here and built a house so that he could keep the peace. He called the place Meshhed—the place of witness. The Sei'ars were the people who caused most trouble, as they do now, but my grandfather had great influence with them and anyone who takes his walking-stick with him can go anywhere in their country. Meshhed is one of the few places where Sei'ars dare show themselves, as a matter of fact there are a couple here now, who came in the night."

He promised I should see them later and in the meanwhile amongst other visitors an old man from Hajarein came in. No one looked too pleased and it was obvious that he was the "club bore."

"Afif bin 'Abdulla al Afif," he announced himself and sat down next to me. He was quite white with what is called white leprosy and plainly in his dotage. The conversation was left to us.

"I'm eighty-one," he said.

"Indeed," I remarked politely, "you must have seen much in your time." This of course is just the remark that the club bore likes.

"Yes, I have," he said. "I remember another Inglizi and his wife coming here." (This must have been the Bents.) "Do you come from London?" he went on.

"Well," I said; "I live most of my time in London when I'm in England, but I come from another town."

"Cardiff?" he asked.

"No, not Cardiff," I said, "though I've been there in the war."

"If it wasn't London it must be Cardiff."

"Why?" I said. "There are lots more towns in England." (Wales was much too difficult to explain.)

"No," he said, "there are only two towns in England, London and Cardiff. My son lives in Cardiff but he has been to London and he has never mentioned any other place. You must be wrong. My son says England is an island and London and Cardiff are its towns. How big are they?"

It was too hot to argue so I gave him an idea of their size and said London was where the King lived. Though I had not Mrs. Bent's book with me at the time I remembered her saying something about an English king in Hajarein and asked him if he knew anything about it.

"Not English," he said, "but Christian, and his name was 'Āmr al Qeis al Kindi. His father was killed in mistake by one of his tribes called the Beni 'Asad. So they came to Dammūn where he lived and told him that they would have him as their king as they had killed his father in mistake. But he refused and went with other Kinda tribes to fight them, but he fought the wrong people, and when he had killed many he cried out that he had avenged his father. He was sorry when he heard he had made a mistake and went back to Dammūn. He was a Christian."

Later when I re-read the passage in Mrs. Bent's book it seemed to me likely enough that he was her informant, for she says: "We saw no more of the leprous Seiyid who told such wondrous tales about the English king who once lived at Hajarein and how the English, Turks and Arabs were all descended from King Sem."

Meanwhile D. returned. There had been a regular reception in a room on the ground floor where women from other houses came in to see the show, wearing long dirty-white cotton cloaks and a piece of blue cloth over their faces. They greeted those seated on the floor by kissing their hands and tops of their heads, sniffing loudly at the same time. These women had their hair done in myriads of tiny plaits and one curl plastered on the forehead. Some had their eyebrows painted bright green, others outlined their eyes with kohl and extended it to their temples and nearly all had smeared their faces with yellow ochre. Hands and feet were hennaed, and they were heavily decked with silver necklaces, anklets, bracelets and ear-rings; even the tiny babies had their ears pulled down by the weight of numerous silver rings hung all round the lobes.

Muhammad proposed we should go out and look at the ruins of Gheibun, where there are three wells. As we wandered about looking for bits of inscriptions and pottery, my eye was caught by a piece of black glass which I picked up, wondering if the ancients could have used it. The small boys, sharp eyed, watched everything I picked up and one came to see what I had got. In a few minutes he and others came with more slivers and I saw that they were obsidian and further that there was a family resemblance between them. They looked like what are known as flakes—pieces of stone knocked off a matrix to make arrowheads, knives and so on.[1] The principal point of interest was that their presence established that Gheibun had contained a factory of implements. I also picked up a sheep's tooth.

"What's that?" asked Muhammad.

"A sheep's tooth," I said, handing it to him.

"This isn't a sheep's tooth," he said. "It's a tooth of the teeth of the sons of 'Ad."

"Why, it's much too big for a man," I argued.

"Ah, the sons of 'Ad were fifty cubits high. They had big teeth. Look at these huge blocks of stone, no ordinary man could build with them."

Muhammad was so sure the matter did not admit of argument, that I felt again that "there were giants in the land in those days."

[1] Since then the pre-historian of the Egyptian Scientific Mission to the Hadhramaut has seen them and expressed the opinion that they are a fine collection of implements including bits of knives, saw teeth and scrapers of neolithic period.

## Chapter XVII

## INTO THE WADI HADHRAMAUT

*I do at length descry the happy shore*
*In which I hope ere long for to arrive;*
*Fair soil it seems from far, and fraught with store*
*Of all that dear and dainty is alive.*       SPENCER.

AFTER lunch we packed up and decided to leave on our donkeys, for the cars had not yet arrived. We went on riding until after sunset and dismounted under some date palms, wanting to stay the night in this pleasant grove. There was a fort just above us on the hill occupied by a few Yafa'i soldiers, and this we thought would be suitable for our followers. But Salih 'Ali was not satisfied and wanted to be in the town of Haura, which he assured me was "here." I let myself be persuaded and walked along behind him under an embankment feeling for some curious reason that there was a railway above it. His constant "here" developed finally into a forty minute walk, tiring as it was on sand. At last we saw the town and turned off among some date palms meaning to camp there. But again we were frustrated, for swarms of the inhabitants came from the town begging us to sleep there. Their invitation was so pressing that we had to give up our green quarter for the roof of a dar belonging to 'Awadh 'Umar Ba Sunkar, where we sat for a long time surrounded by a group of twenty-eight men and boys of all ages. Carpets were spread and everybody was very friendly, though we were tired and wanted our dinner. There was a great Java connection in this town,[1] as in the neighbouring villages, and the

[1] The leading people of the town are townsmen of the BaWazir family, and a very nice middle-aged man, Muhammad bin 'Abdulla bin 'Umar BaWazir, seemed to be the leading spirit in the absence of the local governor, Sa'dallah Faraj, who was on leave. The townsmen of the Hadhramaut, who are derived principally from eighty families who migrated from Iraq with the ancestor of the Seiyids over a thousand years ago, are divided into four classes, merchants, artificers, labourers and servants. They live in the towns, do not bear arms, and are the principal taxpayers.

*(For completion of footnote see page opposite.)*

Java blood of many of the younger people was clearly apparent in their faces.

It was not until seven that we were up next morning, washing and dressing on the roof watched by a group of women standing on a near-by roof who did not move even when I levelled my field-glasses at them, so I gave it up and carried on with my washing and tooth brushing. We had sent the night before to a merchant at Henin said to have a car. In the early morning came the answer to the letter. There was a car at Henin which the owner, Sheikh Muhammad Sa'id Mart'a was willing to put at our disposal but his driver had gone to Mukalla. However, he suggested if any of our party could drive we might take it. So we then decided that a small party should make for Henin and the rest go on to Hauta, to be picked up later by car if possible.

After much talk D., Hassan, Ganess, who had burnt his hand badly in Du'an, and myself left for Henin, the Hauta party starting shortly afterwards. In spite of our protests Muhammad bin 'Abdulla Ba Wazir insisted on coming with us to show us the way. It was as well that we had a guide, for there was a perfect maze of paths amongst the mounds of clayey sand through which we rode. They were only about fifteen feet high but completely blocked the view, and we could rarely see more than a few yards at a time, even when we came across the small patches of cultivation set among them.

The heat was intense, and though the dust rose in clouds Sheikh Muhammad would not leave us, but plodded swiftly along for more than an hour, talking all the time. When finally we saw Henin before us he consented to say good-bye. We shook hands warmly and parted, but he stood looking after us, waving a turban whenever we turned round. There is a proverb in Zanzibar: "If you say 'I know' you will lead the way as long as the sun; if you say 'I don't know' you will rest in peace at home." My experience in the Hadhramaut was that you did not even have to ask the way; people insisted on showing it to you.

The economic life of the country depends to a large extent on them, for the people obtain the necessities of life from them and they form the main link with the outside world. Many are wealthy and have considerable influence in the country. The leading merchants to some extent govern the affairs of their towns and have developed more than a germ of municipal organization. There are also signs of a kind of trades unionism, or rather of the medieval guild system, among the various artificers, and professions are usually, though not exclusively, hereditary.

## INTO THE WADI HADHRAMAUT

It was just about eleven o'clock when we first saw Henin four and a half miles away below the opposite wadi wall, but it looked much closer. Little of the wadi could be seen to the east, but to the west its vast walls stretched away to the distance, seeming to end with massive pillars on either side. I could hardly believe that here at last was the great wadi Hadhramaut I had so long desired to see.

It seemed an age before we reached our goal, though its buildings were clearly visible. At last we came into a belt of cultivation, and then reached Henin with its houses, gaily striped with white-wash, spread out along the foot of the cliffs. We rode towards the largest building, which we were told belonged to the owner of the car, and were welcomed by a group of men standing at the foot of a flight of steps. The owner of the house, Sheikh Muhammad Sa'id Mart'a, like the Sei'ar near whom he lived, a descendant of the Kings of Kinda, was astonishingly hospitable, and at once took us up to a pleasant room in a small house next to his harem. Our host was much distressed at our fatigue and our chapped lips, for we had all been suffering from the herpes, which I find inseparable from changes of altitude. So on we were taken upstairs to a small room well carpeted with mattresses and pillows on which we could lie.

"The car," said Sheikh Muhammad as soon as tea had been served, "is yours, but it is not big and will only take five at a squeeze." He himself insisted on coming and said that he had found a driver so there would be only room for D., Hassan and myself. Ganess, who had been feeling the heat owing to his burnt hand, was left behind to be picked up later.

After our host had said his prayers we went out to the car. It was an Opel, small but comfortably sprung, and we started off, at what seemed an incredible speed after nine days of donkeys, on our first car drive in the Hadhramaut. It was strange to find cars up in the wadi. There are not far short of a hundred of them and they have to be taken to pieces at the coast and carried up on camels. It takes twelve camels to carry one car over the mountains.

Forty minutes along a sandy track brought us to Hauta where we passed Zaidi, Salih 'Ali and the rest in the street. We stopped outside the enormous palace of Sultan 'Ali bin Salah, until recently the Qu'aiti Governor of the Shibam province. Here we were met by one of our future hosts in Shibam, Sheikh Sa'id Bubekr La'ajam, and Sultan 'Ali, a tall, thin young man with a small moustache. After tea and conversation we drove on again with

## SHIBAM

Sheikh Muhammad to Shibam, which we reached in just under an hour.

From a distance Shibam looks like an enormous sand castle, for all the buildings are on a level. It is set in the midst of dates and cultivation, with delightful villas set in beautiful gardens in the rich man's suburb of Seheil under the right bank of the wadi. We first drove into the town, a perilous performance, for the way up to the gate is over steep, rough stone steps. These do not daunt the local drivers, who take the steps at tremendous speed, miraculously avoiding the walls on either side of the narrow gateway. In less than a mile we came to rest beside a high wall with a small doorway leading into a courtyard, where Sheikh Sa'id's villa faced us. It is built in the Singapore style, yet it gave an impression of the Italian Riviera with all its gay colours. Before the entrance was a square stone mounting block bearing a complete Himyaritic inscription:

This had been brought from a few miles away by Colonel Boscawen and Hussein, brother of our host. A double flight of steps led up to the front door, and a short passage gave on to a big hall. At the back of the villa was a small swimming-pool, and upstairs a large room, airy, well lighted and furnished in European style, which became our bed-sitting-room, and where we received a host of visitors.

It was late, nearly seven o'clock, when we woke to the early morning music I love the best, the creaking of a water-wheel, and I went out on to the veranda to watch the team of a man, woman, donkey and ox that were drawing up the water from the well for the garden. Every time the team reached the top of the slope the ox was given a bunch of grass, but why neither the woman nor the ass were rewarded I have never discovered.

The houses of Shibam are amazingly high, six storeys being the average height, but they look like twelve because each floor has a row of small ventilating windows above the ordinary ones. They are built of mud on stone foundations. From upper windows, behind doorways and up side alleys, veiled females peered at us as we passed. Much of the charm of the place is lost owing to the appalling smells rising from the open gutters

## INTO THE WADI HADHRAMAUT

which run down the centre of the narrow lane. I expect I shall always be remembered in Shibam for having asked for the gutters to be cleaned out. The refuse was sold for manture.

The city raised itself aloft on a small eminence close to the right bank of the wadi. It is an ancient town but not so old as Shabwa. It is, in fact, the successor of Shabwa, for when the glory departed from the latter and its shining marble temples fell to ruin, the inhabitants were driven to find another home by the decline of the incense trade and the invading sand. Shabwa owed something to its position as a distributing centre for the incense trade and when that went by sea it became out of the way. This happened perhaps early in the Christian era, but that is not to say that the existence of Shibam dates from that time. There is evidence that there was a settlement there centuries before that date, but it must have been unimportant, not being mentioned by any identifiable name of the ancients. It is not until the time of Hamdani (died A.D. 945) that we have any note of the place. He tells us that Shibam was the chief city of the province. It had thirty mosques,[1] but in his day half the town was in ruins. Its original name, he adds, was Shibat. The sense of Shibat in Himyaritic is rest and quiet, and of Shibam, height.

But there is nothing now in Shibam, at any rate above ground, which is really ancient, though the foundations of the Jama' mosque date from the time of the Abbasides.

But to-day Shibam has great political importance, and the Qu'aiti Government has described it to me as the "eye and backbone of the Hadhramaut." Its province extends westwards to Husn al 'Abr, though eastwards only to just beyond the town, but it includes the lower part of the Wadi Du'an and the Wadi 'Amd, and the Sei'ar country depends on it too. Most of this country is not under direct Qu'aiti rule except for the actual towns of Shibam, Al Qatn, Haura and a few small villages. But he who holds Shibam in fact holds the country, especially if he claims juris-

---

[1] The ill-fated 'Omarah who was strangled in 1174 mentioning the works of the great Yemeni Governor Hussein ibn Salama, who died in 1011, says that he constructed a series of great mosques and lofty minarets from Hadhramaut to the city of Mecca *via* Aden. The first stations were at Tarim and Shibam. Lastly Ibn Khaldūn (A.D. 1332–1406) describing the provinces of the Hadhramaut says, "The largest city of Hadhramaut in the present day is the fortress of Shibam, in which the horses of the king are kept. Along with ash-Shihr and 'Omān, it originally belonged to 'Ad, from whose people it was conquered by the Banu Ya'rub son of Kahtan."

diction over the main routes and protects them as the Qu'aiti does. The tribes cannot do without Shibam as a market to buy and sell, but Shibam could, if necessary, do without the tribes. The present governor of Shibam is in fact a slave, subject to the Qu'aiti Sultan, by name Ferai Sa'id. Being of lower social status than his own townsmen he is regarded with an odd mixture of respect and condescension. For the governor of Shibam cannot, in view of the town's importance, be a nonentity if he has a certain amount of tact and firmness.

Yet though Shibam dominates the whole province, the Qu'aiti Sultan allows autonomy in the towns outside his direct control, and while not interfering with tribal government he has treaties with all tribes in and around his territories. These treaties are of two kinds, which we will call "A" and "B." "A" involves an undertaking by the tribe to respond to the Sultan's call at any time, while "B" is simply an engagement of friendship and an undertaking to co-operate in matters of mutual interest. Thus he has an "A" agreement with a clan of the Nahd, an uneasy tribe half nomad, half settled, and a "B" agreement with the Sei'ar tribe, who are also allied to the Kathīri. The Sei'ar are the wolves of South Arabia, having some 1,700 armed men; they are a name of terror to their neighbours and almost without friends. Being nomads they are elusive and hard to punish, and when they go abroad outside their own territory they travel in small numbers, adopt a hang-dog mien, try to remain anonymous and, taking byways, journey mostly by night.

The day after our arrival at Shibam, Seiyid 'Abdul Rahman al Jifri came to take us to have tea in Seiyun. As we crossed into Kathiri territory, just east of Shibam, he turned to D. and said: "Congratulations on being the first European lady to enter Kathiri territory. Mrs. Bent was the first in Shibam, but you're the first to get beyond."

It took us three-quarters of an hour to cover the thirteen miles of sandy track, for the most part surrounded by date palms and cultivation. Half an hour brought us to Al Ghurfa, where we saw an elaborate system of trenches reminiscent of Flanders, which marked the scene of the fighting that had been taking place almost up to the time of our visit. About five or six years ago trouble arose between the Āl 'Umar and Āl Amr clans of the Kathīri tribe. It began with some of the tribesmen of the Āl 'Umar raiding the inhabitants of Al Ghurfa and generally making trouble. Bin 'Abdat, the Chief of the Āl 'Amr protested and proposed to Salim bin Ja'far, the Chief of the Āl 'Umar, that they should unite to make peace in

Al Ghurfa, but as he was not supported he established control in the town himself. Seiyid Hussein al Mihdhar, at that time the Qu'aiti Wazir, persuaded the Kathiri Sultan and Salim bin Ja'far to join him in trying to force Bin 'Abdat to vacate Al Ghurfa. 'Ali bin Mansur, the Kathiri Sultan, marched against him with one gun, Seiyid Hussein brought another together with troops from Shibam and Salim bin Ja'far brought his men. They bombarded Bin 'Abdat and, as I was told, "they had a good battle but without success." Seiyid Hussein, having successfully complicated things, then retired, and so did Sultan 'Ali, who came to terms with Bin 'Abdat. Thus Salim bin Ja'far and Bin 'Abdat, like Tweedledum and Tweedledee, agreed to fight it out together.

Both sides dug elaborate trenches: Salim enlivened the proceedings by importing a sort of armoured car from Java, and they continued a guerrilla warfare for several years until the Seiyids managed to negotiate a precarious armistice. The armoured car was derelict when we passed Al Ghurfa and was for sale—cheap. So of course the next person who wants to start a small war will not find it as expensive to do so.

A few days later we went to Tarim for the night, borrowing the only car left in Shibam, a Graham Paige, in bad condition and without a driver. D. took the wheel and we left Shibam just before five o'clock. The car had no foot-brake in action, the hand-brake only functioned when practically at a standstill, and the steering-gear was loose. Added to this we ran into a sandstorm when crossing the Shibam landing-ground which continued for some time. The road to Seiyun we had already experienced, but from then onwards the track was new to us and driving was, to say the least, difficult, for the road was full of humps, water channels, crevices and other perils. Hassan and I would almost certainly have been bumped right out of the car if the hood had not been up. After a peculiarly bad one I said jovially, knowing his predilection for a famous London hotel: "Never mind, Hassan, we'll go to the Metropole and have a drink when our journey's over."

By the time we reached Mariama, a small village beyond Seiyun, it was dark. Here we were made to pick up an unwanted escort, a customary form of obtaining money from travellers. After losing the track several times and twice just pulling up on the edge of precipices, we crossed the dry beds of two wadis and a little later we saw afar the astonishing sight of an immense house ablaze with electric light. The walls of Tarim loomed up and it was with intense relief that we drew up at the gate of the town. It was already closed, for it was now a quarter to eight and it was not until

D. had hooted many times that at last two women unbarred the big wooden doors and pulled them apart. It had been a remarkable drive and for my part I did not know which to admire most, D.'s control of an almost uncontrollable car over a nightmare road, or Hassan's control over his cigar which he kept in his mouth despite the most appalling jolts. As it was the year of grace 1934 I felt that it was appropriate that the first European woman to enter Tarim should have done so by driving a car there in a suitable atmosphere of adventure.

We drove over an open space and along narrow roads to a palace decorated with flags and illuminated all over with electric light. As we stepped into this amazing edifice I whispered to Hassan in a voice of awe: "Where are we Hassan, is it real?"

"The Metropole," replied Hassan with an expressive gesture of his hands which reminded me of an obsequious manager receiving a moneyed guest. We were welcomed by our millionaire hosts, Seiyids 'Abdul Rahman, Bubakr and 'Umar al Kaf—the principal members of the wealthiest Hadhrami family in Singapore. A man, whom we got to know later as Hassan, and who combines many functions but for the moment was the head butler, showed us our bedroom and took me along to the bathroom. It was with something more than mere astonishment that I entered this luxuriously equipped room. A marble bath had been built into one corner, a fitted basin with running water stood against the wall, on a ledge near the window had been spread out an assortment of bottles of scent, hair lotion, face creams and other toilet accessories. There was a shower bath, snow-white towels on a rail, soaps, loofahs, a set of pink enamel brushes, everything we could desire, and wonder of wonders a real "pull and let go," an item scarcely to be seen even in Aden.. What was even more wonderful was that *everything* worked. By the time the perfect butler *cum* valet had enquired what hair wash I should like I was feeling distinctly out of place without dress clothes.

The drawing-room was furnished with comfortable chairs and sofas, many small tables, English carpets, gilt mirrors, chandeliers and glass-fronted cases filled with marmalade dishes and things like that. A large bedroom next door had a ceiling of looking-glasses and luxurious furniture. Electric fans, iced drinks and telephones (connecting up the houses of the Al Kaf family) completed my astonishment and I began to feel it would all have disappeared like Aladdin's palace by morning. Seiyid 'Umar pushed a cigarette-box across the table to me. I opened it and took a cigarette, but nearly collapsed with surprise when the box struck up "Rose Marie."

A long table had been laid for dinner in a wide passage-like dining-room. We had an enormous meal beginning with rissoles, followed by chicken, followed by huge piles of rice and entire sheep. Hassan served and we were all given a leg of mutton each. We wound up with a few trifles like caramel pudding and tinned fruit. Seiyid 'Abdul Rahman made a speech of welcome. Soon afterwards we all dispersed to our beds. Ours were brand new, having been unpacked and put together after our arrival. We slept well—save that I had a nightmare after the leg of mutton in which I found myself wandering over the horrid wastes of the Sei'ar country without a compass and believed I was alone on the moon.

Morning brought butler Hassan and early morning tea. Also a sense of relief that the Aladdin's palace had not disappeared in the night. Hearing that there was a swimming-pool we decided to have a bathe before breakfast, and were driven to a house outside the town where we found a perfect bath set in delightful surroundings. There were changing-rooms on one side, a small terrace on the other arranged with carpets and pillows to make an excellent sun bath or drying retreat, and a high wall at one end over which the trees from the adjoining garden gave a very pleasant touch of colour. The bath itself was about thirty feet long, and the water sufficiently warm to be enjoyable and sufficiently cool to be refreshing. In the better baths, like this one, the water is kept running by means of a one-horse-power oil engine. Seiyid 'Umar told me that there were at least a hundred of these engines up and down the wadi for pumping water.

Returning we ate a huge breakfast of boiled and fried eggs, cake and tinned fruit. When this meal had been disposed of we got ready to leave. A surprise awaited us on the return drive for during the night the seil had come down and the two wadis that had been bone dry the night before were now flowing with water. It took some time to get across for the water was deep and got into the engine. We reached Shibam in the evening to find it raining and to make arrangements for our desert trip.

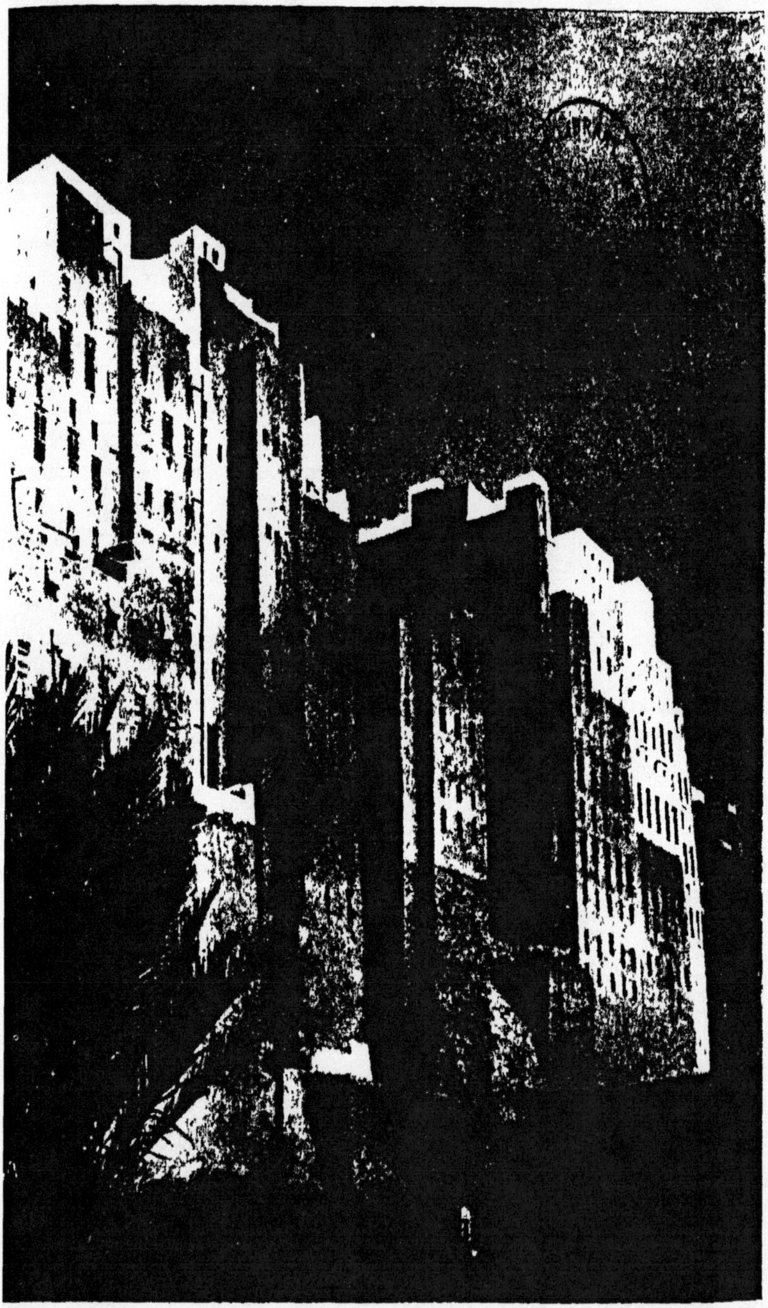

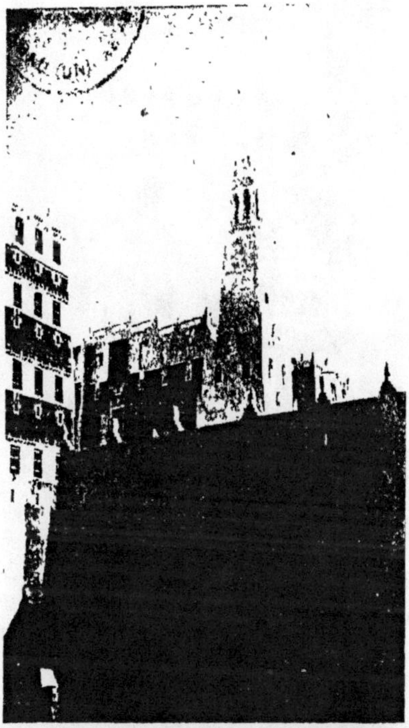

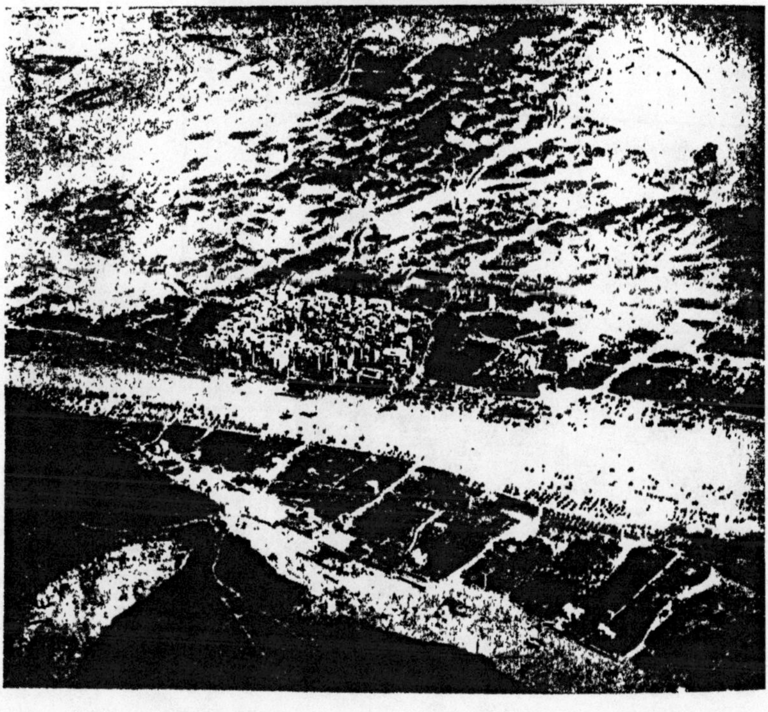

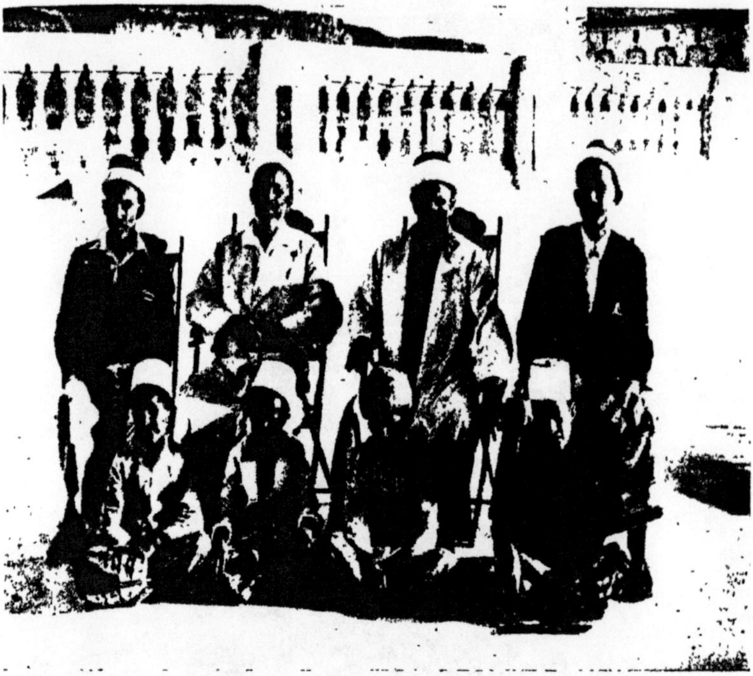

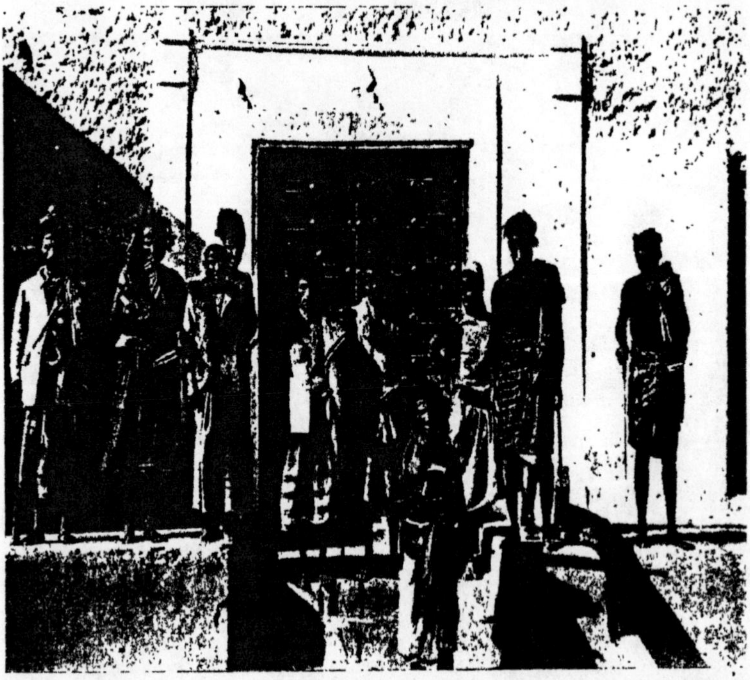

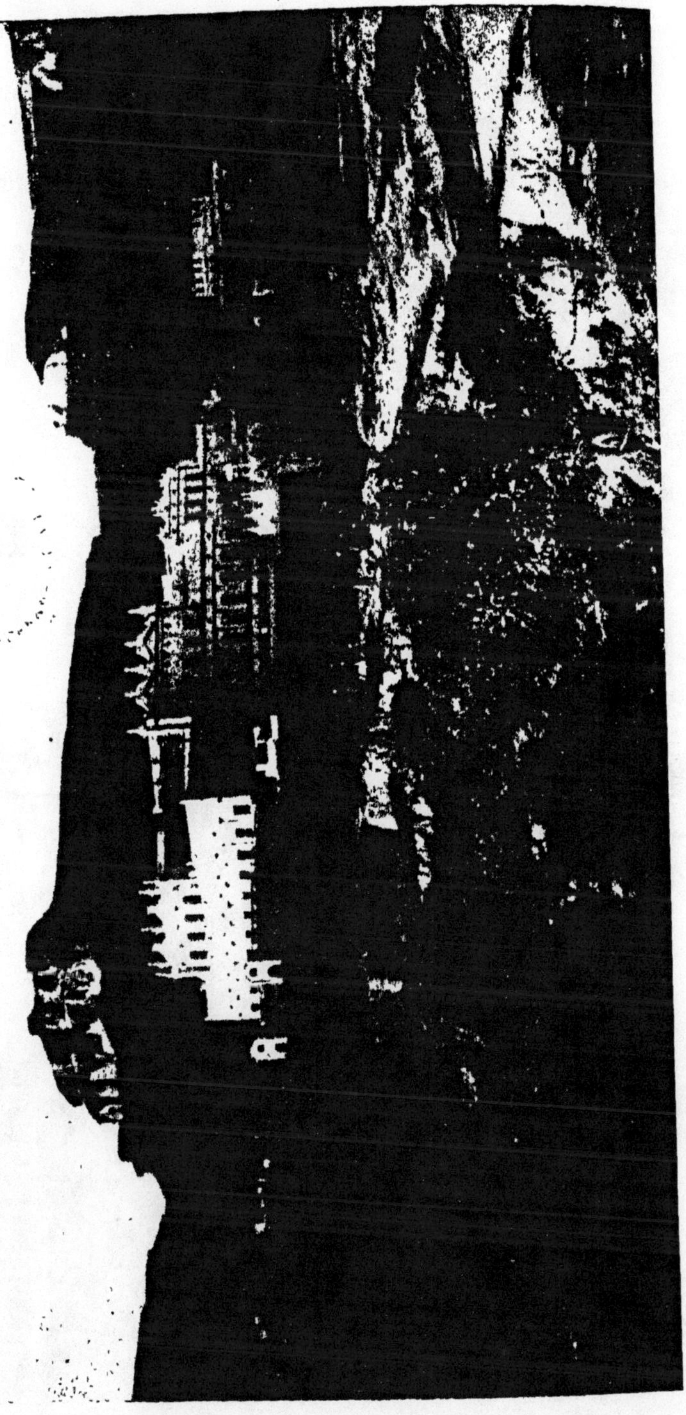

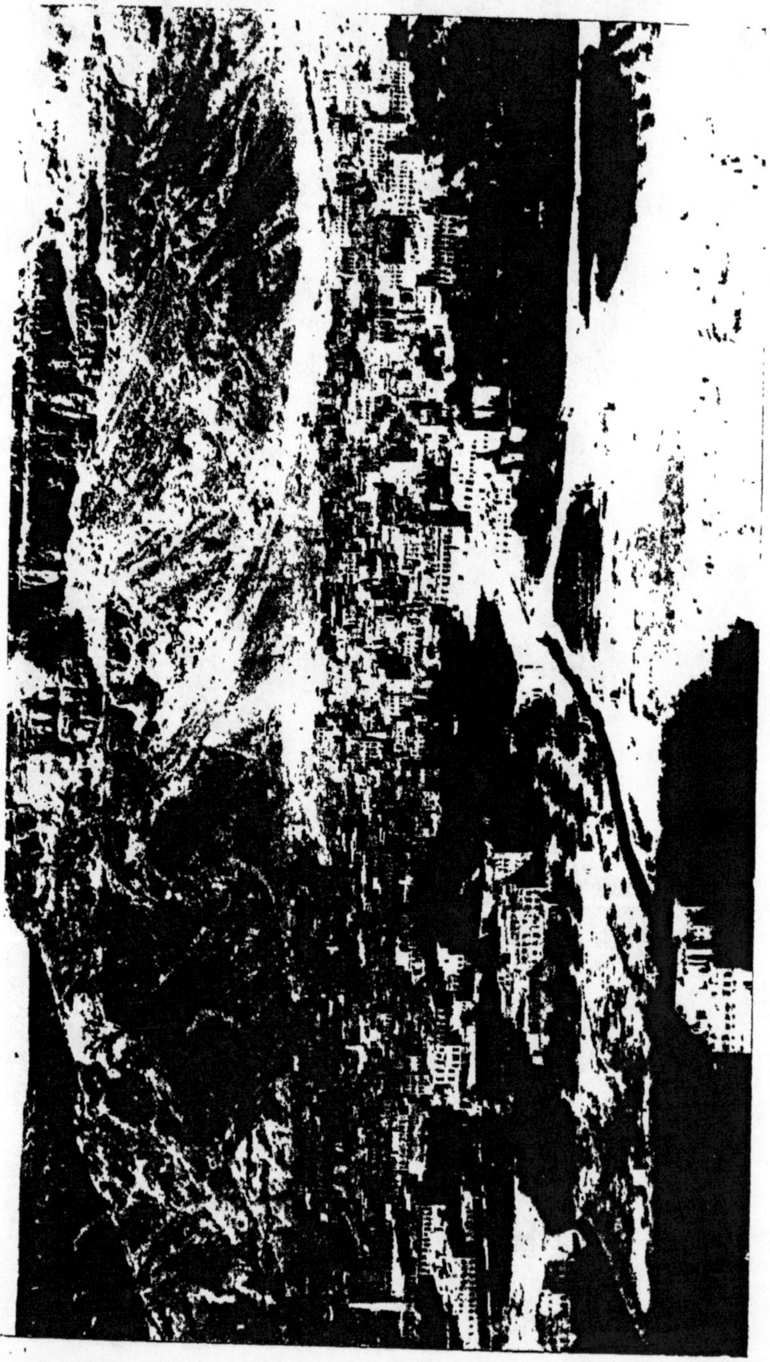

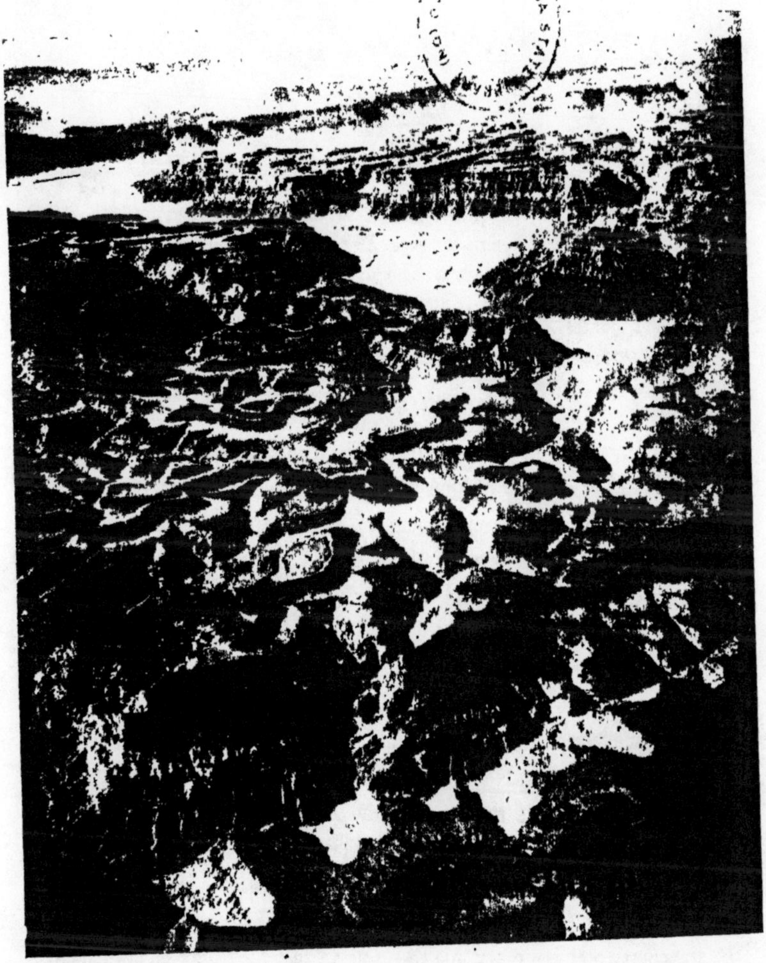

*Chapter XVIII*

## THE TOMB OF SALIH AND THE SEI'AR COUNTRY

*And Salah lived thirty years, and begat Eber: And Salah lived after he begat Eber four hundred and three years, and begat sons and daughters.* GENESIS.

*Towards thee the Polestars led, and there where men's feet had passed a track plain to see that wound by cairns over ridges scarred.*
ALQAMAH.   Trans. SIR C. LYALL.

WITH the exception of Colonel Boscawen, who has left no record of his travels, the Sei'ar country had not hitherto been visited by a European, and never by a Government representative. Enquiries as to possible routes from members of the Sei'ar tribe in Mukalla seemed to point to the feasibility of the programme which I had framed tentatively in Aden, but the more enquiries I made in Shibam and Tarim the longer the journey seemed to become. All together seven different proposals were made by Sei'ars and others to take us to their country and all of them described routes varying either completely or in part. In addition I met some beduin of the Ahl Bùreik in Shibam who invited us to go to Shabwa. The Ahl Bureik are a small tribe of sheikhs turned completely beduin who now own Shabwa. Once they were masters of Shihr and Britain's first treaty with Shihr was with 'Ali Naji, the Bureiki Chieftain. Shabwa has now a local reputation only for its rock salt, and the fact that the beduin have been unwilling to let travellers enter is simply due to suspicion that they may be after their salt. The ancient Sabota is now said to be buried in the sands, though there are some of its walls still standing and built into modern mud huts. There are said to be only four inscriptions visible. As Pliny says, it stands on a wadi hill and was famous among the ancients as the incense capital with sixty temples, so from a personal point of view I should very much have liked to have gone there, but official considerations required the other journey.

It soon became clear that with our limited time we could not do the whole journey to the desert and back to Tarim, and so I reduced our requirements to a visit into the Sei'ar country and a return by another route. Ba

## THE TOMB OF SALIH AND THE SEI'AR COUNTRY

Rumeidan, the home of Sheikh Tannaf bin Seheil bin Rumeidan, one of the principal Sei'ar chieftains, was my main objective. From there I hoped to go to 'Eiwa and perhaps to the edge of the desert. 'Eiwa figured in almost all the routes offered me.

I interviewed a number of Sei'ars with a view to selecting our caravan, and the first candidate for the honour of being our Muqaddam was one of the wildest-looking specimens I have ever seen. He had long straight hair which stuck out like wire all over his head and a scarred face, with red eyes, and a huge nose. He really did look like a human wolf and I saw Hassan's jaw drop about a mile when he was brought in. That evening Hassan was not in the sitting-room, so I went along to find him. He was writing hard in his bedroom.

"What on earth are you up to, Hassan?" I asked.

"I'm writing my will," he said. "If we go with those people we'll never come back."

During the first few days of our stay in Shibam transport had been plentiful. Then came the rain and after it the seil. The coming of the seil is a great event. All Shibam leaves its business and shuts its doors and turns out to see the turgid brown life-giving waters flood into the date gardens. In a few hours there were ten feet of water in some of the gardens outside the city walls. Everyone talked of it, everyone went to see it. As if by magic the camel park of Shibam, usually so crowded, became empty—the beduin had gone off taking their camels for ploughing. There was no transport to be had.

On Saturday, November 24th, our eighth day in Shibam, there was no news in the morning. Hassan went off very early to see if there was anything to be done, and at about ten o'clock he sent a note to say that five camels were ready and others would be there the next day. That afternoon, however, we managed to make a start after much wrangling as to price of camels and duration of journey.

Under the cloudless sky we circled the west wall of the town and passed a mosque just outside the wall. For the next quarter of an hour or so we rode among dates and passed by the large cemetery of the city, and we had been going for more than half an hour when we left them for the sand mounds, dotted here and there with small forts. Presently the wadi became more open, and as we made our way towards the north side of the wadi we passed a number of villages, Ghanima and Huweila being the largest, but the south side was much more cultivated than the north. There had always been trouble, we were told, between Ghanima and Huweila until Sultan 'Umar put a stop to it.

Our beduin maintained a ceaseless conversation. They were incapable of speaking quietly, but at all times and in all places screamed at each other in raucous voices. All carried rifles except the usual small child who seems an indispensable appendage to every caravan. 'Amr the Muqaddam turned out a willing person and anxious to please, though he was never quite sure what to make of us and was not the same lovable personality as Sa'id the piper, to whom we had said good-bye, with many regrets, in Ba Surra's castle. His men were a mixed lot of Sei'ars and Harizis.

Towards evening we entered the Wadi Ser. It is wide at its entrance and guarded by a dar called Dar Salih, at present empty. We had to stop while the beduin yelled in argument as to where we should park. The uproar was increased by the arrival of three men whom the chief, Tannaf, had sent to meet us, one of them his son-in-law, Suleiman bin Yeslem. Tannaf, it appeared, had heard of our intentions and remembering the bounties of Colonel Boscawen was anxious that we too should come to him. After a few minutes we moved on and, as a fresh wind rose from the north-east, yellow and pale pink rays were cast by the setting sun while we crossed slowly to the west side of the wadi and stopped outside the village of Al Atfa. It was an open and barren spot.

The head man of the village came and begged us to use his house where he said Colonel Boscawen had stayed, but we excused ourselves on the plea that we wanted to be off early in the morning. We spent a miserably cold night but dawn and tea came at last to relieve us and, leaving our beduin to wrangle over a change of some of the camels, we started off for the grave or the prophet Salih. It was eight o'clock when we finally got away in a babel of screaming beduin. We started off over a waste with no vegetation and were soon in the Wadi Khonab, sandy but with lines of stones marking where there were once fields. As we passed along the Wadi Khonab the tomb of Salih[1] with the attendant villages of Asanab and Khonab came gradually into sight.

---

[1] Unlike the tomb of the prophet Hud in the Wadi Maseila which is universally venerated, the tomb of Salih in the Wadi Khonab is peculiarly the property of the beduin, and educated Muslim opinion holds that he is buried in the Sinai Peninsula. The beduin believe that Salih was the father of Hud, and if we may equate Salih with Salah of Genesis x and xi, they have some support for their belief, for Hud is generally equated with Eber the son of Salah.

The general appearance of the tomb must have altered considerably since the Bents' day. Mrs. Bent describes it as consisting simply "of a long uncovered pile of stones." It is now enclosed in a long low building with windows down the length of its sides. Up on the hill-side behind the tomb are five other buildings and a mosque; to the right a couple of murabba'as and a siqaya. We entered the tomb on stockinged feet. The roof is low and made of the trunks of date palms, and the windows all the way round have neither shutters nor panes. The tomb is now cemented over so that it has a smooth but undulating surface, and an inscription in Himyaritic is set up on end like a flower label at the head of the tomb. I wanted to copy it, but did not want to give cause for suspicion.

"What is written there?" I said.

"Nebi Allah Salih, on him be peace," straightway replied the custodian.

"Tell me about it."

"He was a prophet of the people of 'Ad and he died and was buried here, and his son was Nebi Allah Hud, who is buried in the Wadi Maseila at Qabr Hud."

"That is very interesting. May I write it down so that I don't forget it?"

"Write, Sahib, write."

So I copied down the inscription, which reads:

|| 𐩡 𐩺 X O | 𐩺 ||
|| 𐩺 | 𐩭 ||𐩺

There were a number of stones and fossils placed loose on the tomb at either end and others embedded in the plaster. Hassan kindly "borrowed" us one of the fossils and, though the beduin assert that anything taken from the tomb will always return to it, so far, apart from its journey with us and to the British Museum (where it was identified as a Middle Eocene Gastropoda Campanile sp. indet.), it has evinced no sign of wandering.[1] We walked all round on our stockinged feet and I think our beduin were

---

[1] Hassan also measured the tomb with his forearm making the length 44¼ dhirras and the width 7¼. This is equivalent to 63 feet 11⅝ inches by 10 feet 9⅜ inches. D. paced it and made the length 55 feet by 11 feet. In height it came up to her hip or 3 feet 3¼ inches. These measurements are different from the Bents' estimate but do not appear to afford any real evidence for the belief that the tomb is never the same length. In any case Nebi Salih was clearly a giant among men.

## HIMYARITIC SIGNPOST

pleased with the reverence with which we treated their prophet's resting-place.

We now retraced our steps and later in the afternoon turned into the Wadi Ser where we camped for the night in a wide open space where two other wadis joined the Ser. Our road next morning led northwards where vegetation changed to a waste of stones, a few bushes and a little cultivated sesame. Gradually we drew into the narrower part of the wadi and reached the Wadi Latakh with the tiny village of Al Had in its mouth. Near-by was the tomb of a weli or saint, and we came on a rough Himyaritic inscription on a massive boulder standing upright at the side of the wadi. So far we had followed the route that the Bents had trodden in January, 1894 and here was the inscription or signpost which Mrs. Bent describes and which was the furthest point that the Bents reached. The seil had, no doubt, removed some stones since they passed this way, and the huts of Al Had may have been rebuilt, but it is plain that little else had changed in the forty years that had passed since they, too, photographed this inscription. I could not make out the word *masabam* (caravan road) though a *mim* and some *bas* appear on it. Still it looked as fresh as it must have done to them, though the last to read its directions had perhaps passed that way more than a thousand years before.

Shortly after leaving the Himyaritic signpost we turned right into the Wadi Sodaf and entered the Sei'ar country. Sand, stones, sumr and harma seems an adequate description of our way. For some distance the wadi was wide, but in its upper reaches it naturally narrowed and, with each successive junction with its tributaries, the track, which had at first been smooth and firm, deteriorated and became so stony that we could not ride.

Now and then we passed small caravans of Sei'ars on their way to Shibam carrying 'elb trunks, charcoal, and saf (*Hyphaene thebaica* (L) Mart.) for making mats. Whenever caravans cross all members exchange greetings as they pass. It is a pleasant custom and I always enjoyed the handshake and the word exchanged. The beduin clap their right hands together with a loud smack and make a kissing noise. Usually no time is lost over these salutations but Suleiman generally stopped to talk, with the result that the whole caravan was often held up. Our camelmen were the noisiest with whom we had ever travelled. They were safely in their own country, free to shout and sing to their hearts' content. As the wadi narrowed, the voices echoed from the steep walls.

A few hours' journey beyond the last tiny village called Dar Sodaf our beduin pointed out a long grave which they said was twelve cubits long and was the grave of Nebu Mola Sodaf, their prophet, though really the tribal ancestor. Here it seemed to me, as it had seemed to the Bents at Qabr Salih, that there was a wonderful continuity of tradition preserved by the beduin. The Wadi Sodaf is quite unknown to the educated people of Hadhramaut and yet Arab genealogies give Sadaf as one of the descendants of Hadhramaut the son of Qahtan.

During the afternoon we were met by 'Awadh bin Tannaf, the son of the Sei'ar chief, whose father had sent him to meet us. I thought there was something a bit ominous in this unusual eagerness and I was not wrong. We climbed steadily all the afternoon while the wadi became narrower and narrower until we reached an 'aqaba. When we had mounted this we found ourselves again on top of the world, for the first time since we had descended to Du'an sixteen days before. It was a brown stone jōl, utterly barren.

By about six o'clock we had reached our highest point on the plateau land to the north of the Wadi Hadhramaut. It was over 3,600 feet and we had climbed a thousand of them since morning. We then descended towards Qā' al Fadhūl near which we camped in an open stony plain with a little vegetation. We were now on the watershed which separates the wadis running south towards the Hadhramaut from those that run north into the Great Desert.

We had now been travelling for three and a half days but had not reached Ba Rumeidan. On Monday and Tuesday our beduin had told us we ought to be there by eleven o'clock to-day, Wednesday, November 28th, but the night before they had hedged about this so that as soon as we had breakfasted I called for 'Amr the Muqaddam and Suleiman to find out the truth. Faced with the direct question it appeared that we could not reach Ba Rumeidan to-day and perhaps not until late the next day (Thursday). Further enquiries elicited the information that it would take us at least three full days to get to 'Eiwa from where we were, four days to the edge of the desert and six into the desert itself. As I was due back in Aden as near the 20th December as I could manage, such a programme was not possible. I did not feel justified in spending the extra time for other reasons, the principal being that as Suleiman, Tannaf's son-in-law, and 'Awadh, his son, were with me, I could get information about their country from them. Hassan had also found out by judicious enquiries from the camelmen that the great idea had been to entice us to Ba Rumeidan. Once there difficulties were to be made about getting to the edge of the desert without large payments, and our camelmen would plead that their rations had been eaten and that we must wait while others were fetched from Shibam. So I decided to return by another route, and while the packing was being done Suleiman and 'Awadh gave me particulars of the Sei'ars' neighbours and of their relations with them.

It was after half-past nine when we mounted and rode northwards over the jōl, which was even more barren and desolate than the way to Du'an. There were a few miserable-looking shrubs but little else, though we soon came in sight of the date palms and the five dars which mark the settlement of Qā' al Fadhūl, home of the Al bā Qarwan section of the Sei'ars. We saw little sign of other life on this jōl though very infrequently a lizard scurried away at our approach. Unlike the jōls we had crossed to reach Du'an, which were edged with trees and shrubs, those up here were quite barren. There were flat-topped hills all around but no peaks to be seen. From an occasional higher level we often had distant but dull views, endless flat, brown, gravelly plateaus varied now and then throughout the day by patches of black. At noon we passed across a shallow depression marking the boundary between Sei'ar and Kathīri territory. When we had reached the level of the flat country on the further side we saw for the first time a feature, a small pointed hill a mile or two ahead, and soon passed the first of a number of groups of ruins. This place was called 'Urum and all the ruins consisted of rough dry stone erections which our beduin attributed to the children of 'Ad. The buildings could not have been big enough to shelter adequately normal-sized human beings, and the absurdity of their sufficing giants did not seem to have occurred to them.

At one o'clock we halted by some ruins near the small pointed hill. Just beyond it was a series of four hillocks, the first three close together and the fourth some distance on, but the whole did not extend over a greater distance than a quarter of a mile. The first three hillocks were crowned with circular ruins and between the third and fourth there were fifteen heaps of stones in a straight line on the crest of the slope. Below the slope was level ground and perhaps a quarter of a mile ahead another row of stones and ruins on a hill. In between, the level ground was sprinkled with chert flakes indicating the site of a factory of chert implements.

For most of the afternoon we travelled over the same desolate landscape, coming eventually to depressions marking the upper reaches of the wadis or sha'bs (small water-courses) in which grew scraggy acacia. We eventually halted at a spot at the beginning of the Wadi Qubhudh down which we were to travel the next morning. The height was only 3,600 feet, but we passed here our coldest night of the whole journey, for the thermometer registered 37.3 at six-forty-five in the morning.

It soon warmed up, however, as we rode down the side of the wadi and near the first of two dars which mark the settlement of Rieidat al Kathiri we met the only inhabitant of the place, a woman with a donkey. She had come to see how her crops were getting on, for the place is only inhabited when the water comes, and the people live for the most part at a spot a few miles away.

Suleiman told a long story about a raid on the settlement in which he had been concerned some years before and our other Sei'ars told us of a raid they were plotting on the Mahra.

After leaving Rieidat we met with increasing vegetation and a few birds, most of them the same colour as the stones and earth, but the track so deteriorated that we had to dismount for the descent to the Wadi bed from which point the wadi belongs to the Āl Hariz tribe of which 'Amr's father was the Sheikh. Such inhabitants as there are live in caves in the walls of the wadi, some of which are quite spacious. The entrances are built up with loose stones and only a small gap left for man and beast to enter. Smaller caves are used for goats, and some are so small that they appeared to be little bigger than rabbit hutches.

During the afternoon we passed junctions with several other wadis and camped in a wide and pleasant spot. There, after dinner, 'Amr explained the marks on the camels, which I regret to say had not all been honestly come by.[1]

Early next morning we passed a small black rock by the wayside with a Himyaritic inscription, so I suppose we were travelling on another ancient route. There was much wild life here; most of the birds so harmonized with their surroundings that they were almost invisible, but we saw one beautiful pigeon, coloured olive green with a darker head, paler chest and a

[1] The Āl 'Aun or Āl Hatim, a Sei'ar section, make a cut between the nose and eyes.
Ad Dumān (Sie'ar clan) make a circle under the ear.
Al Akāsālīn (Sei'ar clan) a ·|· on the cheek.
Al Meshāīkh Āl Ishaq (Sei'ar a ∞ on outside of hind leg. These marks are made by a shaped iron.
Al Kibla tribe a large $\beta$.
Mahris make a circle on the neck.
Al Haras, between Sana' and Hodeida, a circle on the cheek.

yellow rump. In one of the little pools under the boulders D. captured a toad which we tried to keep alive, but it expired a few days later in Tarim and was duly bottled for the British Museum.

Unlike most wadis, which are better as one approaches their mouths, the Wadi Qubhudh became steadily worse, twisting this way and that and cluttered with round smooth boulders, some of them almost as big as cottages. We climbed over, under and round these boulders for several hours while Suleiman kept telling us that the place where we should stop for lunch was close by. He repeated this every few moments while we grew hotter and more bad-tempered slithering amongst the stones. At last we stopped and found shade up the hill-side among some rocks. There was not room for us all to sit together so we found perches one above each other. D. passed a plate down to Hassan and one up to me.

We had only been going a short distance in the afternoon when the wadi gradually became wider: and shortly before five we came in sight of the village of Qubhudh. As we drew nearer two small boys ran out to meet the caravan, kissing the men's hands in greeting. Other children, men and women, soon followed, for this was 'Amr's home, and it certainly looked very attractive with its 'elb trees and dates. We were greeted by 'Amr's toothless father, Salih bin 'Ali, the Sheikh of the little tribe, who gave us a warm welcome.

The next morning I had a long talk with Suleiman and 'Awadh about the Sei'ars and their affairs. They gave me more information about their boundaries and their neighbours and described their system of truces. Practically all the Sei'ar sections are at feud with each other, they told me, and the sections never arrange longer truces between themselves than one month. When the month is over they sometimes renew them and sometimes fight. Suleiman confessed that the Sei'ars had no friends, but he seemed to be on the defensive about it.

"We have no friends," he said. "We don't want them. We manage well enough without them."

'Amr listened anxiously to him and like the mouse addressing the lion said timidly: "Except us."

Suleiman cast a condescending glance at him. "Oh, yes, you," he said. "But you are too unimportant to count."

With the 'Awāmir, they said, there was a year's truce, of which four months were left, with the Kathīri a year, and one month left; with the Hamumi a year, and two months left; with the Murra, Rawashid, Manahil

## THE TOMB OF SALIH AND THE SEI'AR COUNTRY

and Yam there were truces for a year of which eleven months were left.[1]

As there were no signs of Sheikh Sa'id Laajam, who had promised to meet us in his car, we rode on to Juwada, and from there passed again the village of Al Atfa where we had camped on our way up. We had passed it then on the western side, but we were now a little east of it. The dar of 'Umar as Sah attracted our attention under the east bank of the wadi, perched miraculously on a loose boulder which looked as if it would rock at the slightest touch. Soon we reached again the junction of the Wadi Ser with the Wadi Hadhramaut, meeting on the way a messenger from Sheikh Sa'id saying that he would soon arrive. We had hoped to be in Tarim for lunch, but managed to extract some tinned peaches and pineapples from the store box. While resting afterwards a friendly beduin woman came and talked to us. She was dressed in black and unlike the townswomen her dress was long all round.[2] She had a large bundle on her head and stood watching us.

"Come and sit down," said D.

She came nearer but did not sit. Hassan got up to talk to her. "What have you got on your head?"

"My husband's clothes."

"Where are you going?" I asked.

"To Al Juwada."

"And what's this?" asked Hassan taking hold of a long piece of wood with pegs on it, like a huge toothbrush.

"That's the key of my house," she said. "Do you want it?"

I got a picture of her offering it to Hassan. We threatened to show it to his wife.

---

[1] While I was gathering political information, D. visited a tomb which we had seen under the cliffs on the other side of the seil. It was rather an outsize, being 20 feet by 4 feet, and we were told that the tribal ancestor, Nebi Sheikh 'Abdulla Hiteimi, was buried there. He was of the time of 'Ad but does not apparently rank as high as Nebi Sodaf.

[2] This fashion among the beduin women is said to date from Abbaside times when Ma'n Zaida imposed black dresses on the ladies of the country.

## SEIYUN AND TARIM

*Houses are built to live in and not to look at; therefore let use be preferred before uniformity, except where both may be had. Leave the goodly fabrics of houses for beauty only to the enchanted palaces of the poets, who build them with small cost.*
BACON.

*They delight in fine furniture. A room lined with looking-glasses, and with a ceiling of looking-glasses, is thought charming.*
FAR OFF.

THAT afternoon Sheikh Sa'id met us with his car and drove up through Shibam to Seiyun. Here we were welcomed by Seiyid Bubekr al Kaf to his new house, as yet unfinished, for workmen were still busy in the hall and passages under the superintendence of the architect of all the new-fashioned buildings in the Hadhramaut, Seiyid Alawi bin Bubekr bin Alawi al Kaf. Much of it was already completed and it appeared to be far more decorated than any of the other very ornamented houses we had seen. The workmen were local and the man responsible for the decorations had never left Seiyun, but he had only to be shown how to do a thing once after which he did it perfectly himself, as we were able to judge. The walls, like all the houses, are only of dried mud and straw with a lime plaster. For some two-thirds of the way up the walls the plaster is polished with a smooth flint till it shines like marble. In most rooms there were pillars (and in big rooms there is usually a forest of them) as it is difficult for long beams of wood for the roofs to be brought by camels. So Seiyid Alawi, having seen reinforced concrete made in Singapore, was himself experimenting with reinforced concrete beams to avoid too many pillars. Pale green and gold are the principal colours used in the decorations, which mainly take the form of crowns with trailing green strips; these adorn most of the windows and doors. We were also shown a large ballroom attractively designed with a number of pillars down both sides and decorated with gold crowns and coloured ornamentation. There was no ceiling to this room, for it was to be roofed with panes of glass to be brought up from the coast on camels.

## SEIYUM AND TARIM

Several writers have recently deplored the tendency of the rich and travelled Seiyids to bring into the wadi foreign, and particularly European, influence in their architecture. "Architecture" is the one word that describes the quality which makes the Hadhramaut different from any other country and gives it a peculiar cachet of its own. It would be deplorable to let European architects and town planners loose in an Arab town, but what is going on in the Hadhramaut is exactly the converse. It is the Arabs themselves, who, with Arab eyes, are seeing what other countries produce and copying what they think worth copying. They may hit it off wrongly, but gradually innate instinct will lead them right and they will produce something worth looking at. It seems to me that no one can help them in this.

Hadhramaut houses do not last for ever, and indeed it would be happy for us if some of the architecture of the Victorians was expressed in mud rather than in solid bricks. The Victorians, no doubt, thought what they turned out was admirable, and it is true that succeeding generations rarely think alike. Besides, this surely is not the first time that foreign influences have been introduced into the valley. Time and again I saw buildings reminiscent of Assyrian or Egyptian work, and I expect that when the old turreted castles, now mostly in ruins, were abandoned for the rather American-looking ones, the older generation shook their heads and said: "My God, how dreadful."

This was the third brief visit we paid to Seiyun, the capital of Kathīri-land. The Sultan, 'Ali bin Mansur, is one of the most delightful and perhaps the most lovable of the chiefs of the Protectorate. He is also probably the most truly cultured and has a real and earnest desire for peace in his country. He told me that the small revenues of the State were spent entirely on the public service, as he himself lived on private means derived from property in Singapore. The Sultanate, which is under protection by virtue of the Qu'aiti-Kathīri agreement, consists of the directly ruled towns and villages of Seiyun, Tarim, Taris, Al Ghurfa, Mariama and Al Gheil and the Shenafir Confederation of four tribes—the Kathīri, the 'Awāmir, the Jabiri and the Bajri. Large numbers of the Kathīri live in Java so that it is a wealthy tribe. The Āl 'Āmr clan, like some of the Tamimi tribe, have expressed a desire for direct British rule.

After a drink of iced water we started on our way to Tarim. We were now in Seiyid Bubekr's car, for Sheikh Sa'id was anxious to return to Shibam. Our driver was 'Ali, a Somali, who occupies a key position in the

Hadhramaut, being the only person who can put the cars together again when they have been brought up from the coast. We were followed by Hassan Shaibi, the secretary-teacher *cum* perfect butler we had met on our previous visit to Tarim, in a two-seater. We frequently had to diverge slightly from the track in order to avoid large stones placed on the road by beduin who maintain an active dislike of modern methods of transport. The tribesman's prejudice against the motor car is not simply mere conservatism but a dread that motor transport may oust the camel and thus deprive him of his livelihood.

It was already dark by the time we reached the wadis in which we had stuck on our return from Tarim in November, but there was no difficulty now as the wadis were dry. Once more we found ourselves waiting in a car for the gates of Tarim to be opened, then, driving past the cemetery and along familiar roads we came to Seiyid 'Umar's house, but this time all was in darkness save for the faint glow of a lamp shining through the coloured panes of a side window. No one was about, the doors were shut. For some time the driver hooted, but all we could hear in response was a child's voice reading aloud on one shrill note. At length a face appeared at the lighted window and our driver shouted that we were in the car. He was asked to go up, for, as we were told later, Seiyid 'Umar did not believe him, not having expected us to arrive for another four or five days at least.

He came out at once to welcome us, and there were apologies from us for our unannounced arrival and from him because everything was not ready. However, it was all the more delightful for we felt as if we had stepped into a home instead of a formal guest-house. Tea was brought and towels and soap and we were invited to wash and refresh ourselves. We were more than ready for dinner. With the exception of a little tinned fruit which we had eaten in the Wadi Ser, we had had nothing to eat since breakfast at Qubhudh, and Qubhudh seemed now not only miles away but almost in another life.

It was a delicious meal, with plenty of good things such as chopped vegetable salads, pieces of meat cooked in a variety of ways with a variety of sauces and fried eggs, but as no special preparations had been possible it was homely and unpretentious. We felt a great deal better when we left the table to drink coffee in the drawing-room and talk awhile. I thought longingly of a comfortable bed, but was completely overcome to find it furnished with pink crêpe-de-chine sheets, a luxury which I had always imagined to be a prerogative of the most expensive actresses.

## SEIYUN AND TARIM

The next morning Seiyid 'Abdul Rahman took us to visit the site of a Himyaritic tomb which had been accidentally discovered by some boys; and then on to visit Seiyid Bubekr's Tarim house where Seiyid 'Umar promised to show us some stones with Himyaritic inscriptions and carvings. The big courtyard was empty and the house shut up, as Seiyid Bubekr spends most of his time in Seiyun. Passing through a door in the wall in the side of the house we entered a delightful and extraordinarily un-Arab garden. We were first taken to admire the ducks and geese kept in big pens of European pattern with an artificial pond. These birds are very rare in the Hadhramaut and to see them in such surroundings we felt as if we had been carried thousands of miles back home.

There was a wonderful sense of peace in the pleasant walled garden with its green grass, shady trees and sweet-scented flowers, and while we wandered among the fruit trees servants brought out some of the inscribed stones and carvings. I copied some of the inscriptions and photographed others.[1] D. and I drove to the swimming-bath in 'Aidīd. It adjoins another house belonging to Seiyid 'Umar, to which he retires in the heat of the summer. We had a grand bathe, afterwards lying out on a terrace spread with carpets and strewn with cushions.

Next morning Seiyid 'Umar took us to Dammūn to see the celebrations in honour of a successful ibex hunt. Dammūn, though it is not under Kathiri rule, is practically a suburb of Tarim being just outside the eastern wall. The ibex (weil) was a sacred animal with the ancient South Arabians, and there were carvings of them amongst the stones in Seiyid Bubekr's collection. There is no doubt that the dances we saw are extremely ancient and pagan in origin. I think this is realized by the more educated people and for this reason the celebrations are not really approved of.

In the afternoon we discussed arrangements for our journey to Seihut. Seiyid Bubekr considered that we ought to take a Seiyid with us. One had accordingly been summoned from 'Einat and after lunch we interviewed him. We did not take a fancy to Seiyid Muhsin but could hardly refuse

[1] Those I copied read:

## NATIVE GARDEN CITY

his company in the presence of our friend's advice. He turned out to be an unattractive personality and we had more than a suspicion that some of the trouble we had from our camelmen on the way was due to him. He was mean, ignorant and prejudiced, and his chief preoccupation was to see that his hand was duly kissed.

The next day we explored the town. So that we might not be inconvenienced by crowds Seiyid 'Abdul Rahman rang up and asked the Sultan to send us an escort. Three slave soldiers appeared and we set out on foot. Tarim is ruled, on behalf of Sultan 'Ali, by the sons of his uncle. The wealthy Seiyids on leave and in retirement from Singapore find a modest outlet for their business acumen and their money in running the municipal affairs of the town. They do this very well, for they cast a budget, which balances with the aid of a $12,000 annual contribution from themselves. Actually the sum they spend on dispensaries, schools and other public and charitable services is large. They disburse still more on settling tribal troubles. It is worth while mentioning that several of the Seiyids are Justices of the Peace for Singapore. They use other methods to obtain it in Tarim.

Tarim is utterly unlike Shibam and Seiyun. Although it is surrounded by walls it is much more a garden city covering a wide area, and there is little crowding of houses, although there are over two thousand of them. The walls are immensely long and have five gates and twenty-five forts. It is, too, a more aristocratic town than Shibam, having less suggestion of slums and less air of business. There are, of course, many brown mud-built houses of the usual pattern, but the principal features are the large number of stately palaces and the three hundred mosques. One is struck, too, by the presence of telephone lines and pipes with water supply crossing the roads at curious angles. There are sixty motor cars in the town, more than there are in all the rest of the Hadhramaut together. One or two old ruined castles with round towers at their corners stand out conspicuously, built on hills and apparently little different in essentials from medieval European castles.

Near the market were streets of taller houses and between them across the road were slung many hen roosts. Here and there we came across wells and siqayas and, what was really remarkable, public conveniences. Away from the centre of the town a more suburban atmosphere prevails. Tarim is evidently extending for we saw a number of houses in course of building, new villas springing up with pleasant vegetable gardens and groves of date trees.

Talk after dinner that evening turned to superstitions in various countries and Seiyid 'Umar told us these:

> The Hamumi tribe never eat the tongue or eyes of any animal.
> Among the Manahil and Mahra tribes the women never milk the camels.
> If bats come into the house it means that a letter is coming.
> It is very bad luck to meet a one-eyed person first thing in the morning.
> It is bad luck to break down the nests made by the mason wasps in the corners of a room.
> If a cock crows early in the night the people of Tarim say that its owner possesses unlawful money, that is to say, money received by way of interest.
> If a dog holds its head up and barks it is a sign of rain, if it holds its head down and howls it is a sign that someone is going to die.
> If you kick your shoes or sandals off your feet and they turn upside down when they fall it is a sign that you will go on a journey.

Nail pairings must not be left in the house or the owner will become poor. Seiyid 'Umar told us that a rival of his father, Seiyid Sheikh, in Singapore, had secreted some nail parings in his father's house. He waited for three months hoping that he would see Seiyid Sheikh's wealth melt away, but when he saw that his charm had no effect he went and confessed to him, saying: "I thought you would become poor but you're richer than ever before."

It would be hard to equal the contrasts between the modernism—even futurism—and medievalism we found in Tarim. Often in the mornings as we sat in the drawing-room we heard desultory shots. Seiyid 'Umar would go to the window and ask what it was. The answer was always "Bedus." One morning there was quite a big battle and a lot of firing. We watched through field-glasses and saw two parties of beduin firing at each other outside the walls, while from behind the parapets of the ramparts the Sultan's soldiers fired occasional shots to show perhaps that they were there, and that Tarim was not to be included in the battle area. We heard afterwards there was only one casualty—a man hit in the leg—and the *casus belli* was the usual, a blood feud.

Although Tarim is, like Du'an, a place of retirement, Tarim is ultra-modern and Du'an old fashioned. In the west it is not difficult, seated perhaps on what is left of the encircling wall of a medieval town, to conjure up the past, and, with a knowledge of history, even to picture the gradual change in the surroundings and the life of the people from the Middle Ages to the twentieth century. Roads are built and railways laid down. Horses and horse-drawn traffic become less and less as cars appear and fill the roads. The streets dark at night, and the houses dimly lit, gradually grow bright as gas and then electric light take the place of dips and oil. The increasing roar of traffic and the blare of gramophone and wireless are heard.

It is easy living in the present to picture the past, but it is much more difficult to live in the past and conjure up the future. In Tarim we found ourselves in the unfamiliar atmosphere of medieval surroundings and conditions of life, with no friendly policeman and only savagery outside the walls. It was as though men from this past had stepped forward several centuries of time and brought back twentieth century furniture, cars, telephones, electric light, iced drinks, baths and every "mod. con." At night when we sat under an electric fan in a modern drawing-room, the bulk of the population was sleeping in caves, or little stick huts, or in mud dars, every man with his rifle and dagger within easy reach.

*
* *

*Chapter XX*

## THE TOMB OF HUD IN THE VALLEY OF THE FLOODS

> *And unto 'Ad (we sent) their brother Hud.*     QURAN.
>
> *Turn, men of Ad, and call upon the Lord,*
> *The Prophet Houd exclaim'd;*
> *Turn men of Ad, and look to Heaven,*
> *And fly the wrath to come.*     SOUTHEY.

Two days later (Thursday, December 6th) we set out from Tarim along the wadi Maseila[1] to Seihut, on the coast—a distance of just over two hundred miles. Not content with the overwhelming hospitality they had already shown us, our hosts, the Al Kaf Seiyids, insisted on arranging and paying for the whole of the journey, which we expected to complete in little more than a week. Several of our friends accompanied us as far as Masilat as Silma to speed us on our way, and after a farewell conversation, reminiscent of a station platform, we got back into the cars and with waving of handkerchiefs set off towards country till then untrodden by Europeans.

Passing out of Tarim through Al Qōz, Qahir and 'Einat, we overtook one of our camels that had left the previous day and picked up an escort, a child of thirteen complete with bandolier and rifle. I cannot say that we felt much extra security from his presence nor did he seem much worried by his great responsibility, for he sat quite happily clutching his father's rifle in front of the car.

We now entered a zone where the people had many East African connections, and for the next four days I met many who had been in Zanzibar, Mombasa and Dar es Salaam, and was continually having conversations in Swahili. Here we came to the walled town of Qasm, abode of the chief

---

[1] The name Wadi Maseila is applied to the continuation of the Wadi Hadhramaut from Husn Dhiban Maseila, two and a half miles from Tarim.

of the Bin Yemani clan of the Tamimi tribe, said to have a monthly income of $40,000 from Java. A mile and a half further on we came up with the main body of our caravan at Husn as Sufeira, and found them completely unready to move. We had arranged that the baggage camels should go on in advance and meet us at Fughma, where we expected to spend the night, but, of course, they had not gone, the excuse being that the Seiyid and three of the men had only just arrived. After a good deal of grumbling the men started to load up, having wanted to wait until three o'clock. Our men all had long hair reaching to their shoulders, though sometimes they tied it up in a bun behind. Some of them had their hair shining with simsim oil. D. and I, Hassan, Zaidi, Ganess, Salih 'Ali and Seiyid Mushin rode, while Salim, Bukheit, Faraj, and the beduin walked, though the latter seized every opportunity of riding the baggage camels. Donkeys cannot be used down the Wadi Maseila on account of the long stretch without water. They would have difficulty, too, owing to the depth of water at some of the fords, for the track crosses and recrosses the river and in places the water was up to above the camel's girths.

Husn as Sufeira is a castle of the old-fashioned description with turrets at the corners and belonging to the Tamimi chief. Most of the people there had been in East Africa, and while I talked Swahili to a man from Qasm, D. was waylaid by some women who wanted to know if we had news of their husbands and sons in Zanzibar.

At last we got under way. The wadi here was wide, its reddish sand pleasantly broken by the green of rakh. Rakh, rakh, rakh. How tired of it we were to become before we reached Seihut. Our halts were largely determined by its presence, and every morning we were assailed by the sickly stench of the breath and dung of rakh-fed camels. It gave them a perpetual diatrhœa and the camel of anyone riding ahead was a continual offence to the nose and eyes of the one riding behind.

Presently we rode down into the Wadi Hun in which there was water; it is said, indeed, that it is never dry. There was an old lady on the further side filling skins with water and one of the camel-men gallantly carried them up for her into the the village on the bank above.

A little later we came to some mounds, the only relics of ruins again attributed to 'Ad, and shortly after stopped below the imposing mount on which Husn Al 'Ur is built. D. and I climbed up to see the ruins guided by Karama. In its prime the building must have been impressive, and even to-day, when little more than foundations are left, it still gives a feeling of massive solidity. Near the summit is a deep well.[1]

Leaving Husn al 'Ur the track crossed to the riverside, cool and pleasant with dates and cultivation. A large heron stood in the water leisurely collecting its supper; the scenery was Egyptian, colouring soft and attractive with the late afternoon light falling on the date-palms. We could see As Som in the distance and passing through it, halted among sand dunes and rakh a little beyond the village. While our home for the night was being set up, a wild-looking man who had been to Mombasa came to see me and, talking Swahili, asked me when we would have a District Commissioner there, as in Mombasa. He said that the people who had cultivation were tired of perpetual raids by Shenzis (savages) from the mountains who came down when the crops were ready.

In the morning we discovered that the headman, Ma'tuf bin Khashash, had deserted. The mantle fell on Karama.

The flies were still with us, riding on us and buzzing round us. I had a theory that many of them came with us the whole journey from Mukalla and back, for where they could arise from in barren country I could not think. I believe they camped with us at night and started off again on our backs in the morning. We had nothing now to mitigate the nuisance, for we were short of cigarettes and had been unable to buy any in Tarim. Seiyid 'Umar had given us a tin of black Bird's Eye tobacco and some cigarette-papers, and with these we manufactured some powerful smokes at lunch and evening halts.

Now and again we saw the unusual sight of goats perched on the top of quite high bushes browsing on the upper branches. I thought they must have developed the power of flight until I saw a woman picking them up and putting them on the trees.

We did not enter Fughma village but went down to the river and at its junction with the Wadi Yabha settled down, in the shade of the bank, for

[1] We climbed down a shorter but steeper way and found the following inscription high up on the wall which does not seem to have been recorded before:

*Broken, not certain.

lunch. When the baggage animals arrived one of them fell in the water and stuck in the muddy sand. The beduin rushed to its help and unloaded it. They then began digging it out, pulling the wet sand from under it with their hands. One of them had a bright idea and fetching a saucepan tried to empty the river round it. This caused some amusement, but the camel-men, seeing that the idea was not without its possibilities, built a bund round the camel and reinforcing the saucepan with a pail continued to empty the river. Others brought sticks and branches and pushed them under the beast. It was on the point of heaving itself up when Seiyid Muhsin was inspired to invoke the name of Sheikh Bubekr, the famous saint of 'Einat, who was so holy that his name can move anything—so said Seiyid Muhsin. After lunch, however, when we started stirring up the camel-men, even the holy sheikh's name was useless, for nothing short of dynamite will move camel-men before they want to go.

It was not until half-past three that we got away determined to reach Qabr Hud that night. Karama had other ideas and did everything he could to delay us. Just before half-past five we saw Qabr Hud appearing deceptively close and urging on our camels we rode forward. Darkness came down at a quarter-past six, but the thought of spending a comfortable night in the Al Kaf house encouraged us on. Finally, in scattered formation, we came to a halt in the wadi below the village at ten minutes past seven. Salim went off to find the house and its key but without success, so we stretched ourselves out under a tamarisk tree.

The morning broke a little misty and when I climbed above the bank under which we had slept I saw the faint mist drifting slowly away from the gully on the side of which lay the great white tomb of Hud which had been our leading mark till darkness overtook us. Even at a distance of half a mile it is impressive in its calm beauty.

A solitary beduin (it turned out he was one of our party) was descending the broad white flight of steps that leads up to the sanctuary, and I wondered whether our presence here would be resented.

The atmosphere of this most holy spot in the Hadhramaut lost nothing on closer acquaintance. We reached it, not through the little town and up the imposing stairway, but up the side of the mountain by a path leading to the large white-washed platform where there was a many-columned cloister partially enclosing the huge boulder held to be the hump of Hud's petrified she-camel. This cloistered platform is used for prayers. Before stepping on to it we removed our shoes. There was not a soul about and an air of complete peace and calm pervaded the whole place. There was that feeling of reverence and devout worship which hangs like an aura around almost every sacred shrine. This was even more apparent when we had climbed the rough white-washed slope, which half-way up divides into two, one going right and the other left, and came to the dome itself. The tomb extends up the hill-side at the back of the dome: its total length is about ninety feet.

The dome covers the rough unhewn natural rock of the mountain in which is a great cleft. This, it is said, is the place into which the prophet disappeared. The mountain never completely closed after him, and now while the surrounding rock is heavily white-washed the cleft itself is left untouched. Untouched that is to say by paint, but it is worn smooth by countless reverent hands and lips. It was this, perhaps, with the quiet of the fine December morning brooding over the spot, which called back to my mind other ancient fanes where the knees of generations of worshippers have worn away the stones.

It was not easy to turn one's mind to a practical examination of the tomb and its surroundings. Thousands of minute pieces of chewed-up coloured rag or string stuck to the walls and roof of the cupola attracted our attention, and on the grave itself, extending out of the cupola up the mountain, there were numbers of small stones tied round with pieces of rag and suspended from pegs driven into the masonry.

Hud is generally thought to be the patriarch Eber of Genesis and in Muslim theology was the prophet of the giant race of 'Ad. He it was who reproved the haughty Sheddad and warned the 'Adites of their end, after which they were consumed by the devastating wind of the desert. I have not been able to find any reference to the end of Hud in the historians, but legend has it that he was pursued by two infidel horsemen into the gully where his tomb now is. Being hard pressed he reached the rock and said: "Open by the permission of God." The rock opened wide. He entered in and the stone closed on him, but it did not close entirely. His she-camel which he couched near-by was turned to stone.[1]

The pilgrimage to the tomb of Hud takes place on 15th Sha'ban and the

[1] Qabr Hud, like Qabr Salih and other giants' tombs, was probably a sanctuary of the old religion, and it is said that when Seiyid Ahmed bin 'Isa al Mohajir came to the Hadhramaut he searched and made enquiries everywhere for the tomb of Hud. At length one Sheikh Ba 'Abbad, a caravan Muqaddam of Rahia who knew the whole country, offered to show him the grave, but in true Hadhrami style demanded

(*For completion of footnote see page opposite.*)

## PILGRIMAGE TO THE TOMB

town of Qabr Hud is only inhabited for three days in the year. The first act of the pilgrims after arriving and finding their quarters is to go down to the river and wash and pray. Then they return to their houses and after food go out to look at the beduin dances. The fair at which animals, clothing and butter are sold, lasts until sunset and the pilgrims may, if they so wish, do business until this time.

The next day they rise early and going down to the river pray the Fajr beside the water. The ceremonies of the visitation take place during the day. Again by the water-side the pilgrim says: "Verily it is a river of the rivers of Paradise." He then performs the ablutions and prays under the leadership of the Mansab, Sheikh 'Umar al Mihdhar. Then he tells his beads and praises and glorifies, and magnifies, advancing the while to the empty well where he stays a short time. Here he says "Peace be on the Prophet of God, peace be on the Apostle of God, peace be on the Beloved of God." This is followed by the invocation of the peace on all the prophets of importance, the four perfect women, the archangels and the gardener of Paradise.

The pilgrim then prays that out of regard for the prophet Hud, the Prophet Muhammad and others, God will accept his endeavours, be pleased with his deeds, redouble his rewards, forgive him his sins, strengthen his weakness with the protection of faith, raise up his abode and make His pleasure his hope and Paradise his object and goal, that God will keep his record in His right hand, make his deeds good, accept the good deeds of his benefactors and forgive them who sin against him.

Then the pilgrim climbs to the holy tomb where Seiyid 'Alawi bin Ahmed al Haddad prays on his behalf. The prayers are further intercessions by the virtue of Hud and the other prophets, and are followed by the reading of the Chapter of Hud and a reading from the Kawakib of Ahmed bin 'Umar al Hinduan.

how much he would be paid. Burton remarks in a footnote to his *Arabian Nights* "the people are the Swiss of Arabia and noted for thrift and hard bargains; hence the saying 'If you meet a serpent and a Hazrami, slay the Hazrami.'" The Seiyid and his companions replied that they would give him the tithes of the wadis. He led them to the spot and Seiyid Ahmed bin 'Isa after examination was convinced that the prophet was buried there. A cupola was built over the grave with stairs leading up to it and a mosque near-by for prayers. Sheikh Ba 'Abbad became the guardian of the tomb and his descendants hold the office to this day. It is only this cupola that is old; the other buildings and the magnificent flights of stairs are comparatively new and are due to the benefaction of the Al Kaf family.

## THE TOMB OF HUD IN THE VALLEY OF THE FLOODS

The ceremony concludes with a recitation of four fatihas.[1]

Except during the pilgrimage the town is deserted, but shortly before the time it is due to start the Ba 'Abbad Sheikh comes from Al Ghurfa to repair the road where the seil has washed it away, to repair the houses if there is any damage and to fill the tanks of water for the mosque.

An account of these ceremonies of the visitation of Hud is not easily available, even in the abbreviated form I have given them. They seem to me to have some interest as showing how high a place the sanctuary holds in the life and thoughts of the Hadhrami.

With a sense of refreshment we put on our shoes and descended the broad stairway to the village. At the foot we were met by a gentle-eyed heifer which gazed at us for a little while and then turning away with a frisk of its tail departed into a courtyard. Apart from pigeons this heifer was the only living being we met in the place. The large mosque below the tomb was empty, the streets deserted, the houses shuttered. But there was no feeling of decay.

---

[1] The first in honour of Muhammad, Hud and the other apostles and prophets, the second in honour of the Prophet's family and the Imams, this fatiha then invokes the names of the many saints of the Hadhramaut; the third is for guidance, prosperity and help, and the fourth and last seems to reach at the greatest needs of the Hadhramaut: "May God accept from me and from you and from all the visitors of this noble prophet the visits that are made in his honour ... May He bring together in unity the Seiyids of the house of 'Alawi, arrange settlement between them, and cause harmony and unity to reign in their hearts for good. May He raise up for this blessed wadi a just Sultan and bestow on us the desire for co-operation, and give us His assistance to do good deeds and to refrain from bad ones. ..."

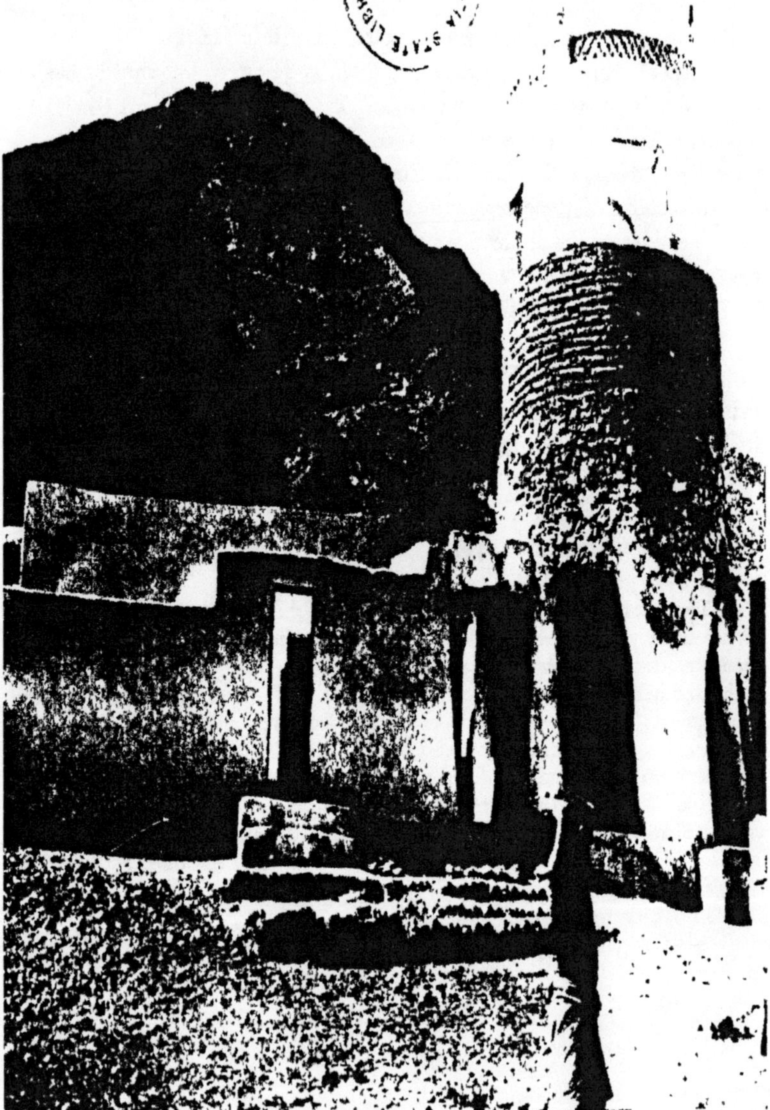

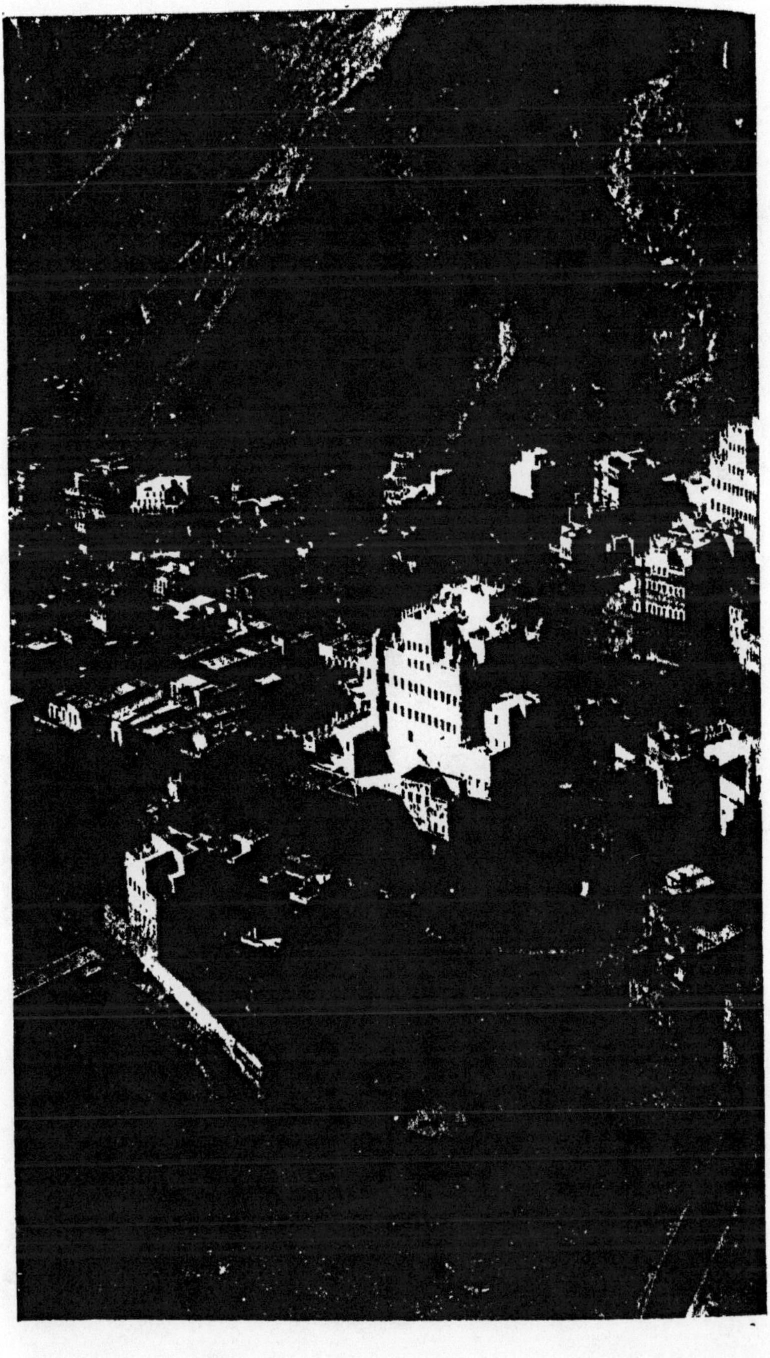

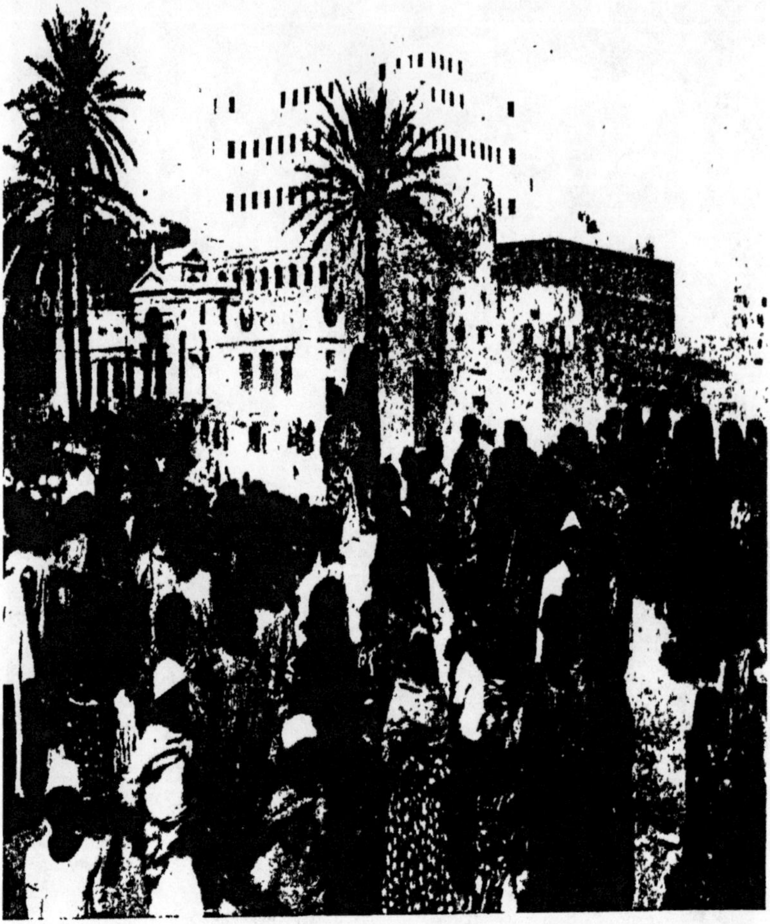

Einat. Mosque

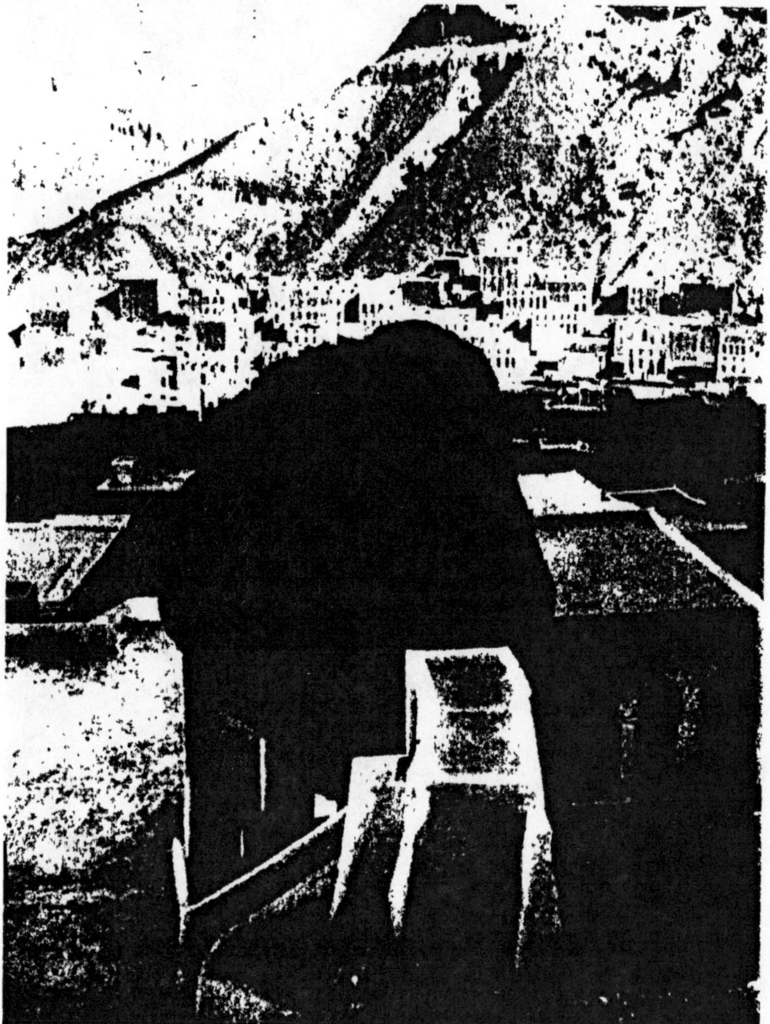

At Qabr Hud
  Standing L.-R.—Salim, Salih 'Ali, Faraq, Bukheit
  Centre—D. I., H. I., Hassan
  Front—Zaidi, Ganess

*Drawing water*
*Cave dwellings at Sena*

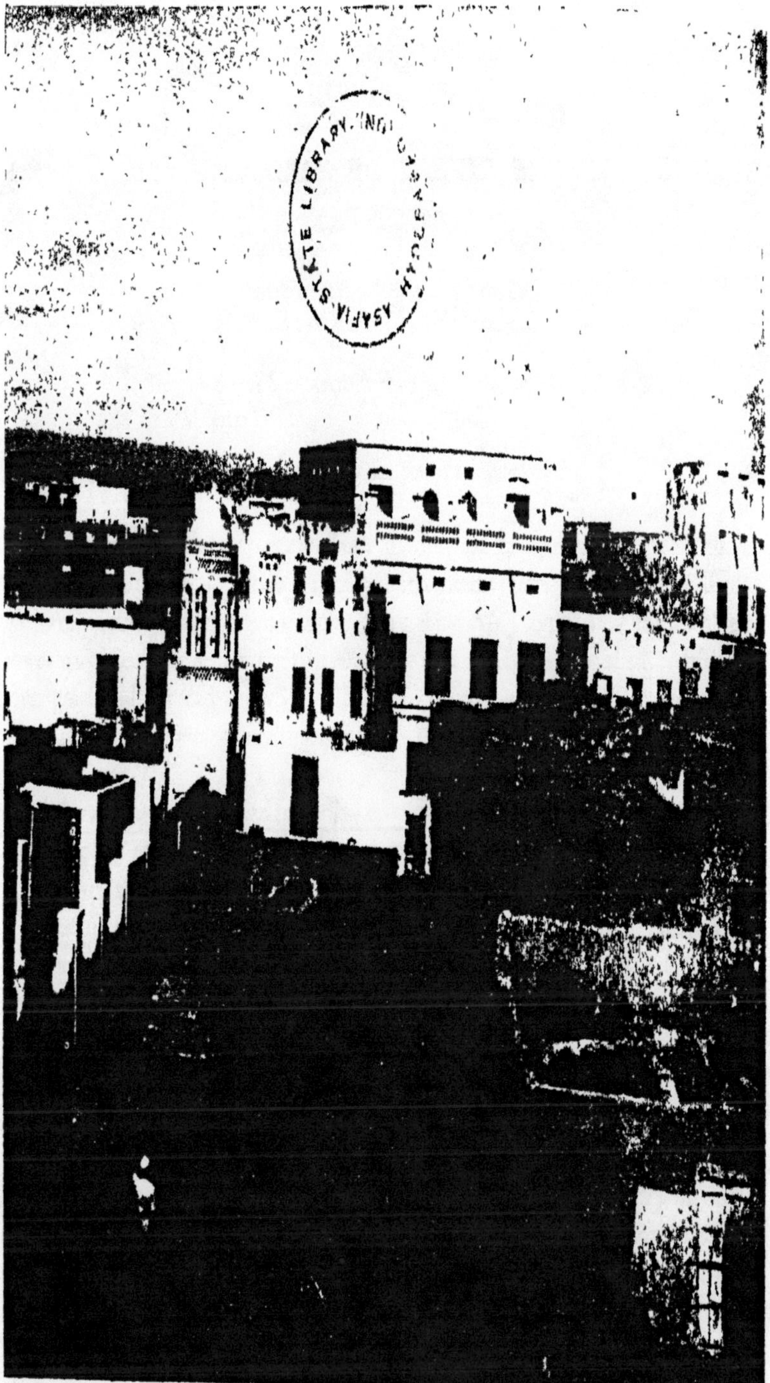

## Chapter XXI

## A RIVER OF THE RIVERS OF PARADISE—THE MAHRA COUNTRY

> *There is a temple in ruins stands*
> *Fashioned by long forgotten hands.* BYRON.
>
> *The thorn trees caught at us with their crook'd hands.*
> Trans. W. S. BLUNT.
>
> *How much alarmed the travellers were.* FAR OFF.

AND now began the last lap and in some ways the best of all; with the thrill of travelling over unexplored country each view seemed to open itself out for you alone. Arabia is a dry country but here was a river flowing mile after mile and day after day with clear green water, banked with grass and trees. This was the part of the wadi of which I had read so long ago in Hogarth's book and I felt in an entirely unjustifiable way that it had been waiting all these years for me.

The wadi was no doubt one of the principal ancient routes to and from the Hadhramaut and beyond. It was also probably the route followed by Malik bin Fahm and his Azdite hordes in their great migration from Yemen to Oman. We found traces of ancient travellers and, as will be seen, among its principal features are the sites of island forts, no doubt designed to protect the ancient incense trade. Throughout the Hadhramaut the ancients seem to have favoured these island sites when available, and Hajarein, Gheibun, Shibam and Husn al 'Ur are examples. Shabwa, as Pliny had indicated, appears to have the same sort of situation.

Geographically the Wadi Hadhramaut is the key feature of the country to which it gives its name. North and south of it the land rises to extensive plateaux forming watersheds. The one to the north, about 3,500 feet above sea-level, has a series of wadis draining north into the sands, and another series draining south into the Wadi Hadhramaut. The watershed to the south consisting in the same way of plateaux, is higher than that to the north,

## A RIVER OF THE RIVERS OF PARADISE—THE MAHRA COUNTRY

rising in the west to some 6,000 feet. From it the wadis drain north to the Wadi Hadhramaut and south to the sea.[1]

Immediately east of the walls of Tarim the wadi changes in all its aspects. Politically it runs again into Qu'aiti territory, but territory not included in any of the five provinces, though there is a Qu'aiti Governor at 'Einat responsible for relations with the Tamimi and Manahil tribes who both have "A" agreements with the Sultan. The wadi therefore remains politically Qu'aiti until it becomes Mahra.

The standard of wealth also changes east of Tarim. It is not to be supposed that this denotes any diminution of business capacity on the part of the Tamimi, for some of them make money in Java and, as has been said, the chief of the Bin Yamāni clan has a large income from Java. The reason for this change in the standard of wealth seems to be that in the course of years the Tamimi have developed much stronger connections with East Africa and therefore succeeding generations find it easier to go there. The Hadhrami in East Africa as a general rule indulge in less remunerative occupations than those in the East Indies.

Occasionally the spate comes down the Wadi Maseila[2] and then much

---

[1] This description is typical of that part of the country through which the wadi Hadhramaut runs more or less west to east, that is to say, from about Husn al 'Abr to beyond Tarim. Over this stretch the bed of the wadi falls from a little over 3,000 feet above sea level to a little under 2,000 feet. On the 49th Meridian, a little west of Mukalla, there is an approximate depth of 106 miles of wadi, mountain and steppe land between the sea and the main wadi, and rather more between that wadi and the desert. As the wadi turns to the south-east, however, it of course modifies these proportions, but the country maintains the same general formation. The wadi finally turns south and breaks through a cleft in the coastal range, which is a conspicuous sight from the sea as you sail by dhow from Seihut to Shihr and from the air. A peculiarity of the river bed is its extreme width near the source and its narrowness near the mouth. At the widest point at which we crossed it on this journey, between Haura and Henin, it was four and a half miles wide, and at Al 'Abr it is forty miles across. In the lower reaches of the wadi, however, we found places where the width was less than a hundred yards. The length of the wadi from Husn al 'Abr to the sea is about 350 miles. The figures given in this resumé of Hadhramaut geography are, of course, approximate, and the summary, while based on observed facts, is deduction in so far as parts of the country unseen by land or from the air are concerned.

[2] The Wadi Maseila receives its first principal contribution of water from the Wadi 'Adim, said to be sometimes dry, and its second a little lower down from the Wadi Hun. The only other important tributary above the waterless part of the

(*For completion of footnote see page opposite.*)

of the route we followed is impassable. We had pointed out to us from time to time the alternative paths used, during the flood, well up the sides of the wadi. At times of flood the volume of water passing through the wadi must be terrific, for we saw high up in the trees debris which had been carried down. Lower in the wadi the high-water mark was twenty feet up the vertical walls. Floods such as these render cultivation in the seil bed impossible, and the Manahil and Mahras carry out their planting on the level surface of the hard alluvium brought down by the river through which the spate has cut its channel, leaving almost perpendicular banks, sometimes as much as twenty or thirty feet high.

After leaving Qabr Hud we gained our first addition to the caravan— eleven camels with their accompanying beduin. We went on gaining fresh recruits till when we arrived at Seihut we were at least ninety camels strong. It was the first day of Ramadhan and I wondered how many of our caravan would fast. Seiyid Muhsin was the only one to do so, and he did it, as he did most things, in a very blatant fashion.

Presently we crossed the river Sena finding on its banks a little garden enclosed by a palisade of date trunks, in which water melons were growing. Across the river we came on the real township of Sena, a group of thirty to forty small cube-like huts of date trunks with no windows and an ever open door. The people came out to watch us and the Seiyid had a magnificent time, for a number of the men kissed his hand twice on the back and twice on the palm.

We camped early near Qōz Ādubi having done barely more than four hours' riding, but the beduin promised that we should do better in future and reach Seihut in time. Our camp lay under a wadi island hill, probably the site of another ancient fort, and in the morning we rode round the back of it where we saw the ancient dam, strongly built of masonry and cement, which Squadron-Leader Rickards had noted from the air. Two men who were roaming the neighbourhood walked some way with us. One of them asked me if there was any magic in my country for a love charm.

Below Tabūrkum with its irrigation plants like jetties at intervals down wadi is the Wadi Sena. From Basa' to Marakhai the wadi is in ordinary times dry and this part is known as Al Liza. Though the aneroid showed diminishing height, we had the impression of going uphill as far as Jebel Qafi from which point it appeared to descend fairly steeply. From Marakhai the river flows perennially to Buzūn, and the principal tributary below Al Liza is the 'Akid. I travelled up a good deal of the Wadi Hajr in 1939 and the description remains accurate. There are valuable agricultural areas on the river and as far as I know it always reaches the sea.

## A RIVER OF THE RIVERS OF PARADISE—THE MAHRA COUNTRY

the river we came to Basa' where the river disappears, and where a man with his wife and child, encamped near-by, volunteered to take us to Sad to see what we understood to be some rock paintings.

After forty minutes' ride we halted under the cliff and climbed up the slope full of anticipation. There was a natural seat and shelter hollowed out three-quarters of the way up the cliff and on the rocky ceiling a good deal of writing painted in red and white. The writing in red looked perfectly fresh, though the white was faded. Later knowledge led me to suppose that the red was painted with "dragon's blood" from Soqotra which retains its freshness indefinitely. The inscriptions had been protected from light and weathering by their situation. Many of the characters were unfamiliar to me though some resembled Himyaritic.[1]

Presently we caught up with the caravan, at least we came across Salih (the beduin) trying with the advice and aid of the other beduin to shoot a couple of sitting birds. The birds were large, guinea-fowl-looking creatures called buri, and they sat on a tree trunk while the preparations went on. Salih had got into a beautiful position for enfilading and, lying at a range of about ten yards, took long and careful aim. Perhaps the birds knew of the prowess of beduin for they did not stir. Silence and stillness were enjoined on us, and we watched with bated breath. At length Salih pulled the trigger. There was a terrific explosion and—the two birds flew unconcernedly away without so much as a

---

[1] I recognized again some of these characters in graffiti when I later visited 'Iryush in Soqotra where they were said to be Ethiopic. Later in England I showed the Sad inscriptions to Dr. A. S. Tritton of the School of Oriental Studies, who had taught me the elements of Himyaritic. He pointed to some resemblances to Ethiopic and more striking still to the *North* Arabian alphabets of Thamud and Safa. On these latter analogies it was possible to suggest the reading of one group of characters which occurred twice as ALF—a thousand. But the inscription, from top to bottom, still remains undecipherable, though it seems more than likely that the characters are in a dead language as yet unknown. All that can be said with comparative certainty is that the language in question belongs to the same group of bygone Semitic languages. It is unlikely that it represents the lost alphabet which was the ancestor of the alphabets of those languages and incidentally of our own, but the exciting possibility remains. Some of the characters *do* resemble our own letters, for instance A and D and H are plain, though they no doubt have other values. The writing of course confirms that the wadi was an ancient route and suggests perhaps the passage of northern travellers through it. The name Sad meaning a dam is also interesting and points to the likelihood that there was in ancient times another dam at this place, but there is no trace of it now.

squawk. They had done all in their power towards contributing to the evening meal.

We made an early start in the morning of December 11th, but after lunch most of us slept, except D. who wrote up some of the journal and Salih (*not* al Khulaqi) who was busy raking the lice out of Karama's head with his jambiya. Seiyid Muhsin told us we were now about half-way between Tarim and Seihut.

Some of the party went on as they heard there was water and presently we sent Bukheit ahead to tell them to get ready. The rest of us started off a bit later and caught up with the caravan who had found a deep pool left by the passing flood.

We met here a man, a woman and a boy with some camels who told us the result of the raid the Sei'ars had planned on the Mahras. They had attacked a southbound caravan, killed one man, wounded another and looted the goods. The news was asked for and given in very much the way that "fans," who have been temporarily out of touch with newspapers, ask for and are given the result of a football match.

From the point where we found the water the Mahras owned the left bank of the wadi and the Manahil the right. As there was a feud between the two tribes our Minhali camel-men announced that in future they were to be called Tamimis.

We woke early among our bushes on December 12th, but as we got further down the wadi there was curious reluctance on the part of our camel-men to move, for they hated approaching the Mahra country. However, we mounted our camels eager to find the promised river again, for we had had our third night on short rations. The morning omens were good for it is lucky to meet a solitary traveller on business and we passed, almost at once, a beduin walking rapidly and carrying his worldly possessions on his back, a rifle, a bundle tied up in an indigo cloth, a straw bag, a wooden bowl and a small iron saucepan.

Soon we came to Marakhai where the river emerges again in a narrow stream beside the left cliff. Frogs and small fishes abounded in the clear water. It was grassy underfoot and the wadi was beautifully green and almost English in appearance, for the tamarisks are much like young pine trees. So, quietly and unobtrusively we entered the Mahra country—the first Europeans to be in its interior—and nature could not have staged a more beautiful entry for us. The branches glittered with dew and birds were singing in the trees. Presently we saw lovely little kingfishers, like

## A RIVER OF THE RIVERS OF PARADISE—THE MAHRA COUNTRY

those I had seen in Zanzibar, standing on poles in the water and feeding off the fish. The morning light lit up the dew-covered spiders' webs and the grass seemed more emerald green than any I had known. The wadi was not more than a hundred to a hundred and fifty yards wide, but, except for the narrow ride of green turf over which we were passing, it and its slopes were packed with trees. There was a riot of variety in the vegetation, 'ithl, 'ais (*Tamarix sp.*), 'ishar, harmal, a little sumr, khuweira, lejāwa (*Zygophyllum sp,*) and a few sār palms, and in all this the ariata soon became the most striking object. There was a fine green copse of these trees ahead, some forty or fifty feet-high, a most unusual picture in this country. It can be imagined how refreshing such sights were to us who had been so long used to barren rocks and sand. Not that I do not love the Arabian landscapes, but even the Arabs say the three best things in the world are running water, green grass and a pretty face.

Dwellings, however, were no more elaborate and Hautat as Seiyid consisted of the usual mean stick huts. These were the commonest type of dwellings in the wadi and were almost universal in Mahra country until we reached Qal'ana. From Qal'ana to Dhubeia the buildings are mostly of mud, only a single storey high.

We came down to the river, full of green water weeds and to grassy pasture where cows were grazing, and later as we climbed the left cliff on the other side we saw below, on the river which had become wide and deep, three black, brown and white wild duck which rose with a whirr and a splash.

In the afternoon we caught up with a resting caravan of forty camels which accompanied us all the way to Seihut. There were six or seven beduin and a woman with an elderly husband and two small children. The man told me that he and his family were off to Zanzibar to seek a living, so I gave him a letter of recommendation. The beduin of the caravan were really Manahil but, like ours, declared they were Tamimis.

We came on some cultivation and a few huts at Bin Qora where there were men sitting in the shelter of a well over which was hung a fishing-net. There were small Soqotran cows and goats grazing near-by and a dog barked at us as we passed. Here the wadi makes a big bend to the north and Karama pointed out a short cut over the jōl for foot travellers. This cuts off in two hours the bend in the wadi that it takes six hours to follow with camels. We camped near Hadhāfa, but the only sign of it when night fell was the light from the fires of its few huts on the sloping cliff behind us.

* * *

On December 13th we were later starting than usual for here, at Al Hadhāfa, we took on our first siyar,[1] 'Aita bin Sa'id, representing the Bin Sahāl clan of the Mahras. He was a pleasant-looking lad of not more than sixteen and the responsibility of taking care of our large caravan sat on him quite lightly. Hitherto our journeys had been for, the most part, through territories of a single tribe where siyars had not been necessary, or along much-used highways where their presence was scarcely noticed. Going into Mahra country with a Minhali and Tamimi caravan reminded me of travelling in an International train where the nationalities of the ticket collectors change at every frontier, for the Mahras seemed a foreign people by their language, clothes, and customs. Their neighbours in the West scarcely regard them as Arabs, though they themselves consider they are of the pure stock of Himyar. Their capital is Qishn but their Sultan lives in Soqotra which has been from immemorial times a foreign dependency of the Sa'd bin Towar branch of the Bin Afrar, the ruling house of the Mahras.

[1] The custom in the Hadhramaut before the peace as elsewhere in Arabia, was that when you travelled through the territory of a tribe you paid a fee to the tribe and took a member of it as guarantee for your safety. He was a kind of walking passport. The system is called siyara.

[2] The other and junior branch of the Bin Afrar is that of 'Āmr bin Towar which rules for the Sultan in Mahraland. The Bin Afrar say they are of the same stock as the Bani Afif of Lower Yafa'. The Mahras are divided into 'usebas, of which there are four, each consisting of a number of clans, and some independent clans, three of which live in the Wadi Maseila. The Bin Sahāl belong with two other clans to the Bin Gesūs 'useba and the Bin Zūeidi with four others to the Shehshihi. One of the principal 'usebas is that of the Bin Sār, for it includes the small clan of Bin 'Ali Muqaddam the peacemakers of the whole tribe. In case of a murder during a period of truce between two clans the Muqaddam of Bin 'Ali deals with it. The murderer is put to death by his own tribe, and, if they fail to do so, it amounts to a recognition on their part that the offended tribe may take revenge. But once a man is declared a murderer by the Muqaddam he is outlawed and may not be greeted by his people. There is an appeal from the Bin 'Ali Muqaddam to the Bin Afrar Sultan. The 'useba of Bin Boqi bin Ahmed is also important for it includes the strongest section and is in close alliance with the 'Āmr bin Towar side of the Bin Afrar. When Bedr Bu Tuweirak, the great Kathīri ruler, was over-running the Hadhramaut, he raided Qishn and Al Gheidha near Ras Fartak and set up his son Ahmed in the latter place. The Bin Boqi combined with Abu Shawarib, the Father of Mustachios, then Sultan of the Bin Afrar, who brought in Yafa'i mercenaries as well and they turned the Kathīris out. The Bin Boqi then said that the Yafa'is were unnecessary and that they would themselves ensure the safety of the country, so Abu Shawarib paid them a subsidy of $480 a year which is paid to this day. The Bin Boqi are

(*For completion of footnote see next page.*)

## A RIVER OF THE RIVERS OF PARADISE—THE MAHRA COUNTRY

I asked a Mahra friend what was the principal trade of his tribe and he said "Raiding." Subsidiary industries are agriculture, a little incense gathering and camel breeding. Mahra camels have been famous for speed and night work since ancient times, and they are said to be extremely intelligent and faithful. A Mahra camel will have nothing to do with a stranger but couches at once for its master.

We started off under Mahra auspices by losing the way and had to retrace our steps, which was annoying as the track was bad with steep ups and downs and many overhanging branches. It took us nearly half an hour to get all our people across the river, for the place where we had to cross had an extremely steep ascent on the opposite side. As each wet camel came from the river the path was made so slippery that fresh earth and branches had to be laid down for the succeeding beast. The climb up the narrowing wadi brought us to the most beautiful views we had yet seen. Long straight stretches of clear green water, fringed with vegetation, flowed over the sandy bed below us. These straight lengths of river gave me the fantastic idea that one day inter-tribal boat races might be witnessed in the wadi!

Below the "aqaba" there was the settlement of Bat-ha where we saw hens pecking outside the huts. We asked for eggs but the people did not understand why we should want them and asked if we smoked them—probably because Hassan as usual had a cigar going.

Passing Adh Dhahoma in the afternoon we were surprised to find the track blocked by a gate which at first sight looked as though it had strayed from an English field: it consisted of six poles fastened horizontally the one above the other and each had to be removed separately. I hope that the

also said to have an agreement with the Sultan of Oman to keep the peace and are paid $120 a year by him. Ahmed, father of Boqi, rests in a weli's tomb at Ras Dargah and his son Boqi was such a mighty warrior that he died with his arm stretched out, rather, I gather, in the manner certain European warriors have adopted, and his tomb is so built as to allow for the salute. His detractors say that his arm got stuck that way as he was so in the habit of begging!

Amongst the independent sections there are several who are said not to be true Mahras, the Bin Qidahi for instance, are those who came out from the sea; the story is that their ancestor was an illegitimate child of the Bin Himr, another independent section, who was thrown into the sea and washed up. The Bin Suleimi are said to be descended from two Indian Christians from Kokun who landed in Khalfat Bay and adopted Islam. The Bin Obtani claim kinship with the 'Awabitha of Hadhramaut. The Bin Balhaf used to be the slaves of Sheikh Johari of Bahwein.

last man closed the gate, but I rather doubt it. Through the gate we came round a corner to the village of Rahta and saw the first sign of comparative civilization since leaving Qabr Hud. This was a domed tomb, the resting place of a weli, Salih bin 'Aqil.

We crossed over to the right side of the wadi where the colour of the slopes changed quite suddenly from brown to black and dark red with lava,[1] and further down came to the wide Wadi 'Akid which is said to be long and to have settlements in it.

We halted near Sifa among the 'ais bushes near the river, and then climbed up to Maqrat on its volcanic island hill through extensive date gróves, surrounded by a palisade of palm trunks.

After crossing the river we met our first upward-bound caravan from Seihut, laden with rice and a few dates for 'Einat, and some dried fish and grain for the beduin in the dry part of the wadi. Mahra caravans rarely serve the wadi higher than 'Einat and Tarim is supplied chiefly by the Shihr route. Following behind was an aged Mahra Darby and Joan travelling up the wadi on foot. The old lady had an enormous nose ring which looked like tin but might have been silver, and later I noticed that almost all the *old* women wore these rings. There was much discussion about D.'s sex, so Muhsin said.

The wadi was now opening out into an immensely wide cultivated plain. Scattered over it were men ploughing and women and children about their several occasions. The place was called Teheir, and settlement after settlement was included in the name. We put up some partridges and I longed for my shotgun, away back with the caravan, to relieve the

[1] The cliffs above the slopes were still the normal colour and the black lava was up to a uniform height of about a hundred feet. A little later there was a gully which broke the continuity of the black stones, but they continued beyond the gully, showing perhaps that the formation of the gully was later than the volcanic activity. Curiously enough there was little of the lava on the left side. The lava ended at the mouth of the Wadi 'Akid on the west side but continued up it on the east side. In the main wadi there was still lava on the right-hand slopes and it was a conspicuous feature of the wadi for most of the rest of its length. Squadron-Leader Rickards' sketch map of the wadi made from an aerial reconnaissance shows a number of small craters and one large crater some way down the wadi from this place. From the distribution of the lava we deduced that the wadis were in point of time older, that they had then been filled with lava to a depth in places of from a hundred to a hundred and twenty feet, and that afterwards the river had carved out a new bed. Much of this country is volcanic, for there are hot sulphur springs at Shihr, and between Shihr and Seihut I have seen extensive lava fields from the air.

## A RIVER OF THE RIVERS OF PARADISE—THE MAHRA COUNTRY

monotony of tinned salmon. After the plain had narrowed away, we came to another gate and as we waited for it to be pulled down we gazed in awe at a mass of rock which made me think that Epstein had been let loose in the valley. The group it formed might have been called "Motherhood," for it resembled an ill-shapen female with a horde of monstrous children crowding up to her. Once past this nightmare conception we could see the high walls sloping down to the valley in spurs with the green foliage and water below and the blue sky above. Actually the bed of the wadi was now only about fifty yards wide.

Everything was quiet and breathless on these afternoon rides, save for the pad-pad of the camels' feet which was the only sound that broke the stillness. There were signs everywhere that there had been a terrific torrent of water for there were branches thrown up high among the bushes and trees uprooted. We camped in a narrow place above the seil bed, heavily wooded and with no sign of habitation near us; nevertheless our young escort climbed up the cliff, as he did every night about half-past eight, and announced to the trees and the echoing rocks that he was our safeguard and we were under the protection of his tribe.

"Who's going to hear that, Hassan?" I asked as we sat at dinner.

"Mon-keys, perhaps," laughed Hassan.

But I do not think there were even monkeys to hear it.

The air next morning was soft and cool, but we found the 'ais and ariata trees very tiresome, for as we pushed aside their wet branches the 'ais in particular left something sticky on one's face and hands, and it became difficult to take a decent sight with the compass. The only sign of habitation was the sound of voices from a village hidden amongst the trees. Once we met a man carrying a baby in a cradle—the only time I remember seeing such a sight in Arabia.

We came out of the forest to see Buzūn in the distance, marking the beginning of the country occupied by the Bin Zūeidi clan of the Mahra tribe. Passing Buzūn we plunged into the shade of the woods again and halted for lunch at Al Bureika, a little village in a clearing on the left side of the wadi. At Buzūn Seiyid Muhsin had collected a Bin Zūeidi siyar, Mseika bin Salim, who was again extraordinarily youthful. He was a cheerful soul who sang continuously, accompanying his singing by the clapping of his hands, but his songs always ended abruptly and with a curious noise like a gramophone that has run down. He wore the black braided coat of the Mahras which is almost a uniform pattern, though the

## SIGNS OF FLOOD AND VOLCANIC ACTIVITY

facings change. (The Bin Afrar wear them braided with silver and the rulers themselves have gold.) Mseika had Mongolian features and his back view with his hair done up in a bun was exactly that of a Chinese woman. He had only arrived at Buzūn from Seihut that day and told us he had taken two and half days on the journey.

At Nedura we left the forest and rode amongst the acacia trees, whose wicked thorns tore our clothes and scratched our hands and faces, till we reached Thei'man where we camped in a magnificent situation raised well above the wadi, and were astir again early on December 16th. As the beduin loaded up the camels, chanting the same words over and over again, frequently concerning one of us, the rising sun lit up the grand walls of the wadi and the sombre bushes below us touching everything with red and gold.

We started off down towards the river and were soon again wrestling with overhanging branches. There were men spreading out ariata leaves to dry and from here on such a sight was common. When dried they are taken to Seihut and sold for camel fodder. The fact that Seihut was now the market town told us more clearly than anything that we were nearing our journey's end.

There were still extensive signs of volcanic activity and we came out into the open with black cliffs on each side of us. They were backed by much higher and older cliffs, curiously patterned with vertical flutings which gave voice to a tremendous echo at the singing of Mseika and the shouting of the camel-men. The level of the flood was at least twenty feet up on the perpendicular cliffs by which we were riding and Mseika said that floods like this happen about once in four years and last some ten days. Anyone caught here by its sudden rush would not have a chance.

The villages now, such as Gheil, were well up on the right slope of the wadi beyond the reach of possible floods, surrounded with date palms and green from the water of springs. These slopes on the right lead up to the high rock wall which appears to be about a thousand feet high.

There were no further villages until we reached Qal'ana with its ruined castle in the traditional medieval style: the houses round it were also broken and deserted. Here, except for occasional pools or when the seil comes down, the river comes to an end and in the afternoon we rode round a large island hill in the middle of the wide wadi crowned with a stone wall attributed by our beduin to the children of 'Ad, and called Husn 'Ad.

We passed a sha'b called Al Kohl which owes its name, according to

Muhsin, to antimony deposits, and halted at Qatāt al 'Abīd, a deserted spot where there was a pool of water. We camped on the other side of the pool under a high wall with well-marked strata, which sheltered us from the wind. It was a good camping place with ariata round us and boulders behind. For dinner we had tomato soup, lean chops, the last of the mutton, with onions and chips, and vermicelli pudding with cherries. Not bad fare for such a spot, but Ganess, who by now had become a complete beduin talking Arabic freely and saddling his own camel, still retained his culinary skill and some enterprise. I sent a letter by messenger to Seihut telling the Sultan's representative that we were coming and saying that we wanted a dhow for Mukalla. We fell asleep to the tune of the pounding of coffee from the beduin encamped across the pool.

We expected that December 17th would be our last day's march and started early in the hope of reaching Seihut in good time. The way was rough, the vegetation sparse, and it soon became very hot. Two men passed by and asked if we were Seiyids. I suppose they were told that we were for one of them took D.'s hand and tried to kiss it. She withdrew it as would have been proper in ordinary society, but the Seiyids allow their hands to be kissed. The man drew back surprised and one of the beduin said: "Nasara", whereupon the man's face blackened with fury. No doubt he felt he had been defiled, and I wondered for a moment if there would be an incident. However, although he put his hand to his dagger he thought better of it and turned away.

After Semarma we left the wadi and climbed up on to a plateau called Al Makad which cuts off a large corner. The country was rapidly opening up and we expected every minute to see the sea. The plateau was barren and the only sight was the grave of another giant, Mola al 'Ain. Seiyid Muhsin, our authority on the saints of the road, did not know when he had lived but said it was a long time ago. He told us that travellers on the sea caught in a storm vow to visit his grave if they are saved.

Wanting to press on we went on ahead of the caravan to Dhubeia which has about a hundred and fifty mud huts, and a good deal of cultivation. A number of people rushed up from all sides to look at us. They seemed friendly. I found one or two who spoke Swahili and they asked me to take a photograph. One man caught hold of D.'s camel as he wanted her to go and see the women. Some yards further on another tribesman rushed forward and he, too, seized the rope of her camel which was the leading one, and was being led by Karama. I thought he was after the same thing

## AN ALARMING INCIDENT

but Karama snatched the rope back and continued on his way. The man shouted something and snatched it again. I was talking to my Swahili-speaking friends and merely thought he was being persistent, but then Hassan and Zaidi made an extremely rapid descent from their camels without even waiting to couch them. I asked what was the matter and Hassan said in a frightened way: "They're going to shoot you."

Then I saw the man take a cartridge from his belt, load his rifle and go off muttering to behind the corner of a house where he was joined by three others; they pointed their rifles at us and somebody shouted that we must stop or we would certainly be shot. There was so much talk that it was difficult to know what was happening but it transpired in time that the Zūeidis had determined we were either to return the way we had come or be shot, for they were not going to have Christians in their country. The rest of the caravan was well behind so we decided to wait until Seiyid Muhsin and Mseika came up and then see what could be done. Meanwhile our Zūeidi friends who wanted to shoot us were still standing at the corner of the house. We dismounted and walked over to one of the houses where we were surrounded by men and women who all appeared perfectly friendly but did not want us to go on in case worse trouble should happen. My Swahili-speaking friends told me that Dhubeia was terrorised by these beduin Zūeidis who had come down from the mountains and ran the place. We learned that the man who first threatened to shoot us was 'Ali bin Hanad,[1] and he and another called Zarkia were the ringleaders in the trouble.

Seiyid Muhsin arrived next and went off to investigate. He explained that we had a siyar and therefore had the right to go through the country and that Zūeidi honour depended on our having a favourable passage. "Siyara was never meant to cover Christians," was the reply.

Presently the rest of our imposing caravan turned up and Mseika and another Seiyid from the village went off to further arguments as the men causing the trouble would not come and see us. Mseika, so the Seiyid said, told them that their behaviour was disgraceful and that if there was any trouble he was going to fight with us. The whole of the rest of the caravan also said they were going to fight with us. Confronted with this the Zūeidis made a face-saving arrangement whereby we were to go on to the

[1] Some months later I was on visits to Qishn and Soqotra. At both places I learnt that soon after our passing, the seil came down and carried 'Ali bin Hanad out to sea and drowned him. This was universally considered a judgment on him for his interference with us.

outskirts of Darfāt and halt for the night there while the tribe decided what should be done with us. As yet we had received no word from the Sultan's representative at Seihut which, I was told, was also in Zūeidi hands, so this seemed the best thing to do.

* * *

We wasted no more time but mounted again amidst the friendly goodbyes of the people who had been talking to us. In a little while we saw the first indications of the sea, the sails of two big buggalows, but the water was still invisible and we did not see it until we were practically beside it. It was two months since we had parted from it. We shouted "The sea, the sea," and I remembered the Ten Thousand and echoed their emotions.

We were riding across the maritime plain with a long stretch of sand-dunes between ourselves and the sea, and hills on our left rising up to the mountains behind. The brown foothills blended with the golden sand piled up against them, and there was even an attraction in the barren plain dotted here and there with green scrub. The sky flecked with feathery clouds was a vivid blue, and every now and again we caught glimpses of the deeper blue of the sea, which seemed to have acquired a new friendliness in our absence.

Ahead of us we saw a man sitting on a stone sharpening his knife and Hassan murmured uneasily: "What does he want?" As we drew nearer the man ran on in front, which he thought very sinister. Soon we reached the outskirts of Darfāt and camped rather dejectedly a little short of the village in a depression where there was a cemetery. Our large caravan declined to desert us and camped near-by.

I sent a letter at once to Seihut and we settled down for the night. By nine o'clock I received an answer to the letter I had written the night before which said: "Your kind letter has been received and both you and your companions are allowed to enter (Seihut) to-morrow morning. May this be known to you."

The new Seiyid from Dhubeia who had joined us told me that the Sultan's representative would send for the Qadhi and Zueidi representatives and probably bribe the latter to allow us to come. An hour later another letter came addressed to: "Our friend who has sent us a letter complaining of what has befallen him on the road and who is now lying at Darfāt."

It said: "Please note that you and your party are under our protection. You need not fear. You are allowed to travel in the country until you come to our part, Seihut, in the security of God and our protection. We will talk the matter over when we see you."

Our last day, December 18th, the camel-men were round for the loads earlier than ever before as there was no grazing for their camels in this barren place. We left in solemn procession at half-past seven and a few minutes later passed through Darfāt, boasting a one-storeyed dar and several mud huts.

Seiyid Muhsin said that the people in the neighbourhood were fanatical, so Hassan played for safety by singing religious chants and telling his beads. We were soon met by Muhammad, son of Sultan Sa'ud the representative in Seihut, a boy of about fourteen in a pink futa and turban, carrying a sword. I dismounted and we greeted each other solemnly.

From a distance Seihut looked quite large. There were one or two minarets and domes and a few two-storeyed houses, but no sign of cultivation. Out at sea we saw plenty of sails and felt it would not be difficult to find a dhow. Many groups of men came out from the town to look at us and fell in behind the procession. One of the first to meet us was a friendly lunatic, obviously mad and obviously friendly, but he had a rifle with which he performed all kinds of antics, occasionally making us feel exceedingly nervous.

We rode to a house belonging to the Sultan's family on the eastern side of the town. Outside the door stood a wild-looking man with much hair and beard, and dressed in an indigo-dyed coat and futa. This was Sultan 'Ali bin 'Abdulla, brother of Sultan Sa'ud who was sick. The lunatic with the rifle was the general manager of the place, for it was he who ushered us upstairs to a room on the first floor. There was no furniture, not even cushions, but filthy mats and one carpet. It was indescribably squalid and dirtier than anything I remembered even in Arabia. However, we sat down on the floor and were quickly surrounded by friends, relations and hangers-on.

After some time two unwashed cups were handed to us and ginger coffee poured into them from a kettle. As it was Ramadhan I thought this was kind, and was glad that the licence to travellers allowed Hassan to keep us countenance. Ganess began preparing lunch in another room, and a live sheep and a dead fish were brought into the "drawing-room" for our inspection before being handed over to him.

Meanwhile Sultan Sa'ud arrived, a very sick man and looking much older than 'Ali. He also looked considerably more respectable. He retired upstairs to rest after a short conversation, and when he left Seiyid Muhsin and another Seiyid began speaking in a curious, half-familiar language. The unknown Seiyid, who had been in Mombasa, subsequently explained it to me. It is an enigmatical way of speaking Arabic. The words are disguised by having extra syllables inserted.

When Hassan returned from enquiring after transport he told me that the large buggalow was off to India, but he had seen three dhows and made arrangements with a bigger one than that originally proposed. The contract was that the dhow should convey our party and baggage as far as Shihr for a hundred dollars. Hassan and I then went up to have a talk with Sultan Sa'ud who was extremely apologetic about the hold-up of Dhubeia. He told me that the Sultan had no control in Seihut outside the door of his house, that the Zūeidis had come down into the town from the mountains a few years ago and now ran the place and took most of the taxes. At first they had stayed in the interior but then they came into the town, gradually usurping more power and then fixing amounts against the merchants. Periodically they elect two Muqaddams and these take it in turn to control the town. In Qishn, he told me, the Sultans of the Bin Afrar have more authority. Sultan Sa'ud was plainly very ill so I did not like to let him talk too long. There was still a large crowd in the room below when I left him, and his brother 'Ali said he would like to come to Aden with us. I agreed and he went off to see his brother, returning a little later with an old man and a large sheet of paper.

"We want an agreement," said the old man.

"An agreement?" I asked. "What for?"

"We want you to sign this paper promising that Sultan 'Ali will be returned to Seihut in safety!"

As we wanted a rest we said we would like to be alone. Nobody was anxious to move, but the lunatic grasped the idea and with much gusto cleared everybody out and proceeded to lock himself and his rifle in with us. Eventually we persuaded him to clear out as well, but he mounted guard outside the door and made it difficult even for Zaidi and Ganess to come in.

More visitors came in after lunch, including Sheikh Hamid bin 'Abdu Rahman Bakareit. His ancestor, Muhammad 'Abdulla Bakareit, is the principal weli of Seihut and the ground on which Seihut stands was given to him a long time ago. On this account his descendants receive an easy income in payments for permission to build and in annual tithes on crops. They also get half a bag of dates for every six bags imported, and two tin of fish oil on every dhow load exported. The story has it that Muhammad 'Abdulla Bakareit was born with a small tree growing out of his head, which continually had to be cut off but always grew again. When he died it grew into a big tree and now grows out of the roof of his tomb.

By now our luggage had been carried down to the beach so we followed it, saying good-bye to most of those who had come to look at us. On the way down to the shore we passed two small date nurseries protected by a fence of fishing nets. Someone with us called out to the gardener: "Come and look at the woman."

"What woman, where?" said the gardener coming up to the fence,

The showman pointed to D. "That's a woman."

The gardener laughed heartily. "Nonsense, that's not a woman. You can't pull my leg like that."

Sultan 'Ali had changed his mind and was not coming with us. However, on reaching the shore he decided to get into the rowing-boat and see us off. On the way to the dhow he decided to come. Once on the dhow when the boat had gone back he decided to go home again. The boat was hailed and returned. Sultan 'Ali then decided to brave the journey and come with us. His luggage was of the scantiest. He had come down to the shore with nothing but what he had on, but in one of the moments when he made up his mind to come with us he had taken young Muhammad's sword away from him and tried without success to borrow his pink turban.

The good ship *Matrab* was anchored about a quarter of a mile off the shore. She was of twenty tons burthen or, as it is put in local parlance, carried 300 bags. She flew a very smart green, red and white silk flag with crescent and star presented by a Hadhrami Seiyid. There were sixteen of us all told on board, the five of us, Salih 'Ali, Salim, Bukheit, Faraj, our wild animal, Sultan Ali, the nakhoda Nesīb bin 'Isa, a crew of three and two boys who cooked and did other odd jobs. One of them was already preparing the evening meal on the box of sand amidships. The rest of us hoisted sail at once to the tune of a shanty and we were off at a quarter to five.

Behind the narrow coastal plain were row on row of mountains, each higher than the last, till they were hidden among the clouds. The summits of those we could see were tipped with purple and crimson by the setting sun which lit up the dars of Darfāt with its straggling row of date palms. The shadows lengthened between the hills as we sailed on into the west,

## A RIVER OF THE RIVERS OF PARADISE—THE MAHRA COUNTRY

passing the imposing break in the range of mountains that marks our never-to-be-forgotten Wadi Maseila. Around us I counted nine sails on the deep blue of the sea, some silhouetted against the sunset.

In this peaceful scene where the soft padding of the camels' feet had given way to the gentle lap of the water against the dhow and the only other sound was the rhythmic pounding of coffee, one of the crew rose up to voice the Call to Prayer.

We watched the land darken and the moon rise up behind us, and reflected how much kindness and how much ignorance there was behind those mountains.

## Chapter XXII

## LAST DAYS IN SHIHR AND MUKALLA

*Peace be within thy walls and plenteousness within thy palaces.* PSALMS.

WE arrived at Shihr early on the morning of December 20th, and when the shops opened and a little life started we went out, escorted by Faraj Maqram, a business man and friend of Hassan's, to explore the bazaar and back streets. The bazaar was still almost empty but we were able to buy cigarettes and smoke once again as many as we wanted. We quickly collected the usual crowd of men and small boys following in our wake with women peering at us from a distance. There are a number of Somalis in the town but not as many as in Mukalla. Their principal occupation is to make mats and look after goats. The main and very obvious industry of Shihr is fishing and the drying of fish, but the town is also celebrated for its looms.

I was told by Sultan Salim and Seiyid 'Abdul Qadir that the present town of Shihr is seven hundred years old. It is certain that it had its predecessors and one of them may well have been the small village of Shiheir a few miles further west.[1] The neighbourhood has had a chequered career and seen many different occupations. About A.D. 821 Muhammad bin Ziyad sent by Ma'mun became master of Hadhramaut, Diār Kinda and Shihr, and levied taxes on the ambergris, still a minor product of the southern shore of Arabia. In A.D. 1012 on the death of Ibn Salama the Beni Ma'n took Shihr at the same time that they possessed themselves of Aden and the Hadhramaut. To the Beni Ma'n succeeded the Suleihis and Shihr later became a province of the Resuli dynasty of Yemen.

[1] The *Periplus* makes no mention of an important post between Cana and Syagrus but refers to the whole of the Shihr coast as the Bay of Sachalites, a word probably connected with the name of Shihr. In the time of the Arabian geographers such as Masudi the expression Shihr included the whole country from the present Shihr coast through Mahra and Dhofar to the borders of Oman. Shihr (shahr) and Mahra are different forms of the same word. In any case the original inhabitants of the country now included in the Shihr province were Mahras who were gradually driven eastward to their present limit marked by Mussena'a.

## LAST DAYS IN SHIHR AND MUKALLA

The first recorded visit by Europeans was in February, 1532, when Manuel da Vasconcello set out from Goa to cruise after Turkish and Moorish prizes in the Arabian Sea and at Shihr captured, among others, a large native craft, richly laden, which he sent in charge of a prize crew to Muscat. This expedition was followed shortly by another of ten ships under Antonio da Saldanha. On reaching Shihr he was visited by the Sultan who complained to him of the proceedings of Manuel da Vasconcello in seizing ships in his port. In 1552 Alvaro da Noronha, hearing that the Turks were preparing a large fleet to fight the Portuguese, sent a spy to Shihr to collect information. The spy confirmed the report but the Turkish fleet was dispersed and several ships lost off Shihr in a violent storm.

It was from Portuguese contacts that Duarte Barbosa obtained the information to compile his short notice of "Xaer." He states that the town belonged to the Mahra kingdom of Fartak. It was very large and enjoyed a considerable foreign trade with India. The imports were cotton cloths, gems, rice, sugar and spices. For many of these articles the place appears to have been an *entrepôt* and the goods were reshipped to Aden. The exports were horses and frankincense. Other products were wheat, flesh, dates and grapes. Earlier, however, than Barbosa's description is that of Marco Polo who states that the great city of Esher had a king subject to the Soldan of Aden. He too speaks of the trade with India and the export of horses and incense and the abundance of dates.[1]

In 1839 Captain Haines estimated the population at about 6,000 and the revenue at about £6,000 a year. In those days it was the residence of the

---

[1] "They have fish in great profusion, and notably plenty of tunny of large size; so plentiful indeed that you may buy two big ones for a Venice groat of silver. The natives live on meat and rice and fish. They have no wine of the vine, but they make good wine from sugar, from rice, and from dates also.

"And I must not omit to tell you that all their cattle, including horses, oxen, and camels, live upon small fish and nought besides, for 'tis all they get to eat. You see in all this country there is no grass or forage of any kind; it is the driest country on the face of the earth. The fish which are given to the cattle are very small, and during March, April, and May, are caught in such quantities as would astonish you. They are then dried and stored, and the beasts are fed on them from year's end to year's end. The cattle will also readily eat these fish all alive and just out of the water.

"The people here have likewise many other kinds of fish of large size and good quality, exceedingly cheap; these they cut in pieces of about a pound each, and dry them in the sun, and then store them, and eat them -11 .1- .... .1......1. 1:1.. .. ...... .1. biscuit."

Hamumi chief. Shihr was an old slave-trading station and must have continued so to a date later than this. I was told that the Āl Bureik, originally from Hureidha, entered Shihr in 1752 at the invitation of the inhabitants and through the medium of the Al 'Attas Seiyids. In 1816 the town was captured by Wahabis under Ibn Kamla. They were turned out by 'Ali bin Naji bin Bureik with whom the British treaty of 1863 for the suppression of the slave trade was concluded. In 1850 Seiyid Ishaq bin 'Aqil bin Yahya al Hadhrami came from Hejaz with four hundred soldiers lent by the Sharif to occupy Shihr and assist the Kathīris against the Kasadis. The Kasadi Naqib assisted the Āl Bureik to defend the place. In 1866 the Kathīri Sultan, Ghalib bin Muhsin, took Shihr on the suggestion of Seiyid 'Aqil bin 'Abdulla bin Yahya.

To-day Shihr is but a ghost of its former glory, though it is attractive and *sympathique*. It is walled on the three land sides and there are two large gateways in the walls, through which cars can pass, and three small ones; there are also thirty-six bastions. The houses are scattered and a great number tumbled down and broken. Close to the inner side of the north wall are a number of huts built of sticks and mats. The streets are wide so that the usual litter does not affect one's nostrils so badly, though the dust is bad. The worst feature of the sanitation is that the drainage of the houses is directed into small pools of stagnant, stinking water.

Two days later we returned to Mukalla. We had left by the west gate nearly two months before, and now we entered by the east, having made a circuit of seven hundred miles. During Ramadhan days Mukalla, like the rest of the country, was silent and its streets almost deserted. But Therb, the camel park, was crowded with camels, for the beduin delay their journey up-country from Mukalla until the very last days of the fast, and then set out, loaded with luxuries, to arrive home for the feast day. Once more we were invited to the palace, and there was much discussion of the growing tension between Italy and Abyssinia of which news had recently arrived. The Arabs with their keen political sense were not slow to see its possible implications.

From Christmas Eve onwards we awaited eagerly the arrival of Besse's steamer, the *Al Haqq*, which was to take us back to Aden. Even the friendliness and social hospitality of our friends could not entirely dispel our anxiety, and as for poor Hassan, he was sunk in vast depression. I tackled him about it.

"What *is* the matter, Hassan, you've hardly spoken a word for days?"

## LAST DAYS IN SHIHR AND MUKALLA

"It's my family," he said. "I think there's something the matter. I've had no letter."

"Well, nor have we."

"Well," he said, solemnly pronouncing judgement, "when we get back to Aden I shall enquire from my cousin in the Harbour Police and if all is well I shall not go home, but I shall go to a hotel in Tawahi and stay there until they all come and kneel before me and beg forgiveness and ask me to return home."

Days of visiting and expeditions went by but the *Al Haqq* did not appear, though there were many false alarms; but on the 29th Cowasjee Dinshaw's ship, the *Africa*, arrived with a huge cargo for Mukalla and Shihr. The following afternoon, however, we learnt that it was to sail for Aden that night, and accordingly we packed our belongings. At ten o'clock Sultan Salim came to take us to the Customs, and when we had taken our leave we left by rowing-boat for the ship which weighed anchor as soon as we were on board. As we steamed slowly out of the harbour we gazed with regret at the lamplit dhows, the line of lights, the dim forms of the houses and the black mass of Qara.

\* \* \*

The morning of New Year's day found us back in Aden, glad to be home again amongst its modest comforts, but such is the fascination of the Ḥadhramaut that we were soon anxious to set out again. As the months went by we missed more and more the guest-house of Mukalla. But in Aden the school and affairs of the Hadhramaut took up most of my time now. All Hadhramaut questions came to me and months were spent on compiling reports on it.

I visited the country again twice before I went on leave, each time by air. It was strange to pass over the scene of so many week's travelling in a few hours, spying out familiar landmarks from a height of 2,000 feet and paying lightning visits to old friends when we landed at Fuwa, the airport of Mukalla. On this first visit I went also to Merbat in 'Uman where the R.A.F. had business, and to Qishn, the capital of the Mahra country, for not only the Hadhramaut, but all the eastern part of the Protectorate was beginning to become my own sphere, and I was to find out somethint about the boundaries between the Protectorate and the Sultanate of Muscas and Oman. I had no official standing in Merbat, but enjoyed the two days there, for there were Zanzibar contacts and the atmosphere of the Wali's house was that of my Omani friends, down to the very coffee we drank.

# NOSTALGIA

To Sogotra, too, I paid a visit, thus seeing the island of the Western Indian Ocean which I had most wanted to know.

Just before going home I made yet another visit to Mukalla by air; Sultan 'Umar had died in India from cancer, and I had to see how the situation was shaping itself for Sultan Salih, his nephew and successor. Things were going to be difficult in Mukalla, for power was passing into new hands; what the future would bring no man could tell, but the situation had elements of promise about it. Such matters would, however, have to wait till the powers that be had decided on a policy for the country.

When the time came to leave thoughts and feelings were torn between England and the Hadhramaut. For those in distant lands the most haunting memories of home are centred oddly around seemingly trivial things.

In my diary I find an entry:

S.S. "Orion"<br>
Port Said,<br>
23rd September, 1936.

This morning a real eastern sun rose out of the sea as we approached Port Said. We have been sitting in a café watching the bootblacks, the galli galli man, the street vendors and all the trumperiness of the Port of Parasites. A tired but tireless violin player and pianist played tiresome jazz tunes, while across the road another indefatigable couple competed with "A Tavern in the Town," "I do like to be beside the seaside," "Red sails in the sunset," and older more time-worn melodies.

For all its tawdriness Port Said still stands for something as the doorway to the East. I remembered fifteen years ago coming back on leave and seeing the canal for the first time and writing something—happily destroyed by that holocaust of the white ants in Mauritius—about hearing a door close behind me. The camels, the Arabs and the wastes of sand seemed so familiar, though I had not then seen them before. They were so much a part of me that they felt like home. To-day it was the same, though I had mingled feelings of sadness in the café. Sadness that it should be so, for I suppose it is not normal in one who still feels as English as I do in sentiment, and sadness because one day I must come to it for the last time.

There are lovely memories to take back—sunset behind Rodney's pillar on the Breidden—coming from London to Wenlock Edge on a summer evening—mornings with my father and mother on the veranda at Shrewsbury, the wilderness of their garden and the greenness of the fields—Severn stream below the school—ghostly Cornovii and Roman legionaries at Uriconium by the river—ghostly monks fishing in their shady pool by the lovely ruins of Haughmond. Again the garden at Maydeken and the lady of the garden, delphiniums at Royston, the downs at Patching and the sound of the lawn-mower, the cawing of the rooks. So great is their power that it takes no effort to recall them, yet however much I let them linger in my mind they can never drive away the yearning to be back in Arabia.

> "We travel not for trafficking alone;
> By hotter winds our fiery hearts are fanned;
> For lust of knowing what should not be known,
> We take the Golden Road to Samarkand."

## PART THREE

*How strangely active are the arts of peace,
Whose restless motions less than war's do cease!
Peace is not freed from Labour, but from noise;
And war more force, but not more pains, employs.*
                                    DRYDEN.

## Chapter XXIII

## RETURN TO THE HADHRAMAUT AND THE FIRST MOVE

*Until the day break, and the shadows flee away, I will get me to the mountain of myrrh, and to the hill of frankincense.* SONG OF SOLOMON.

*... be deaf unto the suggestions of Tale-bearers, Calumniators, Pick-Thank or Malevolent Delators, who, while quiet Men sleep, sowing the tares of discord and division, distract the tranquillity of Charity and all Friendly Society.*

SIR THOMAS BROWNE.

على قطن بالشيم أيمن موبر * وايسره على الستار فيذبل

BACK in Aden, it was pleasant to know that we were definitely going to the Hadhramaut again. Immediately on our first return from the Hadhramaut I had made certain recommendations for the future of the country. In the west of the Protectorate the chiefs and tribesmen had seemed to think that money and a supply of arms was the remedy for all ills. But away in the east where they had not got used to the bounties of Aden, I found grave-faced men who deplored the anarchy of their country and discussed mainly the possibilities of getting the Government to assist in other ways. They considered that they could rightly expect assistance as they were under British protection. They did not appreciate, nor could they have been expected to, that the degree of interest which Aden could take in them varied in inverse ratio with their distance from the seat of Government. Technically, and from the treaty point of view, all the Sultanates and Sheikhdoms comprised in the term Aden Protectorate from Husn Murad in the west to Ras Dharbat 'Ali in the east, and into the interior were on an equal footing: their treaties said that Her Majesty extended to them Her Gracious favour and protection on condition of their not ceding their territories or tolerating any interference from any other Power. In fact, the Qu'aiti, whose Protectorate Treaty was dated 1886, was even more protected, for by an earlier treaty of 1882 he had bound himself to abide by British advice not only in his dealings with foreign Powers but also with neighbouring tribes. But, with the tiny political staff of the Resident of

## RETURN TO THE HADHRAMAUT AND THE FIRST MOVE

Aden, dealings with the tribes whose relations were under the superintendence of the Aden Residency (whence the term *Aden* Protectorate) were necessarily limited mostly to tribes geographically near to Aden, and the Hadhramaut and the Mahra country were left very much to their own devices.

Though the Kathiri country was in the British sphere, it depended little on the Qu'aiti and it was not till 1918 that the Qu'aiti—Kathiri agreement was concluded, whereby the Kathiris recognized the 1882 Treaty as binding on themselves. Such then was the political situation.

The problem was not easy. On the credit side, the country was more advanced than the Western Protectorate, and there was a large and increasing part of the population which had had contacts with the world and seen the benefits of settled administration in the East Indies, East Africa and other places. There was a more than embryonic show of good order and organized government in Qu'aiti territory, and the Sultan had displayed a growing tendency to provide education and social services. In Kathiri circles there was an influential body of opinion which desired to establish peace and good order, and there was also a large expenditure by the rich on public and social services. In tribal circles a desire had been expressed for direct British rule.

But on the debit side there was, outside the towns, a state of internecine war, which had lasted longer than history; and no sort of justice at all. In addition to all the usual tribal jealousies there was mistrust between the two countries of Qu'aiti and Kathiri and the latter, now confined to the interior, was harassed by the former, which was more powerful and, holding the ports, held the key to the situation.

It seemed to me that the first essentials were to establish peace and good order in Kathiri territory, particularly in that part which lay in the main Hadhramaut wadi from just east of Shibam to just east of Tarim, and to remove the mistrust between the Qu'aiti and Kathiri and establish a more helpful attitude on the part of the senior partner in the Hadhramaut.

To this end I recommended that the Kathiri should be helped to establish a force of two hundred Tribal Guards, supplied by us with rifles and ammunition and inspection by a British officer, and by them with a trained Arab instructor. Guarantees were to be given that this force should never be used against the Qu'aiti. Then I proposed that with similar guarantees the Qu'aiti army should be properly equipped and trained at the Qu'aiti's expense. As a condition of this assistance I thought the Qu'aiti should be persuaded to allow the Kathīri to complete a motor road to the sea, and not to impede any measure of development which the Kathīri wished to undertake, such as agricultural development in the wadi. Lastly I recommended that an officer should be appointed for the eastern part of the Protectorate and Adviser to the Kathīri and Qu'aiti Sultans. He would deal not only with Qu'aiti and Kathīri affairs but also with those of the Mahri Sultanate on the east and the Wahidi Sultanates of Bir 'Ali and Balhaf on the west.

These proposals were submitted on the 21st January, 1935: months followed in which detailed reports on the country were prepared (D. typed over 900 foolscap pages in all) and at last in March 1936 we went on leave.

Most of leave was spent on Hadhramaut work: lectures and papers to be written, broadcasting and work on the report. The powers that be decided that help should be given to the Sultans, but it was not yet felt that a political officer should go there. Still I never gave up hope, and then Sir Bernard Reilly, who had more than encouraged my enthusiasm for the Hadhramaut, told me that in the forthcoming winter it had been decided that I should return to inaugurate the new policy. On the last day of leave the final proofs of the report were returned and shortly after it was published—Colonial No. 123. It only remained to go.

* * *

A month or so in Aden sped fast enough. There were the usual preparations for a journey to make and I had my school to look after. We had gone home on leave through the Sudan, Egypt and Palestine, and Winter, Director of Education at Khartoum, had found a first-rate man as headmaster. Thin as a lath, quiet and efficient, I found 'Abdul Qadir Okeir installed there when I returned. The staff was about as efficient as could have been picked; Mrs. Muhsin, as we called the bearded Yuzbashi Muhsin 'Alawi, an 'Aulaqi Sheikh from the Levies, looked after the children better than a mother. We often used to laugh over the early days when he and I had bathed the small boys before putting them to bed. Ahmed and Ghouth, rural teachers from Zanzibar, had done much, especially in producing as fine a small boys' football team as could be found in Aden. It was satisfying, somehow, to find the place running as D. and I had pictured it sitting in the ruins of the barracks, which was now the main college building.

Ramadhan was approaching and with it the end of term. The three biggest and best boys—all prefects—had to think of leaving school, and as they were not very sure of their future I wanted to see more of them and see what school had done for them. On the last night of term I sent for them and asked them what their plans were. They were all rather in the dumps, for the one feeling that everybody in that school had was that they would rather be at school than at home, and we always had a job in repressing applications to be allowed to stay on in holiday time.

"I shall go and stay at the Levies," said Yeslem, an 'Aulaqi. The other two, Muhammad Sa'id the football captain, and Yahya the head of the school were Yafa'is, both of them members of tribes who were in disgrace with Government. They "supposed they'd have to go home."

"How would you like to come with me to the Hadhramaut?"

They thought I was joking and smiled watery smiles.

"I mean it," I said.

Genuine smiles spread all over their faces and Yeslem, begging to come too, was also included.

It was part of my policy that the masters, in their holidays, should tour in the Protectorate, to learn how their charges lived, to advertise the school and to teach football. They had not visited the Hadhramaut, so I invited 'Abdul Qadir and Ghouth to come with us.. Ghouth, who had been born in Zanzibar, was a Ba Wazir Sheikh of Hadhramaut parentage. His father had gone to Zanzibar from Gheil Ba Wazir and his mother from Dis near Hami. It was right he should see his native land.

The other member of the party was Ahmed Hassan, the youngest and one of the brightest of the Residency staff of interpreters.

Again we sailed on the *Al Amin*, a joyful and excited party the night of embarkation, but the morning brought quiet, for all except myself were bad sailors and I passed in solitude a day which was otherwise perfect, blue skies and a wind and sun which whipped and gilded bluer seas.

It was after sunset on the 16th November that we reached Mukalla, to be greeted by the familiar faces of Yusuf Sherif, the doctor, and Ahmed Effendi the Jemadar. It seemed a real home-coming, though the rest of our party were strangers and the boys, clad in their best purple and green kilts, white Scots jackets and purple, green and gold turbans, were shy.

We rowed ashore in the dark. In front of the crowd waiting at the Customs stood a stranger, turbaned, in a long white coat.

"Seiyid Hamid, the prime minister," whispered the doctor to me.

Hamid and I had never met and to me he represented the new Mukalla I had to face and learn.. His predecessor, Sultan Salim, our friend of last

## MUKALLA UNDER A NEW RÉGIME

journey, lay in jail, a private one it is true, but nevertheless a jail, and since I had returned to Aden I had heard disturbing tales of the new regime, and particularly of the influence exerted over the gentle and pious Sultan by Hamid the Seiyid and Ahmed Nasir, who had leapt from being a private soldier to ministerial rank overnight, and who prevented, except in the case of a few courtiers, all access to the Sultan, which is the foundation of Arab justice, and in self-interest was attempting to rule the country in his name. If present history were not as it is, I could hardly write these words. But there was no secret about it and my two friends of to-day know exactly what my opinion of their past is. I never had any personal feelings against either of them, but their villainies had to be stopped.

Seiyid Hamid's greetings were cordial, if rather overdone. He was a young man of thirty or so, well read in poetry, history and religion, and with two years of the Al Azhar behind him. He took us in a new car—the drivers and most of the old regime had disappeared—to the familiar guest-house, where we met the other evil genius—Ahmed Nasir, one of the tallest Arabs I have ever seen. We measured ourselves back to back and I found that with my boots on I could only give him an inch, so he must be just over six feet.

We did not meet the Sultan that night, though as it was the first of Ramadhan we saw him holding a reception below on the open veranda on which I had last seen Msellem and 'Abdul Qadir Ba Faqih checking and sealing up the Mukalla despatches to Aden. A part of the army was already drawn up in the square which was lit with Teriks—those incandescent lights which are now used all over Africa and Arabia. I had not before seen them in full dress, blue and gold laced tunics, scarlet breeches with a broad blue stripe and squat tarbushes, looking like something out of the Balkans or what is supposed to exist in Ruritanian States. The Sultan's car drew up before the guard, His Highness stepped out backwards, the band played "God Save the King," and His Highness made his way to the carpeted veranda where a long procession of his subjects kissed his hand and congratulated him on the arrival of the sacred month. The ceremonial ginger coffee of south-west Arabia was then handed round. Hardly a word was spoken and the ceremony did not last long. His Highness got up, the band played again and, when he had departed, led the forces away.

## RETURN TO THE HADHRAMAUT AND THE FIRST MOVE

Mukalla had been soon after Sultan 'Umar's death, when I had interviewed Salim to ascertain what the reactions would be to Sultan Salih's accession. Salim's report had been favourable and Sultan Salih had been accorded recognition, the title of Highness and a salute of eleven guns. Great things were hoped of him. He was good and pious and was expected to remove many of the oppressions of the last reign. He had had to wait so long for the throne of his ancestors that he was already an old man of sixty; he was about six feet tall but his massive bulk prevented him taking much exercise, and he could not be sufficiently mobile to superintend the many activities of his state.

Nothing is more difficult than to sort out facts and truth from a tangled mass of oriental intrigue, and I found before long that His Highness, absent from Mukalla for many years, was almost as confused about the state of affairs as I was. He knew that the two men on whom he depended were loyal to him personally, but he was disturbed at the rumours which had reached him of the dissatisfaction they were causing in the country. That was beyond dispute: it was not only merchants' talk in Aden or its echo in the Egyptian Press. Wherever one went in the wide expanse of the Hadhramaut from coast to desert the tale was the same, oppression and injustice, and this could not be neglected even if it was difficult to get at cast-iron facts. In truth no one dared to bring forward real evidence for fear of the consequences, and though the country welcomed me as an independent investigator they knew that our policy was one of non-intervention in domestic affairs, and that if they complained all I could do was report to the Sultan, and they feared that all he would do would be to call in his ministers for an investigation.

I told the Sultan much of what I had heard.

"Mr. Ingrams," he said, "find me one honest man in Mukalla and I shall put things in his hands. I have been here months and I have not found a soul on whom I can rely, not one."

It was a gloomy outlook politically, but I took great comfort in the fact that confidence daily increased between us and that I found His Highness full of ideas for the improvement of his State. It was there that his real interest lay, not in the pettiness of Arab politics.

The variety of subjects which we discussed through a fortnight's interviews shows the wideness of his interests. In agriculture he asked for an expert to come for six months to advise on agricultural development. He wanted also a practical man to teach the planting and preparation of cigarette tobacco and the manufacture of cigarettes. He wanted an expert to advise on the construction and equipment of a hospital, and another to advise on a possible new motor road through Du'an to Shibam. He wished to purchase a beacon buoy for the harbour and a two-ton crane for the Customs. He wanted a new wireless set for Mukalla and to establish a station at Shibam. He wanted a steam-roller and had ordered a sixty-horse-power Diesel engine to supply the town with electric light. He was anxious that the mineral resources of his country should be explored and showed me an interesting collection of geological specimens which he had made himself. He was anxious to proceed with a scheme for the development of the fisheries; to obtain teachers from the Sudan and to send boys there for training. He had also a great scheme for developing Fuwa with its aerodrome, as there was little room for further building in Mukalla. It pleased me greatly when he said to me each time: "Mr. Ingrams, I want your help in so many things."

As it was Ramadhan the bulk of my work was done at night, though most mornings found me at the Palace discussing all these matters with the Sultan. In the course of a fortnight I met and talked with nearly all the leading characters of the place.

Night after night I left the guest-house to keep some pre-arranged appointment, walking through dark, narrow streets where shrouded forms of women flitted silently by, accompanied by servants carrying lamps. After ten o'clock the streets were silent with just an occasional passerby, bound, like myself, on some unusual errand. But through the often shuttered windows and the cracks of doors lights gleamed. I dare say most of the inhabitants were intent only on the usual Ramadhan exercises of reading and praying, but the secrecy of my own movements gave me the feeling that everyone else was in like case. In fact, many of them were.

Stepping cautiously amidst the litter and ordure, one would arrive before some barred door. A gentle tap was followed by a glance from an upstairs window, the shuffling of bare feet and the soft sliding back of wooden bolts. I followed a servant with a lamp through long passages, up narrow stairs to a guest room, and then sat for hours in *tête à tête* conversations with someone who was bound to pour out incredible tales of intrigue. Such care was taken by those I interviewed that our meetings should be secret, that I was always surprised at the trust apparently placed in the silent servants who perpetually entered with fresh glasses of sweet, milkless

Java tea. Indeed, sometimes the samovar from which the glasses were replenished steamed away in the room where we sat.

I cannot, of course, describe who all my informants were, but the biggest villain of all was 'Abdur Rahman bin 'Othman, then a kind of judge in political causes, employed principally in the rather vain hope that if he were paid he would be loyal to the Sultan and his country. One night when I went to see him, he was suffering from rheumatism and was in bed, on a ferrash on the floor. He had the light behind him and as I listened, hour after hour, to the vitriolic scandal which poured from his lips in an increasing flood, I was hypnotized into the feeling that there sat before me a hooded vulture, for the silhouette of his beaked nose and the folded ridge of the green shawl half-way over his bald pate reminded me of nothing so much as the bird of carrion, and so to this day he is always known as the Vulture.

In this atmosphere of intrigue I felt I could do very little. We found ourselves surrounded by spies in the house and outside the house; even 'Abdul Qadir, a stranger from Sudan, remarked on the first night of our arrival: "Is this a choky in which we have found ourselves? No one is allowed to come and see us and whenever we talk there are people listening." Of course it did not take us very long to clear out this band of amateur detectives, and I always insisted on going everywhere unaccompanied, but there was no doubt that certainly in one quarter there was uneasiness at my presence and determination to thwart my every move.

## Chapter XXIV

## OVER THE HILLS TO TARIM

*Whither have ye made a road to-day?* SAMUEL.

It did not seem possible that I could achieve much in such an atmosphere, and we set out for the interior via Shihr with a feeling of relief. This time we hoped to be in Tarim in a matter of a few days, for our old friends, the Seiyids of Al Kaf, were to send cars for us which would reach a point less than forty miles from Shihr.

The completion of the motor road was one of the main objects of my journey, and I was anxious to see exactly what remained to be done, both from a constructional and political point of view. It seemed probable that the latter aspect would be more difficult. As a general rule difficulties easily cause an Arab to tire of a long undertaking, but the persistence with which Seiyid Bubakr bin Sheikh Al Kaf had stuck to his road-making and poured out $180,000 in compensations and encouragements and on labour, not for himself but solely for others, had impressed me on our last visit as one of the surest auguries for success in developing the Hadhramaut.

He had started the road perhaps ten years earlier and at the most difficult end of all, by pushing the road up the steep cliffs of the Wadi Hadhramaut itself. Hadhramaut wadis, it will be remembered, have almost perpendicular sides: here and there the cliff in bygone ages has fallen away, and up the steep sides of a shab such as this, Seiyid Bubakr began his road. He was lucky in having a man who was equal to the task. 'Ubeid, his foreman, had worked on roads in Zanzibar and in Somaliland, and the little knowledge he had was dangerous, because he never knew where a task was impossible and thought motor-cars could go up anything—rather like flies—provided only that they had a flat surface as wide as themselves with stones on each side. Later on when 'Ubeid was building the remaining part of the road, I told him that the part behind him, completed years ago, was in bad repair. "Get some bazaar loafers and put them on it," he said, "I only look ahead, I cannot turn back."

He was perhaps sixty years old, short and stocky and somewhat hump-backed, with a grizzled bearded face and loin cloth well tucked up, and he earned the nickname of Al Ingliz (The Englishman) because of his astonishing feats in road construction and, later on, in the building of landing-grounds. Once you gave him a job, he barely waited to drink a cup of tea, but, long staff in hand, was striding in swift, jerky steps on his way. 'Ubeid, then, just went bald-headed at that wall and the road climbed nearly a thousand feet in 1.4 miles. At least half a mile of that was on the flat—an overhung ridge which he found half-way up—and it had more hairpin bends than ever I care to remember. There was just room for a car on the straight parts, but to get round corners they had to reverse. The corners were so steep that the passengers had to put stones behind the wheels each time the car halted.

Once at the top of his mountain, 'Ubeid had a hundred miles of fairly easy going before him. At that moment, Sultan Salih, then in Mukalla (it was early in his uncle's reign) wrote and asked Seiyid Bubakr to make peace between the Qu'aitis and Hamumis, the most feared tribe of the country. Seiyid Bubakr did it at his own expense—it cost him $7,000—and out of it gained friendship with the Hamumis. He proposed to take the road through their country and they promised that it should be safe "on their faces" for cars, and for Qu'aiti and Kathiri soldiers, while for the public it was to be safe even if there were war between the Qu'aitis and Hamumis.

Mukalla, however, was nervous about the road passing through the Hamumi country: perhaps they remembered their own treachery towards the Hamumis in the past, and they asked Seiyid Bubakr to take his road through the Ma'ara and Ba Hasan of Ma'adi tribes. Arranging this cost him $15,000 but he agreed, and the work started and went on favourably. Seiyid Bubakr asked that Mukalla should arrange its passage through Ma'adi: he knew the Ma'ara but not the Ba Hasan, and this was agreed. An expenditure of $30,000 took 'Ubeid and his merry men through the friendly Ma'aras to the borders of the Ba Hasan and there the latter stopped the work. Sultan Salih had gone back to India and Sultan 'Umar had come to Mukalla. Our old friend, Sultan Salim Ahmed, was Governor of Shihr. Sultan 'Umar, however, told Salim Ahmed to arrange matters and he asked Seiyid Bubakr for money to do so. Seiyid Bubakr sent him $10,000 and waited results.

All he got was a letter from Sultan Salim, on behalf of Sultan 'Umar, stating the Qu'aitis were responsible for any interference by their tribesmen with the work. At the same time Salim told him to send the workmen. So 'Ubeid went down to the Shihr end. He had barely forty miles to go to link the coast with the road from the interior. Eight days brought him over easy ground to the southern borders of the Ba Hasan where he was stopped again. He was idle for ten days and then Seiyid Bubakr paid $4,000 to Sultan Salim to bribe the beduin. Work began again in difficult country, but, after a month, the armed beduin stopped it. A further $1,000 and work went on for ten days and was stopped. The pay of the coolies over the period was $8,000.

Seiyid Bubakr's agent in Shihr advised him to give up the enterprise, for he was sure the Qu'aitis never meant to press the beduin. That this was so, I learnt from the beduin later. They were bribed not to allow the work to go on but to stop it. The Qu'aiti Governor of Shihr had found a very profitable milch cow.

Later Seiyid Bubakr went to Shihr and demanded his money back. Salim Ahmed said he was sorry, but the wazir, Seiyid Bubakr al Mihdhar, father of my friend Hamid the present wazir, was backing the beduin. He suggested that Seiyid Bubakr and he should go to Mukalla to see the Sultan. There Sultan 'Umar was told Salim's story and he ordered the wazir to see the work was carried on. The wazir promised Seiyid Bubakr he would do this, but persuaded him to ask the Sultan to order that Salim should have nothing more to do with the work. Sultan 'Umar gave the order and then left for India.

Al Mihdhar then asked Seiyid Bubakr to send the workmen and some more money, as Salim had all the other. Work started again when the wazir had had a *douceur* of $5,000. But again the beduin stopped it. Then the wazir sent fifty soldiers and while they were there work went on for two months, and Seiyid Bubakr spent another $8,000.

But Salim was sad to see this good money go by. He wrote letters to Sultan 'Umar in India of the misdeeds of the wazir. Probably they were true. Anyone could write true tales against a Mukalla wazir. Sultan 'Umar returned from India. Seiyid Bubakr al Mihdhar was dismissed and the work stopped for good.

This is the complete story of an intrigue heard in various versions from the three parties most concerned, Seiyid Bubakr, the beduin and Sultan Salim. I tell it because it contains the elements of every great undertaking in the Hadhramaut, the selfless, tireless Seiyid Bubakr, helpless absentee sultans, grasping officials and greedy, troublesome beduin.

I think of those $180,000 every time I pass up and down that road, but draw comfort from the fact that it has gone through, and like it many other undertakings with all the same elements in them.

A messenger went off up-country to Seiyid Bubakr asking for five cars to meet us beyond the Ba Hasani country on the 28th November, and we left Mukalla on the 25th. I had only been given six weeks in which to do all I had to do, and could spend no more time in the intrigues of Mukalla. To do good one would have to stay much longer, and I felt I had a better chance up-country where there was Seiyid Bubakr and where we were looked on with less suspicion. I had hopes, too, of travelling overland from the Hadhramaut through the Mahri country to Gheidha beyond Ras Fartak. The Sheikh of Fartak had given me introductions and it would have been easy. But it needed a clear fortnight and I did not see much chance of squeezing that out of my six weeks. Even though we were destined not to return permanently to Aden, the journey still remains to be done.

We left Mukalla in a car with a lorry and one of the famous hotel omnibuses, and were soon speeding along the familiar track to Gheil Ba Wazir. There we stopped in the pleasant garden bungalow for lunch, and bathed and boated in the bath which had been filled for us. The late Sultan's favourite pastime here was to have twenty or thirty of the frailer sex tobogganing down the water-chute into his arms, while he stood and bellowed like a sea-lion in the water beneath.

At sunset we were in Shihr and breakfasted and dined *au clair de la lune* on the familiar roof-top, where poor Salim had so hospitably entertained us two Ramadhans ago. He had been particularly fond of Shihr and as the palace, Dar Nasir, had not been permanently inhabited since his time, his presence still seemed to haunt it.

There were callers, but none of the old friends. I went out by night to see them and found them all timid and fearful of what would happen. Seiyid 'Abdul Qadir Ba Faqih, our historian friend, had, however, feared nothing and was the only one to stick by his former master. Yet he intrigued in nothing against the present régime, and when at last Salim was allowed to depart, minded his own business and helped, when asked, in things profitable to his country. Still, though things were not satisfactory, it was pleasant to feel the friendlier atmosphere of Shihr. The Governor was a Kasadi of the old Yafa'i dynasty, always loyal to Government and so had survived several changes of dispensation.

At Shihr the Ba Hasani chiefs who were to conduct us through their country had arrived. A colleague from the west later said that the Ahl Haidera Mansur of Dirjaj, whom we had met years earlier on our Fadhli trip, and who were considered as almost sub-human, were "positively Mayfair compared with the Ba Hasan," and certainly I had seen little more uncouth.

On Saturday morning, the 28th November, we started off with the usual procession of cars and lorries, and twenty-four miles brought us to "railhead" at Ma'adi. Some of the beduin with their camels and donkeys had already arrived. Presently an aged Ford clattered and clanked in a cloud of dust up the road we had come. It had no radiator cap, and its tank was spurting up like a geyser in full eruption, with showers of boiling water and clouds of steam. Out of it stepped 'Awadh, whom we had met at Shihr, and three other villainous-looking, half-naked beduin—the captain and his staff joining the ship. Immediately all was bustle and after the usual wordy battles, during which I almost got shot by a Ba Hasani for attempting to take his photograph, lots were cast and the cameleers chose their loads.

We were mounted on donkeys and proceeded down the narrow track on the side of a deep and precipitous wadi, the bottom of which was filled with date, coco-nut and areca palms of different shades of green.[1] At the bottom of the valley, beneath the one solitary dar of the Ba Hasanis—most of them live in caves on the valley side—we stopped and came into first contact with the commercial instincts of our savage friends. They demanded two dollars a skin for the water we had to carry with us. Prominent among the shouting beduin was a curious figure. All the men were naked to the waist, but this one person wore a shirt and jambiya tucked into the belt, t was, in fact, a woman, but she preferred to be known as Sheikh Salim. She had once visited a saint and the saint had told her that henceforth she should live and dress as a man.

---

[1] Ma'adi is the only place in the Aden Protectorate where betel nut and pepper vine are grown, and their cultivation is a considerable source of profit to the Ba Hasanis. In Zanzibar the betel and pepper vine were known as *tanbul* and the Ba Hasanis are nicknamed as Tanbuli. The leaf of the vine with a small segment of the areca nut in it, together with a smear of lime, is consumed mostly by the people of Shihr, and many of them have the redstained teeth so familiar to me in Zanzibar. The new Governor of Shihr, 'Umar bin Salih, not only had a large and bushy hennaed moustache, but carried round with him a vase into which a steady stream of red juice poured from his lips. I have never known a man who could fill a spittoon in so short a time.

The opposite side of the valley was even more steep and precipitous, and I wondered how on earth a road was to be made, but then I had not yet met Al Ingliz. Just about sunset we reached the Hadhramaut "railhead," a matter of only thirteen miles from the other. There were no cars so we settled down to camp for the night. Practically all our kit had gone up by camel to Shibam, so that we were short of food and other comforts. During the two days we stayed on this barren jōl, 3,500 feet above the sea-level, we were exposed to sun and wind by day and icy cold and dew by night. We found little to augment our rations except coco-nuts, which we had to buy from the beduin at exorbitant prices and toasted over our fire.

On the second day the beduin received news from a passer-by that some of their friends had killed a man of the Ba Habab the previous night, and so, expecting a night attack, they set to to build forts. We helped them and with the united efforts of both parties two quite respectable little round forts were built by nightfall. As it was the beduin who were in danger, we suggested it was only fair that they should pay for our labour, but needless to say the proposal did not receive a favourable response.

In the night we thought we ought to make alternative arrangements for moving on and bargained for camels and for a messenger to go to Tarim, and there was nothing for it but to agree to their exorbitant demands. Next day, however, 'Abdul Qadir and some of the boys with 'Awadh, sitting on the hill above the camp and watching the empty white road which stretched away over the narrow Backbone jōl, as it was called, saw clouds of dust moving in the distance.

"The cars, the cars!" they shouted, and 'Awadh came dashing down to claim the *bishara*, the fee for bringing good news. We packed up at once, and soon five cars with Hassan Shaibi in charge came tearing down the hill. In half an hour we were away, driving over the barren jōls. The views on either side of the Backbone Plateau were magnificent. Away to the south we could still see the Gulf of Aden, shining in the sun, while Dhubba and Dhubdhub, between which lies Shihr, and Qara, the hill of Mukalla, were easily visible. On our right hand lay a deep wadi. But, after that, the scenery became monotonous as the road dodged endlessly round flat-topped hills and wadi heads.

In two hours we came to Reidat al Ma'ara, the country of the Ma'ara tribe, a collection of small scattered villages in country intersected by shallow wadis which offered some chance of cultivation. Here we stopped for petrol and there was the usual clamour for medicine. D. gave a woman some Epsom Salts and after that everybody wanted it, till a pound or two had been distributed.

"I can't think what that place will be like in the morning," said Ahmed Hassan as we drove away.

We saw little more of the way that night for darkness fell soon after, and we drove on for interminable hours. All I could do was take sights with my illuminated compass and shout out the bearings and the mileage to D., in the back of the car, to write down. We stopped in a narrow defile beyond Heru at about eleven o'clock. Ganess turned out a good dinner and we were soon asleep in the wadi bed.

In the morning I awoke to the raucous voices of beduin arguing with Hassan Shaibi. We found that they had built a barrage across the road and were determined we should not pass on till we had paid $100, $20 for each car. We were unarmed and it was useless to do more than argue, so we paid them $10 and started off again.

Four hours in the pleasant warmth of the morning brought us to the top of the Tarim 'aqaba, and it was grand to look down on that friendly sight once more—the white palaces and minarets of the first city of the Hadhramaut shining in the morning sun. Hassan borrowed a rifle and fired several rounds to announce our arrival. The drivers tied up their brakes and we began the perilous descent. At the bottom we were met by the Sultans and the Seiyids and taken into the town in procession and out to the suburb of 'Aidid, where we found a perfect Riviera villa with cool colonnades, a sparkling bathing-pool and garden of palms and flowers awaiting us. We were at home again.

## Chapter XXV

## TRIBAL WARFARE AND SEIYID BUBAKR

*But Traynings of Men, and Arming them in severall places and under severall Commanders, and without Donatives, are things of Defence, and no Danger.*
BACON.

*The Arabs are so unforgiving and revengeful they will seek to kill a man year after year.*
FAR OFF.

OUR first days were filled with a social round and much work. On the first two days I had to make two successive journeys to Shibam. I started off there within an hour of our arrival to meet Meryem Besse, who came in her father's aeroplane, the first woman to fly to the Hadhramaut and the first Frenchwoman to see it. She brought me news that next day Royal Air Force machines would bring Beech, the sapper Captain, to survey the Sultan's new motor road. This was an unexpectedly quick response to a telegram I had sent from Mukalla, and so Beech, learning nothing at the coast, came up to Shibam. As he said on arrival, he had trod on the snake and had to go back to the starting place. He had no interpreter so 'Abdulqadir volunteered to go with him and they started off the next day after Farnhill, in charge of the machines, had marked out a new landing-ground for Tarim on about the most unpromising bit of land ever chosen for such a purpose.

These days, too, marked my initiation into the constant wearing of Arab clothes. Hitherto when on the road I had worn a turban for practical reasons. It was infinitely more comfortable than a topee and served a variety of purposes—shade by day, warmth by night, a sieve for water, a bag for goods, and, being brimless, it enabled me to take bearings without having constantly to push my hat up. This time I had worn it since leaving Mukalla, even in the towns.

As it was Ramadhan, our friends could only ask us to meals after dark. They knew we did not like to eat in splendid isolation and dinner was tiresome for them when they had had a meal at sunset. In a day or two I was asked to the sunset breakfast by Seiyid 'Abdur Rahman.

## INITIATION INTO THINGS ARABIAN

"Would you mind eating on the floor—Arab food?" he asked doubtfully. I explained that I very much preferred it and that I was used to such meals in Zanzibar days. Next day it was at Seiyid 'Umar's. I saw the brothers and others in whispered consultation, plainly about me. 'Alawi, the architect, came over and asked me to come out of the room with him. He produced a fine new sarong. "We should be very pleased if you will wear it." Having adjusted it to his satisfaction, we returned to the room to be greeted with pleased smiles and exclamations of "Wallahi! 'Arabi. You are no longer an Englishman, you are a Hadhrami." Seiyid 'Abdur Rahman said: "We have always treated you and Duri as of the family, now we feel that you really are."

I did not at first wear the garb by day, but every house I went to provided me with a new sarong, so that soon I never wore anything else. Indeed, from the point of view of comfort, I should be sorry to return to trousers again, and the fashion has spread so that every member of the Air Force garbs himself in sprightly skirts when off duty in the Hadhramaut, and a European is hardly seen in any other dress. It has won universal favour in the country and is taken as a compliment even when the wearer speaks no word of Arabic.

When Ramadhan was over I do not think that either D. or I had another European meal outside Mukalla, and we should consider that we were badly in disgrace if it were not taken for granted by the family we were staying with that we shared whatever they had.

Seiyid Bubakr, the Sultan and I soon started talks. I had let it generally be known that I had good news and that the Government was to give them help. We settled down in the villa one morning and began. There was a pleased anticipatory smile on the Sultan's face.

I described the Tribal Guards scheme in detail.

"Is that all?" he asked. The pleased smile had disappeared in the most comical way.

"Oh, no," I said, "Government will allow you to buy a wireless set and train the operators for you. Then your sons can go to school at Aden and dispensers can be trained there. The Qu'aiti will allow your road to go through. You will no longer be cut off from the world."

"But the wars in the country?"

"Your soldiers will stop them."

Sultan 'Ali laughed rather bitterly. "What will a band of troublesome retainers armed with old French rifles do?"

"When they are trained and disciplined, they will do a great deal."

"And who will pay them?"

"Well, I hope the Government will pay a bit and you'll have to pay the rest."

"What am I going to pay them with? I have no revenue. All that we get is from Seiyid Bubakr and Seiyid 'Abdur Rahman. Are they to go on paying for ever?"

I asked what they had expected and found that what they wanted tactically amounted to the taking over and putting in order of the country by the British Government. Nothing would happen, they were certain, unless force were available.

I explained that it was useless to hope for the Government to do all this. The Government's policy was not to intervene in internal affairs beyond what was necessary. If they wanted the Government's help at all, they must realize that their best way of getting it was by showing they were prepared to help themselves. Talk alone would bring them nothing.

"But every day there is murder and robbery on the roads," said the Sultan. He described a particularly bad case that had just occurred. Some Kathiri travellers from a tiny settlement ten days' journey away to the north-east among the Mahras, had come down on one of their rare visits. As they left Seiyun on their return journey a party of the 'Awamir, who had the worst reputation for murder of any tribe in the main Hadhramaut wadi, had ambushed them and killed four. The Al 'Ali Kathiris had no quarrel whatever with any of the people in the Hadhramaut, but the 'Awamir, believing they were Mahras, had thus, as they considered, settled a murder due to them by the Mahra. This case of mistaken identity was no doubt genuine, but it was little consolation to the relations of the murdered men. Sultan 'Ali demanded air action against the offenders.

I agreed it was a bad case, but explained it was a month or so old. Nobody in the Hadhramaut had ever expected the Government to intervene and we could not weigh in on an old case until the people knew that we were taking a real interest in the peace. Perhaps if a case occurred in future the Government would intervene, but each case would have to be decided on its merits, and I was sure the Government would do nothing unless the Sultans also did all that was in their power.

It was agreed that we should discuss all the proposals I had brought at further meetings in Tarim or Seiyun.

I knew that if anything was to happen it would be through Seiyid

Bubakr. More foreseeing and thoughtful than is usual with Arabs, he knew that the regeneration of the Hadhramaut was not a matter that could come to pass in days.

"With my health and my wealth (hali wa mali) I will help you," he said, "and together we will bring peace and order. But you cannot rely on Arabs; they have no patience and expect everything to happen in a day."

I was particularly anxious to try to make peace in the wadi and had decided in Aden that the question there to be settled was that of Al Ghurfa, of which I had learnt on our previous journey. A perpetual feud was kept up by Bin 'Abdat, who, as I have recounted, had possessed himself of Al Ghurfa, and Bil Fas, who lived just outside the walls. The town had long been closed and traffic had to skirt the walls. Between the two rivals lay a small plain across which rival systems of trenches had been built. In sorties by night both sides had pushed forward small forts connected with their bases by communication trenches. Even a small mosque had been captured and turned into a fort.

The townspeople had a deep, wide and long trench, which stretched out far towards the centre of the wadi with forts at intervals, and down this they had to go to their fields. The only fields which could be properly cultivated were those out of accurate rifle range. On the southern wall of the wadi below which Al Ghurfa lay, first Bin 'Abdat had built a fort surrounding Bil Fas' houses, and then Bil Fas had seized the heights above and built a fort commanding Al Ghurfa itself. The feud had continued for many years —now and then came stalemate and comparative quiescence, but some fresh murder always cropped up to fan the flames and stimulate both sides to fresh outbursts of hostility.

While I was yet in Tarim another case took place a few miles on the road to Seiyun. A silversmith, one of the unarmed classes, went up to a tribesman of the 'Awamir and asked him to settle a debt, and the tribesman murdered him then and there on the road.

There was nothing unusual about the state of affairs; later on when the peace had come people made careful estimates and said that we had saved, at the least, ten lives a month in the Hadhramaut wadi country alone. Every tribesman in the place was armed, and armed not with old-fashioned, worn-out weapons, of which, of course, there were a great number among the beduin, but with modern express rifles selling for between 600 and 1,000 riyals apiece, prices which were within easy reach of well-to-do tribesmen who had made money in the Far East. It was an old complaint. Rifles could only come in with difficulty through Mukalla, for permits from Aden were necessary, but from Sana there was no difficulty, except the dangers of the road which did little more than put the price up. Modern rifles came in dozens with each caravan from the Yemen, of German, Austrian, Italian and Belgian manufacture. I had asked Sultan Salim on my last journey to do something to suppress the traffic, but he had said it would "not please the beduin!"

In circumstances such as these it was not surprising that people did not see immediately how two hundred of the Sultan's retainers, who were always unruly and had on several occasions gone on strike, armed only with second-hand Legras rifles, were going to make much difference.

Seiyid Bubakr and I had long discussions. Seiyid Bubakr is one of the most remarkable people I have ever met. He was born in Singapore, where his grandfather had gone to found the family fortunes. In those early days the Al Kaf family were not well off: even now they are not all rich and it is only that section living in Tarim and Seiyun which has shared in the vast fortune of which Seiyid Bubakr's grandfather laid the foundations. He had left the Hadhramaut, as so many do, for the East Indies and there obtained a position as a clerk. When he had saved enough money he bought a small house and let it, and then another, and so it went on until the property of the family in Singapore is worth the best part of two million sterling, and in Java a similar amount or even more.

Seiyid Bubakr stayed in Singapore until he was about thirteen, when he came to the Hadhramaut, and there his heart has always been. He paid a further visit to Singapore, a short one, and in that time, he tells me, the Government of the Straits Settlements, wishing to make road improvements in Singapore, found that a mosque stood in their way. The Government offered the custodians to put up another mosque in an even better situation, but they were advised that according to Muhammadan law once ground had been consecrated to the use of a mosque it could never be anything else. They therefore gave it up, and this attitude on the part of the Government, who had all power and strength behind them, so impressed Seiyid Bubakr that he felt that the one Government which could be trusted to help the Hadhramaut was the British Government.

Some of his friends have told me of how, long ago, he sat on the edge of the jōl overlooking Tarim, sorrowing over the condition of his beloved valley, and said that he would use all his endeavours to bring the British Government to lend their assistance. For twenty-four years he had laboured in the cause of peace, spending and overspending his fortune, and sparing no effort; fruitlessly for the most part, alas! because the only weapon with which he had to fight was money, and you cannot buy permanent peace with money.

I have never known Seiyid Bubakr say a really unkind word about anybody, and perhaps his greatest failing in affairs is that he always has hopes that the bad people will have a change of heart, and this never alters, although he has been let down time and time again. He is a very religious man in the broadest sense, for there is nothing of a fanatic about him, and his personal religion is one that anyone might wish to share. He is no formalist, though he is strict about observing the compulsory prayers and fasts prescribed, and usually reminds others of their religious duties. He says his prayers devoutly, but does not prolong them: in fact, I heard it said several times with a chuckle: "Seiyid Bubakr gets over his prayers pretty quick, but it doesn't matter because he's 'accepted' anyway."

His wife, to whom he has been married for thirty years, is as kind and charming as he is, and although, of course, she is not seen, men say to you confidentially: "There's only one other person in the Hadhramaut like Seiyid Bubakr, and that's his wife," because her influence spreads out unseen. He is the simplest and most generous of men, and although his charity is done without a flourish it is so widespread that he is called the Hatim Tai of Hadhramaut. I think everybody who has stayed with him will agree that he is the best of hosts, and while he provides extremely comfortable and well-fitted rooms with all European comforts for his European guests, he himself sleeps on a mattress on the floor.

There is, indeed, no other man I know in the country who has more rightly earned widespread confidence, because Seiyid Bubakr thinks merely of the common good and not of his own or of that of any particular party. He spends his money as freely in promoting peace among the Qu'aiti people as among the Kathīri, and he more than any other has tried to bring an end to the long-standing mistrust between Qu'aiti and Kathīri which is now, happily, almost a thing of the past. Certainly no decoration was ever better deserved than the C.B.E. which Seiyid Bubakr received in a recent New Year's Honours List.

The only people who work against Seiyid Bubakr are those who are unmistakably out for themselves, and in a country so long used to relying on the spoken word for its news and its opinions, rumours and lies have their brief successes, though, as Seiyid Bubakr says, lies and cruelty cannot last.

There was plainly no better person with whom I could concoct plans of peace, and he suggested that we should go on to Seiyun and gather together those most likely to help us.

*Chapter XXVI*

## VISITS TO THE TRIBES AND THE FIRST PEACE CONFERENCE IN SEIYUN

> ... *the mighty,*
> *Smoked the calumet, the Peace Pipe,*
> *As a signal to the nations.*
>                                         LONGFELLOW.

BEFORE we went to Seiyun I had a remarkable caller, 'Ali bin Habreish, paramount chief of the Hamumi, who came with some of his followers to interview me privately in the villa.

The Hamumi are a large tribe of over 7,000 warriors who have long been on bad terms with the Qu'aiti. There is no doubt that the Qu'aiti Government on the coast had suffered much from them, but equally, no doubt, that the tribe had been badly and unwisely handled. Eighteen years before, the advisers of the Qu'aiti Sultan had thought that the best way of settling the Hamumi question was to invite all the chiefs to a party in Shihr and there murder them. This was done and 'Ali bin Habreish's father, whom he had succeeded, was amongst those murdered. From that day 'Ali bin Habreish had not entered Shihr, though from time to time the Qu'aiti Government had purchased a year's truce from him at the price of two thousand dollars a year. His history rather explains 'Ali. He was of medium height, unkempt and covered in indigo. Under no circumstances would he consent to wear more than his indigo-dyed loincloth and another cloth wound over his shoulder like a shawl.[1] On his head he wore the triangular bandage-like cap of the out and out bedu. Furthermore he *never* washed. He hated the towns and for the most part hated buildings, though he owned two dars at Gheil bin Yomein, and Al Khamt. The latter place had no other building than his solitary dar perched on a spur of a wadi, and I do not think there was another in all that desolate landscape within fifty miles of it. In the towns his eyes were always fearful, suspicious and shifty. Only once in our talk did I see that expression leave his face

---
[1] Later he invited me to stay with him, but insisted that I too should wear indigo and a loincloth.

and that was when he offered me mounts to his fastness and hospitality there: then I saw the look of the wild animal take its place as he described his distant home. He could, of course, have owned a palace like the one we were sitting in, for he had great wealth in camels and flocks, and I have heard his date palms numbered in many thousands. But it was always difficult even to learn where 'Ali was, for he preferred the open air and his tribe wandered over 2,000 square miles of country.

The gist of his talk was: "I do not want the Qu'aiti Government—they have wronged me, and the Qu'aitis think we are just wild beduin to be treated like animals. They are preventing us from making our living by carrying goods from the coast to the interior, for we cannot enter Shihr. I do not want the Kathiri Government for the Kathiri Sultan has not the strength to help me. I do not want the English Government for I know nothing of them beyond the fact that they are friends of the Qu'aiti, and would help him against me and have done nothing for me. I have heard of a new Government called Injerams which is wanting peace in the Hadhramaut. Will you give me protection so that I may have a port of my own in our own country that we may earn our living? If you will not I must go to some other Government."

Unhappily there was little I could do. I had no powers and there was, as usual, the obligation on me to support local rulers, good or bad. I knew it was useless to say, as I probably ought to have done, that the case should be referred to the Sultan, so what I said was this: "These are foolish words, oh 'Ali! The Hamumi are a tribe under British protection and I am a servant of the British Government. The great Government will never agree to your bringing other Governments into the country under their protection. I am not denying that the Qu'aiti Sultan may not have treated the Hamumi tribe well in the past, but equally I know that the Hamumi tribe has caused trouble to the Qu'aiti. As for Salih bin Ghalib, know that he is a good man and a pious one, and does not desire that oppression should exist in the country, and the British Government is interested in the cause of peace in the country. If God wills you will have it. As for me, all I can do is assure you that I shall use all my endeavours to see that a just solution to your complaints is arrived at, whether the decision be for you or against you."

'Ali shook his head. "I might have saved myself the trouble of coming to see you: I can never trust the Qu'aiti. I know that Salih bin Ghalib does not desire evil, but the men who are round him and the Yafa'i are not those who will give us justice. We are beduin. We do not know how to talk, but we do know justice. I shall have to go elsewhere."

"I am sorry, 'Ali," I said, "I cannot say any more, but I advise you to keep the peace and I repeat that whatever I do, whether I meet you again or no, I shall see to your affairs."

That night 'Ali and his few followers slipped away from Tarim. Neither of us knew that when we next met, in a few months' time, I should be in a better position to help him.

Seiyid Bubakr suggested that the people we ought to rope in who were not immediately present with us were Sultan 'Ali bin Salah, the Governor of Shibam, as representing the Qu'aiti, and Sheikh Salim bin Ja'fer al Kathiri, who was a friend of both Qu'aitis and Kathiris and had been concerned in the making of the Qu'aiti-Kathiri agreement. So I started off on a small tour, and I went first of all to visit the 'Awamir, the tribe who had killed the four beduin Kathiris near Mariama and murdered the silversmith a day or two before.

We drove along the same road as far as Tarba, where the 'Awamir live, and then turned off up the Wadi Tarba to where the chief, Muhsin Bukheit, lived at Seheil Muhsin. Presently we came to an impasse and I got out of the car and walked, asking some of the tribesmen who had collected to lead me to his house. Young men sped on to tell him I was coming, and I had barely walked half the distance when the old man and the other sheikhs, with a crowd of followers, came out to meet me and started off the conversation by saying they would surrender their arms if I would come and rule them. I had, however, come to talk about the murders, and Muhsin led me to his house, where he and I sat on the floor of the private chapel and discussed the matter.

"You must surrender these murderers," said I. "Be well assured that if this sort of business goes on the Government will punish you and your tribe. I am sure you cannot approve of wanton murders such as these, and the 'Awamir have the worst name for murder in all Hadhramaut."

The old man, who was so fat he could not walk upright, took this in good part, treating it as rather a joke that he and his tribe should be dubbed murderers. He informed me that he would punish them himself and that such things would not occur again, but he was somewhat stumped when I asked him why he had not yet done anything.

"Who will try them," he said, "and how?"

I made the usual political answer: "The Sultan, according to the Sharia."

I felt I had fallen a little in his estimation.

"'Ali bin Mansur is not our Sultan and we do not recognize him, neither do we recognize the Sheria. Our cases must be tried according to the '*urf*—the tribal law—but if you will try the cases, then we shall be satisfied."

We argued inconclusively for half an hour, and I left him saying that he might be quite sure that the matter would not be allowed to rest there. At the moment there was nothing else I could say.

After a day or two in Seiyun we left by car for Hureidha. On the way I was to call and see Salim bin Ja'fer and Sultan 'Ali bin Salah at Shibam.

\*  \*  \*

All the little tribal villages in the Wadi Hadhramaut contain complete sections of a tribe. In this they differ not at all from any other tribal village in the Protectorate, but these sections are wealthy and their houses well built and imposing in their height and dazzling whiteness. Each of them is a feudal stronghold. In the biggest dar dwells the sheikh and his family; in the others, his tribesmen. Each is ruled, more or less, by the sheikh and the elder brethren, and their strength naturally depends on their numbers and on their wealth. If they are wealthy, as was Salim bin Ja'fer, they have good arms and many retainers. Sometimes, like Al 'Uqda, the home of Salim bin Ja'fer, the village is surrounded by a wall.

It was a pleasant little place with plenty of trees of all kinds within and without the walls, and the great dar showed up well from the distance. Our arrival created quite a sensation, for though some of the people had met us elsewhere, we came unexpectedly.

Salim bin Ja'fer was old and slight, deliberate of speech, honest but not, I felt, a strong character; indeed, Seiyid Bubakr told me later that he was even afraid of his wife. I never knew the old man travel without his water-pipe, and after receiving us he was soon puffing at it again. While tea was brewing we discussed mutual acquaintances and when the glasses were put before us we started serious business. I explained my mission—good will between Qu'aiti and Kathiri and peace in the Hadhramaut. Salim told me all the history of the Qu'aiti-Kathiri agreement, of which he was a signatory. He told me of the many and fruitless efforts that had been made by him and by others to make peace. He was an out and out pessimist, but I left him having secured a promise that he would come to Seiyun with me on my return from Hureidha and that we should discuss matters there.

We stuck a long time in the sand outside Al 'Uqda, but at last came at evening to Seheil, outside Shibam, to the familiar little guest-house where we stayed so long on our first visit, and where, since then, Freya Stark had lain ill. There came many of the same friends to see us and we talked of old times, above all it was good to see the ever-friendly Laajams.

After dinner I went across with Hussien Laajam in the car to Shibam. We had to leave it in the square and made our way through the dark streets with a lantern, endeavouring to avoid the ordure and the unknown liquids which fell from the houses above. The filth of the streets of Shibam always astonishes me, for, owing to the compactness of the town, it is much more concentrated than elsewhere. It was another Laajam house to which we went, overlooking the city walls, comfortable and clean inside. A light supper, tinned fruits and sweets, was produced and 'Ali bin Salah and I discussed matters.

'Ali bin Salah was tall and exceedingly thin. He wore a moustache and his hair was always long. Though he had never been out of the Hadhramaut he was inclined to Western habits, and had a number of chairs and tables in his house at Al Qatn. His dress, too, was more the dress of the Arab in contact with the West than the born Hadhrami, for he wore a tarbush. I felt that the undoubted influence he had with some of the beduin was due chiefly to the reputation of his father, who had entertained the Bents, and to his mother who was a Sei'ar. As I got to know him better these impressions were strengthened: his own weak face did not belie his character. The rather overbearing voice of authority, which he put on when dealing with those who could not answer him back, barely concealed indecision and an extraordinary lack of political sagacity. He was badly handicapped too by greed, while his authority continued largely because he was the representative of the Qu'aiti Government. Still I always found him amicable even when I felt, after constant trials and fresh starts in which he promised to run straight, that I could no longer trust him. He had come back to power on the accession of the new Sultan, but was not on good terms with the two ministers in Mukalla and only had one friend there—the Vulture.

We talked first of our earlier meeting and of Freya Stark. I then produced a letter to him from the Sultan directing him to help me, and I found no difficulty in roping him in for the prospective peace conference in Seiyun. He promised to come with us on our return from Hureidha in two days' time.

* * *

## VISITS TO THE TRIBES AND THE FIRST PEACE CONFERENCE IN SEIYUN

We went on to Hureidha next morning. No escort was necessary, for it was the Ramadhan truce and during that month both Nahd and Ja'da suspend hostilities; though unfortunately the truce did not extend to friendly intercourse, otherwise there might have been some chance of its becoming permanent. It is a pity most people do not realize the virtue of personal contact. I get most of my fun out of learning other people's languages and living among them and sharing their life. If you know and understand people you rarely want to fight with them. I think the greatest compliment I was ever paid was in Mauritius, where I was described as international. To be aggressively English always seems to me the most unpleasant form of "patriotism."

At Diar al Buqri some of the Nahd came out and intercepted us, demanding we should come and have some refreshment. Their reputation for hospitality is such that they have been known to fire on cars, if the occupants did not stop for a meal, and I learnt later that they had brought a cook from Java in the sole hope of being able to entertain Europeans. The Buqri dress completely as beduin, but the entertainment they give you is on the most lavish and varied scale. I have eaten dinners there as good as I have eaten anywhere. Breakfast and tea are always my favourite meals and the Buqri won my heart by producing teas in the best schoolboy tradition. Cakes, honey, and sweetmeats, several varieties of tinned fruit, Huntley and Palmers' biscuits and Sharp's super-cream toffee.

News travels fast in the Hadhramaut and the Buqri knew I was after peace, though, like the rest, they had little hope of its achievement.

"The British are the best of the Governments," they said, "but we don't like them because they leave us to the mercies of these Sultans. We want a Government here who will enforce peace."

I assured them, very earnestly, that the Government really was interested in peace, and next day on our return the old men met us and, taking me in silence to the top of their tallest dar, showed me the country.

"There lie our enemies," they said, pointing to the western wall of the wadi. "We can shoot at them from here. All this country round was once green with date palms, but they have destroyed them by pouring kerosene on them, and we too have destroyed theirs. If you will come and govern the country and give us peace we will give you that house to live in," pointing to another tall dar a few yards away.

At Hureidha we stayed with Seiyid Bubakr bin 'Abdulla al 'Attas, with whom we had travelled as far as Hodeida on our way home on leave.

"Uncle Bubakr," as I know him now, is a kindly old man, but like most of the Al 'Attas Seiyids he has little political sense. His solutions for difficulties, if they were adopted, would undoubtedly result in even greater confusion.

We had a great dinner-party that night with all the principal Seiyids of the place, for Hureidha is a town inhabited only by Al 'Attas Seiyids and their dependents. It has a "Parliament," as Uncle Bubakr called it: all the various families were represented and its decisions were recorded. He said it was about a hundred and eighty years old.

Here, in Hureidha, the talk too was of peace, though the situation seemed more hopeless than anywhere else, for the Wadi 'Amd was more torn with feuds than any other part of the country. Seiyid Bubakr said it was ridiculous that I should stay only six weeks, and when we left next morning he handed me a letter which he had written to Sir Bernard asking that I might stay longer.

Everywhere outside Mukalla I was begged to stay in the Hadhramaut, because I think they really believed I could give them peace. Very often there was the suggestion "if you do not stay something else must happen." This was a strong undercurrent which was not immediately apparent on the surface. Personally I never anticipated such a wide anxiety for me to remain in the country. When I passed through Seiyun for the first time since my return and halted in the market place talking to people in the crowd, an old man came up and said to me: "Is it true that Ingrams is coming?"

* * *

There was great excitement in Seiyun when we returned with 'Ali bin Salah and Salim bin Ja'fer. Both brought their staffs with them, and it was an imposing procession of cars which entered the town about five o'clock in the afternoon. Everybody knew what was afoot, and my comings and goings had always created considerable interest as there was a current fear amongst the common people that unless the British did something, some other force would. Much of this fear was due to Philby's visit. They had thought he was the forerunner of a Saudian invasion. I was told that he had removed stones from the road and that no one had attempted to stop him, because, they said, Ibn Sa'ud chops off the hands of those who interfere with the road. Then, too, there was everywhere the fear that the Italians would come into the country. We were often blamed for not having stopped them from taking Abyssinia and there were some who thought they would take the Hadhramaut also.

## VISITS TO THE TRIBES AND THE FIRST PEACE CONFERENCE IN SEIYUN

Sultan 'Ali gave a grand dinner-party that night, and after it the plenipotentiaries withdrew to a private room where peace proposals were put before them. My ideas were vague enough. Everybody said that peace could not be achieved unless there was real British intervention, and I could not promise anything like that. The furthest I could go was to insist that the Government really was interested in the maintenance of peace, and that if it were made it was possible they might intervene to deal with anyone who broke it, if the circumstances of any particular case warranted intervention, and if they were sure that the people were doing their best to help themselves.

Finally the period of a truce was discussed. I should have liked ten years, for in that time I felt one could be sure that the country would be organized and at peace. The tribal representatives thought it was possible that six months would be obtained, to be renewed if they saw that the Government was going to help. This, of course, was useless, and they raised the period to a year. But I declined to come lower than three. Rapid thinking as to the difficulties to be faced politically and to the work involved in training forces and in measures of development, made me realize that no shorter period could be of any use. I had in mind, too, the inevitable delays there would be in dealing with the Government where, at this time, there was no conviction that help was possible or even entirely desirable.

At length they agreed to try for a three years' general truce.

The following night in Seiyid Bubakr's house, with tempting trays of Ramadhan delicacies before us, we discussed how the matter should be tackled. It was of particular importance that there should be machinery for dealing with past disputes. Nobody was going to sign on to a general truce for three years unless they could have some sort of assurance that the causes of their existing warfare would be examined and settled. As for future breaches of the peace, they tried their level best to inveigle me into a promise that they would be dealt with by the Government, but I could go no farther than I had gone before, except to say that offences occurring on the road would no doubt be treated as they were in the western part of the Protectorate.

As for the old offences, we decided to recommend the setting up of a Board to deal with them. Of those who were present we agreed that 'Ali bin Salah and Salim Ja'fer should be members. I was anxious that the others should not be ornamental, but had to agree to the appointment of

## PEACE BOARD NOTIFICATION

the Sultan's relative, Sultan 'Abdulla bin Muhsin who, with his brother, was nominal ruler of Tarim. 'Abdulla bin Muhsin was fat and good-natured but had little real interest in administration. Two other members were chosen on Seiyid Bubakr's recommendation, 'Awadh bin 'Azzan of the Bin 'Abdat, and 'Abd 'Alawi bin 'Ali the Bin Yemani Muqaddam of the Tamimi. They were all extremely anxious that I should be a member, but I could not do this and could only promise that I should be there in the background to help them. In the same way Seiyid Bubakr felt that he, too, should not be a member.

So we drew up the following notice to be published after the truce had been achieved, and if Sultan Salih gave his approval. This I promised to do my best to obtain when I returned to Mukalla.

### PEACE BOARD NOTIFICATION

Whereas His Britahnic Majesty's Government desire a general peace in the Hadhramaut and are interested in the mutual co-operation between Sultan Salih bin Ghalib bin 'Awadh al Qu'aiti and Sultan 'Ali bin Mansur al Kathiri in the maintenance of this general peace and whereas this co-operation has actually taken place in the presence of Sultan 'Ali bin Mansur al Kathiri and Sultan 'Ali bin Salah—representative of Sultan Salih bin Ghalib bin 'Awadh al Qu'aiti—therefore now as a preliminary step towards the establishment of this peace desired by His Britannic Majesty's Government, both the said Sultans have arranged a three years' truce between the Shenafir themselves, Al Tamim themselves and between Al Tamim and Dolat Al 'Abdulla and other tribes of Hadhramaut in accordance with their usual customs of peace commencing from Dhul Hijja 1355.

2. In order to achieve the desire of His Britannic Majesty's Government, both Sultan Salih bin Ghalib bin 'Awadh al Qu'aiti and Sultan 'Ali bin Mansur have formed a Board composed of five men whose names are given below:

1. Sultan 'Ali bin Salah.
2. Sultan 'Abdulla bin Muhsin.
3. Sheikh Salim bin Ja'fer.
4. Sheikh 'Awadh bin 'Azzan.
5. Sheikh 'Abd 'Alawi bin 'Ali at Tamimi.

in order to study the problems and solve them during the truce, either by means of compromise or arbitration and to endeavour to establish a permanent peace among the people of the Hadhramaut. So all should accept the decision of the said Board.

3. Both Sultans desire the said Board to report to them every

breach or violation done by any of the tribes and propose to inform His Britannic Majesty's Government of such violations.

Sd. SULTAN SALIH BIN GHALIB.
SULTAN 'ALI BIN MANSUR.

We all took away copies of the draft document to study, and met again the next morning at the Sultan's summer palace of 'Izz ad Din. At that meeting the first item on the agenda was the drawing up of the form of truce which was to be signed. I had agreed that this should follow the usual outlines of a Hadhrami truce document, and most of the argument that took place arose from my resistance of the proposal that my name should also be included in the document with those of the Sultans. It would in many ways have been better if I could have agreed to it, for the Arab as a rule has little use for abstractions and always prefers individuals. However I agreed in the end to the preamble starting "Whereas His Brittannic Majesty's Government desire peace in the Hadhramaut."

When the terms of this document were settled, Salim bin Ja'fer and the Sultan astonished me by raising the question of what form the announcement of the result of our meeting should take. I reflected that the Hadhramaut had little to learn from European Chancelleries in these matters. Indeed, the draft of the Peace Board Notification of the previous night, which we had slept on and agreed to that morning, was passed round to be initialled by all those present. Finally a communiqué in the following terms was drawn up:

"It is understood that at meetings held in Sultan 'Ali bin Mansur's palace at Seiyun, at which were present Sultan 'Ali bin Mansur the Kathiri Sultan, Mr. Ingrams the First Political Officer, Sultan 'Ali bin Salah representative of Sultan Salih bin Ghalib at Shibam, Seiyid Bubakr bin Sheikh Al Kaf, Sheikh Salim bin Ja'fer al Kathiri, and Sultan 'Abdulla bin Muhsin al Kathiri, it was decided to recommend to the tribes of Hadhramaut a three years' general truce, and the setting up of a Board to deal with their disputes."

When this had been corrected and discussed down to the last comma, it was taken into the general *majlis* next door where the élite of Seiyun sat drinking tea, and published by being read to them, for Seiyun as yet does not boast any newspapers. Copies were then made and sent off by special messengers to the various important tribes and tribal leaders of Hadhramaut.

## Chapter XXVII

## AN INCIDENT AND THE TRIAL OF THE BIN YEMANI TRIBE

*Look now on that adventurer who hath paid
His vows to fortune:*     WORDSWORTH.

WHEN the Sultan's letters enclosing the communiqués had been sent off there was nothing much to do except sit back and wait for reactions. These were on the whole favourable, but there was considerable doubt as to whether the Government really would do anything to help if occasion arose. This doubt was not to be wondered at, considering that hitherto contact had, as the Sultan said, usually been confined to short visits when "Salaam aleikum" and "Fiamanillah" (How do you do? Good-bye) had been about the only conversation. I remembered the conference the Sultan and the Seiyids had asked Lake and myself to attend in the 'Izz ad Din in November, 1934. After speaking with great earnestness on the desire of the Hadhramaut for peace, Sultan 'Ali and the Seiyids had apparently expected some more encouraging reply than the words of thanks they got from us for their hospitality and an assurance that they would be treated with equal hospitality in Aden should they visit it. The patience of despair with which this kindly speech was greeted, convinced me as much as anything of the earnestness of the leading people of the country and determined me, if ever I could, to help them.

One answer came back saying "If just one bomb goes off on a mountain in the Hadhramaut" people will believe that peace will be assured. A letter which I sent to the all-important Nahd tribe brought the following answer from the venerable Sheikh, Hakm Mbaruk bin Muhammad, paramount chief of the Nahd tribe:

"We have received your letter, wherein you state that the British Government is interested in the maintenance of peace in the Hadhramaut and desires to arrange for a three years' truce during which permanent peace will be established, and that the Qu'aiti and Kathiri

## AN INCIDENT AND THE TRIAL OF THE BIN YEMANI TRIBE

Governments will co-operate with each other for the maintenance of peace and the British Government will assist them.

"Please note that we like the peace and settlement but we cannot find anyone to co-operate with us in it. We do not agree with interfering with the trade routes. If settlement and peace were really arranged with certain rulings which will not be violated, we would like them and agree to them.

"Please note that the inhabitants and tribesmen of Hadhramaut are without any Government and they lack cultivation and the poor classes live in fear, and strife continues.

"The Nahd tribe, such as Al Rodhan, Maqarim, and others, claim certain murders among themselves and no one can settle the case of anyone else. Their cultivation, water channels, etc., are in a disorderly condition. Both the Qu'aiti and Kathiri Sultans are well aware of the tribal customs and rulings and the harmful acts going on amongst the Nahd.

"We proffer our thanks to the British Government and the Qu'aiti and Kathiri Sultans for bringing peace and arranging settlements in the Hadhramaut, and we will assist in the establishment of peace. Greetings."

While we had been in Shibam I had received a letter from Beech saying that his job on the Du'an–Shibam road was almost completed, that he would come back to the Hadhramaut to advise on how the road should cross the deep Ma'adi pass, and to fix the longitude and latitude of Tarim. Shibam he had already fixed. Though it would clash with the 'Id, Hassan Shaibi and the drivers kindly undertook to go down to meet him and Abdul Qadir at Ma'adi.

On the 15th December news was brought to me that his car had been fired on by the Bin Yemani section of the Al Jabir living at Risib. Risib we had passed in the night, but the Bin Yemani were the people who had held us up near Heru a few miles further on. These people had an exceedingly bad reputation for holding up caravans and cars. Six years before they had fired on a Seiyid in a car, and that very Ramadhan in which the discussions were taking place, they had looted two caravans bound for the wadi and had the goods with them at their settlement of Risib. The new incident took place at night and the highwaymen fired a first shot which was mistaken for a backfire, and then another at the lights of the car. The bullet, which was fired from a few yards ahead directly at the car, passed through the radiator and the steering column, and the driver and Hassan Shaibi, who was with him in front, were both slightly wounded. As usual the miscreants were after money. Beech and his companions spent the night with some friendly sheikhs at Husn Heru and came on to Tarim.

Within ten minutes of getting this news Seiyid Bubakr and I were on our way to Tarim. We talked little and only stopped once, at Tarba, to find a man who would take a message to the coast. My thoughts were chiefly of how the situation was to be dealt with, if the news of the hold-up were true. After all my talk I felt that my efforts would go for nothing if the Government felt unable to take cognisance of the matter.

At Tarim I was relieved to find neither Hassan nor the driver seriously damaged. The former had only a scratch on his arm, which required no more than the dab of iodine which Beech had given it, and the latter, a Somali, had a slight wound in his calf which had been bandaged. But it had been a close shave. The beduin had fired head on at the lamps, hoping, as he afterwards said, to "put its eyes out" and the driver might well have been killed.

I took statements from Beech and all the other witnesses, including a sheikh who had been near-by and had come on with the party. Beech said that when the car was hit, Hassan fell out yelling on one side and the Somali on the other. 'Abdul Qadir, undisturbed in the back, had remarked: "Well, they can't both be killed with one bullet and they can't be badly damaged or they wouldn't yell so lustily."

I drafted a long message to Aden explaining the circumstances, the history of the tribe, their relations with the Sultan, and so on, and sent it by our camel messenger who guaranteed to be in Shihr in two days—it plainly was not safe to send another car. At Shihr the message was to be sent by car to Mukalla and from there to Aden by the new wireless.

Beech and I returned to Seiyun to await developments.

All Hadhramaut was awaiting them—watching and asking would Government help? Everybody regarded the matter as the crucial test of what I had been saying, and the issue was plainly peace or the continuance of the age-old tribal warfare.

On the 22nd aeroplanes arrived. Beech and I donned trousers and went off to meet them at Shibam, where I got a letter from which I gathered that something might be done but I must go back to Aden for discussions.

On Christmas Eve we started. I had to go on crutches because I had an inflamed foot. The Sultan and the Seiyids came much of the way to see us off and we parted in a palm grove—rather a sad parting as we did not

## AN INCIDENT AND THE TRIAL OF THE BIN YEMANI TRIBE

really know what was going to happen. Amongst the last things that were said to me was that I must impress on the Government the necessity for entering into the affairs of the Hadhramaut with a firm policy. I had told them all that I knew, that the Government was genuinely interested in the maintenance of peace, but that help only came to those who helped themselves. The Kathīri Sultan promised all the assistance he could give if the Government came in, and that was mainly confined to banning the offending tribe from his towns. Seiyid Bubakr alone really believed that the Government was interested in peace, and he said to me: "The way that the Government deals with the Hadhramaut is the way that a woman flirts with a man. She wants an affair but she's afraid of the burden she may have to carry."

At Mukalla Sultan Salih came out to Fuwa to meet us. He promised his help and signed the peace notification. Up again and on to Aden. In the west they had another disturbance and we turned inland to demonstrate in aid of Ham (Hamilton, the 2nd Political Officer) who was dealing with the trouble between the Fadhlis and the Yafa'is. We dropped him a plum pudding and a round robin of Christmas greetings and flew on to Aden.

\*   \*   \*

In Aden I gained as usual all possible help and encouragement from Sir Bernard Reilly. In common with all south-western Arabia the Hadhramaut owes perhaps more than it realizes to him. I was interested to discover that the possibility of British help to the country had been in Sir Bernard's mind as far back as 1918 when the question of continuing the post of British agent at Mukalla, then held by Lee Warner, was under consideration. In 1933 he went on the first visit a Resident of Aden had made to the Hadhramaut, and if other duties prevented that first visit being, superficially at any rate, of more than the "How d'ye do—Good-bye" description, no more important visit was ever paid, for from it arose directly my own first tour and all that has since transpired. Speaking at a meeting of the Royal Central Asian Society in London on June 24th, 1936, Sir Bernard had said:

> "My own knowledge of the interior of the Hadhramaut is limited to a journey of a few days, when I visited the three towns of Shibam, Seiyun, and Tarim.... We have had treaty relations of long standing with the Qu'aiti Sultans of Mukalla, but our relationship with the Kathīri is much more recent, and is based upon a treaty that was made during the Great War. The Kathīri then made a treaty with the

## BRITISH HELP FOR THE HADHRAMAUT

Sultan of Mukalla, and agreed that the Hadhramaut should become one entity, and further that by virtue of their treaty with the Qu'aiti, the Kathiri Sultan would come into the sphere of the British Protectorate. But no direct treaty between ourselves and the Kathiri was made then, nor does a direct treaty exist even now, and until recently it was not practicable to visit the country.

"But it had come into our orbit, and we therefore felt, not only an interest, but also responsibility for people who had wished thus to come into our sphere of influence.

"The pioneer work in opening up the country we owe to the Royal Air Force, who made surveying flights, and have now a landing-ground at Shibam. But still we remained very ignorant of this territory, and it was desirable that something should be done to fill the gap in our information.

"That gap was filled when Mr. Ingrams came to Aden, and he, with Mrs. Ingrams, was able to explore the Hadhramaut in detail.

"In his lecture Mr. Ingrams has not explained the value to the British authorities in Aden of the report he brought back. We feel now that we have details and a knowledge of the conditions of the country, on which to form our policy in dealing with that outlying region."

I feel there has been more than a mere coincidence in the combination of forces that have led to the possibility of a brighter future for this country, which all its inhabitants love so much and under whose spell all visitors fall. While Seiyid Bubakr was seeing in the attitude of the Straits Government over the mosque in Singapore the omens of sympathetic help to his country, and while I was learning of and yearning after the Hadhramaut from the talk and encouragement of Bin Sumeit in Zanzibar, Sir Bernard had the constant feeling that something could and should be done to help when the time arrived.

The day of help drew nearer when the Colonial Office took over the Protectorate. Such is the spirit which animates the Colonial Office and Colonial Service that I believe it to be impossible for any territory coming under their control to fail to benefit in some way, unless the very strongest political pressure is exerted continually to maintain some other end, and even then the interests of the people are steadfastly fought for. In twenty years' experience of the service, with two periods of work in the Colonial Office, I have not found a file in which the first consideration was not the welfare of the people of the territory concerned, even in priority to the interests of the home country itself or the empire at large. And yet there is rarely any actual clash between these interests, for the interests of the

## AN INCIDENT AND THE TRIAL OF THE BIN YEMANI TRIBE

empire at large are in the end surely best served by the prosperity and welfare of each constituent part.

"That which is written on our foreheads we must indeed fulfil," and Seiyid Bubakr holds that it was "maktub"—written—and destined that all this should be. I would not presume to think him wrong.

There were long conferences at Aden, at which it was decided, if necessity arose, to use air action to compel the submission of the offending tribe. Before any country can become prosperous it is necessary that security to life and property be obtained, and nothing is more important than the security of the roads. This is nowhere more accepted than in the religion of the Arabs, for the roads are held to be Haq Allah—belonging to God for the use of all.

Before ever air action is brought into use every possible means of settling the affair without it are explored. The affair is examined in all its lights, and the decision to use air action is always contingent on the exhaustion of all political means first. Used sparingly as it is, it is far the most effective and humane weapon possible: it leaves none of the rancour which may be caused by an expedition as it is so completely impersonal and the casualties are very few: more often than not there are no casualties at all, and the commander who gets through his operations with fewest casualties is the one who receives the most praise from his superiors. Of less importance is the matter of cost, but air operations cost far less than ground operations.

There is one other important point: the use of air action has always the strongest support of public opinion. The complaint of the Arabs in the Hadhramaut has not been that air action is used, but that it is too little used. There has been the fullest possible co-operation between tribes and the Royal Air Force. A further, and probably to many people a most extraordinary, feature of operations is the total lack of rancour on the part of those who suffer punishment, and the curious fact that in several cases those whose lands have been bombed have afterwards expressed their thanks for the action. To an Arab nothing is more important than the "saving of his face"; if one of his relations is murdered, he will regard it as a blackening of his face, which can only be whitened by the killing of one of the assailant's relations. But he suffers no blackening of his face when aeroplanes knock down his house, because no one can expect him to have an answer to such action. Indeed, he receives a certain amount of enhanced reputation from it. People think he is a stout fellow to have

## REGARDING THE PEACE NOTIFICATION

ndured it. They do not sympathize with him, but they tell him he was brave. Now they are beginning to tell him he is a fool to stand out and get bombed when he knows he has got to pay up in the end for his misdeeds. So it happens that there is a recognition that the game is not worth the candle, and once the beduin knows that and knows that he is being protected and that he is no longer regarded as a pariah, I have found no keener supporter of peace.

Still I know of no political officer worth his salt who will not use every possible means of avoiding having his people's villages bombed, even if they are empty.

Not only did I have the promise of his support, but Sir Bernard also sanctioned the issue of the following notification, which I drafted to go with the Peace Board Notification of the Sultans:

1. The Resident commends the Notification approved by the Qu'aiti and Kathīri Sultans regarding the general peace and co-operation which they are establishing in the Hadhramaut, to the attention of all the people of the country.

2. The British Government is sincerely desirous of seeing peace and prosperity established in the country and that the peoples of the Hadhramaut should flourish under the rule of H.H. the Qu'aiti Sultan and the Kathīri Sultan working in co-operation, with the approval of the British Government, the Protecting Power.

3. The Resident greatly regrets the recent incident of interference with the roads by the Al Bin Yemani of the Al Jabir tribe and advises all wrongdoers to take heed of their case and the action that is being taken against them, for those who interfere with the roads will be punished by the British Government supporting the Qu'aiti and Kathīri Sultans.

When I returned to Mukalla I had another job to do. An Egyptian paper had started a *canard* that the Hamumi had ceded the small port of Asadi al Fay to the Italians. This was repeated in the English Press, though Aden, Government and bazaar, knew nothing of it, nor indeed did they know where Asadi al Fay was. I did not either, but D. discovered a note about it in the old papers of our first journey. It turned out to be on the coast not far from Reidat al 'Abdul Wadud and Quseir. At Reida there was a Royal Air Force landing-ground and there, and at Quseir, Qu'aiti posts. It is true that Hamumi inhabited Asadi al Fay, but it would have been about as possible for them to cede it to the Italians as for the inhabitants

## AN INCIDENT AND THE TRIAL OF THE BIN YEMANI TRIBE

of, say, Peacehaven, to offer their beach to the French or Germans. However, I flew off to Reida and having ascertained that Asadi al Fay still stood where it had always stood, went up to the Hadhramaut.

D., who had reached Aden in five hours from Seiyun, had certainly trodden on a pretty long snake and it took her many shakes of the dice box to get back. Leaving Aden by ship on the 31st December, she travelled from Mukalla on the old Du'an road with some Seiyids of the Mihdhar family, and it was not until the 28th January that she re-entered Seiyid Bubakr's house, looking, as Ham said, as if she had just come in from a walk round the park.

I arrived in Seiyun on January 2nd complete with a wireless set, and Ham arrived a little later to form the Kathiri Tribal Guards for which we had all been endeavouring to raise recruits.

In consultation with the Sultan, summonses to the offending Bin Yemani were drafted out in the approved form. They were charged generally that they had been guilty of continual acts of highway robbery, and specifically:

1. That on the night of Tuesday, the 16th Ramadhan corresponding with the 30th/31st November, 1936, a man of the section, to wit, Salih bin Sa'id bin Ismail bin Jahim bin Yemani, built barricades across the road near Al Khurob and prevented from passing cars belonging to the Seiyids of Al Kaf in which Mr. Ingrams, the First Political Officer and his party were travelling, and demanded money by menaces.

2. That on the night of Tuesday, the 30th Ramadhan corresponding with the 14th/15th December, 1936, near Risib, a man of the section, to wit, Sa'id al Ma'arri or another, fired on a car belonging to the Seiyids of Al Kaf in which Captain Beech, a British Officer, and his party were travelling and damaged the car and wounded two men.

Further that a man of the section, to wit, Sa'id al Ma'arri or another demanded money by menaces from the party.

These summonses were sent out on the 6th January and they were ordered to appear before their Sultan and myself at the palace of Seiyun on the 15th January to answer them. When news was received that the offenders were coming, steps were taken to prepare for their trial. The large audience hall of the palace was arranged for the day like a Court of Justice, with a table for the Sultan and myself at the top end. On the right sat the 'aqils of the Bin Yemani together with their principal tribesmen, some twenty men in all. On the left stood the witnesses who recited their

## COURT PROCEDURE

account of events. The procedure of the court was explained and the Bin Yemani were told that the witnesses would all be brought in one by one, the remainder being out of earshot, and that they would be allowed to question them on their evidence. The court was simply packed with the public, including tribesmen and chiefs who had come from considerable distances.

The evidence, of course, was conclusive and the Bin Yemani, in fact, admitted their fault. The sentence was carefully assessed, having regard to their ability to pay, the necessity of making sure that it would be sufficient to discourage them from further similar crimes, and that yet it would not be so severe as to cause them any real hardship by depriving them of means of living. So they were ordered to hand over ten sound she camels, thirty serviceable rifles, a hundred goats, and twice the amount of money and goods taken from the parties mentioned in the charges, namely, thirty Maria Theresa dollars. They were also to provide six hostages, two from each of their sections, which were to be kept by the Kathīri Sultan at Seiyun as long as Government considered necessary, but could be changed at the desire of the culprits provided satisfactory hostages were given in exchange.

The hostage system we copied from the Arabs in this case. The Imam of the Yemen keeps order in his country principally because he has hostages from tribes of whose loyalty he is doubtful. The beduin in the Protectorate realize, I think, that under British influence their hostages would not be used for their theoretical purpose, but they can never be quite sure, so the system acts satisfactorily enough and the hostages are kept in comparative luxury.

The proceedings of the trial were generally considered most impressive. A common comment afterwards was: "If this is the English *kanun*, it is also the Muhammadan sheria, and it would be well if all cases in future were tried in the same way." The Bin Yemani were told that they had until January 28th to pay the fine, failing which their villages and fields would be liable to air action until they did pay.

After the formal proceedings of the court I went and had coffee with the Bin Yemani in the more friendly atmosphere of the Sultan's bungalow where they were being entertained. I urged them to make payment, and so did Seiyid Bubakr and the Sultan, explaining that once they had submitted to the terms, and thereby made amends for their crime, we should hope to be friends in future, though the Government would no longer tolerate interference with the traffic of the roads.

## AN INCIDENT AND THE TRIAL OF THE BIN YEMANI TRIBE

When they left Seiyun we thought they would probably pay, though we did not relax our efforts at persuasion and sent them constant letters, Seiyids from among their mansabs, and fellow Jabri tribesmen, to impress the necessity on them. The real difficulty was again that of rubbing into people that when the British Government said a thing it meant it, and that its decisions were not the empty threats to which they had been accustomed.

## Chapter XXVIII

## ROYAL AIR FORCE ACTION AND THE SUBMISSION OF THE BIN YEMANI

*Give peace in our time, O Lord.*

*They, indeed, help their friends not only in defensive but also in offensive wars; but they never do that unless they had been consulted before the breach was made and, being satisfied with the grounds on which they went, they had found that all demands of separation were rejected, so that a war was unavoidable.*

SIR THOMAS MORE.

THE business of keeping the country informed of events took up a good deal of time. Rumours of the most extravagant descriptions flew round and, as a result of the general relief that the Government was intervening, the most extravagant stories of how the Bin Yemani would be dealt with were circulated and used to threaten habitual offenders on the road, like the Awamir. The effect of these was bound to be on the whole worse than the efforts of the few mischief makers like Bin 'Abdat's nephew, 'Ubeid Salih, who had seen the Bin Yemani and told them not to pay up as the Government was only bluffing. The 'Awamir, too, had told them the same; the wish was no doubt father to the thought, for their consciences were uneasy and they were not quite sure if anything was going to happen to them.

The dissemination of "straight news" and exposés of Government's real intentions went hand in hand with general peace propaganda and arrangements for the first peace meeting, to which part of the Kathiri tribe were invited to come and sign on the three years' truce document.

The first meeting was to be held at Hautat al Ahmed bin Zein on 24th January. This was decided at a meeting of the Peace Board held at the Seiyun Palace on the 18th. We made the choice because the place was central for the sections invited and was neutral ground. The village—a small town on Hadhrami standards—belonged to the Habshi Seiyids and was the scene of an annual fair at which, if you reached it without being shot at, you were safe, for the place was a sanctuary. It lay on the south side of the wadi

285

on the road from Seiyun to Shibam, just a few miles short of the latter. The mansab, Seiyid 'Umar, inspired universal respect in the country. I remember at one party when he got up and left, an Arab sitting next to me pointed at him with his pipe and said in English the one word "Gentleman." So he was in all the meanings of the word. Grave and courteous to a degree, honourable in all respects, Seiyid 'Umar had a fine figure and presence and was always extremely well dressed. He was about sixty years of age with a neatly trimmed beard and moustache like that of a French nobleman, bushy eyebrows and ascetic features, and twenty years before had been esteemed as one of the finest horsemen in Hadhramaut. His clothes were always an ensemble of some quiet colour—blue or a delicate shade of beige. His coat buttoned up to the neck like a forage tunic, and he wore a long coat of the same colour. Round his neck was a fine long chain of amber beads, and on his head a white turban. I delighted to watch him seated on a coloured silk ferrash with a background of carved panelling like some figure in a Persian miniature, his long fine fingers turning over the leaves of one of the many manuscripts in his library. Though he steered clear of politics, he exerted influence simply by precept and his religion and I suspect his faith was very real. He talked to me once of our common humanity, and his courtesy and friendliness to me were always very sincere but in no way familiar. I appreciated it greatly when, at a later date, Seiyid 'Umar travelled to see me, for he did not often leave his home, simply to thank me for what I had done. Having done so, quite quietly taking my right hand in both his, he made his good-bye and stepping into his car returned home. Truly a great gentleman.

His house was my headquarters for this first peace meeting. Seiyid Bubakr had thought it best not to come, so 'Ali bin Salah and I conducted the proceedings. The Bin Yemani case was the chief topic of conversation and I was able to explain much by question and answer. There was some uncertainty about the truce. There were the usual doubts as to whether the Government was bluffing or not, but the principal difficulty was that this was the *first* gathering. If those present signed on, would others? Would those who signed be safe from those who might not? Most of those present had Bin 'Abdat and Bil Fas in mind. 'Ubeid had been mischief making and nobody felt it would be much good for the "small fry" to join in if the "big noises" were going to stay out. However, by evening most of the sections there signed on, though there were a number of abstentions.

I was rather cast down by this, for a partial truce would be no good; no one would feel safe. Still I persisted in preaching and writing about peace, while at the same time I sent constant messengers, Seiyids and tribesmen, to the Bin Yemani, whose time was running out and who showed now no sign of paying. The two people who helped me most were Siyid Muhammad Midheij of Reidat al Ma'ara who knew the Bin Yemani well, and Salih 'Umar, chief of the Bin Dhobani section of the Al Jabir. Something, too, had to be done about 'Ubeid Salih and his mysterious uncle, Umar 'Ubeid Bin 'Abdat, known as the "Jinn of Al Ghurfa." Here I had great assistance from Nasir 'Abdulla al Kathiri.

Nasir had been one of my "Shihiri" friends in Zanzibar. Some time after I left Zanzibar there was trouble among the Shihiri in which Nasir Abdulla was considered the principal ringleader. The ringleaders were deported for varying periods of which Nasir's was the longest—twenty years. He came back to the Hadhramaut leaving four wives behind him and a large business gone to ruin. His dhows lay idle, for there was no one to carry on for him in his trade, which was the supply of meat to Zanzibar. Nasir's share of this fell to his competitors and instead of being well-off he was now poor. On our first journey I could not find him for he returned from a journey to the Far East just as I was leaving. It was a great joy to us both to meet again. I remembered him as a man with an enormous belly. He seemed to me positively slim when I met him again outside Shibam. Now that my eyes have grown used to his contours again, I still find that he has an enormous belly, so what it can really have been like in Zanzibar I do not care to think. But though it was ten years ago, the old fire still shone from his eyes and he was as full of quick repartee and dirty stories as ever.

People in Hadhramaut say that Nasir's heart is good but that his tongue leads him into trouble, and this is true, for though he would be willing enough to get his own back on anybody, I do not think he would use underhand methods. When we had picked up the threads of past friendship and got back on to the old familiar footing, Nasir's tongue loosened and finding me now dressed and living in the same style as himself, he talked perhaps more freely than he would have done before. I was surprised to find he had no grudge against the Zanzibar Government, or against the Sultan. He said he had been foolish, but that his troubles were mostly due to *fitina* (intrigue) on the part of his rivals. He did, however, feel rather hurt that he had been put out of Zanzibar by what he described as "a lot of

## ROYAL AIR FORCE ACTION AND THE SUBMISSION OF THE BIN YEMANI

knock-kneed policemen," and invited me to join in a little expedition he proposed. He wanted us to go to Bin 'Abdat, who was a great friend of his, borrow twenty-five husky slaves with big sticks, borrow a dhow, and go down to Zanzibar where we were to beat up the police and be off to the Hadhramaut before they woke up. I rather discouraged this plan, but when Nasir discovered that I had determined on peace in the Hadhramaut, he found work of a quite congenial nature. Although he was over sixty he constituted himself a firm ally and stumped up and down the wadi preaching peace and saying that what I said had to go. His language was so forceful and picturesque that he made himself really useful.

"We Hadhrami," he said, "have always a devil sitting on our shoulders. When we go abroad the devil gets off and sits on the quay at Mukalla. If we're away five years or twenty years he waits just the same, and as we land again mounts our backs and comes up country with us. Now we've got to leave the devils for good and all and behave ourselves in our own country as we do abroad. Anybody who makes trouble," and here the old man would pull out his dagger and feel the blade, "Ingrams will have his ... off. So, if you want to say good-bye to them—ayah!"

Nasir could neither read nor write and besides Arabic only knew Swahili, except, as he said, bad language and that he knew in every tongue. Non-Arabic speaking visitors were sometimes startled to hear him burst out with "Goddammit—Bloddifool—Schweinhund—Mascagliono."

Nasir came up against it badly when he found that his friends at Al Ghurfa were intriguing against the peace. I never saw a man so affected by the pull between two loyalties, for he quarrelled with Bin 'Abdat until the latter agreed to sign the truce. He seemed to age perceptibly, and I remember him stumping into Seiyun one evening at sunset, dirty and utterly weary, to tell me of some point that needed to be dealt with, and declining to drink even a cup of tea before he stumped off again in the dusk to tackle Bin Abdat again.[1]

\* \* \*

As the Bin Yemani had not submitted to the terms by 28th January, notices were issued to them, by hand with Seiyids to explain them, and by

---

[1] I am glad to say the Zanzibar Government have now forgiven Nasir for his sins in Zanzibar and let him go back on account of his good work in Hadhramaut. I confess I did not report the suggested expedition there, but I feel sure their decision was as wise as it was generous. It was a gesture that was highly appreciated in the country, for it was just the kind which appeals to Arab sentiment.

## SCENE OF PUNITIVE AIR FORCE ACTION

ir, telling them that their places would be bombed on 1st February. The notices warned them either to submit before that date or to leave the villages until they were told they could return. They were also told that the waterholes at Heru would be safe as it was not desired to cut off the water from them.

Bombing began on 1st February, and propaganda was continued in all directions. Salih 'Umar was there when the bombing began, persuading them to pay up. Seiyid Muhammad and the broker of the Bin Yemani at Seiyun had arrived on their last visit to Risib on Thursday, 28th, and Salih arrived at midday on the Friday. He left on Tuesday the 2nd and on arrival at Seiyun recounted to the Sultan, Seiyid Bubakr, myself and others what had happened. The people simply would not believe that anything would happen and scoffed at Salih.

"They won't do anything," they had said, "the aeroplanes have been here every day and what have they dropped? Papers, which you and Seiyid Muhammad have read to us."

As a gesture of bravado, they had decided to celebrate twelve weddings simultaneously.

"I was with them," said Salih, "and in the afternoon we were sitting in a small valley where the people were dancing and beating drums and firing rifles and so on and enjoying themselves. There may have been a few people left in the houses but most of the population was at the dance."

Suddenly someone had cried: "The aeroplanes are coming!"

Five machines flew over the place three times.

"Run away," cried Salih, "they are going to drop bombs. They won't drop them on people so clear out all together."

"Nonsense," the chiefs had answered, "lies, they won't drop bombs."

Then a bomb dropped and there was smoke.

"Look," said Salih, "look at that! What did I say?"

"It's nothing, it's only paper."

There was another smoke bomb and then a real bomb was dropped. It was a small one and it fell in the cultivation without making a big explosion.

"Run away," shouted Salih.

"This is only a threat," replied the chiefs, still unwilling to be convinced.

"Well, I'm going."

"No, if we die we die together."

Another bomb dropped and the women ran to their houses but the men remained in the valley.

Then more bombs dropped; big ones with loud explosions. The men ran away and scattered and there was yet more bombing, all in the fields at a distance from the houses.

"At sunset," said Salih to me, "when the areoplanes had gone, we all returned to the houses. I went to the house of the Sheikh of Beit al Haji and then we went to the Bin Yemani and had a meeting of the section in the home of 'Umar Tuheish, the chief. There we heard of five casualties which had taken place from flying splinters among those who were running to their homes."

I can hardly describe what my sensations were when I heard of these casualties. I could not remember that these people were all at the bottom of, and mixed up in, road outrages and thought nothing of even killing unarmed travellers for loot. I tried to say what I felt, but the Jabri chief and other tribesmen simply could not understand that I worried about it.

"The devil take them!" they said. "What does it matter?"

Salih resumed his story. "I spoke to the meeting," he said, "and I said 'Pay the fine.' The sheikh supported me. Bin Hotali said he would pay five camels and the other five were to come from Bin Akshat and Bin Hizer, two and a half each. I went to Bin Akshat and he at once agreed to pay for two and a half. Then I went to Bin Hizer and he also agreed but said: 'I cannot produce them at once for I have nothing with me.' These proportions were to apply to everything except the hostages who were to be two from each section. I tried to collect the fine, even from unsound camels to be changed afterwards, but I was unable to do so. An hour before dawn on Tuesday, 2nd February, I left with my two sons and my brother."

The meeting broke up, but I remained sitting there with my head in my hand. When the others had gone Sultan 'Ali came over to me and putting his hand on my shoulder said: "There is nothing for you to worry about. Perhaps you think differently of these things to us. What do a few lives matter if we're all going to have peace? And, anyway, it is nothing to do with you—it is from God." And that was the most consolation I ever got out of it.

I had written a letter to Bin 'Abdat. With his brother in Singapore he had started a favourite line that he was the third independent chief of

## BIN 'ABDAT ACCEPTS THE TRUCE

hramaut. His lawyers in Singapore, not knowing Hadhramaut
ics, had written letters stating their client claimed he was an "indepen-
Rajah." I wrote to Bin 'Abdat that he was "recognized as the head of
Bin 'Abdat of Al 'Amr of the Kathīri tribe, part of the Shenafir Con-
ration, of which the Kathīri Sultan of the Al 'Abdulla is recognized as
an, and that you have no independent status. We take this opportunity
dvising you in your own best interests and with a view to preserving
r *heshima* not to persist in attempting to get your independence recog-
d, for the British Government will never recognize it.

"We entertain personally the most friendly feelings for you and are
ious to see you taking a lead in peace matters in the Hadhramaut. For
reason we hope very much that you will at once engage in the three
rs' truce now being negotiated in order that you may win the respect
thanks of the British Government and of all the people of the
lhramaut.

"We beg you will not be misled by lies and false hopes: someone
new that Bin 'Abdat would know to whom I was referring) has misled
Al Bin Yemani of Al Jabir into believing that the British Government
uld not act and bomb their places; but to-day they are seeing that the
tish Government means what it says, for their places are being bombed,
. we hope that you will listen to our friendly advice before it is
late."

That evening I got a message from Bin 'Abdat imploring me to go and
him for five minutes. I was there with him within the hour. No
nder he was called a Jinn, for he was a most peculiar little old man to
k at, with one large protruding eye, one half closed, a turned-up nose
l cleft palate. Now, however, he agreed to accept the truce and help
to persuade others to do so. He had doubts about it being kept and
pressed on me that I alone could see that it was. "We Arabs don't
st each other."[1]

Bil Fas had already undertaken to sign if Bin 'Abdat did. My discussions
h him had taken place in Seiyid Bubakr's drawing-room and the manner
his agreement is worth recounting. As we were talking a broker came

---

[1] Bin 'Abdat kept his word until his death, and I had no more loyal supporter.
was a pleasure to go over to Al Ghurfa for lunch or tea. The windows were
ays open, for Bil Fas' forts were no longer manned, and a real peace seemed to
e entered the heart of the old man, his last days being spent in a kindliness and
piness he did not know before.

## ROYAL AIR FORCE ACTION AND THE SUBMISSION OF THE BIN YEMANI

in with some old dollars, for he knew I collected them. I turned them over as we talked and saw on one the inscription: "DA PACEM DOMINE IN DIEBUS NOSTRIS." I read it out and explained it and spoke of mankind's constant prayer for peace. It was an omen and taken as such, for straight away Bil Fas promised his consent and his help.

The day after I had seen Bin 'Abdat I went to meet Walmsley, who was in command of the Royal Air Force detachment operating from Fuwa, at Shibam, and we decided to give the scattered Bin Yemani a chance of reassembling and thinking things over. So letters and Seiyids were again sent to them telling them they had forty-eight hours for this purpose. They were advised to collect the fine at Heru and when they had done so to wave a large white sheet we sent them to show reconnoitring aircraft that they were coming.

On Sunday, 6th February, the Sultan and the Seiyids and myself went across the wadi to Buheira for the second peace meeting. Bin 'Abdat and his nephew, 'Ubeid, Bil Fas and everyone of importance from the Kathīris was there, as well as the Tamimi Muqaddam, a member of the Board, and his head men. By this time most of the defaulters from the previous meeting had joined in and to-day there were no dissentients. A number of houses had been cleared for committee meetings, meals and so on, and in the evening all the clans assembled before our headquarters where the truce and all the adherents were read out. It was a long and imposing list and as it got longer enthusiasm waxed stronger. I have never before witnessed, as it were, the birth of a new hope taking place before one's eyes. I sat next to 'Ubeid while this reading was going on. He was still suspicious I thought, for I picked up his automatic and found it was loaded. Later I learnt he never parted from it.

I made a speech promising all the help I personally could give, and thanking them all. I believe that at the moment they were genuinely thankful. They still are, but I know that the thanks and plaudits fade, not only among Arabs but others. Still there is no reason for ceasing to hope and pray that the peace established that day was really the beginning of a new era.

As we were getting into our cars Seiyid Muhammad and Salih came dashing up in a cloud of dust and a motor-car: "The Bin Yemani have collected their fine and are moving to Seiyun!"

Thank God the bombing had finished. That it had been necessary no one could fairly doubt and it had shown that there was power behind.

## MANY JOIN IN THE TRUCE

t was indeed a day of new hope and named by all "Peace Day."

\* \* \*

After the Buheira meeting news of the truce was circulated throughout country, and headmen of all sections and clans were pouring into un asking for truces, and there were deputations thanking the Sultan the Seiyids and myself for what had been done. Even the beduin 1e 'Awamir from the northern steppes between the Hadhramaut and the )'al Khali came asking to be included in the truce. The Tamimi wrote to as follows:

"On Saturday we attended the meeting held at Buheira and saw the Al Kathīr sections there who have signed the three years' truce. We have ascertained that this excellent action has been done, and will be continued, by your efforts which are in the interest of the general peace, for which acts you are much thanked. We personally thank the British Government and your honour as well as Seiyid Bubakr al Kaf.

"We further inform you that the Tamimi tribe and all Beni Dhanna agree to these arrangements which we heartily like, and all the people of Hadhramaut as well are very anxious for this peace.

"There are at present some cases to which we would like you to pay due consideration and full attention and dispense justice and equity. These are the cases of Al Qaseir, a clan of Al Tamim, and the beduin of Beit Hamuda, and some of Al Sheiban who fought against each other last month on two occasions. We can see that when they meet each other they will fight, whether it be on a main road or elsewhere, because each one of them wishes to take retaliative action against his enemy on account of former blood feuds existing between them. We can see that the cessation of fighting among themselves is impossible, hence all of them should sign the truce document.

"The Sei'ar tribe (the beduin), who have been banned from the localities of Ar Rasma, as well as Al Sheiban and Shemlan of Al Tamim, have been at feud since ancient times (with murders, looting of property and burning palm trees). The inclusion of such a tribe in the peace arrangements will be very difficult as the men are robbers and looters who raid the localities of Al Tamim and when no attention is paid to them, they at once loot and kill anyone they find.

"The Al Hamum, who also have declined to have a truce with our men, will, when we see them within our boundaries, not be left in safety because they would not come to our country unless for the purpose of killing, looting and intercepting the people.

"If the truce is signed by all the tribesmen in the Hadhramaut it will result in a general peace and in the safety of souls, roads and property, but the tribe which disobeys and does not sign the truce document should be considered against the people, and whoever has a claim against them must take retaliative action wherever they may be.

"It is necessary that a notification to this effect duly signed by all tribesmen be published and distributed, stating that 'whosoever commits any offence contrary to the peace arrangements, or interferes with the roads, or transgresses against anyone, will himself be held responsible and no doubt he will be punished by the aeroplanes, etc.'

"These are our observations which we submit to you, and we are leaving for our country this morning and hope to see you shortly. In conclusion we convey our high regards. Greetings."

The Hamumi and the Sei'ars were certainly the biggest fences left, for all Hadhramaut was interested in them. There was hardly a tribe from the coast to the desert that had not some score against the Sei'ar. As we met each section and explained who had joined they all ended up by asking: "And the Sei'ar?"

Then came the Bin Yemani surrender ceremony attended by Sultan 'Ali bin Salah and chiefs and notables from all over the country. It will probably give the best idea of the crowds if I say that "every hotel in the place was full." People came on foot, by camel and by donkey and never had there been seen so many motor-cars in Seiyun. The ceremony was preceded by an enormous luncheon-party given by Sultan 'Ali in the palace, at which the chiefs and the Royal Air Force were the guests of honour. Nothing was too good for the Royal Air Force, and I am told that many a damsel of the damsels of Seiyun cast longing eyes upon them from the safe shelter of their voluminous robes and thick veils. Space on roof-tops was sold to witness the ceremony and the demonstration which the Royal Air Force had promised afterwards before they left for Aden.

The ceremony, carefully planned, was short and simple. The Sultan and I sat before a table in the doorway of the palace; the notables and the R.A.F. sat on our right and left, and before us in successive rows were the 'Aqils, the hostages, the camels, the rifles and the goats.

The charges against the Bin Yemani were read out. The 'Aqils of the tribe were summoned by name and answered in person. The fine was examined and approved. The hostages were produced and the ceremony ended with a proclamation:

WHEREAS the full penalty has now been paid by the 'Aqils and people of Bin Yemani of Al Jabir and whereas the hostages demanded have been surrendeted.

Now therefore the ban on their entry to the ports of Shihr, Mukalla and all ports of the Qu'aiti Sultan and the towns of Shibam, Seiyun and Tarim and all markets and towns of the Qu'aiti and Kathīri Sultans is removed and their submission is accepted.

Let them and all men take heed that neither the Tarim-Shihr motor road nor any other trade route whatever may be interfered with on pain of similar penalties which will be inflicted by the Great British Government and by the Qu'aiti and Kathīri Sultans.

The roads are Haqq Allah for the use of all and the Great British Government under whose protection you are and which supports your Sultans—the Qu'aiti and Kathīri Sultans—will not countenance interference upon them.

Bombing is a very terrible thing, for the bombs destroy houses and crops and drive the people from their homes. The Great Government wishes to be friends with the people. It does not want to bomb them but it wants all people in the Hadhramaut and in the whole of the Protectorate to be safe to live in peace so that they may pursue their work and achieve prosperity, but the cutters of the road will always be punished by the Great Government and by the Qu'aiti and Kathīri Sultans.

But there were also three unrehearsed items. The Sultan stood up fumbling in his pockets produced a long scroll and a pair of spectacles. 1en he had adjusted the latter he began:

"Oh, respectable guests, I stand now in this delightful ceremony in order to welcome all the visitors present. I take this opportunity to express my great rejoicing at the sincere affection existing between you and myself.

"The political assistance rendered by the British Government to my native land, the land of my respected forefathers who reigned in it hundreds of years ago, is of great help and proof of the unique friendship and firm affection existing between the officials of the British Government and myself.

"I, therefore, express my great pleasure and warm thankfulness for the efforts and assistance rendered by those honourable men in the maintenance of peace and suppression of troubles in this province.

"There is no doubt that the confidence exchanged between Aden and Hadhramaut will result in great interest to both parties. I entertain a great hope that this great friendly contact will help me to discharge my peaceful obligations towards my country and nation, which has continued, since a long time ago, in tribal disturbances but which have recently been suppressed. Such disturbances spoil the establishment of peace and security.

"I confirm that I appreciate the assistance of the British Government which I can only recompense by the preservation of the continuance of British friendship and be loyal friends to them. I wish to see to the welfare of the Hadhrami country during my time and the nation must be educated and developed in its social and economic administration by virtue of the peaceful arrangements which have been established to-day, on account of the efforts and assistance rendered by the 'Friend of Hadhramaut,' viz., Mr. Ingrams, the First Political Officer.

"I trust that my beloved nation will, in completion of their education and progress, remember this favour and preserve it for the sake of the welfare of the country. God, the Supporter, may help us to perform good acts and for peace."

Then a herald stood forth and proclaimed as follows:

"As Sultan 'Ali bin Mansur bin Ghalib al Kathīri has bestowed the title of 'Friend of Hadhramaut' upon Mr. Ingrams, every person of the people should address him by this title.

"May the 'Friend of Hadhramaut' live long! (Thrice shouted out)"

Henceforth it was by this title that I was addressed in all correspondence in the Hadhramaut and I confess it has pleased me more than any other. Afterwards, the extravagantly-minded called me al Mahdi, and on the coast I was hailed as Rasul as Salaam! The beduin among themselves, when they did not call me Gerāms, referred to me as Al Muslahi—the Settler (of disputes). There is no better feeling than the feeling of friendship one gets from being treated as an equal. The "Sahib" suggests Government, and while they respect the Government, it is an abstraction miles away from them, and oneself is just any Nasrani belonging to it. As Gerāms we had everything in common. The one name I do hate is "The Mister," which gets handed out to me by the "effendis" sometimes.

Then the beduin made their speech. They dictated it to Seiyid Muhammad Midheij and he pronounced it for them:

"Oh Sultan and Ingrams, we are beduin and do not know how to speak nor the rules, but anyhow we will speak as far as we know.

"Please excuse us for what we have done, and we thank Ingrams for his advice which we did not accept, for we did not believe that we would be put into great trouble. Now we should like to speak with Ingrams, and on this day we say 'Al Hamdulillah,' everything is all right."

## "YOU DID WELL TO BOMB US"

When all this orgy of speech-making was over, I took the Sultan to [e] of the Bin Yemani present and we shook hands with them all. The [ter] was finished with, I declared. Henceforth, I hoped, we should be [ids]. That evening 'Umar Tuheish and his friends came round to [id] Bubakr's house and after dinner invited D. and me to go and visit [n].

"You did well," they said, "to bomb us. And we thank you. If we given in before, people would have said we were cowards. We [t] peace too now we know you'll keep it. Come and stay with us."

## Chapter XXIX

## THE SIGNING OF THE TRUCE

*Where small and great, where weak and mighty made*
*To serve, not suffer, strengthen, not invade;*
*More pow'rful each as needful to the rest*
*And, in proportion as it blesses, bless'd.*

POPE.

*The mountains also shall bring peace: and the little hills righteousness unto the people.*
*The kings of Tharsis and of the Isles shall give presents: the kings of Arabia and Saba shall bring gifts.*

PSALM LXXII.

NEXT day Seiyun emptied. Uncle Bubakr from Hureidha, his son 'Alawi, the Mansab of Meshhed and his brother and other 'Attas Seiyids had been staying in the house. They were anxious that I should go up the Wadi 'Amd and sign on the Ja'da, but there was still much to do in Wadi Hadhramaut and I promised to go later on. In the meantime they took D. off with them and she and 'Alawi were to go up the wadi and see what the situation was.

From Hureidha they visited every village up the wadi to 'Amd, the capital. 'Alawi and his Javanese servant rode one camel and D. and Jamila, the Al 'Attas maid and a woman of character, rode the other. Jamila taught D. beduin war songs and when she had learnt them they proceeded up the wadi singing duets. D. took down details of thirty-two major feuds in the wadi. Almost everywhere the villages were divided against themselves and everywhere the cry was the same: "Give us peace." One gentleman discussed the matter from a second-storey window. He apologized for not coming down but explained he was busy carrying on a war single-handed against all his neighbours. Another had said: "We want peace, we're sick of fighting. Bring us peace and settled Government."

During the next few days I visited Tarim where in two days the whole of the Tamimi signed on and in following days came the Jabir, Bajri, 'Awamir, Johi, Ma'ara and Madhi. The truce in fact had become more infectious than an outbreak of measles. Nothing could have been more

:cting than the arrival of a deputation of the Al 'Ali Kathīr, from far to north-east, who live among the Mahras. It was late at night and the :e men clad in long brown kamises, an unfamiliar garb in Hadhramaut, 1e and kneeling down and stretching out their hands said: "We have rd of the peace in this country, please give us a share of it." It was y who had had four men brutally murdered by the 'Awamir a few rt months before, and they went away after signing on the three years' ce with an invitation to me to visit them, to make landing-grounds in ir country, and a promise that the Board would investigate their case.

The chief of the Tamimi tribe, Al 'Abd bin 'Ali bin Yemani, sent me following letter from all al Tamim and Beni Dhanna:

"The three years truce document has to-day been concluded and signed by the Tamimi tribe. This was done through your good efforts and great endeavours for the maintenance of peace within our beloved home, the Hadhramaut. We proffer our great thankfulness to His Majesty's Government and your honour for the same, as well as to his honour Sultan 'Ali bin Salah and the honourable Seiyid Bubakr bin Sheikh Al Kaf.

The Tamimi tribesmen are extremely pleased with this truce which will give relief and rest to the people from killing and fighting, and all of them wish to maintain security on the trade routes. During the truce period all people will attend to buildings and agriculture, which the inhabitants of Hadhramaut have neglected for a long time owing to the lack of peace existing among the tribesmen. Now all the people entertain confidence in the British Government only. Had such a truce been made by others they would not have felt confident.

"We have heard your explanation yesterday when we asked you at the first meeting held at the palace of Seiyid Bubakr bin Sheikh and you hoped to be always beside us and render us assistance in the preservation of peace and dispensation of justice, for which we are very grateful and obliged. We would like soon to see the British flag hoisted on one of the palaces in which you have been staying in one of the Hadhramaut towns. Complete tranquillity will have to be given to all the inhabitants of the country.

"As regards the tribesmen who have not yet signed the truce document, such as the Sei'ar, 'Awamir, Manahil, some of Al Jabes, Al Hamum as a whole, Mahra, Simah and others, please note that their tribes are at feud with us and each of us has certain murders against them. The custom has been that the beduin bringing caravans from the coast and fuel, charcoal, and saf (from palm trees) from the Hadhramaut mountains, always pass along the trade routes. If they see an enemy on the road they kill him and if they find goods and riding camels they will carry them away and cut down the palm trees. We wish to have your opinion as to what we should do if we meet them on the trade routes, should we be handicapped and allow them to do anything they like with us on the plea that they are wayfarers? We await your reasoned opinion on this dangerous subject.

"Please accept our high regards."

On 25th February the truce party consisting of Sultan 'Ali bin Salah, the Seiyids of Al Kaf, the mansabs of the Nahd and myself, left for Qa'udha, the capital of the Nahd. The Nahd and the Ja'da were the biggest fences left. The Nahd had twenty-one continuous years of feudal strife behind them and a system of trenches as elaborate as that of Al Ghurfa. Only fifteen yards separated the nearest houses of the principal warring sections and there were people in those houses who had not been out of them for many years.

Hakm Mbaruk, the paramount chief of the Nahd, was a fine old patriarch with a long beard and a voice that seemed to echo up from his belly. He has a wide and enviable reputation for dispensing real justice, but as he himself said: "Real justice unsupported by strength does not satisfy everyone." The Nahd are a distinctive tribe, well-built, not small of stature, and their many elders all seem to have enormous bellies and resonant voices.

Signing on went well at Qa'udha, and after the truce had been read out with all its several hundreds of signatories, we moved on to the Al Thabit of Nahd next door. They were the real cause of the Nahd trouble, for their village was originally part of Qa'udha and they had split off and now waged relentless warfare. They were led by a young man, hot-headed and violent, and I noticed that nearly all his supporters were young too.

We were in for a tough job. All day long the argument went on. Each of us would take apart a few and explain and argue and press. Finally most of them were willing to sign. The young chief and the others withdrew together. An hour passed—two hours. At last they came out. No, they would not sign. More argument and more withdrawal. At eleven o'clock at night they had still decided not to sign. It was the chief and one or two others who held out and it must be all or none. That was their attitude.

Finally, in simulated wrath, I took up my stick, a good heavy tamarind from Zanzibar, and, sitting in front of our side, faced the young man sitting in front of his. Beating the floor within an inch or two of his folded legs till the dar shook, I told him what would happen to him and his people in

world and the next. In the midst of it all I heard Seiyid Bubakr behind
whisper to his neighbour. "I'm afraid he'll laugh in a minute." It
all I could do not to, but I kept it up, never letting my eyes off the
ng man, and describing what a fate he would bring on himself and his
ple.
"Not that I mind about you," I said. "But do you suppose all your
: are going to like being the only outlaws in Hadhramaut?" I wound
by saying that I and all my friends now proposed to leave his dar for
r and never set foot near him again.
The tribe withdrew again. Five minutes later they returned and
ed. We had decided to sleep out on the sand in the fresh air. It
all we could do to persuade them we were not leaving, but we promised
ie in for breakfast.
Under the moon lying in our blankets on the soft sand, we talked of
day's events. Once or twice before I had given to the 'Awamir what
rid Bubakr called my No. 5 speech. "It's the stick that does it," he
handling it, 'Asa Nebi Allah Musa—Moses' Rod." And to this day
Hadhramaut knows my walking-stick by that name.
It was an amicable party that assembled for breakfast—coffee, black
id and honey.

* * *

What a sight it was that morning to see the Nahd emerge from their
ses and their trenches. It reminded me of the Christmas in the Great
r when Germans and English came above ground and exchanged greet-
;. One man had not come out of his house for eighteen years; another
ked a few yards to a house to see his sister whom he had not seen for
nty-one. But the desolation of all these years' enmity, in which most
:hose present had grown up, was as bad as that of France. Before,
:e villages had stood in flourishing date groves; now nothing remained
a few dead trunks, for each side had killed the other's palms by watering
n with kerosene. That very morning talk began of regenerating the
lens.
We packed up and went on to Hureidha, meeting on the way Ahmed
sein, the mansab, with two of his sons, trotting along on ponies. At
:eidha all had been prepared for us. We were to have the most com-
able house in the place, belonging to one of the mansabs, Hassan bin
m, a great traveller still away from the Hadhramaut. The house was
n, large and well furnished in purely Arab style. Hassan's wife had a

301

name as an excellent housekeeper and everywhere there was evidence of her overseeing eye.

It was odd how we organized ourselves like any diplomatic mission. Each of us had our own suite in which we slept and had our various committee meetings. There was one big assembly room where the meetings of tribesmen were held, and another smaller veranda which was also a public room, where we signed on in batches each section. We took our meals except breakfast outside, the whole mission being entertained at lunch or dinner by different notables. Each morning, after I had bathed in refreshing icy water from the big jar in my bathroom, a maidservant came in to clean and tidy up, very black and rejoicing in the name of "Happiness." Her husband's was "Good Luck," in spite of which he suffered terribly from dangerous poisoning in his foot, and I gained their gratitude by sending him off to Aden where they amputated it and gave him a good wooden one on which he can now stump about.

The day of our arrival was a fair day in honour of 'Attas ancestors in the domed tombs below the town. The Seiyids had me all dressed up in my best, with the long abba and jambiya I only wore on State occasions. The mansabs took me by the hand and led me behind the banners and the beating drums in a long and dusty procession to the tombs. A display of riding by Ahmed Hussein and his sons brought the visitation to a close.

All day long deputations from the various sections had been arriving. They would stand beneath our house, fire off rifles in salutation, and then sit down and wait their turn. The well-meaning but extremely undiplomatic Ahmed Hussein thought he would help by cutting the proceedings short, so he started haranguing the different sections and telling them they had to sign straight away, all gathered together in the big assembly room. Luckily Nasir was there and he came dashing up to where Seiyid Bubakr and I were discussing an incident which had just taken place near Hureidha. By the time we had got down Ahmed had the crowd well by the ears and they were starting to quarrel amongst each other. None of them like discussing their private affairs in front of their adversaries, and the only way to success was to take them section by section.

The incident that disturbed me was the shooting and wounding by one Ja'di section of a member of another a few days before. Luckily I was able to bluff the offenders into depositing $300 with me as a guarantee of future good behaviour. This sent my stock up a lot, and all the Ja'da and other tribes of the Wadi 'Amd signed in three days.

). had prepared the ground well, and all these wild tribesmen spoke
tly of her, referring to her as the "Nonya"—Malayan for a Chinese
. After the Ja'da signatures had been read out there were the most
aordinary scenes of rejoicing, so much so that the women were openly
ping for relief in the streets.

Many amusing incidents also took place in Hureidha that day, most
hem at the expense of Seiyid Talib, one of the 'Attas patriarchs. We
·d him Sinbad the Sailor, for he claimed to be ninety-two and had
elled extensively, even as far out of the track of Hadhramis as Capetown.
en Seiyid Talib's beard goes bright red and he is wearing silk clothes
know that he is going to marry again. He claimed to have had fifty-
it wives and he had them all recorded in a book, for otherwise, he said,
would forget them. He had the distinction of being the only man in
·eidha who owned a bed, which had to be admired by all his visitors.
Before we left Hureidha we copied out a truce form and sent it on to
Ba Surras of Du'an, with full directions for its completion, for I felt
ain that we could leave it to them to manage their area. We then went
c into the Wadi Hadhramaut to Henin to finish off the Nahd. We
not arrive till nearly two o'clock in the morning for, as usual, the
ple of Diar al Buqri had held us up for dinner, and when we left them,
n extremely distended condition, we continually got stuck in the sand
were in no state to afford much help to the unfortunate drivers.

At Henin we stayed in the house of Bin Marta'. Not only the rest of
Nahd but some of the settled Sei'ar sections also signed on there, so
there was little trouble when we returned to Seiyun at four o'clock in
afternoon.

\* \* \*

Deputations and letters of thanks came from almost every section.
n the women sent to say how grateful they were, for in the old days
7 always lived in fear that when their menfolk parted from them they
;ht not see them again.
Here are two examples of the many letters:

*From Al Hakm Mbaruk bin Muhammad bin 'Ajaj, paramount chief of
the Nahd, and his men of Al 'Ajaj of Nahd.*
"We write this to express our pleasure in the settlement and peace
maintained by you because you relieved the people from disturbance
and trouble. In the meantime everyone will do his own work peacefully. We are peacemakers. There is nothing other than to proffer

## THE SIGNING OF THE TRUCE

our thankfulness to the British Government as well as to His Excellency the Resident of Aden and all the officials of His Majesty's Government.

"As regards yourself, we thank you as well as the Sultans of this part, the Qu'aiti and Bin 'Abdulla, and the Seiyids of Al Kaf, for the service and endeavours rendered by them to the interests of the Muslims. May God reward you all for the same and perpetuate the peace and tranquillity.

"At present, as you know, we carry personal arms, but know that we do not carry them except on account of the harmful acts being made, otherwise no one is in favour of inconvenience and trouble, but we are afraid of our souls and ourselves and if peace has generally been maintained we need personal arms no longer.

"We therefore request you to continue your assistance and be always at our side so that we may dispense with arms and that success may always be ours. May God preserve you. Greetings."

*In the Name of God the Supporter.*
*To be submitted to His Excellency the Resident of Aden.*

"We beg to submit the following:

"The interest taken and the attention directed by His Majesty's Government towards our sacred home and the present assistance for the establishment of peace and security within our province, and the safeguarding of the nation from disturbances and troubles which destroy the country and subject it to despair and worse, that such interest taken by His Majesty's Government for the removal of all these things will make the future of Hadhramaut bright and prosperous, and it is expedient on us to express our great appreciation and thankfulness in our hearts which direct us to submit our hearty thanks to His Majesty's Government and Your Excellency, oh Honourable Resident.

"We do not forget to express the great thanks felt in our hearts for the Friend of Hadhramaut, for the excellent services rendered by him for the reform of the conditions in our beloved province.

"Hadhramaut history will perpetuate the valuable assistance rendered by the British Government to the nation and Government of Hadhramaut. It is certain that it will be a great foundation for the improvements which are expected in the Hadhrami country for the progress of the people and future civilization which men of learning and earnest peacemakers in the Hadhramaut have endeavoured to bring about and made great efforts in that respect.

"Now nothing remains but to express our sincere and appreciative thanks from the bottom of our hearts for the interest taken by His Majesty's Government in the welfare of our home. Also we entertain the hope that our best compliments, thanks and gratitude will be conveyed, on our behalf, to the Great Government of London which we hope may continue to be the source of peaceful arrangements and good actions. Please accept our high regards."

*Signed by all the Seiyids of Al 'Alawi.*

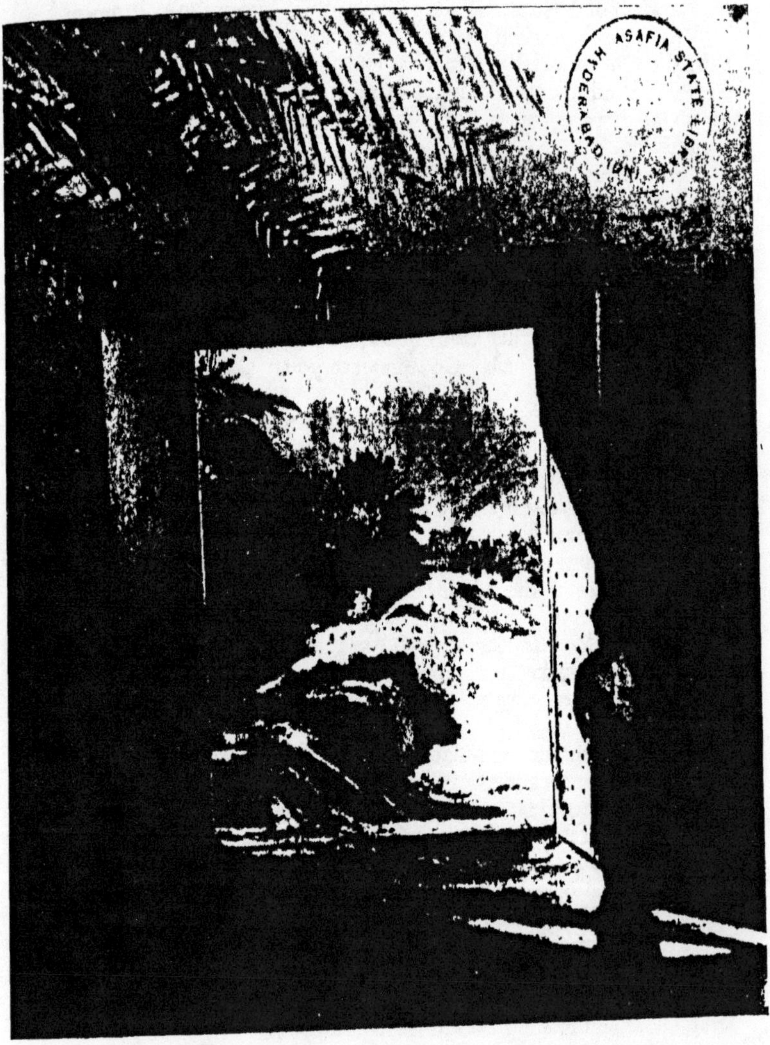

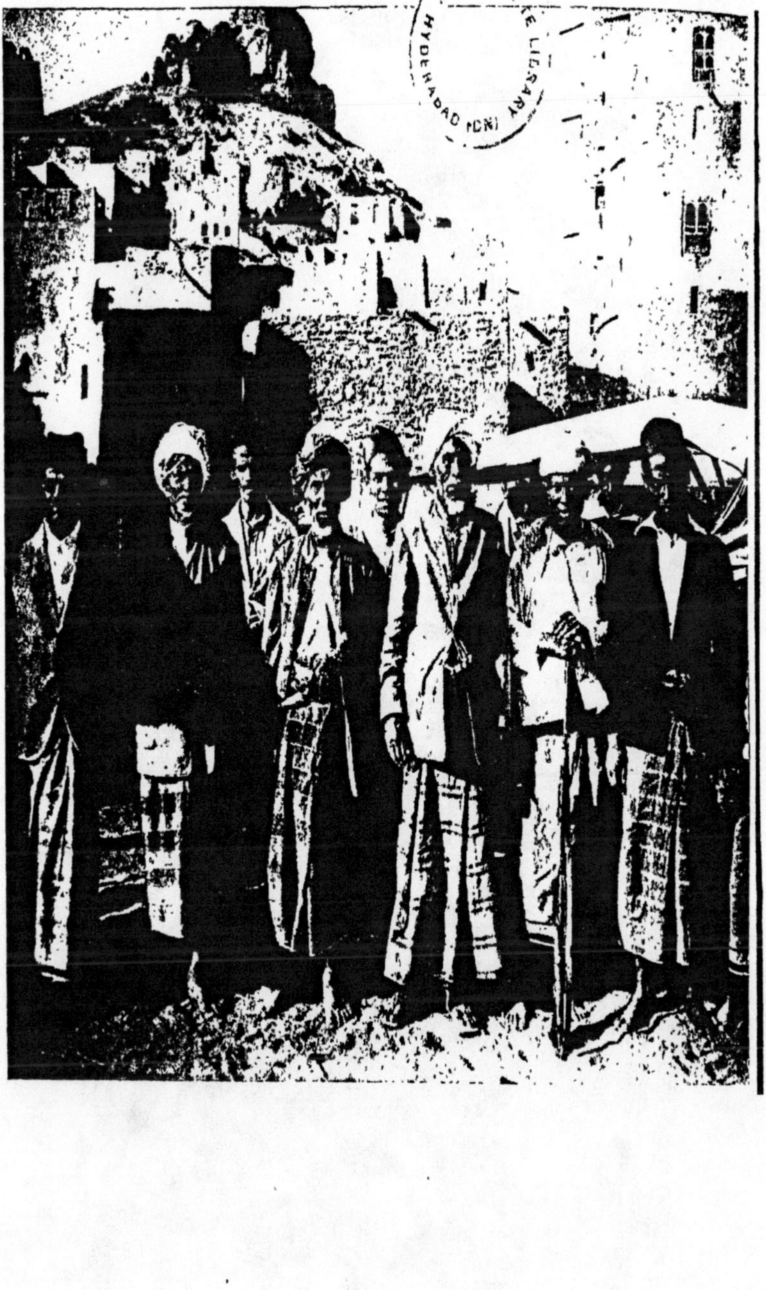

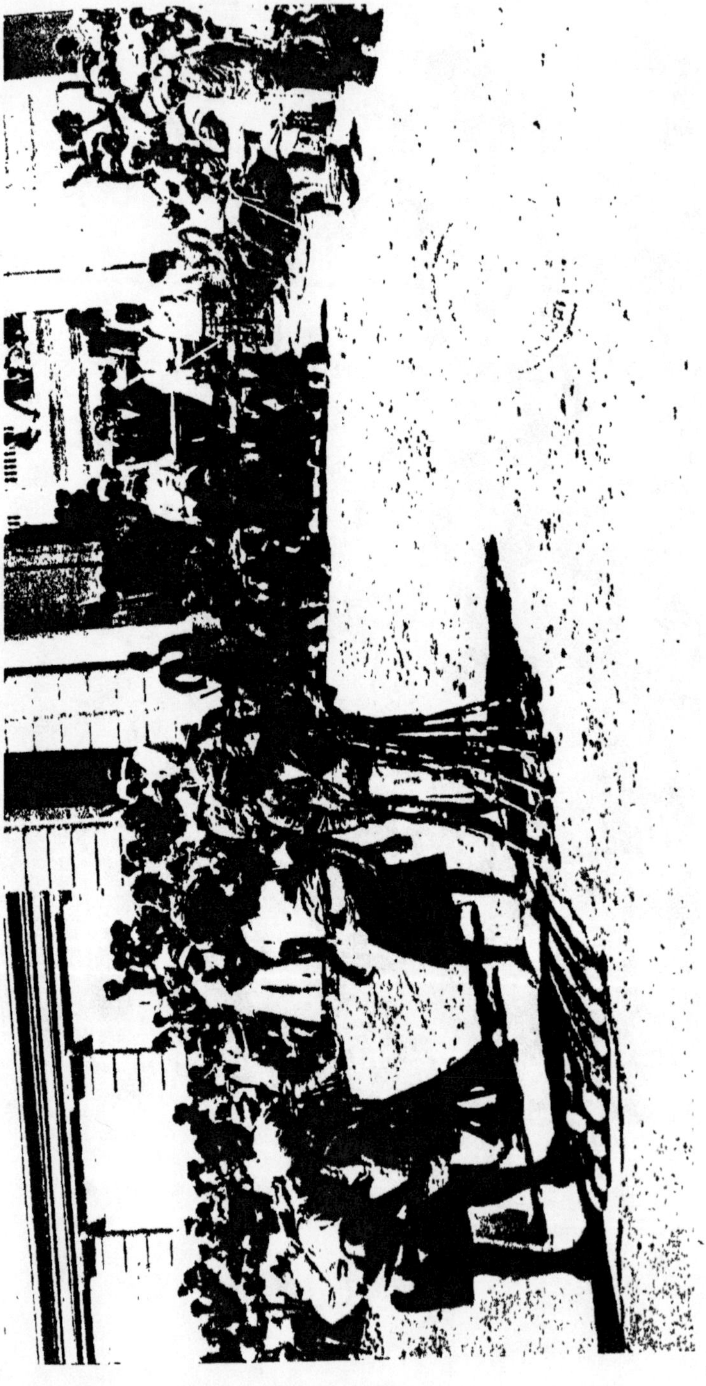

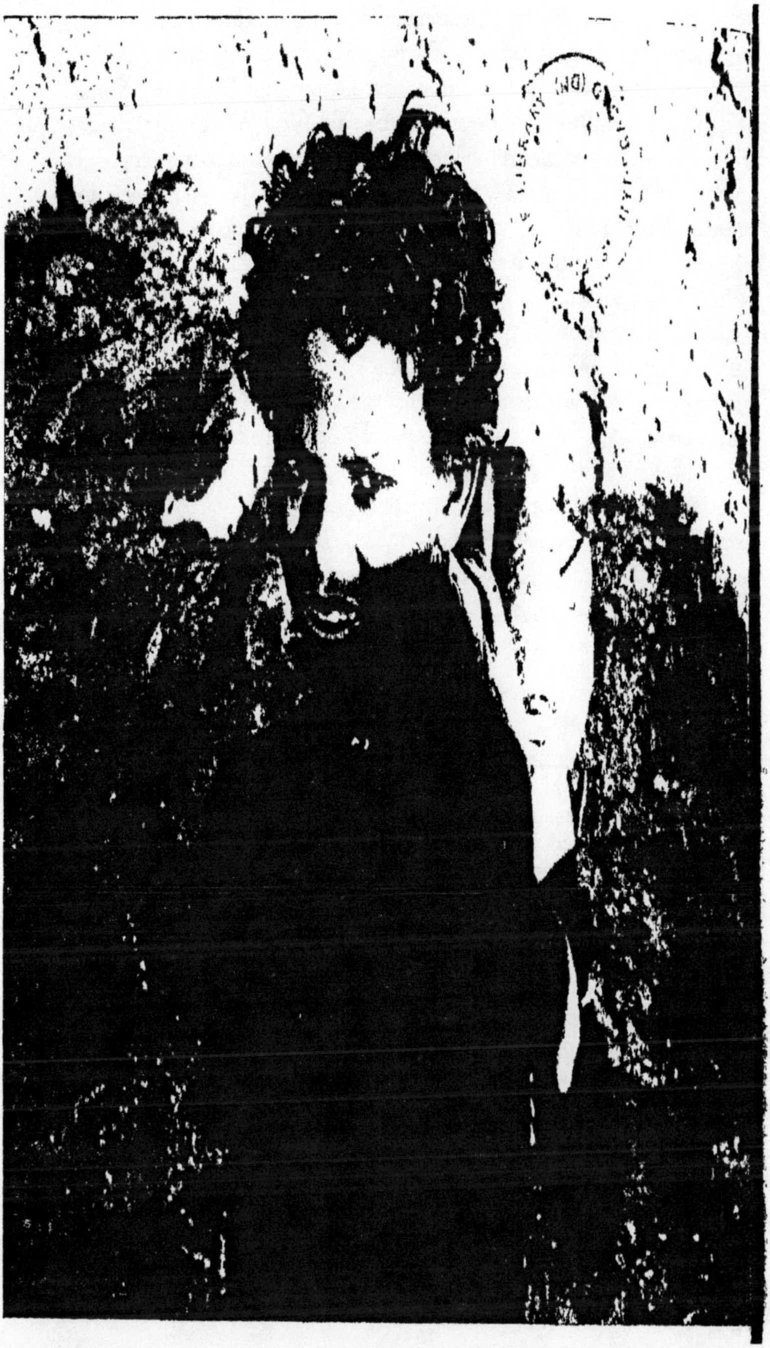

## SLUMP IN ARMS TRAFFIC

One of the most striking indications of the changing attitude of the country was the slump in the sale of arms; many of those coming in from Aden were returned unsold and rifles that a short time before had fetched from 400 to 700 dollars could not now be sold for 150 dollars. Another sign was the mild speculation which began in house property, for there was a conviction that many people would return from Java and that prices would rise enormously. One huge house changed hands at $15,000, the purchaser assuring me that he would have no difficulty in getting $100,000 for it in the near future.

I had for some time been anxious to return to Mukalla as Sultan Salih had already left for India, but before going I arranged that the Peace Board would begin to hold further meetings for the settlement of disputes as from 1st Muharram (14th March) and urgently counselled the members to start work early and to work hard.

The Board took offices in Seiyun with a "brass plate" outside the door. A secretary was appointed, Seiyid Muhammad bin Hashim, who had started all the Arab schools in Java and later became a constant friend. He had written books on the history of Hadhramaut and was preparing another. He addressed the following letter to me:

"I have already studied Hadhrami history from 500 of the Hejira up to the present time, and I have read numerous books and enquired from learned and knowledgeable persons about the general peace in Hadhramaut, and from strict enquiries made I cannot find that Hadhramaut, from border to border, has ever had universal peace at any period, either in ancient or recent times.

"The great, powerful and just Sultans of Hadhramaut, 'Abdulla bin Rashid who died in 615 and Bedr Bu Tuweirak who died in 977, compelled everyone to submit to them but the tribes continued to have trouble amongst themselves.

"As regards recent times, I have enquired from learned persons about the peace arrangements which used to be concluded among the tribes and found one vital point, namely, that Hadhramaut has never known, for many centuries, the meaning of 'universal peace.' There were truces between two or three sections but the others continued their disputes.

"When one of the notable men of Al 'Attas died there used to be a one year, or less, truce concluded between the Ja'da and Nahd only. When one of the notable men of either Al Habashi or Al 'Abdulla bin 'Alawi al 'Aidarus died there used to be a truce between the Al Kathir and Al 'Awamir only, and when one of the great men of Al 'Aidarus or Al Sheikh Bubekr died there would be a truce amongst the Tamimi and so on.

"In 1320, during the lifetime of the Mansab 'Abdul Qadir bin Salim al 'Aidarus, he remained for one month endeavouring to arrange a truce and after great difficulty concluded a one year's truce.

"To conclude, universal peace on the roads and among the tribes in the province has not been known in Hadhramaut for many centuries.

"I have written a note at the end of my history saying that it is essential for historians who may come after us to announce their delight and strike their drums at the establishment of universal peace in the country."

A Legal Adviser was also appointed in order that the Sheria should not be overlooked in coming to decisions, and as far as possible taken into consideration in settling them. The members of the Board and others were so anxious that I should be a member that finally a compromise was arranged whereby I should see the decisions before they were promulgated. I drew up rules for the Board which, besides providing for matters of office routine, such as the filing and numbering of cases entered, prescribed how each case should be dealt with. Difficult cases requiring research might be referred to sub-committees. In all cases the chairman of the sub-committee was to be a member of the Board unconnected with the dispute, but sub-committee members might be appointed who did not belong to the Board. All cases, whether referred to sub-committees or not, had to be considered by the Board itself. Over six hundred cases were entered in quite a short time, and a large number of them disposed of satisfactorily.

\* \* \*

Perhaps one of the greatest surrenders of those days was that of the royal wives at Seiyun. Sultan 'Ali was completely under their thumbs and it was extraordinarily difficult to get them to consent to send their sons to Aden to the Chiefs' College. D. conducted a campaign in the background as she could carry it well into the enemy's trenches. Finally they gave in and Hussein, the eldest son, and Majid were selected to be educated. It was not easy to get Hussein as he had already been booked for a girl aged fourteen or fifteen by an anxious mother who thought it was high time she was married.

I myself had an embarrassing number of proposals of marriage in these days, but Nasir was generally with me and, being a great admirer of D.'s, said, when one chief even emphasized how white his daughter was: "He

;n't want your dirty daughters; he's got a perfectly good wife of his
1 who's clean about the house." He was completely flabbergasted
:n D. told him she didn't mind how many wives I had. But he didn't
:ve her.

With the party of us that set out for the coast on 6th March was a
oner in irons. Shortly after the Bin Yemani affair he had held up a
rid with a loaded camel merely in order to get his masters into trouble.
: masters seized him and brought him to me for judgment. This was
ible, and if he had been content to stay three days in jail, as I ordered,
matter would have ended there. However the Sultan's guards let him
.pe. The Sultan was worried lest I should know and set out with two
dred men to recapture him. The culprit had armed himself and was
pared to stand a siege. But 'Awadh bin 'Azzan persuaded him to sur-
der again and I felt he would be safer in Mukalla jail. Settling small
:s like this, mostly with the invaluable advice of Seiyid Bubakr, helped
1gs a lot. Other cases had settled themselves. I sometimes heard of
:s in which a threat that they would be brought to my notice was enough
nake aggressors settle. Even children were heard to settle their disputes
saying: "Shut up, or I'll tell Ingrams." I was told in Seiyun that cases of
elty to animals had practically ceased, owing to threats of the same
ure, but this was probably due to D. having dealt with a small boy who
; roughly handling a puppy.

An important item in our caravan was Seiyid 'Abdur Rahman's lorry. I
; anxious to take a lorry to show the beduin we considered ourselves
: to take anything we liked. My policy was to protect the beduin
ffic, but I was determined it would be protected because I said so and not
:ause they thought we were afraid of them. So the lorry came with
beid and his hearties from Tarim to finish the road under my protection.
roposed to stop two days with them at Maadi and that they should start -
the easy end, i.e., the end furthest from Shihr and work towards Shihr.
ranted to be sure of getting the greater distance done in case of more
uble. Seiyid Bubakr counselled otherwise. "Put them at the Shihr
1 and let them work towards home. They will work faster and can be
re easily provisioned from Shihr." Of course he was right.

The first night we fulfilled our engagement with the Bin Yemani at
sib. They gave us a wonderful reception. 'Umar Tuheish and all the
jils with a long line of tribesmen were drawn up at the roadside when
: cars came to a halt and fired *feux de joie* in great abandon. When I had

shaken over a hundred indigo-dyed hands, they led us across the valley and fields to their dars firing off rifles at our very ears as we went. We were taken to their guest-house built of loose stones, like all their huts, and innocent of windows. After a rest in the gloom they took us round to see the damage from the bombing. I had spotted a badly-damaged house in the distance but that, they told me, was ruined before the bombing. One bomb they said had "broken six houses." We went to see it. It was the usual kind of conglomerate dar—a tall husn, untouched, in the centre and a number of loose stone dwellings piled round it. From a European reckoning they were just rooms for they all had party walls. On the corner of these a bomb had fallen. One room or "beit" required repairs, but all the bomb had done otherwise was to displace some stones. They were rather apologetic that there was so little to see.

While we were waiting in the gloom for dinner a cousin of 'Ubeid al 'Ingliz regaled us with the history of the Bin Yemani in couplets. No one enjoyed it more than our hosts, who picked out and repeated the bits where they were praised or made fun of.

Dinner came; vast quantities of boiled mutton on rather wet and stodgy rice. I was hungry and made a good meal, but even then they thought I put up a poor show. It was kind, warm hospitality and now I always spend an hour with them if I can, and the Bin Yemani are always ready to make themselves known and do small services when we meet them on the roads or in Shihr or Hadhramaut.

I would have liked to be able to help them and some day I hope to get them a well. It was water they wanted. Their waterholes were almost dried up and on the morrow they were to move with their flocks to find water elsewhere. Like the man at Ma'adi who had wanted to shoot me and had then demanded that I should make the rain fall from a cloud to which he pointed, they too asked me to bring the rain.

"The rain is from God," I said, "Inshallah the world will rain before long."

We went on in the morning to Reidat al Maara widening the 'aqabas for the lorry as we came to them.

At Reida they have a fine tree which gives plenty of shade to men and beast. It is a sanctuary, and he who reaches it is safe from pursuit. There they hold their tribal meetings and beneath it we held our peace meeting. They and the Yafa'is living in their midst signed on to the peace.

At Ma'adi I heard that 'Ali bin Habreish was at a tribal rally at 'Arf in the Wadi 'Arf on the old caravan road. I sent a message to the 'Aidarus seiyids, Hussein and his brothers, to meet me the next day at the other "rail head," and in the morning started off with the labourers to Ma'adi. Here they started work while I explained to the Ba Hasan Tanbulis that they were not to be interfered with. I also tried to persuade them to sign the truce, but pleading that some of the 'Aqils were away, they gave me a pledge on their faces to sign at Habs, where formerly we had visited Salim Ahmed's garden, on the 15th.

When we got to the head of the pass on the Shihr side, 'Ubeid had finished about a hundred yards of new road and the seiyids were there to meet me. I had not yet met Seiyid Hussein and I was not sure of his identity, for he wore rather the clothes of a tribesman with a dagger at his waist. His red-bearded brother Zein looked more like a Seiyid to me, and 'Alawi, the youngest, carried a rifle as well as a dagger. I knew that these seiyids, rather than the Mansab of the 'Aidarus—Seiyid 'Abdur Rahman—had influence with 'Ali, for there was a family quarrel and the Qu'aiti Sultan had persistently backed the old man and his son Muhammad, which was a tactical error and cost him a lot more in payments for truces.

As it was late I proposed to motor to Shihr for the night. The seiyids displayed some uneasiness about this, for Hamid Mihdhar was in Shihr. They feared that the move would not be popular.

Hassan Shaibi reassured them: "All that has changed. No one can change his mind from what he decides to do."

We went to Shihr. Hamid was as agreeable as ever but I did not discuss my plans. Next morning at six we mounted donkeys and shortly after nine had reached 'Arf, riding up the stony wadi, the object of much speculation from the Hamumi gathered in force at the various villages on the banks.

'Ali bin Habreish was holding a reunion at the tribal meeting-place under a huge boulder on the side of the wadi. We took up our quarters in the house and presently he and his merry men advanced across the wadi singing and halting every now and then to fire a volley of greeting. 'Alawi, the young seiyid, stood on our roof and fired in answer.

When 'Ali arrived we talked and my companions impressed on him the story of Hadhramaut peace till lunch arrived. Most of his contribution to the talk was grunts. I was anxious to eat with 'Ali and was amused that the same thought was in his mind. "There is now salt between us," he said as we plunged our hands into the rice.

After lunch we got down to serious business. There was much argument

## THE SIGNING OF THE TRUCE

and I never found a man so suspicious. He did not seem to trust a word I said, and every now and then he and the seiyids withdrew, but none of us seemed to make much progress.

"I want peace and justice and honour," said Ali. By "Sheraf" he meant money. I meant the other kind.

"Peace I bring you," I said. "God willing I will get you justice as I promised you before. Honour you will have from the Government and Qu'aiti and all men if you make and keep peace."

We discussed also further peace with the Qu'aiti. They had just purchased a year's truce for $2,000. The seiyids and I proposed that he should throw in another three years for nothing, as well as sign the general tribal peace.

Evening came and nothing was yet settled. I told him he must sign or I would go. He promised and then withdrew, so I delivered "Speech No. 5." The Hamumi tribesmen round were astonished to see me speaking thus to 'Ali. I got up and went. He pursued me. "In the morning I will sign." I mounted my donkey and went, after a whispered word to the seiyid. We reached Shihr late, but at dawn the seiyids returned with the two documents signed.

On the 15th I met the Ba Hasan Tanbulis of Ma'adi at Habs as arranged. They signed there as did the Sha'amila that day. A few days later we heard from 'Ali bin Salah in Shibam that various tribes near the Nahd and some of the Sei'ar and some of the sections in the Wadi Rakhia had come to find me and had signed also. I received back the documents from the Ba Surras duly signed by all the tribes of Du'an. Other chiefs and tribes came in to Mukalla and signed, while to others, more distant, went messengers with letters.

There were extraordinary ovations in Shihr and Mukalla and one of the best pieces of news I heard was that owing to the security, imports of goods had largely increased in the last three ships and that there was a drop, in some cases of as much as 50 per cent, in transport charges on the road.

Our exclusive seiyid discovered in a book of the Traditions on the night of our arrival, a saying of the Prophet, peace be upon him, which he interpreted as meaning that Peace would not come to the country save through a stranger. This he had generously broadcasted and that too had its effect.

In Mukalla the truce between the Qu'aitis and 'Ali bin Habreish was arranged, and an effort was also made to clear up the long outstanding bitterness. I got the Qu'aitis to agree to entertain 'Ali in Shihr and, what

as more difficult, persuaded 'Ali to accept. The man was so suspicious
at he still thought he would be murdered like his father. At last he agreed,
I went out to meet him and brought him in. On the 5th of April I drove
it from Shihr through silent crowds. Not a man believed that 'Ali
ould come. I took a car and a big lorry for the fifty tribesmen he told
.e he would bring. They were waiting at the rendezvous. 'Ali stepped
to the car nervously and sat between Seiyid Hussein and myself. We
ere afraid that even then he might "do a bunk" and the driver had orders
tat once he started he was not to stop till he reached the Shihr palace! I
t him see his men climb into their lorry—all armed to the teeth—and we
ere off. There were nervous looks backwards from 'Ali. We told
im stories and flattered him by letting him tell us tales of his prowess.

I was very relieved when we reached Shihr safely. There were yells
om the gates of "He's come, he's come!" and we drove to the square
/here an enormous shouting crowd parted to let us drive up to the door.
took 'Ali by the hand. Out stepped his bandits, firing from modern
fles and matchlocks the salutes of greeting as we entered the palace. 'Ali
in Habreish was the guest of honour of the Qu'aiti Government. There
rere huge dinners served in the palace and all night Shihr made merry.
1 the morning 'Ali was given a present and robe of honour. The old feud
ras buried.

Thus the three years' truce includes the whole of Qu'aiti and Kathiri
omains from the sea to the desert, as well as part of the Wahidi country.
ill together there are between 1,300 and 1,400 signatories, which shows how
isunited the country was, as many of them represent only small sections.

\*   \*   \*

On 28th March the rain had begun to fall all over the country and
ong before it ended it was generally said that it was the heaviest rain for
ifteen years: later it was generally declared to have been the heaviest in the
nemory of man and a blessing from the Almighty as a reward for peace.

So far so good. That was in April, 1937. It now remained to see
vhether this truce could be kept and peace secured.

*Chapter XXX*

## THE NEW ROAD

*And an highway shall be there.*   ISAIAH.

ON one of the occasions when I was visiting Shihr in connection with 'Ali bin Habreish's affairs, I was sitting with His Excellency 'Umar Salih when a Yafa'i of the Al Ardhi tribe approached me with a petition regarding an act of oppression by Ahmed Nasir, who had a share with him in some land at Gheil Ba Wazir. Ahmed Nasir, it appeared, had come to Gheil with soldiers of the Sultan, seized all the crop and had it sold on his own account. Neither his partner, nor the cultivator who was working the land on a share basis got anything. The Governor said the complaint was true, but shrugged his shoulders and said: "I can't do anything. Ahmed Nasir is the Government himself; perhaps you can help."

The use of Government soldiers for personal ends struck me as an appalling misuse of authority, and next day, on my way back to Mukalla, I called at Gheil, saw the land and the people concerned, discussed it with the local Governor who confirmed the whole story and returned to Mukalla, where I spoke to Sultan 'Awadh who was acting as his father's representative. 'Awadh told me that he had heard of the case and had tried to intervene, but that Ahmed Nasir had torn up his letters and forbidden him to speak to me about it. I promised him support and we wrote a letter from him ordering the Governor of Gheil, an honest Qadhi, to hear the case "without fear or favour, affection or illwill." The court thus appointed was at first hesitant: it said that it would only look ridiculous because its judgement would not be enforced. Support, however was promised. The case was heard with due form and order and on the one count, of using the soldiers without authority, Ahmed Nasir was sentenced to be dismissed from Government service, and on the other, concerning the property, was ordered to restore what he had taken and pay a fine of $100.

On the 4th of April Ahmed Nasir was summoned to hear the judgement which had been passed on him. He tried, however, to avoid this by going on board the *Al Amin*, by which ship he was to go to Aden, but Sultan Awadh ordered him to be brought back to the palace where the judgement was read and sealed.

Thus I felt one of the last serious obstacles to the spread of peace and justice had been removed, and it had the important effect of generally enhancing the Sultan's prestige.

On the 7th of April we flew back to Aden to meet the Sultan of Zanzibar and the Sultan of Mukalla on their way to the Coronation. It was a great joy to me to see my old Sultan again. He had wired from Zanzibar asking me to meet him and I had learnt that his ship was due in at five o'clock in the morning. As usual with old friendships, the years fell away, but though I tried hard somehow I could not talk Swahili to him and our conversation was all in Arabic.

We visited the Tanks and the other sights, and the college where he talked to the Zanzibar masters. I then took him to call on Sir Bernard Reilly, now the Governor, for the Colony of Aden was ten days old.[1] We returned to the ship to have breakfast with him and afterwards we sat on the deck. He had a "Good morning" and an enquiry for everyone that passed, and a pat on the head and a kindly word for every child that came up. There was delay about the ship sailing and our launch getting away, but although he was tired, he could not be moved from the deck by his doctor and when at last we went he stood waving his handkerchief until we were out of sight.

On the 14th came the Sultan of Mukalla, Sultan Salih, with Khan Bahadur Sheikh 'Ali Baakza, his able and charming secretary in India. Sheikh 'Ali's family had left the Hadhramaut over 400 years ago. Sultan Salih approved the dismissal of Ahmed Nasir and gave me a paper in which he dismissed Hamid also. He seemed very grateful for what I had done, for he had had full news in India.

I felt that I returned to the country with the full support not only of the people but of the Sultans, for both Sultan Salih and Sultan 'Ali bin Mansur wrote and asked the Government that I might remain in the country as their adviser.

\* \* \*

[1] On the 1st April, 1937, Aden ceased to be a part of India and became a Crown Colony. An Order in Council came into force that day which gave it a constitution and another Order in Council gave a constitution to the Protectorate which had hitherto had no formal existence. Sir Bernard Reilly achieved the unique distinction of being the last Resident, the only Chief Commissioner and the first Governor of Aden.

## THE NEW ROAD

There was plenty to do in Mukalla for our office had to be organized. Hitherto when at the capital we had stayed in the guest-house, but the Sultan kindly put at our disposal a house which had been built by his predecessor before he ascended the throne and had since been used as the local "No. 10." Here we were very comfortable. The façade was imposing and there was a delightful portico under which cars could drive. The bottom floor was well fitted up as offices and above we had reception-rooms, including a large "diwan" for Arab guests. Our living quarters were on the second floor.

Tribal affairs gave way for a time to an enormous number of written and verbal complaints of injustices from the inhabitants of the coastal towns. Our office hours were 7.30 a.m. to 8.30 p.m., with an hour off for lunch and two and a half from four o'clock for air. In the midst of this we started to set Governmental services on a better footing, but it was difficult as there was little local experience, though plenty of good will, and my only personal staff consisted of my wife, a voluntary worker, and three Arab clerks, of whom only one had sufficient experience to make him useful.

In April Colonel Robinson, who was in command of the Aden Protectorate Levies in Aden, came to advise on the reorganization of the Mukalla Regular Army. I was extremely glad he was able to come for he had put the Sultan of Lahej's army, the Lahej Trained Forces, on a sound basis. He was always ready to help, and I have never appealed to "Robby" in vain. He had already helped me over the foundation of the college, and was to help much with the armed forces of the Hadhramaut.

Amongst other things, the Regular Army had to be medically examined and weeded out. It was a strange assortment including a "recruit" with twenty-five years' service and another aged sixty-nine with nine months, and quite a number of sexagenarians. The artillery, whose average age was about sixty, it was decided to retain. They were such delightful old gentlemen and as they fired the Coronation salute of twenty-one guns in just under four minutes, no greater efficiency could have been asked of them.

Later we formed a bodyguard of lancers for His Highness, mounted on camels, who looked very well in their scarlet and blue uniforms with scarlet pennons. They were recruited from the Nahd tribe and it was extraordinary how soon a dozen of the rawest beduin youths settled into being smart soldiers. Not the least of Colonel Robinson's services was sparing one of his officers, Captain Hopkins, to help us in reorganizing and training

## OPENING OF THE ROAD

Mukalla Regular Army for six months. In that period Hopkins put [s]plendid service and the force made great progress.

I pressed too for work to be put in on the new motor road to Shibam [via] Du'an, on which the Sultan was very keen, and we used to drive out of [an] afternoon to see how it was getting on. The rains had done a good [dea]l of damage to the early work, but it was soon repaired, and at one [pla]ce D. found a new track to take part of the road out of a wadi bed. [Th]e particular pass is now always called 'Aqabat Ingrams.

Then, too, I paid visits to Shihr and to 'Ubeid al 'Ingliz, working on the [ma]rim road. He had developed an excellent system of security. On the [stre]tch on which he was working he erected a red flag at each end. The [bed]uin asked why. He said that if either flag came down it sent wireless [wo]rd to me and I should be along in an aeroplane at once. Though several [agi]tators tried to stir up the beduin to interrupt the work, the latter always [sa]w that the flags were kept standing, and in three months 'Ubeid completed [hi]s thirteen-mile gap and joined the coast to the Hadhramaut. It was a [re]markable piece of work across the deep valley. The gradients were [no]t too steep and the corners on the hairpin bends wide enough to take a [lor]ry. ('Ubeid had kept a lorry with him to be sure it could go round [cor]ners without reversing.) I came back from Seiyun just as there was [ab]out a mile left. Over this we managed to drive in the first car that had [ret]urned to the coast since it had been carried thence in pieces on camels.

The opening of the road gave good cause for celebration and in July [Sir] Bernard kindly came to perform the ceremony accompanied by Air [Co]mmodore McClaughry, the Air Officer Commanding. It was the hottest [tim]e of the year and ten days' travelling in the Hadhramaut was no joke, [bu]t Sir Bernard did it as he did anything which was likely to help us. After [a f]ew days he, like the rest of us, adopted the sarong, and at dinner-parties [was] enthroned in state on purple cushions. He had a great and enthusiastic [we]lcome which was absolutely spontaneous, as he had specified no official [rec]eptions and this must have shown him how much his help had been [ap]preciated. McClaughry was always regarded with affection in the [Ha]dhramaut, where he was known as the aerial beduin. He was clad, [us]ually, in a sarong, tucked up fairly high like a bedu's, and carried in one [ha]nd—perpetually—a large cigar and in the other a fan. He looked rather [lik]e a mikado gone wrong and was an endless source of affectionate amuse[m]ent to everyone, for not even the most correct and formal seiyid could [res]ist him.

315

## THE NEW ROAD

After the opening we drove along the road to Hadhramaut and there followed days of sightseeing and entertainment in Tarim, Seiyun, Shibam, Hureidha and Du'an. The enormous banquets included one of 400 to dinner at Sultan 'Ali's palace in Seiyun. As a matter of fact Sultan 'Ali had not intended such a party. He had invited Shanfari chiefs to come with one or two friends and few of them brought less than ten. , At Al Ghurfa Sir Bernard called on Bin 'Abdat. Afterwards the lunatic 'Ubeid took Sir Bernard by the arm to show him the sights. In his free hand he carried the famous revolver—loaded as usual—which was waved about from house top to minaret and from Sir Bernard's abdomen to his nose. I wondered how many Colonial Governors would have stood that without a qualm—at any rate a visible qualm—in the cause of friendship. Such was the hospitality that Sir Bernard was glad to get back to Aden for a rest. He complained he had always thought there was too much entertainment in Aden, but that the Hadhramaut had it completely beat.

The Al Kaf road, named, of course, after the family that had spent so much money on it, was made a toll road administered by a Board, and I arranged that half its revenue should be accumulated for capital works and improvements and half should be spent on maintenance. The maintenance expenditure was very heavy as the daily buses did a lot of damage. The fees for the use of the road were designed not only to give revenue but also, in conjunction with minimum fares, to protect the bedouin camel traffic. In fact goods were not allowed to be carried by road unless they were perishable, too heavy for camels, or urgent, in all of which cases the freight charged had to be higher than that which would be charged for camel transport.

\*      \*      \*

Early in August I went to Aden to meet His Highness on his return from the Coronation. During his stay we discussed a new treaty between the Sultan of Mukalla and His Majesty's Government by which the latter agreed to provide a Resident Adviser on the lines adopted by the Sultans of Malaya. The treaty also provided for the stabilization of the succession to the Mukalla State, and was signed by Sir Bernard and the Sultan on the 13th August. My appointment as Resident Adviser to His Highness and to the Kathiri Sultan followed with effect from the same date, and I was also given political charge of the three other Sultanates of the Eastern Aden Protectorate, namely, the Wahidi Sultanates of Bir 'Ali and Balhaf and the

## NEW SCHEMES AND A GOVERNMENT LOAN

ahri Sultanate of Qishn and Soqotra.[1] The Balhaf Sultan was already a iend of mine and had a son in the Aden Protectorate College, and a few onths later the Balhaf Sultan persuaded a number of the Wahidi sections sign the truce. His Majesty's Government also very generously promised loan of £20,000 to assist in developing schemes for which His Highness as so eager, and in developing agriculture in the main Wadi Hadhramaut.

[1] To these were added in 1938 the Sheikhdoms of 'Irqa and Haura, two tiny :aty principalities on the 'Abdul Wahid coast.

## Chapter XXXI

## TROUBLE WITH THE SEI'AR AND OTHER TRIBES

*Though we had peace, yet 'twill be a
Great while ere things are settled:
Though the wind lie, yet after a storm
The sea will work a great while.* SELDEN.

*Pleasure and revenge,
Have ears more deaf than adders to the voice
Of any true decision.* SHAKESPEARE.

SHORTLY after His Highness returned in September to India to see his mother, who was seriously ill, trouble started with some of the foreign Yafa'i mercenaries. It will be remembered, perhaps, that the Qu'aiti dynasty is itself Yafa'i, and that Yafa'i had come to the country about four hundred years before. The families that had long settled there had become as Hadhrami as the indigenous Hadhrami themselves, but others had been in the habit of coming for a period of years from the Yafa'i mountains and enlisting as mercenaries. They received eight dollars a month pay and, being like all members of their tribe good money makers outside their own country, had settled down to screwing money out of the local inhabitants in no very scrupulous ways. Some of the leaders realized that, as good order and Government were now on a fair way to being established, they would be likely to find their wings clipped. They therefore started intrigues which, later, were to cause considerable trouble among the Hamumi tribe.

I was anxious too about the big desert tribes. As I have said, the Sei'ar were always the biggest problem. I had learnt how far they raided on my first journey, and enough has been said here to show that all the tribes who signed the general truce were suspicious of the Sei'ar. They wanted to have unlimited licence to shoot Sei'ars on sight, but it would have been a poor sort of peace if the Sei'ars were to be out of it and were to be counted no more than animals. A few of them had signed on and a few came to me

## LOOTING CAMELS FROM THE MANAHIL

...mplaining of murders in their own country. I promised to do what I ...uld, but for long months that was very little. Then a Sei'ar section of ...e Al Hatim called Al 'Abdulla bin 'Aun, with the encouragement of the ...hers, looted forty camels from the Manahil. The actual miscreants were ...fficult to get at for they were pure nomads and kept the looted camels at ...e distant well of Husn Al 'Abr where they were seen by Minhali spies.

It was because of their relations with the Sei'ars that the Manahil,[1] ...ho were the most north-easterly tribe in Qu'aiti domains, had failed to ...gn the truce. Their relations with the rest of the Hadhramaut were ...irly good, but if they were not sure that their Sei'ar affairs were settled, ...ey would have felt insecure with a one-sided peace. The Manahil ...elonged to the same confederation as the Tamimi, the Beni Dhanna, but ...hereas the Tamimi were all settled, the Manahil were all Bedus. Never-...eless they were more united than any other Hadhramaut tribe and their ...oung chief, 'Aidha bin Tannaf, a very fine lad of about twenty-five, had ...em completely under control. Surprisingly he held them back from ...taliation on the Sei'ar, and I promised to do my best to help them to ...et their camels back if they signed the truce. This they did and waited ...atiently for months while I negotiated with the Sei'ar.

Public opinion demanded that something should be done about the ...ei'ars, so in order to find out more about them and their country as quickly ...s possible, the whole country was explored by air. I accompanied all the ...econnaissances, of which the first were made in October 1937. So that ...e might start over ground that we knew we followed first of all the route ...hich D. and I had taken before. From Shibam to the entrance of the ...Vadi Ser took us three minutes; this journey had taken us exactly two hours ...n camels, and twenty minutes by car. After sighting the tomb of the ...rophet Salih in the Wadi Khonab, we turned into the Wadi Ser and at the ...outh of the Wadi Latakh I recognized the Bents' Himyaritic caravan ...gnpost. Then we went up the Wadi Sodaf and from Qa' al Fadhul on the ...il at its head took directions previously given to me by beduin for Ba

---

[1] The men of the Manahil, Mahra, and those distant sections of the Kathiri ...ho live up amongst the Mahra on the confines of the desert, take their mothers' ...ames and not their fathers. Ordinarily of course Arabs call themselves Hassan bin ...Iuhammad for example, but these people say Hassan bin Maryam. The Manahil ...nd the Hamumi and some of the other tribes are almost exclusively monogamous ...nd the women, who in some parts are not veiled, are extraordinarily free. A man ...roposes marriage to the woman direct, and her father will say it is not his concern. ...ride price is very high, but the bride brings a lot of stock with her.

## TROUBLE WITH THE SEI'AR AND OTHER TRIBES

Rumeidan, which we found. This was the residence of Tannaf, the principal chief of the Al Baqi Msellem of the Sei'ar. From the air I saw plainly that just before Qa' al Fadhul we were over the northern watershed, from which deep-cut short wadis ran south-south-west to the Hadhramaut and long shallow ones in an east-north-easterly direction to the sands. There was very little habitation over this part of the country, and most of the inhabitants lived in caves.

After just over forty minutes' flying from Shibam we found ourselves between two short wadis that ran out into a broad channel of sand which it took us two minutes to cross, and beyond it was a broken mass of rock that stretched away to the north-east. The channel itself ran out into the desert just west of the course of the flight, and the distance from Shibam to this point was calculated at sixty-nine miles. The visibility was perfect. Air Commodore McClaughry, who was with the flight, noted the high mass of the Seiban mountains at least one hundred miles away to the south. To the north an unbroken sea of sand stretched wave on wave far away to the horizon, coloured with a rosy red that was quite unforgettable and quite unbelievable. It was about three-quarters of an hour short of noon local time, so that the colour owed nothing to early morning light. After a few minutes over the desert we turned back to Shibam. The same afternoon, Seiyid Bubakr asked me to go with him and one of his brothers and a son to Qabr Hud, where the great annual pilgrimage to the tomb of the Prophet was in progress. When we had gone there on foot in December, 1934, the place was empty; now it was crowded. We flew there in the Arabian Airways machine chartered by Seiyid Bubakr, and this, as he said, was the first pilgrimage by air.

Next morning we left Seiyun at a quarter to nine on an almost due northerly course. On this outward flight the same facts were observed, deep short ravines that ran nearly south to the Hadhramaut, and more shallow wadis that ran almost east-north-east past the paler-coloured jōls of the watershed to the sands. In the upper reaches of the southern system we saw a few poor settlements of the 'Awamir and a caravan of some fifty camels plodding its way southward.[1] After exactly an hour and a quarter's

---

[1] The whole jōl from west to east was heavily scored with well-marked tracks and I noted, as I had also noted on aeroplane journeys over the Wadi Maseila, that east of our course and some fifty miles north of the wadi as it went towards Qabr Hud, there was a considerable rise in the ground, almost a range of mountains. This was probably the Jebel al Wuti of Von Wissmann's map.

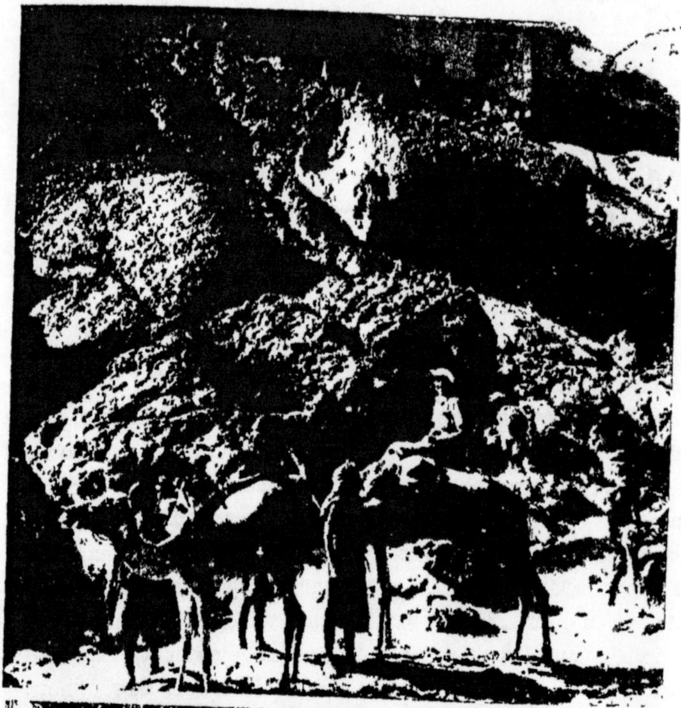

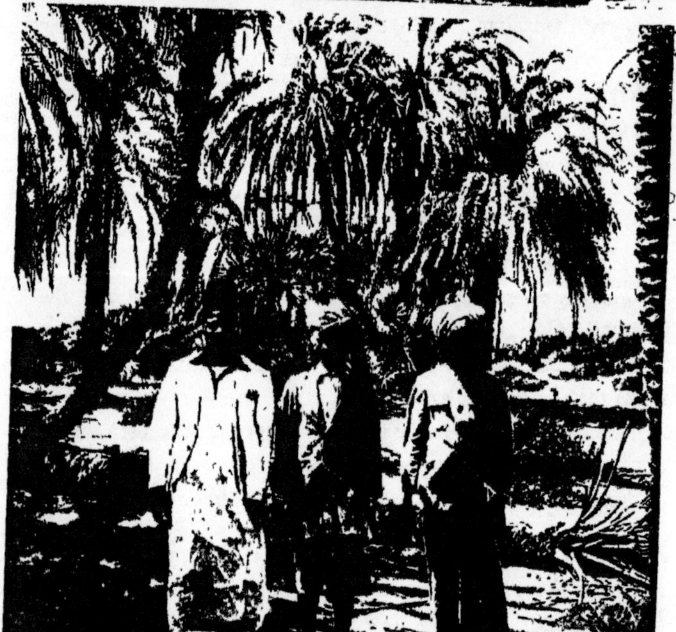

Rumeidan, which we found. This was the residence of Tannaf, the principal chief of the Al Baqi Msellem of the Sei'ar. From the air I saw plainly that just before Qa' al Fadhul we were over the northern watershed, from which deep-cut short wadis ran south-south-west to the Hadhramaut and long shallow ones in an east-north-easterly direction to the sands. There was very little habitation over this part of the country, and most of the inhabitants lived in caves.

After just over forty minutes' flying from Shibam we found ourselves between two short wadis that ran out into a broad channel of sand which it took us two minutes to cross, and beyond it was a broken mass of rock that stretched away to the north-east. The channel itself ran out into the desert just west of the course of the flight, and the distance from Shibam to this point was calculated at sixty-nine miles. The visibility was perfect. Air Commodore McClaughry, who was with the flight, noted the high mass of the Seiban mountains at least one hundred miles away to the south. To the north an unbroken sea of sand stretched wave on wave far away to the horizon, coloured with a rosy red that was quite unforgettable and quite unbelievable. It was about three-quarters of an hour short of noon local time, so that the colour owed nothing to early morning light. After a few minutes over the desert we turned back to Shibam. The same afternoon, Seiyid Bubakr asked me to go with him and one of his brothers and a son to Qabr Hud, where the great annual pilgrimage to the tomb of the Prophet was in progress. When we had gone there on foot in December, 1934, the place was empty; now it was crowded. We flew there in the Arabian Airways machine chartered by Seiyid Bubakr, and this, as he said, was the first pilgrimage by air.

Next morning we left Seiyun at a quarter to nine on an almost due northerly course. On this outward flight the same facts were observed, deep short ravines that ran nearly south to the Hadhramaut, and more shallow wadis that ran almost east-north-east past the paler-coloured jōls of the watershed to the sands. In the upper reaches of the southern system we saw a few poor settlements of the 'Awamir and a caravan of some fifty camels plodding its way southward.[1] After exactly an hour and a quarter's

---

[1] The whole jōl from west to east was heavily scored with well-marked tracks and I noted, as I had also noted on aeroplane journeys over the Wadi Maseila, that east of our course and some fifty miles north of the wadi as it went towards Qabr Hud, there was a considerable rise in the ground, almost a range of mountains. This was probably the Jebel al Wuti of Von Wissmann's map.

*D. (on camel) in Sei'ar country*
*Zaidi, Salim, and Ganess*

*Sei'ar chiefs*
  *Nazir bin Muhammad*
  *Awadh bin Tannaf*

*Suleiman bin Yeslem*
*Muhammad bin Musaid*

'ar types

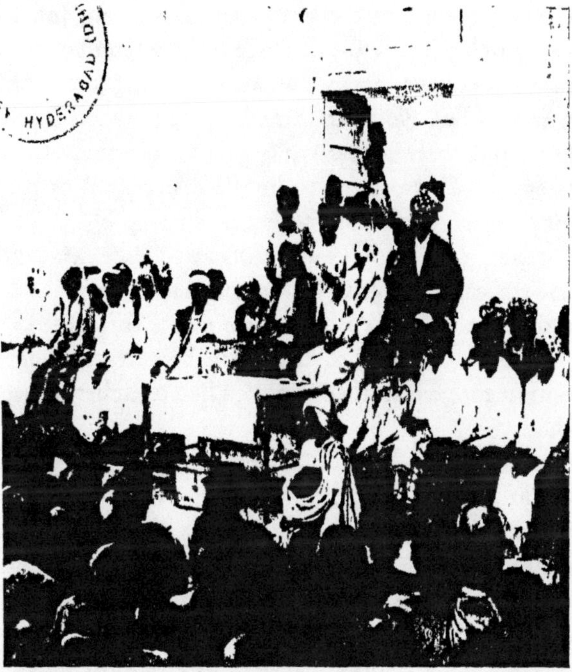

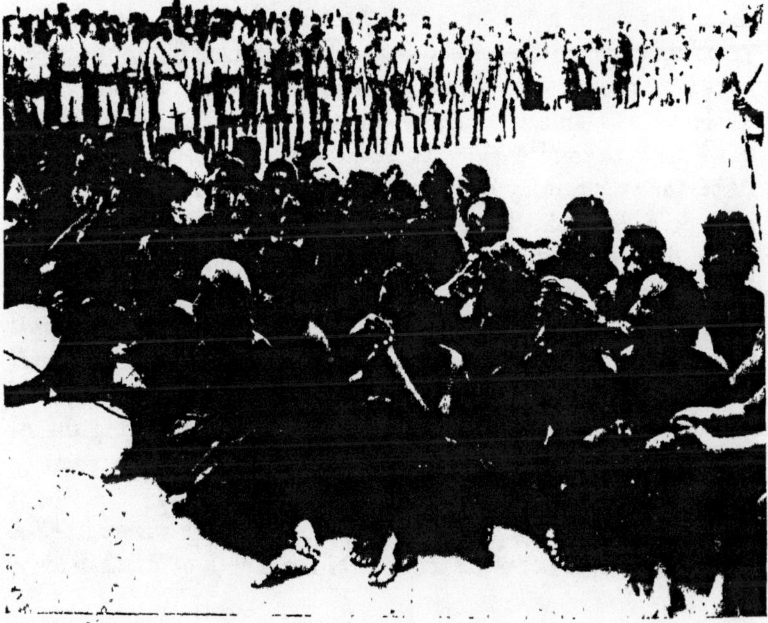

passed over the edge of the steppe and the desert, just by a con-
arge white patch of sand, the distance from Seiyun being calculated
iles. Again there was the same wonderful sight of endless rosy
sand, though when we were directly over the sand I noticed that
ich ochre. Just west of the white patch a channel of desert sand
ito the steppe. This proved to be the eastern end of the channel
en the day before, separating a long broken-up island jōl from the
. Its situation and shape were sufficiently like Madagascar for
it that, and the name seems to have stuck in local usage. We turned
ls along the line that just divided the desert from the steppe and
ie larger wadis ran out into the sand there were wide stretches
ed vegetation that from the air looked like stretches of green scum
the sand.

ie western end of the "island," much broken with gulfs and with
inds lying off it in the desert, our flight turned to the south-west, a
he west of the point which had been reached on the previous day's
ssance, and we explored the western part of the Sei'ar country, the
of the Al Hatim of which Bin Jerbu'a and Bin Mulhi were the
This was the heart of the Reidat as Sei'ar, and turned out to be
gly thickly populated and cultivated. On almost every bank of
is were villages consisting of the usual type of Hadhramaut beduin
ierate dars, with a tall tower in the centre, and small contiguous
, each called a Beit, clustered round it. Subsequent flights made this
very familiar, and with the aid of a Sei'ar, one of the most intelligent
guides, I was able to identify almost all the dars. On several
is we flew beyond Reidat as Sei'ar over uninhabited steppe to
l'Abr, and on clear days saw Shabwa away in the distance.

r the Sei'ar had raided the Minhali camels, the rest of Hadhramaut
to ban them from their places, though they insisted that something
; done as they would be in great difficulties if the Sei'ar should attack
nd they had to retaliate. I therefore invited the four principal
f the Sei'ar to come down and discuss "peaceful arrangements."
aid that the Minhali camels would have to be restored, but that if
ilhi, the chief who was mainly responsible for encouraging the Al
la bin 'Aun in their loot, was unable to compel the restoration he
at any rate come down and help in any way possible.
messenger returned in due course with favourable answers. The
ill said they would come on the fifth of the month of Break-fasting,

i.e. five days after the end of Ramadhan. It was odd they should talk of Break-fasting for they never fast. Nor do they pray, as they have themselves told me. Once Seiyid Bubekr asked them why they did not fast and they said: "Your grandfather (i.e. the Prophet himself) told our grandfather that we needn't as we had saved him from his enemies."

On the appointed date came Tannaf bin Seheil Ba Rumeidan and 'Aidha bin Terjem, the two chiefs of the Al Baqi Msellem, but there was no sign of Bin Mulhi and Bin Jerbu'a the Al Hatim chiefs. We all took a fancy to the Al Baqi Msellems and their party and after a few cordial days they went away having promised every sort of assistance, and left a young sheikh as their "consul," as he was called in Seiyun, with whom we could discuss matters. Curiously enough, without any prompting they begged we should make landing-grounds in their country to facilitate future visits.

Like all beduin the Sei'ars are really remarkably acute. At least one of them thought I was very simple. I suppose he had never heard of Castles in Spain, but he came up to me at a conference and whispered: "I've got seven wells in the Rub' al Khali of which nobody else knows the existence. I'll sell them to you cheap if you like and I'm sure you'll make a good profit out of it."

The Al Hatim had been "got at." Unfortunately Sultan 'Ali bin Salah, a weak though charming personality, had turned sour and for the hope of gain, which he could never resist, had started intriguing against the peace and encouraging the mercenary Yafa'is. As the Al Hatim told us later they had been convinced they had only to appear in Seiyun to have their throats cut.

A further letter was sent telling them that they must come and that if they did not they would be held responsible for the raiding and suffer air action. This brought them down to the wadi. The threatened date for air action came near, but they were plagued by messengers telling them the usual lying stories of what would happen to them if they came to Seiyun. On the eve of the date fixed, I went out to find them and after a long day's chase in a car from village to village where they had been heard of, I ran them to earth at Al Qara, north of Shibam. I found them in a state of complete panic and Seiyid Bubakr and I did our best to reassure them. Finally I gave a pledge "on my face" that nothing but honourable treatment would be accorded to them in Seiyun and Bin Mulhi came in the car with us to Seiyun.

## SEEKING AN ALTERNATIVE TO AIR ACTION

t was late at night when we got back but we dined and in the morning
k coffee together and we showed him he had nothing to fear. Thinking
eep 'Ali bin Salah under my eye, I had picked him up at Al Qatn, on
previous day's paperchase, and he was there in Seiyun too. After
kfast Seiyid Bubakr and I took him to see Sultan 'Ali bin Mansur, and
n we came out of the palace a car drove up with 'Ali bin Salah's principal
ator in it, a fat Nahdi called Bin 'Abri. They whispered together and
bin Salah then told me he had to get back to Shibam, as there was a
1di case. I doubted it, but let him go. Later Seiyid Bubakr and I
rned home and found Bin Mulhi gone!

It transpired Bin 'Abri had been there and talked to him and later we
nt again that he had been told by him that arrangements were being
le to slaughter him in the market-place. I straightway sent Nasir
dulla and some soldiers to bring the rest of the Sei'aris at Al Qara to
/un, as I wanted if possible to avoid the necessity of bombing their
:es. Next morning they came back with all the Sei'aris except the
er chief, Bin Jerbu'a. He had been in such a panic that he had got out of
vatory window in the night and fled.

The companions of the chiefs were ashamed of their behaviour and
:red to write that they should be put to death. They said that in any
nt they would be deposed. They agreed themselves to stay as hostages
Seiyun, and we gave them a house and did them proud.

After this there was no alternative. As he had declined to come and
1r himself of the charge of inciting the Abdulla bin 'Aun, Bin Mulhi, after
:ry possible warning, had his house knocked down. If we had not done
we should of course have been called bluffers again. There were no
ualties and it was an excellent object lesson, approved by the Hadhramaut
1 even by the other Sei'aris themselves.

The next thing was Al 'Abr itself where the guilty Al 'Abdulla bin 'Aun
re reputed to be. The Al Baqi Msellem had given us permission, as far
they were concerned, to occupy it and put a post there to protect the
lls and the travellers. On our part we undertook that the garrison
)uld not interfere with the beduin on their lawful occasions.

So one afternoon Seiyid Bubakr and another friend and I started off in a
: for Al 'Abr. We took also two lorries of retainers and workmen. The
ainers were of the Mukalla Regular Army and intended as garrison, and
: workmen from Tarim had all the material to rebuild the ruined fort.
Our plans were kept secret till the last possible minute and the lorries

went ahead. Seiyid Bubakr and I arrived at Henin about sunset and after prayers started off westwards. Dr. Pike, who with Mr. Wofford had arrived a month or two before to conduct a geological survey, had driven part of the way and we followed his tracks for a start. Those made by Mr. Philby had, of course, disappeared. It was difficult finding the way in the dark, but we caught up the lorries at half-past eight and all of us sat down to dine together, just near the village of Sur and under the two mountains called Thukmein, which form a conspicuous landmark from the air for a radius of seventy or eighty miles around. This was twenty-seven miles from Henin, and we were in a country with which there had been practically no contact. It must have been alarming to the beduin: a noisy party in lorries, which they had never seen before, and ourselves in cars, shouting directions to each other in the night and firing Verey lights to show each other the way; but the beduin materialized out of the darkness, most surprisingly without rifles, directed us time and again on our way, and pushed our cars out of the sand. Of course no one knew I was there—and no one knew Seiyid Bubakr. On one of these pushing parties I heard Seiyid Bubakr say to some of the beduin: "Why aren't you frightened, and why haven't you got rifles?"

"Why should we be frightened?" one said, "we walk in the peace of God and the peace of Ingrams."

After Thukmein, which we left about half-past eleven, we had no great difficulty in moving on as the moon was up. We drove on for some hours and then stopped to let the rest of the party come up. It was bitterly cold and the keen wind cut through us as we huddled together trying to sleep on the sand, but we did sleep and woke to a marvellous dawn. The sunset of the night before, the brilliant moon, and the sunrise are three enduring memories of that night.

The four flat-topped hills of Al 'Abr lay about ten miles ahead of us, and although only one of the lorries had arrived, the other having had one of its many breakdowns, we decided to go on. It was hard sand on which a speed of 50 m.p.h. was easy and we quickly left the lorry behind. We made our way into the wadi bed, myself acting as guide as I was the only one who knew the country even from the air. There were one or two Bureiki sheikhs about with camels, and rather reluctantly they told us that the 'Abdulla bin 'Aun were also there with the camels. A few minutes' driving up the hard wadi brought us to the ruins of the fort, said by the Al 'Abdulla bin 'Aun to have been built by them.

he dozen or so beduin round the well looked extremely surprised
the car drew up. I suppose they were hardly awake, as the morning
still chilly and they were all wearing their sheepskin coats. A few
iki sheikhs came down and bade us welcome. The rest of the beduin
ed to belong to every tribe except the 'Abdulla bin 'Aun. Some said
were sheikhs, some claimed to be Daham, a Yemeni tribe, and some
i, but there were a good many shifty looks and in the course of the
ning we sorted out nine who had given themselves away and who
ly admitted to belonging to this raiding section. There were only
-three males all told of the 'Abdulla bin 'Aun, but from the amount
ouble they had given in the past it was well worth getting them under
rol. They had no houses or settled habitation and were about the
people of the Hadhramaut who had goatskin tents.
When the lorries came up I installed the wireless and settled the garrison
temporary quarters. There was nothing at Al 'Abr except the ruined
, of which only one wall still stood, a small stone murabba'a, one of the
: cube-shaped shelters used by travellers all over the Hadhramaut, and
it built of branches of trees and grass of which there was a great profusion.
:re was also a new weli's tomb decorated with ibex horns, and one of the
eiki sheikhs took us there and slapping the tomb addressed its lately
onized occupant and introduced us. We put the garrison into the
is hut, as the murabba'a was occupied by a woman who had been bitten
a snake and the sheikh asked us not to disturb her: it was part of her
itment that she should not be seen. A thin trail of ash had been sprinkled
nd the building to keep other snakes away.
During the day we collected more of the 'Abdulla bin 'Aun who came
l watched us from a distance in little groups. Somehow they seemed
be fascinated by us, for although they would not come when we shouted
them, they made no attempt to move or to resist when we walked over
them and told them to come along with us. Few of them were armed,
1 neither were we until the garrison came along. There were a couple
wells in commission and I was told that at one time there had been as
iny as eighty-one. Some of the beduin showed us on the wall of a cliff
le columns of holes bored in soft stone. You counted up the holes and
en stepping that number of paces from the column found yourself on a
:ried well.
Having explored the neighbourhood of the fort we went to see the
e for a landing-ground which had been previously decided on from the

## TROUBLE WITH THE SEI'AR AND OTHER TRIBES

air. Unfortunately it had to be at some little distance from the fort—two or three miles—but it was a marvellous landing-ground and greatly pleased the Royal Air Force when they came along later in the day and flew Seiyid Bubakr and myself back to Seiyun.

On later visits I had the opportunity of seeing all the surrounding country from the air, and I was struck by the truth of the saying that Al 'Abr is the "Key of the Hadhramaut," for, behind the mountain, tracks radiated out in all directions to Nejran, the Yemen, and Shabwa and the Western Aden Protectorate. From Al 'Abr eastwards there was only the one track. I visited Al 'Abr five times on the ground and passed over it many times by air, and on each occasion I was struck by the large number of caravans which halted there for water. For a week or two after our occupation there was some falling off, as the beduin were not certain of our intentions, but after that they seemed to come in greater numbers than before; they had a sense of security which was previously lacking when the Al 'Abdulla bin 'Aun were constantly looting. I myself, as well as responsible Hadhrami, believed that before long a town would spring up there, as it formed an ideal place for a market and there was plenty of good water.[1]

The skilled builders from Tarim set to work at once to rebuild the fort. They also opened another well or two and I hoped that if the money could be found we would eventually open more, for the beduin greatly appreciated these increased facilities.

Among the visitors who came were a large number of women. Thereabouts they were unveiled and talked fearlessly and freely with me. I found these girls very charming and full of courage. They thought nothing of journeys alone with camels across the desert, from the Jof for instance, and it was the women throughout the Hadhramaut who most appreciated the peace.

In due course the Al Hatim came in with the two chiefs, Bin Mulhi and Bin Jerbu'a, now deposed, and the two candidates they proposed to elect

[1] The Wadi Hadhramaut is certainly one of the most extraordinary river beds in the world for it must be at least forty miles from its northern or left bank to its southern or right bank at its source near Al 'Abr. It narrows rapidly to four miles or so at Henin and at its mouth near Seihut is about 200 yards wide. Politically Al 'Abr proved a most useful place, for it enabled me to keep easy touch with our own beduin tribes such as the Nahd, Sei'ar, Kerbi and Al Bureik, and also enabled me to make friendly contacts with our neighbours such as the Daham and 'Abida. These latter tribes asked me to extend the peace to them, but I could only reply that they must apply to the Imam of Yemen.

:ir places. They gave declarations that they would assist in preserving
eace and confirmed the arrangement by which we kept a post at Al
. So all ended well and from that day to this there has been no trouble
with the Sei'ar, but they have on the contrary been uniformly friendly
elpful.

* * * *

While the Sei'ar affair was being finished I had also to deal with two
ages of some importance.

The first was concerned with the long-standing grouse of the people of
m against the Tamimi tribe. Tarim lies under the north wall of the
li Hadhramaut, just before the great wadi becomes the Maseila. West
t is the Wadi 'Aidid and to the north-east Dammun. In the Wadi
lid is the tomb and shrine of Mola 'Aidid and the suburb called after
. This is Kathiri territory, but the other suburb is Tamimi and as far
t as 'Awamir borders and east of Tarim to Manahil borders lies Tamimi
ntry. The Tamimi are a Qu'aiti tribe so that Tarim is a Kathiri island.
also is the little walled village of Al Ghuraf, west of Tarim on the road to
yun. Within the walls of Tarim is another "state." This enclosure,
ich contains a few houses inhabited by the Seiyids of Al Haddad, is ruled
their mansab under some ancient right. His subjects are completely
der his jurisdiction, and even if they commit offences in the city of Tarim
: not tried by the Sultan but handed over to him. The intelligentsia of
rim call him the *Baba* (the Pope) and his state the *Fatikana*.

Though Tarim is a garden city there is no room in it for extensive
ltivation, so the people have their date gardens in Tamimi country outside.
ere are no beduin sections to the Tamimi, and they all live in the wadi
d emigrate largely to East Africa and the East Indies. They are, however,
astonishingly disunited tribe whose sections were constantly warring
ainst each other, mostly over land questions. Of course the Tamimi,
ing tribesmen, carried arms, while the Seiyids and townsmen of Tarim
ere without them.

A long time ago the Tamimi started an institution called 'Shaim, which
as really a complete replica of a Chicago racket. A Tamimi would come
ong to a garden owner and say: "That's a nice garden of yours, but there
re a lot of thieves about, you know. Give me so much per cent of the
rop and I'll look after it." The Tarim gentleman realized he had no
ption and gradually the racket grew, till of late years as much as 75 per cent,
nd in many cases 100 per cent of the crop was taken as "protection fees."

## TROUBLE WITH THE SEI'AR AND OTHER TRIBES

In no case that I met was less than 25 per cent taken. Furthermore, although the trees were acknowledged the property of the owners, they could only sell them with permission of the Shaim holders, and could not cut them down even if they wanted to.

With the peace this had to stop, though I felt it reasonable that if proper agreements were made the Tamimi might suitably be appointed as watchmen. I therefore arranged for a Board of independent non-date owners to examine all the cases, and those who were accused of illegality were summoned to appear. With one exception they came and admitted that their proceedings were unlawful. The exception was brought in by the police. As he resisted by arms a fine was levied and he was threatened with the demolition of his house if he refused to come peaceably. He came and paid. New agreements were then made providing for a reasonable remuneration for genuine protection.

The second incident that occurred at this time was a series of outrages by different sections of the Hamumi tribe on the Al Kaf road. There were five cases of shooting on cars and looting, and two murders, including one of our Qu'aiti Governor of Gheil Ba Wazir. At the same time there were also two camel caravans looted by the Hamumi.

I was at a loss to understand these, for I was on excellent terms with the Hamumi chief, and they had no reason to interfere with the traffic on the road, because, as I have explained, every possible care was taken to protect their own traffic. I wrote at once to 'Ali bin Habreish asking him to come and to discuss a settlement at once before matters got more serious. Unfortunately the trouble had been stirred up by agitators, in particular the Yafa'i, who were hoping that they would be called in, as in the past, and paid vast sums of money in cash and arms to settle the trouble.

It was an outrage that had to be dealt with and the Hamumi chiefs were summoned to answer the charges. They failed to appear and air action was undertaken after the usual warnings had been given. As the people are practically all beduin and nomadic, these warnings took time to deliver. One day during the bombing I went myself to an empty wadi round which it was known that there were Hamumi of the guilty sections, and I compared my feelings with those I had experienced when I was in Hazebroucke being bombed by Taubes during the war. A small bomb was first dropped in the wadi, where the only signs of life I could see were a few goats. After giving anybody who might have been in the neighbourhood enough time to get a long way away, five machines spent half an hour dropping bombs

andy wadi bed. The noise was terrific and multiplied by those echo-
ls, but on this particular day no damage was done. It seems strange
)lice bombing such as this can have the effect it does, but discussing it
ribesmen who have been bombed, the fact of the matter is that it is
ie noise, the moral effect, which makes them surrender, for they
what it would be like if the bombs fell on them.

e fine imposed on the whole Hamumi tribe was 100 camels and 100
and, as usual, twice the amount of loot taken. This amounted to a
deal—about 6,000 rupees worth in all. The operations produced the
l effect, though unfortunately there were three casualties. When,
ver, it is considered that we were up against the whole tribe of about
armed men and operating over 3,000 square miles of territory, it is
kable there were not more, and is a fine testimony to the care the
l Air Force take to avoid damage to human life. The Hamumis
elves thought nothing of the casualties and they themselves had
two men.

ie chiefs of the ten Hamumi sections came into Shihr with all the loot,
)f the fine, two hostages from each section and the miscreants. There
he usual surrender ceremony and they fully admitted the justice of
had been done. We made friends and I gave them periods up to
a month in which to pay the balance. It was all paid in the time fixed
nstead of 100 rifles, 270 were brought as the people said they had no
of rifles if there was going to be security. The balance of the rifles
some extra camels were allowed against the cash fine. The actual
lerers were tried and sentenced by His Highness's court to imprisonment
fe.

n interesting feature of the Hamumi operations was again the whole-
ed co-operation of the tribesmen and townsmen against the offenders,
the economic blockade, which was willingly enforced by the people
hihr and the Hadhramaut and the neighbouring tribes, was a great
r in compelling their speedy submission.

While I was in Shihr negotiating final terms with the Hamumi, a Seiyid
d brought me a document which shewed that these were not the only
)tiations going on at the time. The document, which had just been
:luded by the Seiyids of Shihr, was a sort of treaty of alliance by husbands
nst the extravagance of wives. My friend told me that the Seiyids
: always having trouble with their wives who were trying to outvie
other in dresses and in entertainment, much to the detriment of their

## TROUBLE WITH THE SEI'AR AND OTHER TRIBES

husbands' pockets. The treaty was an agreement, signed, sealed and delivered, that in future no husband would spend more than, I think, ten dollars on a dress for his wife or more than two dollars on the "elevenses" she provided for her lady friends. I heard later that the ladies had been quite equal to the occasion and agreed that if any husband refused his wife the frock she wanted, all the wives would refuse their favours to their husbands.

## Chapter XXXII

## THE SOCIAL ROUND

*Therefore doth heaven divide
The state of man in divers functions,
Setting endeavour in continued motion;*   SHAKESPEARE.

[WRI]TING of the events between November 1936 and April 1938, when I [wen]t on leave, has given me the feeling of living them all over again, and [the s]peed at which I have written brings back the speed at which I lived them. [As I] look back I seem to have been continually on the move, on ship or [boa]t, on camel or donkey, in an aeroplane or in a car—once even in a [pala]nquin. Weary of mind and body, footsore, never getting away from [tri]bal politics, dashing to stop one trouble, with another starting. On [the] road I would be stopped constantly with requests to settle disputes [ove]r a camel, a goat or a piece of land. In houses where I stayed the same [wou]ld happen though the disputes were usually more serious. Never [bein]g off duty, night or day, sleeping hard and eating anything, I acquired [whe]n travelling a power of more or less immobilising my body, so that I [kne]w unaware of it though my thoughts were seldom at rest. Some sort [of] discipline like this was essential if one was to endure the hot endless [jour]neys up and down the wadis and the Al Kaf road. These journeys [wer]e rarely uneventful. Accidents usually happened on the long dry [stre]tch between Heru and Tarim: once it was two burst tyres and a cut [hea]d as I was flung against the roof: once it was only six punctures: and [onc]e when Sir Bernard came up the road some of the cars broke down and [the] occupants were reduced to drinking radiator water. On New Year's [Eve] my car dried up at eleven-fifteen at night, twenty-three miles from [Tar]im. I walked it thinking that most people I knew had probably chosen [mo]re pleasant ways of welcoming the New Year, though D. was having a [sea]sick passage in a dhow to Aden. Every now and then I lay down [exh]austed on the roadside and slept till the cold drove me on. I got to [Ta]rim at eight-fifteen in the morning; and now whenever I get to the top [of] the aqaba and the first sight of the city I remember the quotation: "Tarim and then thou desirest no more." Often D. came with me, but often she was tied to the office at Mukalla. She, too, had a fair share of mishaps. Once she and Zahra, of whom more later, made a forced landing in an aeroplane between Aden and Mukalla. I got her message by a fisherman at four in the afternoon, having waited hours for her on the landing-ground, and by means of car and donkey reached the party at 2 a.m. on a barren piece of coast where they were sleeping under the wings of the machine. We returned in the morning to Mukalla by a small fishing-boat.

Much of our time was spent in Mukalla. Like every seaport it is thoroughly cosmopolitan and in its bazaars you find representatives of Arabs from all the coastal parts of South Arabia and the Red Sea and Persian Gulf, as well as Somalis and other Africans. One curious strain of not infrequent visitors were the long-bearded Mongolian pilgrims who would flourish incomprehensible Chinese passports at me and, speaking no Arabic or other language which could be understood locally, would appear to demand onward travel facilities. There were quite a number of Indian visitors and residents too, including Banian shopkeepers, and in the upper layer of Mukalla society the various races, Indian and Arab, mixed quite happily. We all attended each other's parties and the Government servants of Mukalla started a good club. Amongst various festive occasions one of the best was the celebrations for the Coronation. The streets and house-tops were gay with flags and I can remember no more beautiful sight than the illuminations that night. The Palace, the Residency, the Government Offices and the principal mosques were outlined in coloured lights. That night I imagine Mukalla burnt almost as much incense as Pliny complained of Nero burning at the funeral of Poppæa. Almost every house that had no coloured lights heaped incense in piles along its roof parapets, and the coloured lights and the flaming incense were wonderfully reflected in the waters of the harbour, while clouds of smoke filled the streets with a sweet-scented fog and completely obliterated the smell of the dried fish. Soon afterwards Mukalla was reflected in the water every night, for electric light was introduced and the greenish glow of the street lights was visible far away.

Sometimes in Mukalla we took an afternoon off from the office and went picnicking up the Du'an road, never more lovely than after the rains, when the hills are green and the streams run down by grassy pastures against a background of purple distances and rugged cloud-topped mountains.

A day or two after the Coronation we started up inland on a journey ch was intended to be more social than political, for our old friend Ahmed Hussein, the mansab of Meshhed, had pressed upon me an invitation he great fair.

We stopped at Shiheir—Little Shihr—on our first day to have lunch ı Salih 'Ali al Khulaqi, who had been a constant friend since our first ney round the Hadhramaut. His little garden I have described before, it was there, under the shade of the coco-nuts with a slight breeze wing, the ground laid with mats and carpets and plenteous cushions, : we had our al fresco lunch to which there were some twenty guests. On the way we stayed in that happy family atmosphere of Seiyid ɔakr's house. Many people have enjoyed his kindly hospitality in the : as Salaam, and during the hot weather nothing was more delightful n to sit in the swimming-pool in the evening and listen to the strains the B.B.C. Empire Orchestra. (When the Arabic broadcasts started y were extremely popular throughout the Hadhramaut, and people re soon setting their watches by Big Ben.) Bathing over, dinner would laid on carpets by the side of the bathing-pool. We rarely sat down than twenty at meals in Seiyid Bubakr's house, and very often it was ty.

I left D. at Seiyun. They, too, had had Coronation festivities of which heard the account. Seiyid Bubakr told me that the small boys in the vn had been convinced that the celebrations were for my wedding! I not hear who the bride was.

Driving on to Meshhed, I saw a sight at Al Qatn which seemed a full ompense for all the recent trouble we had had. The whole width of the di was green from side to side with a waving sea of well-grown millet. ver, I was told, in the history of the Hadhramaut had such a sight been n, for the constant warfare had prevented it. Peace followed by rain had de it possible.

At Meshhed I had a great welcome from old friends and the mansab's ther lent us a house where we had continual receptions. Throughout : two days of the fair parties came in from all sides, and each of the portant new arrivals had a ceremonial entry into the village. In our turn : were met outside by the mansab with his banners, drums, and a vast wd of singers and sightseers. The mansab had a number of small rtars for which a phenomenal amount of gunpowder must have been d. Every time a gun went off it was blown several yards away and , of course, added to the entertainment. I was taken on a solemn procession to the tombs of the saints and introduced to each of them separately. The Fatiha was recited and the mansab, with typical courtesy and generosity, introduced me to them as "Ingrams whom God hath sent to bring peace to the Hadhramaut."

When this was over we repaired outside the tombs and made speeches on the benefits of peace to the assembled beduin. After our respective receptions we all turned out in a mass to greet later arrivals and followed them round on their visitations. The amount of dust I swallowed in those two days seemed unbelievable, but it was a happy visit and drew me closer to these kind people who had made me so much one of the family.

Amongst the various things I settled in Seiyun was a case of slavery which came to light and which was to concern particularly D. and myself. A Kathīri section had owned a male runaway slave of a Thelūd Yafa'i section and the latter had a female runaway slave of the former. The affair had caused a regular feud and on a previous visit I had directed, at Seiyid Bubakr's suggestion, that both should hand the slaves over to me. They were now in Seiyun and I decided that both should be freed but that neither might return either to the original owners or to the ones with whom they had sought refuge. The male slave was the genuine African variety, but the woman was a tribeswoman of the Sei'ar and should never have been enslaved. Early in her life her father had died leaving her and her blind sister to the care of a seiyid "friend." When the girl grew up we discovered that her guardian had sold her and that she had passed from hand to hand. Now she was still only about twenty and had a little daughter of about one year old. The child was a pathetic little object. It looked as if she was not long for this world as a result of malnutrition and neglect. She had bad rickets, her tiny legs and arms were like match-sticks and her distended tummy had flopped from lack of condition. She could not stand and sat cross-legged in silence all day long, when her mother was not feeding her, for she was not yet weaned. The mother did not want her. I asked her what she did want and she hung her head and said "I want a man." So D. and I agreed to take the child. A document was drawn up, which said she was transferred from her mother's conscience (on which I am afraid she had never been a burden) to mine, signed and witnessed and sealed by the Sultan. And thereupon Hassan Shaibi and I sallied forth to the Seiyun bazaar to buy her clothes and toys.

She howled at us impartially for several days and we referred to her as Jemima. There were great consultations with the harem and with Seiyid ubakr as to what she should be called and finally we fixed on Zahra. What feed her on was a problem, for neither D. nor I knew what was appropriate; it recollections of advertisements in London omnibuses came to me and e wired for a consignment of Glaxo and cod-liver oil. Under this treatment she thrived and was soon crawling all over the place. Now she has become a normal child. Watching her develop into a noisy ordinary baby made me reflect that it was probably only their tummies which caused the præternatural gravity of most Arab children, for there was nothing to distinguish Zahra's activities when she regained her health from those of European children. Objectively Zahra represents an experiment in long-range educational policy! The idea is that she should be brought up as a doctor, but as things are it seems more likely she will become an Arab Shirley Temple, as she is a complete little mimic and she has large gazelle-like eyes with long lashes which should be the envy of a film producer. It may yet be that we shall be able to retire and be kept by Zahra.

I was not the only one to think there was profit in her. Her male parentage was doubtful. Mama said her father was a sheikh of the Al Bureik. Seiyid Bubakr said that was probable as her hair is bronze-coloured and not black, and the Bureikis are said to have that coloured hair. Anyway there were several claimants for the honour of being father. It looked as there might be money in it. The Yafa'is at Mukalla had instigated one of them, and an intercepted letter said that "she was now a Christian." Poor little Zahra, at two years old! Needless to say when the time comes Zahra will be brought up in the faith of her forebears, and if she has nothing much to thank them for, she can always be proud of being a daughter of Kinda, the ancestor of the earliest of Hadhrami kings and of the Sei'ar tribe.

At Mukalla entertainment, Arab and European, increased with Arab inner-parties, and the visits of the Royal Air Force and other guests. It was a great pleasure to see Freya Stark come back again with Miss Caton Thompson, whom I had met years before, and Miss Gardner. The Hadhramaut soon called them all by their Christian names, and I did not know who Seiyid Bubakr was referring to when he spoke of Ali Nur until I realized how well Eleanor translated. Adela Broome was, of course, 'Adila: I often think how much her presence helped us in the days of Hamumi wars and Yafa'i intrigues. D. and I were worn to a frazzle, but Adela brought an air of calm and peace with her and it seemed infinitely restful to sit after dinner and watch her doing something so normal as knitting while we

## Chapter XXXIII

## PRESENT AND FUTURE

*New times demand new measures and new men;
The world advances, and in time outgrows
The laws that in our fathers' day were best;
And, doubtless, after us, some purer scheme
Will be shaped out by wiser men than we.*

LOWELL.

WHEN I began this story the term Hadhramaut was itself an amorphous conception, and the Governments of its Sultans vague and undefined. Though there was a Government of Mukalla, it might have been difficult for anyone used to governments in the ordinary sense, to recognize it as one. From the time of the signature of the Treaty of 1937 the term meant the Qu'aiti Sultan as advised by his Resident Adviser, and gradually under His Highness's leadership organized Government departments grew up, with departmental heads responsible for them. The Government took a definite, though constantly developing, form on the 1st April, 1939, when its first budget came into force. The estimates provide now for a civil list to H.H. the Sultan, Secretariat, Provincial Administration, Treasury, Customs and Harbour, Judiciary, Police, Prisons, Army, Medical Services, Education, Agriculture, Electricity, Public Works, and other services common to any Government or peculiar to the needs of the Qu'aiti State.

In February 1939 the Kathiri Sultan too signed a treaty on the lines of the Malay Treaties, by which he undertook to follow the advice of the Resident Adviser in all matters except those concerning Muhammadan religion and custom, and so the term Government of Seiyun took on a meaning which it had not had before. In fact there never had been any Government in the Kathiri State and progress there has not been so rapid as in the Qu'aiti State, owing to lack of staff.

The same month happily saw the conclusion of an Anglo-Qu'aiti-Kathiri Agreement reconstituting the Qu'aiti-Kathiri Agreement of 1918 and removing the sore points of the old agreement. Thus the hatchet, in fact buried this year or even earlier, now received ceremonial interment.

and incidentally it may be mentioned that at the same time an agreement for a postal union between the Colony of Aden and the Hadhramaut States was signed.

For several years the term Hadhramaut has been taken to mean politically the territory included in the Qu'aiti State of Shihr and Mukalla and the Kathīri State of Seiyun and these two States are now referred to as the Hadhramaut States. It has been necessary to import some trained officials from other dependencies for some of the more important posts in their Governments, but for the most part they are staffed by local people who have had little or no experience of Government work, and a tribute is due to them not only for the work they have achieved but for the spirit of loyalty and trust they show towards the British Residency. In other dependencies, these officials local and imported would no doubt be in subordinate positions, though many would be drawing larger salaries then they do in the Hadhramaut. I feel that to expect real responsibility you have to give it, and to a remarkable extent it is already being accepted. One would have to look far for a finer officer than Subedar Major Lal Khan of the Regular Army, or a man more energetic than his adjutant Ahmed Effendi. (Ahmed Nasir, once the villain of the piece, is now Chief of the Muqaddams of regulars and his political sense is as sound as anybody's. Hamid, his Mondam partner, has remained in private life as much from his own choice as anyone else's, but he is now a great personal friend.) Msellem is still State Treasurer and with the chief accountant Salim as his mainstay now runs his accounts on the orthodox colonial model. 'Alawi al 'Attas of Bureidha manages the electricity department and monthly obtains new customers. Where could we find a better Chief of Customs than Jehan Khan, who drafts his own decrees and what is more has completely reorganized the customs without antagonising the merchants? These names come to me at random, but I could think of many more. I should be very far from claiming that the Mukalla Government was yet efficiently staffed, but the will to carry on is there and the Residency is there to supply the knowledge and experience within the limits of its capabilities.

As time goes on it will be more and more possible for the Residency to restrict itself to purely advisory functions, but I think I can truly say that the help it gives to the local administration is appreciated. The staff of the Residency now consists of the Resident Adviser, a Political Assistant, a Military Assistant and a Secretary, together with seven clerks. A lady child welfare worker has recently joined us and an Arab Educational Assistant

## PRESENT AND FUTURE

is soon about to do so. A Financial Assistant and State Treasurer for Seiyun and perhaps a Medical Assistant will complete the staff. But there is also an Agricultural Officer for the whole Protectorate who spends six months of the year with us. Of course the bulk of the work of the Residency is and will continue to be concerned with the Hadhramaut States, potentially the richest area, but east and west of them there are Sultanates as backward as any to be found in the whole country.

The Protectorate is now divided into two areas, the Western Aden Protectorate and the Eastern Aden Protectorate. The latter consists of the Hadhramaut States, the Wahidi Sultanates of Bir 'Ali and Balhaf, the Mahri Sultanate of Qishn and Soqotra and the Sheikhdoms of 'Irqa and Haura, and apart from his work in the Hadhramaut States, the Resident Adviser is responsible to the Governor of the Protectorate for British relations in all these territories, an area covering between 60,000 and 70,000 square miles, but containing perhaps only 300,000 people. This area is bounded on the west by the Wadi Sanam separating the 'Abdul Wahid tribes from the 'Aulaqi, and on the east by Ras Dharbat 'Ali separating the Mahri from the Qari tribes and the Aden Protectorate from the Sultanate of Muscat and 'Uman.

Here I have tried to tell the story of our travels and labours in the two Hadhramaut States. Though I cannot include it all it is not the whole tale and one or other of us has now visited most if not all the territory. In particular D. made two long solo journeys over partly untravelled country to the heart of Hajr and through Du'an and Reidat ad Deiyin to the Wadi 'Amd and the Wadi Bin 'Ali. Beyond the States we have not been idle. Visits to 'Azzan, one enlivened by crashing in an aeroplane, and Balhaf led to more peaceful conditions there and the acceptance by the Sultans of advisory arrangements which have increased prosperity. In a journey over the main incense road from Bir 'Ali to Shabwa I made many new contacts and broke fresh territory. There have been journeys to Soqotra and up the Mahra coast, even one beyond the Protectorate to Merhat in Dhufar. Figgis and Kennedy also roamed far afield and had adventures in 'Amd and Wahidi country. With the recent travels of Freya Stark, of Van der Meulen and Von Wissman and of Pike and Wofford little of the 70,000 square miles of the Eastern Aden Protectorate has not been seen in the last seven years.

\* \* \*

## Chapter XXXIV

## THE FUTURE OF THE HADHRAMAUT

As I rewrite this last chapter the Empire has been at war for twenty months and one of the most encouraging things to us working in Aden and the Protectorate has been the loyal support of the people, and, even in the darkest hours we have so far gone through, their consistent and steady confidence in our ultimate victory. Day by day during the French collapse and when at our doors our forces had to evacuate Somaliland, the people of the Protectorate never faltered in their belief of final British victory for which constant prayers were said in every mosque. On all the occasions on which His Majesty has called the Empire to prayer special congregations, thousands strong, have met in the mosques of Aden even though the general day of prayer was a Sunday and not a Friday.

It is good, therefore, that in these days when urgent and important matters connected with the actual prosecution of the war take up so much of our time, we should still have been able to continue, even on a lesser scale than we should otherwise have hoped to do, our help to the Hadhramaut, though of course it is only to be expected that progress in war time cannot be the same as it will be after the war.

The Hadhramaut general truce came to an end on the 1st Dhul Hijja 1358—the 11th January 1940. The Hadhramaut leaders did not think it would be possible to achieve the same unanimity in negotiating a further truce. This was not because the people did not want it, in fact after living through such an unprecedented period they were only too anxious for it to continue, but the three years had proved too short to do all that we had hoped to set things on a stable basis and although many cases had been decided and settled a great many of the tribal feuds could not be brought to a satisfactory conclusion in the time. In these cases it would have been difficult to obtain the unanimous consent of all the 1,400 signatories to the first truce formally to accept an extension. However, much canvassing was done and with very few exceptions all the important leaders signed a paper asking the Sultans and Government that the truce should be extended.

341

## THE FUTURE OF THE HADHRAMAUT

The Sultans therefore, supported by the Governor, proclaimed a ten years extension and this extension has been accepted by the vast majority of the tribes and people, though unfortunately there have been two or three cases in which considerable trouble has been caused, notably by 'Ubeid Salih bin 'Abdat of Al Ghurfa and by the wild Hamumi. But still, on the whole, peace is maintained and the number of murders is infinitesimal compared with five years ago.

I propose in this chapter to try and indicate the lines on which one may hope the future will shape itself. I have told how I felt that three years was the minimum period in which the foundations of progress could be laid. With peace gained the immediate objectives were the stabilization of security, ordered finances, and a scheme of agricultural development to give the people an alternative interest to discord and fighting. Social services, the improvement of health and the betterment of education had also to be provided for. In some ways the progress made was phenomenal—ample justification for the belief that the people not only needed but wanted it. The Residency staff was small, but much was nevertheless achieved. But nothing much could have been done if it had not been for the desire of the people and the co-operation of some of their leaders, and here I must pay tribute to the wonderful support and trust that was given to us by His Highness Sir Salih bin Ghalib. If we had had a suspicious unwilling ruler to work for the difficulties would have been endless, but we met with nothing but sympathy and a fine desire to co-operate.

Sultan 'Ali bin Mansur, who to our great sorrow died in 1938, and his brother Ja'far who succeeded him, have been good and loyal friends, but the bulk of the tribal work in the interior was and is still borne by Seiyid Bubakr, wisest of counsellors, best of friends, a man whose like in East or West one rarely meets.

These names are outstanding, but I could quote scores more of people in more or less humble positions who, according to their talents, helped and supported us.

In other ways progress which could have been made was delayed, owing sometimes to lack of funds and sometimes to obstruction, such as that which was encountered at a period from the irregular soldiers. The more serious obstruction disappeared, but lack of ready cash delayed us in work which could have been further advanced than it was. First of the needs of the country before permanent peace could be considered safely blished I placed the stabilization of security. I put this even before ordering of the finance because, cost what it may, in a country used to violence, peace has got to be kept before people can feel secure. ing the truce the peace was kept by political methods, backed only the distant presence of the Royal Air Force, and, as I have explained, one wants to use air control a second longer than is necessary. Nor in event is it practicable to use a sledge hammer to crack a walnut. Our derers were obtained by diplomacy. Luckily there were not many. haps a dozen in the three years compared with the ten a month there l to be in the main wadi alone. But policemen there have got to be justice has to be brought within the reach of everyone. One cannot on for ever settling cases by political means or expect to get judgnts executed without some organized forces.

As far as possible the aim was to build on existing institutions and I 'e already referred to the Mukalla Regular Army, the Irregular soldiers l the Police[1] and some idea of the state of these forces will have been hered from what I have said about them. One of the officers told me t since Sultan 'Umar had said he only required the Regular Army for emonial purposes they had all lost heart. Colonel Robinson's visit l Captain Hopkins' work gave them a new interest. This was followed a weeding out of unfit and unsuitable men, new recruits were taken and increases of pay granted. The force was re-equipped, re-armed and racks were provided out of loan funds and it was given a new outlook yond ceremonial parades. It has however still far to go. Sufficient y cannot yet be afforded to attract the men to a life of whole-time diering and discipline and efficiency are as yet by no means what they ust become. The regular army will be used as a reserve of power hind the ordinary police forces of the Qu'aiti State in cases of emergency d serious disturbances, and although it has still a long way to go to fill this le satisfactorily it has improved very considerably: not only has its own eas of its usefulness changed but others are realizing its importance.

The interior towns of the Qu'aiti State, such as Shibam, 'Einat, Haura, enin, towns in Du'an and Hajr, and the coastal villages beyond Shihr such Hami, Dis and Qusei'ar and many others in the State were always policed irregular soldiers, either Yafa'is or slaves. These irregulars were also

[1] Full details as to the defence forces of the Qu'aiti State and as to the general ndition of the country as it was in 1934 and up to 1936 will be found in olonial No. 123.

## THE FUTURE OF THE HADHRAMAUT

used in tribal areas and if they were Yafa' always caused trouble. There were about 1,400 Yafa' and until Figgis finally drew their teeth in 1938 they were a serious menace to good government. They still need careful handling and are now being gradually transformed into the Qu'aiti Gendarmerie to be used in the policing of Qu'aiti towns and not in tribal areas. The irregulars can usually be relied on for defence purposes in towns where trouble is anticipated and in an Arab country it is often safer to depend on things done in an Arab way rather than a European.

In the Kathiri State there was no sort of organized force till 1937 and the Sultans had merely a large number of undisciplined slaves in the towns (outside them, in tribal areas, they could do nothing) who when so disposed obeyed their orders, though they took their choice within what limits they obeyed them. Early in 1937 the Kathiri Armed Constabulary was formed mainly from these slaves and has since then become uniformed and armed. Shortage of staff has hitherto prevented its progressing much. It is at present nearly 100 strong and it is intended to bring it to a strength of 200 to police Seïyun, Tarim, the villages belonging to the Kathiri Sultan and the roads in between them. It can also be used as a military force if occasion requires.

One small body of men arose out of the Hamumi incident. The Al Kaf road is run independently of both Qu'aiti and Kathiri States. It is an "international" affair and a key road which was also, as will be remembered, a keystone in the new policy approved for the Hadhramaut. The road incidents showed that policing of the road was necessary and we therefore recruited a patrol of six men consisting of representatives of the Hamumi, Ba Hasan Tanbuli, Bin Yemani and Ma'ari, through whose territories the road runs. They are armed, uniformed, mounted on camels, well paid, and under the command of a Shaush obtained from the Aden Protectorate Levies. Their duties are to see that the road fees are paid, to check traffic generally, to see that the beduin do not put up barricades and to provide intelligence of the road and find out the feelings of the beduin towards it. The patrol gives the people themselves a share in the road as their duties include the supervision of those rules made in the beduins' interests regarding the carrying of goods.[1] Incidentally they are intended to be very much "courtesy cops."

It will be seen that the forces now in existence will, when trained, provide for the security of the whole country except for two important

[1] See page 316.

;, the nomadic and semi-nomadic tribes and the settled tribesmen.
country we usually refer to the former as beduin and they are immed-
distinguishable from the rest of the population in that except for the
: tribes, who wear long once-white qamises, they are all painted with
o and wear one black futa round their waists.
1ope it may be possible to recruit from the settled tribesmen themselves
: for each tribe, and already the subject is under discussion. The
in present a different problem and their needs are now being met.
had long heard of the Desert Patrol of the Arab Legion in Transjordan.
: creator, Major Glubb, kindly invited us to stay with him and see
, and in 1938 the Colonial Office generously gave me an extension
we to do so. The Arab Legion is a well-known force and I had read
1eard much of it before I saw it, but after I had seen its Desert Patrol
)gnized that that and the system of tribal control which it operates were
·ly what were required by the beduins of the Hadhramaut. On my
n to Mukalla I showed the Tribal Control laws to friends who could
: and was told that they might have been written for the Hadhramaut.
'he force is indeed a living memorial to the genius of its creator and
ilful blending of organized police and military training with Arab
tion and custom. The men are clothed in a uniform which is simply
larized tribal dress and most impressive they look. An Arab takes
.gn instruction absolutely literally, and here the old maxim that the
.er's best friend is his rifle from which he should never be parted is
n so that even while he eats his meal he holds it in his left hand.
no Arab likes being tied down to a definite period of service, so
he is not tied but good pay and a realization that the Legion is the
of Transjordan keeps him in it. Also no Arab likes our idea of a
:ve by which the Government keeps a hold on him after he has left.
the other hand competition to serve in such a force is naturally so keen
the establishment could be filled several times over and the waiting
becomes, as Major Glubb calls it, a "backwards reserve." The men
t come up for training once a year and mobilization finds no absentees.
The Legion is the beduins' own force into which only the pick of them
accepted. It is well armed and trained. Force has rarely been called
and all its efforts are directed to avoiding it. Suppose that one
1 steals another's camel, an incident of no great rarity in Arabia and one
ch often used to lead to bloodshed. Nowadays the complainant goes to
)st or patrol of the Legion and makes his statement. Legionaries go out

to fetch the defendant and while the complainant waits he stays with the patrol as the guest of the Government. When both parties are present the sergeant hears the trouble, settles the complaint and if both parties are satisfied they sign his decision as accepted and go their ways. If they are not satisfied they can remain as guests until Major Glubb comes along, but he tells me that these days he practically never has an appeal.

But the Legion's activities do not end with this sort of work for teachers are attached to some of the posts who hold schools for the beduin children. There is a doctor of the Legion for the beduin and at each post are men trained to deal with simple diseases and injuries and a supply of drugs. The Legion also improves waterholes and takes an interest in agriculture. In fact there is no aspect of beduin life in which it does not help.

Finally it collects taxes of twelve piastres a year on camels and five on sheep and goats and the sum collected amounts to no less than £50,000 a year. Tribes are told to bring their stock to specified wells at specified times and there they are taxed. Few wait to pay the double taxes demanded of those who fail to turn up. It must have taken a few years for this precision in payment to be attained, but the secret of the matter is of course that practically all the money returns to the beduin in wages and other services.

This description of the Desert Patrol is not really a diversion for it is on those lines that the Hadhrami Beduin Legion, which started its career early in 1940, is being trained to work. Major Glubb generously found the officers from N.C.O.s in the Desert Patrol. Major Northfield, formerly of the Arab Legion, came to Mukalla as military assistant to the Resident Adviser, and the Hadhrami Beduin Legion is now functioning on an experimental basis.

So, Inshallah, security will be provided for, and as security in the Hadhramaut States increases so does the desire for it spread east and west. I have mentioned the beginning of truce in the Balhaf Sultanate and the unruly Dhiyeibi were suppressed in the autumn of 1939. Earlier in the year the Sultans signed an agreement to follow advice and the Customs at Balhaf were put under proper control with an imported clerk. There is now a force of Tribal Guards commanded by an officer of the Aden Protectorate Levies. Balhaf affairs started under the watchful eye of Kennedy, who has travelled over more of the country than any other European.

Towards the end of the three years' peace the most urgent question on the lips of Hadhrami was "would it be permanent," and I have spoken

efforts that have so far been made to make it so and to establish
y. The answer to the question depends of course to a considerable
on whether these security forces can be brought to such a state of
cy that the tribesmen will see that they are sufficient guarantee for
aining peace in the future. When this happens the truce will no doubt
to a permanent peace. That will mean the giving up of arms altogether
h the tribesmen have already seen that their use is far less general
it used to be. There has been some recrudescence of arm bearing
the first three years came to an end, but the market value of arms is
ery low for few buy them. Here in Sana, whence many of the arms
I find that the traffic is negligible compared with what it was a few
ago, and in the Hadhramaut there was no opposition to the promulga-
f decrees controlling the buying and selling of arms and ammunition.
is one even bigger pre-requisite to the establishment of permanent
. The British Government has no intention of setting up direct
h administration in the Hadhramaut and the administration has got
pend on the inhabitants. In 1939 I made an extensive tour of Malaya
udy the Adviser system in the Unfederated States. In the early days
Ialaya the position was much the same as it is to-day in the Aden
ctorate and the people were just as backward as the Hadhrami beduin.
Adviser system in Malaya has proved a wonderful example of co-
ation between the few British Advisers on the one hand and the Rulers
people of Malaya on the other. I do not speak here of the situation
e Federated States for there the system has been a barely disguised
of direct administration. No doubt in its way and in its material
ts this is more efficient but in its intangible results it is not nearly so
ing as the system in the Unfederated States. It is this system that we
at in the Hadhramaut but in order that we may achieve it it is necessary
the rulers and people should give the same co-operation as the Malays
done. As I have stated this co-operation has been willingly and freely
n by the rulers and by such outstanding men as Seiyid Bubakr, but
ne who has worked in Arab countries knows how difficult it is to obtain
peration even in such a comparatively small area of Arabia as the Hadhra-
t. I finished up my tour in Malaya by visiting the Arab communities in
and in Hyderabad. At the latter place I had the pleasure of meeting
Sultan, Sir Salih bin Ghalib, in his Indian home and there His Highness
e recognised leader of the Arab community. There are 80,000 of our
lhrami in the Netherlands East Indies and I visited communities of

them Batavia, Cheribon, Tegal, Pekalongen, Solo and Surabaya. We shall never forget the warmth of the welcome we received nor the very general approval of what we had done in the Hadhramaut and the expressions of gratitude we received for it.

The expressions of gratitude were, as I say, for what we had done and it met with general approval that the British had organized peace in the Hadhramaut. Those we met took the same line as the majority of people in the Hadhramaut, i.e. that if the British would step in, make peace and keep it, everybody would be perfectly happy. There was no suggestion that the people should do otherwise than acquiesce in everything that was of advantage to them, and little thought that they should rouse themselves and co-operate amongst each other to put government on a proper basis. In other words most of the people in the Hadhramaut would much prefer a direct British government which saved them all the trouble. On the other hand a small body of individuals presented a demand for independence of the Hadhramaut on the Egyptian or Iraqi models. The Adviser should restrict himself solely to the function of advising and everything should be left to the two governments with legislative assemblies and all the other trappings of self-governing units. Those who advocated this programme had very little personal experience of the Hadhramaut—some of them none at all. One of the signatories came to me and asked for the independence of a small village of five houses in the Wadi 'Amd. The fact of the matter was, as I pointed out to my advanced friends with the evident approval of others present at the meetings, that there were getting on for 2,000 separate governments in the Hadhramaut—the 1,300 or 1,400 tribal units who had signed the truce and a large number of autonomous villages belonging to sheikhs and seiyids of the unarmed classes. That is the real problem of the Hadhramaut. It is necessary that all these heads of sections and villages should surrender something of their independence to central governments and should rule their little units as parts of larger entities. When successful co-operation on such lines is assured, the greatest difficulty in the building up of peace and sound government in the Hadhramaut will have disappeared.

There are other requirements almost as basic as the need for mutual co-operation between the leaders and classes of the Hadhramaut. Of these none is more important than the improvement of the courts and the provincial administration. The foundation has been laid by the enactment by His Highness of a series of decrees setting up a system of State and Tribal and laying down the boundaries of Liwas (Provinces under Naibs) ...stricts (under Qaims). The personnel has also been improved and ...re schemes for the training of Qadhis and District staffs. One very ...ant step taken in 1939 was to set up a State Council on the lines of ...alayan State Councils. It is presided over by His Highness and the ...members are the Resident Adviser, the Heir Apparent, the Assistant to ...sident Adviser, the State Secretary and two nominated Arab members. ...ouncil is the Sultan's cabinet and has proved most successful.

...ave mentioned that the Qu'aiti State now has its annual bugdet. ...ear 1938–39 ended with a deficit of about Rs.40,000, 1939–40 with a balance of about the same figure and at 31st March, 1941, the estimated ...s was about Rs.190,000. Salaries though still low have been sub-...lly improved and scales introduced. Some extension has been made ...penditure on social services and on services designed to increase the ...ue-producing resources of the State. Qu'aiti finance owes much to ...reful supervision of Figgis who organized the State Treasury on regular ...as well as the Sub-Treasuries at Shihr, Gheil, Shibam and Du'an. Kathiri State has only a skeleton budget as yet, but the two small ...s—the Al Kaf road and the Balhaf organization—are working on ...ized finance; the latter started rather shakily but now has a balance ... favour. The old system of farming the Customs out at Shihr for ...1,000 a month came to an end in April 1939. Excellent Customs ...:rs have been obtained from Somaliland and Zanzibar, and the Customs ...pts mount steadily. It is hoped to bring all the ports of the Eastern ...1 Protectorate into a Customs union, and though this may take some ...such an arrangement should prevent much of the smuggling due to ...rent tariffs and act to the benefit of all the partners.

:Iere in parenthesis, before I speak of social services, something should ...aid of a change that is coming over local society, namely the gradual ...ppearance of slavery. There are probably 4,000 or 5,000 persons in a ...nical state of slavery in the country, most of whom are of African descent. ...ar the largest number of cases the state is purely technical: the slaves ... in fact free to do anything they please. In many cases, such as those ...he slaves belonging to the Kathiri Sultan, they have often shown them-...es too powerful and really uncontrollable. They have occasionally ...sed real trouble, just as the Zinj slaves did in 'Iraq in the Middle Ages. Many slaves rise to high positions: we have under the Mukalla Govern-...nt several who are Governors, and the slaves of the Qu'aiti Sultan are on the whole extremely loyal, and the Muqaddams of the slaves I have generally found most helpful. Still, there are a number of cases where slaves held by beduin tribes, such as the Ja'da and the Mahra and the Wahidi, have not been well treated.

Men like Seiyid Bubakr do a lot to move towards a general emancipation of slaves: he, for instance, has spent large sums of money in buying slaves and freeing them, or in buying families and freeing them because he does not approve of families being broken up.

In 1938 we made considerable progress, though a general emancipation may take time because the slaves themselves would resist it as much as anyone. But we now have agreements signed by many chiefs—the Hadhramaut Sultans included—declaring that the slave trade is illegal, and the Hadhramaut Sultans have also agreed that any slave who asks for his freedom shall have it. The Resident Adviser was given powers of manumission and we have freed a fair number, for those who want it can easily approach the Resident Adviser, if they are afraid of going to local governors. In this way any slave who is oppressed can get redress. A scheme also exists whereby slaves who desire to leave the country can do so and settle elsewhere. In 1938 a Slavery (Regulation) Decree was enacted by His Highness the Sultan for the Qu'aiti State which gives statutory effect to the arrangements described above and contains other provisions of a manumissive character.

Education is making strides. The services of Mr. Griffiths, the Principal of the Bakht Er Ruda College in the Sudan, were kindly lent by the Sudan Education Department and with a noble sacrifice of part of his leave he toured the country studying its present resources and future needs, and his report, approved by the Colonial Advisory Committee on Education in the Colonies, is being put into force with further generous assistance with staff from the Government of the Sudan. The main features of the report are a large school at Seiyun with an agricultural bias and one on the coast with a commercial bias, but training of teachers, female education (for which there is already a small demand) and technical training all find a place in it. The leading spirit in Hadhrami education is now Sheikh Gaddal as Sa'id Gaddal from the Sudan who is Educational Assistant to the Resident Adviser. Sheikh Gaddal has recognized the keenness of the local staff to improve education and with their eager co-operation a new spirit has been infused into the schools. His teachers' training courses are inspiring even to a layman. Plans have been prepared for the Seiyun school

## AGRICULTURE AND THE FUTURE

Seiyid 'Alawi al Kaf and many improvements in the coastal schools
already been made. One new teacher has been engaged from the
an.

The Medical Department has also extended for there are two more
tors, one at Shihr and one at Shibam, and Mukalla has also a sanitary
ector, a local and energetic seiyid trained in Aden, who has a corps of
epers under him. His chief delights are mosquitoes, latrines and the
nerators built by Figgis on Nigerian pattern. They are artistic domed
irs, very like a saint's tomb, and tone in well with the local architecture.
: first is generally known as Weli Khumur after the sanitary inspector.
:n Miss Viney, a qualified nurse with much experience, has joined the
;idency Staff as Child Welfare Worker, and after her survey is completed
hope it will be possible to see the way to reducing the appalling mortality
:hildren. There is scarcely a woman whom D. has asked who has not
one or more of her children die. A small hospital is in the programme
when funds are available it will be one of the first things taken in hand.
will be remembered that a hospital was one of the first things which
Highness desired to see on his accession.

Hitherto I have described not the building of the foundation and walls
he new Hadhramaut, but in effect only the clearing of the ground and
digging of the foundation, for the true structure of Hadhramaut pros-
ity must rest on agriculture. I must confess to a personal hope that
1eral wealth may not be found in the country. This may be a strange
1ark to make, but it is just because the rewards are usually greater than
dangers to a growing country are also greater. The production of
nerals may provide work for many, but it provides often so much money
t many prosper without the work. I feel myself that the gains from
rking the land result in a happier and more moral population, and
it is good to know that the Hadhramaut possesses several hundreds
square miles of land as rich as any in the world, for it consists of æons'
:umulations of alluvial silt. For an Arabian country the Hadhramaut
ucky to have two rivers and water easily available in many cultivatable
as at no great depths. In January 1939 I spent an absorbing month
velling round with Mr. Beeby Thompson, the Consulting Engineer,
l Hartley the Agricultural Officer. War had broken out by the time
it Mr. Beeby Thompson's report was received, but it indicated that the
ospects of extended agriculture in the Wadi Hadhramaut are not un-
rourable if the water which is probably there can be raised economically.

## THE FUTURE OF THE HADHRAMAUT

Boring experiments are required and these need money—more money than the Hadhramaut can afford—so that it may be we shall have to wait till after the war for a final decision.

In 1938 the tobacco specialist desired by His Highness was found by the Government of India and Mr. Paul has since then been engaged with an interesting experimental station at Gheil Ba Wazir—the heart of the Hamumi or hubble-bubble tobacco-growing industry—where he is trying out varieties of cigarette-tobacco obtained from Mauritius and other Empire tobacco-growing places. The results have not been unfavourable and experimental crops of cigarette tobacco have been produced. Experimental blends of tobacco have been made in Aden with the co-operation of Mr. Nicholas Athanassacopoulo of the Aden Tobacco Company. The imported tobacco monopoly was abolished early in 1937 and a customs duty substituted. This caused the cigarette-smoking fraternity to increase. If Mr. Paul produces a suitable cigarette the duty will be increased and also, I hope, the profit to growers and to the revenue from excise duty.

Samples of cotton and castor-oil seed, which grow practically wild in the Hadhramaut without irrigation, were sent home for examination and the reports on them were favourable. Much further investigation and experiments will be necessary before it can be decided whether their cultivation can be profitably undertaken, but they are two possible lines and Hartley is now busy starting an experimental station at Seiyun. Of course in agriculture the first thing will be to increase the home production of foodstuffs and to improve stock, but if it is possible we would like also to produce something for export. If we can it will profit the beduin who at present bring their camels back from the interior unloaded.

Hartley has already prepared a scheme for the rehabilitation and development of the Meifa area—the delta of the river Hajr—and the preliminary steps to put it into force have been taken. Meifa has long been considered potentially rich from an agricultural point of view but fever has made it unpopular and not nearly so much is made of it as might be. It is proposed to reorganize the water furrows, to replan and rebuild the straw huts in which the villagers live, to start an experimental plot, clear the workers of debt and develop the place on a share cropping basis. Much of interest should appear from this experiment for even the little examination we have started has shown us that there are certain problems of which the solution is necessary preliminary to real development. These are debt, the alienation of land to non-agricultural classes, the determination of

## SCOPE FOR THE FUTURE

boundaries of land, much of which hitherto has been valueless, and the large shares taken by landowners from share croppers who do not get even a fair subsistence in some places. The investigation and solution of these questions may be both long and difficult but it is hoped to tackle them early.

Serious though these difficulties are and serious though the financing of the provision of water may prove, there are hopeful auguries for the success of agriculture apart from good soil and water even though it cannot be expected that the Hadhramaut can become a rich country. From the development point of view the Hadhramaut is fortunate in possessing a balanced and enterprising population. Its enterprise is shown by its success in making money abroad. All the Hadhramis who live abroad keep touch with their homeland and hope to return to it. One may expect that if security and a reasonable chance of finding a livelihood at home is offered to them many will take it. The population is well balanced in that there are classes or "castes" which fit into every stage of the cultural and economic structure of society. If we had tribesmen alone the matter might have been difficult for there are many occupations in which tribesmen will not engage. But in the Hadhramaut even tribesmen seem to take kindly to agriculture and many nomads or semi-nomads have become settled in recent generations. Peace has already made a difference to the landscape. On my tours of recent years I have found everywhere new houses being built, new wells being dug and new palm trees planted. In one place at Fuwha, west of Qa'udha, in what was once desert area to which none penetrated without fear of danger, and which I had previously known from the air only as a barren spot, I saw in 1939 about a hundred newly opened wells and a large acreage of well-grown wheat. Near-by at Qa'udha Figgis settled the differences of the Nahd, and new palms were planted in place of the thousands formerly destroyed with kerosene.

Apart from agriculture there is extra promise in the abundant harvest of fish to be found off the coast, and consideration is being given to developing the industry to the profit of the large fishing community.

Taking all these things into consideration it is perhaps not too much to expect that the Hadhramaut of the future may consist of a well-ordered community of states with an increasing population, of whom most will be cultivating the soil and making not wealth but a living out of it. There should be a living too for the business man and increased prosperity for the beduin carriers. This at any rate seems an end worth working for. That there are many difficulties ahead is not to be doubted

## THE FUTURE OF THE HADHRAMAUT

and that development will make strange changes in society must be expected. To-day the man of wealth is the remittance man: to-morrow the hard-working, agricultural classes may find themselves better off. Where influence in the future will lie no man can tell, but it is likely that it will lie neither with violence nor superstition. It is a grave business undertaking the regeneration of a country, but the benefits of peace, of ordered Government, of education and of science must be at the disposal of those who want them. How they use them must depend to some extent on how they are introduced to them, but mainly on themselves under the Providence of God. Whatever dangers there may be in the "benefits" of modern civilization, it is certain that no man, if he wants them, may be denied access to them. That does not mean that every effort should not be made to avoid "spoiling" the country and its character and I think I have made it clear that that is one of our primary aims.

It is an Arab country and Arab it must remain. It should never be necessary for any large number of aliens to be in it either for administrative or other reasons. Those of us who are there respect the customs and life of the people. We do not set ourselves up as the rulers of the country but merely try to pass on to them any experience or knowledge we have which may be of value. If the week-end visitor of the future goes away having seen Arabs dressed as Arabs and living in houses of Arab architecture and does not find endless outward and visible signs of European occupation our labours will not have been in vain, and we who know it will hope that inwardly and spiritually the character of the Arab has not suffered by our presence.

One thing that will not change in the Hadhramaut will be the word of God as it was revealed to the people by their Prophet, and I believe myself that, if they follow the spirit of their faith, there shall no harm come to them.

# INDEX

Abd 'Alawi bin 'Ali, Muqaddam of the Tamini, 273.
Abdali State, 103-4, 108-9; Sultan of, 111, 117.
Abdul Karim, Sir, *see* Fadhli Sultan.
Abdul Krim, Riff chieftain, 71.
Abdul Qadir Ba Faqih, Seiyid, 235, 254.
Abdul Qadir Okeir, headmaster Aden College, 245-6, 250, 256, 276-7.
Abdul Rahman al Jifri, Seiyid, 189, 191-2, 307, 309.
Abdul Rahman, nephew of Yeramis Sultan, 125-6, 128.
Abdul Rahman al Kaf, Seiyid, 191, 206-7, 210, 258-60.
Abdulla Ali, interpreter, 13-14, 97, 122, 125, 128.
Abdulla bin Bubekr, Sheikh, Fadhli official, 115.
Abdulla bin Muhsin, Sultan, 273.
Abdulla, Sultan, son of the Yeramis Sultan, 124-8.
Abdur Rahman bin 'Othman, 250, 268.
Abyan, dams at, 93, 114; settlement, 134.
Ad, giant race of, 140, 183, 188n, 196, 202, 211, 214; Mola Motar prophet, 167; tomb, 213-6.
Aden, xi., xii., 5, 49, 64, 66, 82, 84-90, 104-5, 108, 137, 148-9, 151, 163, 172, 191, 193, 232, 236-8, 243, 247-8; the Tanks, 84, 89; college for sons of chiefs, 99-105, 245, 306, 317.
Aden Protectorate, xii., 91, 137, 179, 243, 255, 341; Western, 91, 326, 340; levies, 98, 102, 346; Residency, 244; made a Crown Colony, 313n; Postal Union, 339; Eastern, 340, 349.
Adh Dhahoma, gates of, 224.
Adim Wadi, 218n.
Afif bin 'Abdulla al Afif, 181.
*Africa, ss.*, 238.

Afzel Khan Monen Khan, chauffeur, 155
Ahl as Sa'd tribe, the, 179.
Ahl Bureik, tribe of bedouin Sheiks, 193.
Ahl Fuleis, Arab tribe, 111, 118, 131.
Ahl Haidera, Mansur of Dirjaj, 111, 118, 120, 131, 255.
Ahmed, nephew of the Yeramis Sultan, 125-6.
Ahmed, Sultan, C.I.C., of Lahej, 104.
Ahmed, teacher, Aden College, 245.
Ahmed, the slave, 122.
Ahmed Ba Gheish, Quaiti sub-Governor, 178.
Ahmed bin Abkr bin Sumeil al 'Alawi, Seiyid, 43-5, 71-2.
Ahmed bin Sa'id, founder of the Albusaid dynasty, 9.
Ahmed bin 'Umar bin Ahmed Ba Surra, Sheikh, 170, 173-5, *see also* Ba Surras.
Ahmed Effendi, the jemadar, Mukalla, 246, 339.
Ahmed Hassan, interpreter, 246, 257.
Ahmed Hassan, a Nakhai, 128-9.
Ahmed bin Hussein bin Harun al 'Atlas, Mansab of Meshhed, 178-80, 333.
Ahmed Nazir, Arab minister, Mukalla, 247, 312.
Ahmed Sa'id Baziad, butcher, 40, 42.
'Aidarus, patron saint of Aden, 88.
'Aidarus bin Muhsin al Afifi, Sultan of Lower Yafa'i, 119, 130-4, 179.
'Aidarus Seiyids, 143, 309.
'Aidid, Wadi, 327.
'Aidha bin Tannaf, Chief of the Manahil, 319.
'Aidha bin Terjem, Chief of the Al Baqi Msellum, 322.
Akid river, 219n, Wadi, 225.
Al 'Abd al Muntassar, 106, 108.

# INDEX

Al 'Abd bin 'Ali bin Yemani, chief of the Tamini, 299.
Al Abr, see Husn Al Abr.
Al 'Ali Kathīr, deputation from the, 299.
Al Amin, ship, 246.
Āl 'Amr, Kathīri clan, 189, 204.
Al Ardhi, tribe, the, 312.
Al Baqi Msellem, Sei'ars, 320, 323.
Al Gheil, 204.
Al Ghuraf, walled village, 327.
Al 'Ghurfa, trenches at, 189-90, 300, 204, 261, 291n, 316; Jinn of the, 287.
Al Haddad in Tarim, 327.
Al Hadhāfa, 222-3.
Al Halāf, 162-4.
Al Hamum tribe, 293, 299, see also Hamumi.
Al Haqq, s.s., 237-8.
Āl Hariz tribe, 195, 201.
Al Hatim, Sei'ars, 319, 321-2, 326.
Al Jabir tribe, the, 204, 276, 281, 284, 287, 298-9.
Al Kaf Seiyids, the, 240, 251, 257, 282, 300, 302, 304; the new road, 316, 328, 331, 344.
Āl Kathīr, see Kathīri.
Al Khamt, dar of 'Ali bin Habreish, 265.
Al Khor, 134.
Al Khurob, 282.
Al Liza, river, 319n.
Al Makad, giants grove at, 228.
Al Qara, near Shibam, 269, 323.
Al Qōz, 210.
Al Quf, tobacco nurseries, 156.
Al Sheiban tribe, 293.
Al Tamin tribe, see Tamimi.
Al Uqda, home of Salim bin Ja'fer, 268.
Āl 'Umar, 189.
'Alawi bin Ahmed al Haddad, Seiyid, 215.
'Alawi al 'Attas of Hureidha, 339.
'Alawi bin Bubekr bin 'Alawi al Kaf, Seiyid, architect, 203-4, 206.
Albusaide tribe, the, 13.
'Ali, author's servant, 86.
'Ali, Somali chauffeur, 204-5.
'Ali, Sultan of Tarim, 207, 259, 275, 316.
'Ali bin 'Abdulla, brother of Sultan Sa'ud, 231-3.
'Ali bin Hanad, a Zūeidi, 229.

'Ali bin Mansur, see Kathīri, Sultan of.
'Ali bin Salah, Sultan, Governor of Shibam, 267-274, 286, 294, 299, 300, 310, 322-3.
'Ali bin Salim Albusaidi, Sir, 79, 81, 115.
'Ali, Seiyid, Sultan Grand Comorro, 71.
'Amd, Wadi, 188, 271, 298, 340.
'Amr al Queis al Kindi, 182.
'Amr bin Towar, branch of the Bin Afrar, 223n.
'Amr the Muqaddam, 194-5, 198, 200-1.
'Amudi tribe, the, 177n.
'Anana Wadi, the, 162.
Ankedum, Wadi, 166.
'Aquabat al Hibil, Du'an Wadi pass, 169.
'Ar Rashid, Du'an town, 169, 175.
Ar Rodha, Wadi Yeramis, 122, 124, 128.
Ar Rasma, 293.
Arf, Wadi, 309.
Aroba cliffs, 166.
As Saila, 132.
As Soda, landing ground, 97.
Asadi al Fay, port in Hamumi territory, 281-2.
Ash Shūara, 166.
Athtar Sharquan, guardian of temples, 167.
Audhali country, the, 138.
Aulad al Imam, royal family of Muscat and Zanzibar, 13, 336.
Aulagi tribe, 340.
'Aura, Du'an tribe, 169, 170, 173.
Ausan, kingdom of, 4, 142.
'Awadh, chauffeur, 255-6.
'Awadh bin Azzan, Sheikh of the Bin Addat, 273, 307.
'Awadh bin Tannaf, 198-9.
'Awadh 'Umar Ba Sunkar, 184.
'Awamir tribe, the, 201, 204, 260, 267, 285, 293, 298-9, 305, 320, 327.
Azania, near Zanzibar, 5, 49.
Azzan, 340.

Ba 'Abbad, Sheikh, 216.
Bā 'Āmr, resident of Zanzibar, 55-9.
Ba Habab tribe, the, 256.
Ba Hasan tribe, the, 252-5, 309-10, 337.
Ba Khāmas plateau, the, 168-9.
Ba Rumeidan, in Sei'ar, 194, 198, 319-20.

## INDEX

a Surras of Du'an, 164, 177n, 178, 180, 303, 310; *see also* Ahmed bin Sa'id *and* Muhammad bin 'Umar bin Ahmed.
a 'Ubeid, beduin broker, 157–9.
a Wazir family, 184n.
ab el Mandeb, 109, 140.
ackbone plateau, the, 256.
ajri tribe, the, 204, 298.
akezebur, Mukalla's reservoir, 155.
alhaf, Sultanate of, 5, 245, 316–7, 340, 346; the Sultan of, 336.
ana, Wadi, 129–134.
ani Afif, Lower Yafa tribe, 223n.
ara as Sida, Mukalla, 149.
arghash, Sultan of Zanzibar, 10, 51, 65.
Basa', 219n, 220.
Basra, 57, 59.
Bedr Bu Tuweirak, Kathīri ruler, 223.
Beech, Captain, R.A., 259, 276–7, 282.
Beihan, Sharif of, 92–3, 336.
Bein al Khorebtain plateau, the, 166.
Beit al Ajaib, 63.
Beit al Haji, Sheikh, 290.
Beit Hamuda, beduin, 293.
Beni 'Asad tribe, 182.
Beni Dhanna tribe, the, 293, 299, 319.
Bent, Mrs., author of *Southern Arabia*, 116, 138, 178, 181–2, 189, 196, 269, 319.
Bent, Theodore, xiv., 116, 178, 181, 269, 319.
Besse, A., 88, 147.
Besse, Meryem, 147, 259.
Bil Fas, 261, 286, 291–2.
Bin 'Ali, Muqaddam, Mahra tribal peacemakers, 223n.
Bin 'Ali Wadi, the, 340.
Bin 'Abdat, chief of the Āl 'Amr, 189–90, 261, 273, 285–6, 288, 290–2, 316.
Bin 'Abri, Nahdi agitator, 323.
Bin Afrar tribe, the, 223, 227.
Bin Akshat, Yemani chief, 290.
Bin Hizer, Yemani chief, 290.
Bin Hotali, Yemani chief, 290.
Bin Jerbu'a, Al Hatim chief, 321–3, 326.
Bin Marta, 303.
Bin Mulhi, Al Hatim chief, 321–3, 326.
Bin Sahāl clan, the, Mahra clan, 223.
Bin Sumeit, 279.
Bin Yemani, section of Al Jabir tribe, 276, 281, 285–8, 291, 307–8; trial of, 282–4; bombing of, 289–92; peace, 292–5.
Bin Yemani, section of Tamimi tribe, 211.
Bin Zūeida, Mahra clan, 223n, 226, 229–30.
Bir 'Ali Sultanate, 5, 245, 316; Sultan of, 336, 340; the incense road, 340.
Boscawen, Colonel, 138, 187, 193, 195.
Bourdonnais, Mahe' de la, 66, 75.
Broome, Adela, 335.
Bubakr al Kaf, Seiyid, 191, 251, 253–4, 259–60, 262–4, 268, 277, 279–80, 282, 286, 289, 291, 299, 301, 307, 320, 322–4, 326, 333–5, 342, 351.
Bubakr al Mihdhar, Seiyid, 253, 282.
Bubakr bin 'Abdulla al 'Attas, Seiyid, "Uncle," 270–1, 298.
Bubekr, Sheikh, saint of Einat, 213.
Budha, capital of the Amudis, 177.
Bugamoyo, 53.
Buheira, peace meeting at, 293.
Bukheit bin Mansur, porter, 160, 211, 233.
Bureiki sheikhs, 324–5, 335.
Buzūn, in Mahra, 226.
Bwana 'Abdulla, 34–7.

Camel markings, 200n.
*Canton* s.s., xi.
Cavadee, pilgrimage, 74–5.
Chake Chake, town in Pemba, 29, 30, 32–3, 35, 37, 42, 47–8, 65.
Charlewood, Port Officer, Zanzibar, 60.
*Chitral*, s.s., xi.
Chole island, now Mafia or Monfiyeh, 7.
"Cokkai," Sheha of Potoa, 26.
Cole, Sir Lowry, Governor of Mauritius, 80.
*Colonial Appointments* pamphlet, xv.
Comorro islands, 7, 63–4, 66, 69, 71.
*Corfu*, s.s., 85–6.
Crofton, R. H., chief secretary in Zanzibar, 78.
*Cupid*, s.s., 12, 35, 60–1.
Curzon of Kedleston, Marquess, 31.

Daham, Yemani tribe, 325.
Dammūn, 206, 327.

## INDEX

Shibam, 187; tea in Seiyun, 189; by car to Tarim, 190-2; pagan dances at Dammūn, 206; journey to Seihut, 210; tomb of Hud, 213-16; exploration in the Wadi Hadhramaut, 217-30; arrival at Seihut, 231; by dhow to Shihr, 232-4; by ship to Aden, 238; on leave for England, 239-40; return to Aden, 243; visits the Sultan at Mukalla, 247-9; completion of the motor road, 251-3; by car to Ma'adi, 255; arrival at Tarim, 257; Tribal Guards Scheme, 259-60; tribal visits, 267-71; peace proposals, 272-4; letter from the Sheikh of the Nahd, 275-6; Bin Yemani, summoned to appear for trial, 282; meeting of the Peace Board, 285-8, 292; bombing the Bin Yemani, 290; the three years' truce, 293; created Friend of the Hadhramaut, 296; signing the truce, 299-306, 311; dinner with the Yemani, 307-8; office work in Mukalla, 314, 332; opening the new motor road, 315-16; appointed Resident Adviser to Sultans of Mukalla and Kathīri, 316; settles Sei'ar trouble, 318-27; air action against the Hamumi, 328; visits Ahmed bin Hassan, 333; adopts a slave child, 334-5; organizes Government in the Protectorate, 338-40; extension of three years' truce, 341-2; tour of Malaya, 347.
Iraq, 185n.
Irqua, Sheikh of, 92, 340.
Isma'ili clan, 13.
Itsandro and Bambao, Sultan of, 71.

Ja'bil bin Hussein, Sultan, nephew of the Yeramis Sultan, 124-9.
Jabiri tribe, 204, 276, 281, 284, 287, 298-9.
Jackson, Sir Wilfred, Governor of Mauritius, 75.
Ja'da tribe, 270, 300, 302-3, 351.
Jama' Mosque, Shibam, 388.
Jamila, 'Al Attas maid, 298.
Java, 45, 49, 172, 190, 305, 347.
Jebel al Whuti, 320n.

Jebel Hadid, college, 102.
Jebel Qafi, 219n.
Jebel Shamshun, Aden, 87-8.
Jebel 'Urka, 167.
Jebel Warwah, 106-7.
Jedda, 103, 184.
Jembiyani, 49.
Jezirat Borraka, islet, 5.
Jibuti, 66.
Johi tribe, 298.
Jōl Ubeid, plateau, 168.

Karama, Arab boy, 40-2, 45, 211-13, 221-2, 228-9.
Kargos, Punch and Judy show, 49.
Kasadi family exiled, 52-3.
Kathīri, 'Ali bin Mansur, Sultan of, 138, 143, 145, 190, 204, 266, 268, 273-4, 306, 338; tribe, 172, 189, 199, 201, 206, 223n, 260, 263, 276, 278, 282, 293, 296, 305, 313, 323, 334, 349; Ghalib bin Muhsin, Sultan of, 237; country, 244, 327; Tribal Guards Scheme, 244, 282; treaty relations, 278-9, 281; three years' truce, 285-6; Resident Adviser, 316; Constabulary, 344.
Khalf, centre of fish curing industry, 150-1.
Khama clan, the, 157.
Khoreiba, Du'an town, 169-70, 175.
Khormaksar, 87.
Khan Bahadur, Sheik Ali Baakza, 313.
Khan Jehan, 339.
Kilindini harbour, 79, 81.
Kilwa, 7.
Konduchi village, 49.
Kuweit, 57-8.

Laajam, Hussien, 269.
Lahej, H.H., 'Abdali Abdul Krim, Sultan of, 85, 92, 103, 133; his Army, 104-5, 314.
Lahej Protectorate, the, 93, 103, 130; visited by the Ingrams, 103-5.
Lake, Colonel, xiii., 97, 138, 275.
Lal Khan, Subedar Major, 339.
Lancaster, Sir James, 7, 8.

# INDEX

ang, Andrew, 72.
atakh Wadi, 3, 9.
atham Island, 60.
ee Warner, W. H., O.B.E., British Agent, Mukalla, 278.
eisar Wadi, 177.
ower Yafa'i dispute, 113–19, 179; letter from Sultan, 129–30.
usb, village and wadi of, 162.

Ma'adi tribe, the, 252, 255, 276, 309; cultivators of betel nut, 255n.
Ma'ara tribe, the, 252, 298.
Ma'afir tribe, the, 4.
Madagascar, 7, 64–6, 71, 321.
Madhi tribe, the, 298.
Mahra country, 64, 138, 219, 223, 236, 238, 244, 340; tribe, 221, 235n, 260, 299, 319n, 350.
Mahri country, 254; Sultanate Qishn and Soqotra, 340; tribes, 340.
Makunduchi village, 48.
Malacca, 4.
Malaya, the Adviser System, 347.[1]
Manahil tribe, the, 201, 218–19, 221.
Manawarih, near Mukalla, 155.
Magrat, volcanic island, 225.
Maraduka, 65.
Marakhai, in Mahra, 219n, 221.
Marashida clan, the, 157.
Mariama village, 204.
Maseila Wadi, 195n, 196, 210–11, 218n, 223n, 234, 320, 327.
Masilat as Silma, 210.
Mathews, General Sir Lloyd William, his ghost, 51.
Ma'tuf bin Khashash, headman, 212.
Maulis, Muslim clan, 31-2, 35–6.
Mauritius, xi., 7–9, 63–4, 66, 82, 84, 86–7, 168, 176, 239, 270; Muslim festival, 69.
Mayotte island, 64.
Mazruis, tribe in Pemba, 30, 80.
Mbaruk bin Rashid, Sheikh, 30.
McClaughry, Air Commodore, 315, 320.
Meifa, development of, 352.
Merbat in 'Umar, 238.
Merhat in Dhufar, 340.

Meshhed, 176, 179, 181; Mansab of, 178–80, 333.
Milner, Lord, xvi.
Minhali, tribe, 223, 319–21.
Mkanjuni, 32–4.
Mkokotoni, in Zanzibar, 18, 19, 28–9, 165.
Mkumbu Peninsular, 32, 35.
Mocha, 4.
Mola 'Aidid, tomb of, 327.
Mola Matar, 166–7.
Mroni, capital of Mauritius, 71.
Msasani village, 49.
Msellem Bal'ula, Treasurer at Mukalla, 148, 152, 247.
Mtumbatu tribe, 28.
Muhammad, carpet dealer, 55–6.
Muhammad, porter, 160, 181–3, 185.
Muhammad, Sheikh of the Albusaidi, 13.
Muhammad, son of Sultan Sa'ud, 231.
Muhammad bin 'Abdulla Abu Haidera, "Uncle" Fadhli, C.I.C., 121, 125–6, 128.
Muhammad bin 'Abdulla bin 'Umar Ba Wazir, 184n, 185.
Muhammad bin Ahmed Ba Zaid Bazara, 175, 176n.
Muhammad bin Hashil, Sheikh, 48–9.
Muhammad Ba Harūn, Seyid, 176, 178.
Muhammad bin Hashim, Secretary of the Peace Board, 305.
Muhammad bin 'Umar bin Ahmed Ba Surra, 170.
Muhammad Sa'id Mart'a, Sheikh, 186–7.
Muhammad Midheij of Reidat al Ma'ara, Seiyid, 287, 289, 292, 296.
Muhammad 'Umar Bazara of Du'an, 165, 172, 176n.
Muhsin, college usher, 102.
Muhsin af Einat, Seiyid, 206, 211, 213, 219, 221, 225–6, 228–9, 232.
Muhsin Bukheit, chief of the Awamir, 267.
Mukalla, xi., 5, 41, 88, 139, 147, 154, 159, 164, 193, 212, 228, 238, 254, 262, 269, 273, 277–8, 295, 305, 331, 335–6, 345; description of, 149–52; slaves, 154n, 349; Tribal Guards Scheme, 259;

# INDEX

Ser Wadi, 139, 195, 197, 202, 205, 319.
Sha'amila tribe, 310.
Shabwa, 188, 193, 326; incense road, 340.
Shanfari chiefs, 316.
Sheba, ancient state, 4.
Sheikh Othman, Aden, 87, 143; gardens, 82; mission, 87.
Sheikhs, the, 177n.
Shenafir, confederation of tribes, 204, 273, 291.
Shery Bā Salam, Subian village, 150.
Shias tribe, the, 6–7, 67, 69.
Shibam, Province of, 41, 44, 139, 143, 146, 164, 177, 186–93, 197, 199, 204, 207, 217; town of, 187–8, 244, 249, 269, 316; R.A.F. landing ground at, 258, 279; political importance of, 188–9; motor road, 258, 315.
Shiheir, 156, 235.
Shihr, province of, 5, 46, 143, 146, 148, 172, 193, 218n, 232, 251, 253–6, 276–7, 287, 295, 307, 309, 312, 329, 333, 343, 349, 351; treaty with, 193; sulphur springs, 225n; town of, early history, 235–6; motor road, 314.
Shihr, Sultan of, 147.
Shinen bin Sa'id, 165.
Shin Kao, temple oracle, 74.
Shiraz, Hassan, Sultan of, 7.
Shuqra, 115–16, 120.
Sidr or Elb tree, 165, 171, 197.
Sif, 178.
Sifa, 225.
Simah tribe, the, 299.
Singapore, xi., 172, 187, 191, 203–4, 207, 262.
Siyara or passport system, 223n, 229.
Sodaf Wadi, 197, 319; grave of the prophet Nebu Mola Sodaf, 198.
Soqotra, island of, 140, 142, 220, 223, 229, 239, 340; Sultanate of, 317, 340.
Spurrier, Dr., 50–1.
Stark, Miss Freya, xiii., xiv., 269, 335–6, 340.
Subeihi, Arab tribe, 94, 109, 111, 138; Rija'i Sheikh of, 92, 111; Makdumi, Sheikh of, 111.
Suleiman, Liwali of Chake Chake, 31–4.
Suleiman bin Mbarek al Mauli, Liwali, 30.

Suleiman bin Nasir al Lemki, Sheikh, 53–5, 115.
Suleiman, bin Yeslem, 195, 198–200.
Superstitions, 208.
Sur village, 324.
Sūri Arabs, 45.

Tabūrkum, 219.
Tahir-bin Abubekr al Amawy, Sheikh, 47.
Ta'iz, 103.
Tamimi, a Qu'aiti tribe, 142, 172, 204, 211, 218, 221–2, 273, 293, 319, 327–8; Ben Yemani clan, 211; sign the truce, 298–9; letter from the Chief, 299, 300.
Tanganyika, 138, 155, 172.
Tarba, home of the 'Awamir, 266, 277.
Tarim, 41, 139, 172, 176, 190, 193, 201, 204–5, 207–10, 218, 221, 225, 244, 251, 257, 260–2, 267, 277, 295, 298, 307, 316, 323, 326, 331; description of, 207–9; motor road, 315.
Tamimi dispute, 327.
Taris, Kathīriland, 204.
Tawahi, Aden, 87.
Teheir, Mahra, 225.
Thei'man, 227.
Therb, camel park, 150, 159, 237.
Thompson, Beeby, consulting engineer 351.
Thompson, Miss Caton, 335–6.
Thukmein mountains, 324.
Tiban Wadi, Lahej, 105, 107–8.
Tila as Sufla, 159–61.
Tritton, Dr., 220n.
Tumbatu Island, 28.

'Ubar as Shab'a, 130, 133.
'Ubeid al Inglis, road foreman, 251–2, 307, 309, 315.
'Ubeid Salih bin 'Abdat of Al Ghurfa, 285, 287, 342.
'Uman, Sultanate of, 340.
'Umar, Seiyid, Mansab of Hauta, 286.
'Umar, Sultan, 139, 148–51, 159, 194, 239, 248, 243.

## INDEX

'Umar al Kaf, Seiyid, 191–2, 205–6, 208, 210, 212, 259.
'Umar al Mihdhar, Sheikh, 215.
'Umar bin Salih, Governor of Shihr, 255, 312.
'Umar Tuheish, Chief of the Bin Yemani, 290, 297, 307.
'Umar 'Ubeid Bin Abdat, Jinn of Al Ghurfa, 287.
Upper Yafa, 92.

Van der Meuhen, 72, 139, 164, 178, 340.
Viney, Miss, 351.
Virginia, Mabel Anna, xiv.
Von Wissman, 139, 164, 320.
Vundive Island, 50.

Wa Arabu, Arab tribe, 16.
Wahadimu, aboriginal tribe, 18, 23, 29, 49, 50.
Wahidi country, 311; Sultanates, 340; tribe, 351.
Walmsley, Wing-Commander H. S. P., O.B.E., 292.
Wa Manga, Oman Arabs, 16, 23, 38.
Wangika, tribe, 30.
Wapemba, aboriginal tribe, 29.
Warneford, Captain, 99.
Wa Shihiri tribe, the, 16, 39, 43, 45, 49, 50.
Warwah Jebel, 106–7.
Watts, Alan, xiv.
Watumbatu tribe, the, 28.
Wavell's Arab Rifles, 43.
Welsted, J. R., xiv.
Weti, Pemba, 13, 15, 16, 18, 25, 30.
Winter, R. K., C.M.G., Director of Education at Khartoum, 245.
Wofford, Mr., 324, 340.

Wrede, Count A. von, author of Reise in Hadhramaut, 178.

Yabha Wadi, 212.
Yafa'i tribe, 53, 119, 143, 145, 223n, 254, 308, 335, 343–4,; soldiers, 178–80, 184, 312, 322, 328; mercenaries, 318; Thelud section, 334.
Yakut, geographer, 29.
Yam tribe, the, 202.
Yemen, the, 4, 6, 12, 69, 86, 98, 109, 217, 262, 303, 326; ancient history of, 143; Rēsuli dynasty, 235; Imam of, 285.
Yeramis Haidera, Sultan of, 115, 122–9; disturbance, 119; mortgage dispute, 120; wadi, 122–3, 129.
Yusuf Sharif, Indian merchant, 152.
Yusuf Sherif, Doctor, 246.
Yuzbashi Muhsin 'Alawi, Sheikh, Aden College, 245.

Zaghoul Pasha, 99.
Zahra, adopted slave girl, 334–5.
Zaidi, Ingram's servant, 26–8, 49–51, 63, 65, 70–1, 75, 77, 86, 104, 115, 121, 162–3, 186, 211, 229, 232.
Zanzibar, xi., xvi., 4, 8–10, 12, 15–18, 28–9, 31, 37–8, 40–66, 68–71, 77–9, 84, 101, 115, 147; bombardment of, 27; its growth, 51; bazaars, 52; Arab Girls' School, 78–9; proverb, 185–6; Sultan of, 313.
Zeidi Imam, 95.
Zeidi, Muslim sect, 6, 95, 141.
Zemen as Saghir, rest house at, 165.
Zenj or Zinj Empire, 7, 65; slaves, 340.
Zinjibar, 122, 133–4.